Rebecca Manley Pippert

D0474454

out of the saltshaker

and into the world

Inter-Varsity Press

INTER-VARSITY PRESS
38 De Montfort Street, Leicester LE1 7GP, England
Email: ivp@uccf.org.uk
World Wide Web: www.ivpbooks.com

First British edition 1980
Reprinted thirteen times
Revised edition 1999
Reprinted 2000

British Library Cataloguing in Publication Data
A catalogue record for this book is available from the British Library.

ISBN 0-85111-646-9

Set in Garamond
Printed and bound in Great Britain by Omnia Books Limited, Glasgow

*Inter-Varsity Press is the publishing division of the Universities and Colleges
Christian Fellowship (formerly the Inter-Varsity Fellowship), a student movement
linking Christian Unions in universities and colleges throughout Great Britain,
and a member movement of the International Fellowship of Evangelical Students.
For information about local and national activities write to UCCF, 38 De Montfort
Street, Leicester LE1 7GP, email@uccf.org.uk, or visit the UCCF website at
http://www.uccf.org.uk*

Contents

To Jim and Ruth Nyquist,
whose faithfulness to God
and exuberant love for people
have touched so many lives,
including my own, with the
beauty of God's grace

Introduction

Twenty years ago, when this book was first published, I thought I knew who my readers would be – my parents and grandparents were good for two copies; certainly Christian students, since I was involved in Christian work among them at the time and I knew that world best; a smattering of American Protestants (considering that was my own point of reference); and those who had a special interest in the area of evangelism. Knowing that the word *evangelism* carried a negative connotation for many believers, I assumed the general readership would be small.

But now I am delighted that *Out of the Saltshaker* has reached a wider and more diverse audience than I had ever thought possible. Because of the book, I have been invited to teach Catholic nuns, priests and laity; Protestant clergy and churches of every denominational stripe; Christians from around the world; and those who struggle to be a witness where they are placed, be they business people, prison inmates, university lecturers or even golf pros!

Why has a book about evangelism reached such a wide audience? I hope it is partly because this book offers an understanding of evangelism that respects seekers and desires to have authentic relationships with them, and that encourages a style of witnessing that is true to one's own being. But I think there is a more basic explanation: regardless of our tradition or nationality, fear permeates most of our attitudes about evangelism.

Fear, not ignorance, is the real enemy of evangelism. We fear that our friends will reject or marginalize us if we speak about our faith; we fear that what we don't know will be exposed; we fear that our beliefs will be challenged. Back then, as well as today, we resisted shallow techniques for communicating truth to complex human beings. If nothing else, sheer frustration compelled many to explore fresh approaches to the subject of evangelism.

When Andy Le Peau from InterVarsity Press asked me to do a revision for the twentieth anniversary of *Out of the Saltshaker,* we talked about what would be involved. Freshen up the language, take out dated examples, add new stories where appropriate, and write one or perhaps two new chapters. Nothing to it. But then Andy proceeded to ask me several compelling questions: 'What have you learned in these past twenty years about evangelism that you didn't know when you wrote the book? Has the fact that we live in a very different culture from when you wrote it (after all, "New Age" wasn't even an identifiable category back then!) changed your approach to evangelism? Has your understanding of evangelism been altered, having now taught Catholics, mainline and evangelical Protestants, and Christians from many other countries?'

As I pondered those questions, I began to realize this would not be a revision – this would almost be a new book! I want to thank Andy for the penetrating questions, and even more for not panicking when I turned in so many new chapters! This proved to be one of the most wonderful writing experiences I have ever had.

So while the first half of the book updates and expands on what I wrote earlier about Jesus' life, values and lifestyle, on practising the presence of Jesus and on the practical issues of conversational skills, what else is *different* about this version? Well, for one, I am. When I wrote *Out of the Saltshaker,* my work had been almost exclusively tied to student work. But in these past twenty years God has given me extraordinary opportunities to teach and dialogue with believers from many different traditions and walks of life. That has enlarged and enriched my thinking enormously. And like almost everyone else, during the past twenty years I have read more, thought more, prayed more and suffered more.

But the times are different too. And different times demand a rethinking and re-evaluating of how best to communicate the gospel. We do so not to create a gospel that matches itself up to current trends, but we pay attention to our cultural context so that we may rediscover and proclaim the gospel with fresh power and clarity for 'such a time as this'.

Another difference comes from lessons learned from doing evangelism training these past twenty years. For example, one question I always ask people at an evangelism conference is, 'Where do you get stuck in sharing your faith?' The answers never vary. Whether I'm in Paris or Peoria, with Methodists or Mennonites, their answers always fall into three categories: 1% say it's their fear of being asked questions they can't answer; 1% say they are uncertain about the mechanics of evangelism, such as how to lead a person to Christ; the other 98% percent say they feel their communication skills are inadequate. For example, this last group wants to know how to bring up the subject of God without seeming awkward, or they are worried about offending someone. Just that feedback alone tells us how important it is to provide not merely the content training of the gospel but the communications skills as well.

So chapters 11–13 deal with such questions as these: What is the role of truth and how can we speak in the power of God's truth? How can we practise the presence of Jesus and mediate his love as we share the gospel?

At one conference, however, a woman raised her hand and said, 'If evangelism is essentially a spiritual activity that is predicated on the supernatural power of God, then how do I tap into the Spirit's power? What is the role of prayer and fasting in evangelism? What are the spiritual tools I need to deal with spiritual deception or hard-heartedness?'

What stunned me about her comment was that it was the first time anyone had ever raised this issue in all the years I've done training. Why is this? I think in part it is because we live in a culture so saturated with self, in which humans have placed themselves in the centre for so long, that our natural tendency, even as Christians, is to focus on the human aspects of evangelism and not the divine. Yet it is God who takes the initiative to pursue seekers, it is his Spirit who converts, it is his gospel that saves. Evangelism is God's business from start to finish.

So I have included in this new edition, especially in chapters

14 and 17, the role of the Holy Spirit in evangelism and what we can do both to depend upon and demonstrate the power of God's Spirit.

What else has changed? In the original version the chapter on apologetics was geared more to answering the 'modern' sceptic who shared a common understanding of truth. And I still deal with those types of questions in chapter 15. But today the 'postmodern' person often approaches truth in a very different way. Therefore chapter 16 offers an apologetic for the postmodern person, who often cares more about whether something is experientially 'real' than whether it is true.

Furthermore, we live in an age that is more conversion-prone than we did in the 1970s. It's in vogue to consider oneself 'spiritual' today. However, in the paradoxical 'absolute relativism' climate in which we live, we quickly discover that spirituality is more akin to a 'flavour of the month club'. When I wrote in 1979, the alternative forms of spirituality were hardly a blip on the screen. Today they are commonplace. So chapter 17 includes new material on how to witness to those involved in New Age and other alternative forms of spirituality.

Last, when I wrote *Out of the Saltshaker*, my experience had been almost entirely with parachurch ministry. But the past twenty years have been rich in church ministry. Therefore the discussion of evangelism and the local church, in chapters 18 and 19, has been expanded dramatically.

Out of the Saltshaker had its beginnings before I became a Christian. Even then I had definite thoughts about the way people communicated what was most important to them. I remember once encountering a zealous Christian. His brow was furrowed, he seemed anxious and impatient, and he sounded angry. Then he told me God loved me. I couldn't help noticing the difference between his message and his style. His message was arresting (me, a sinner?) but ultimately appealing (there is a God who loves me deeply). But his style put me off. I recall thinking, *If God is so good and loving, then why is this guy so uptight?* Surely the way we communicate a message of good news should be as marvellous as the message itself. This book is about getting our message and our style together.

Jesus tells us in the Sermon on the Mount that we are the salt of the earth. And he challenges us not to lose our savour – our

7

The Critical Path

Conservators don't like being the centre of attention, but that's just where I had put Abigail Quandt: in the public eye and subject to its scrutiny. If you work on Leonardo's *Last Supper*, Michelangelo's *David*, or the unique witness to the thoughts of Archimedes, you'd better not slip up. Everybody tells you what you should be doing, but only you can do it. And no one had any idea of the problems that Abigail faced. They do now, but they didn't then. Hers was not only the critical path, as programme manager Mike Toth had characterised it; it was also the most important and the most onerous. Like Reviel, you are going to have to wait until you get more of the *Method*. This is Abigail's story.

You are probably thinking of Abigail as a book conservator, and that is what she is. But Abigail is not a normal book conservator. Most book conservators work with paper books; very few work on parchment manuscripts. There are good reasons for this. First of all, there are many more paper books in the world than there are parchment ones. Second, in general, paper books need conservation treatment much more often than parchment books. This is particularly true if they are printed on bad paper, with a high acidity. Such books are literally self-destructing in libraries across the globe as we speak. Many are the paper conservators who fight this battle. Parchment does not have this acid problem, and it is much tougher than paper. One essential difference between parchment and paper, however, is that parchment is much more sensitive to changes in temperature and humidity – it is skin, after all. If you lay a sheet of parchment ov your sweaty hand it will quickly curl. Actually, it will curl into the shape it had on the back of the animal from which it came. With finely illuminated manuscripts, such as those at the Walters, this can have serious repercussions. The pigments in the illuminations do not change shape with the parchment as humidity changes and after a while the pigments flake off. Abigail had been working on parchment with this kind of problem for more than twenty years. She was a parchment expert, and very few people have her skills. This was why she was almost uniquely qualified to work on the Palimpsest.

Normally, the best thing to do with a historic object is absolutely nothing – which is what conservators do most of the time. Don't touch it; secure and monitor its environment. After all, a codex that has survived a thousand years is unlikely to degenerate much further if it is not handled and if it is not subject to pollutants or extremes of climate. In the past, even well-intentioned treatments have resulted in permanent damage and the loss of important historical evidence. In the nineteenth and early twentieth centuries many palimpsests in particular were wrecked by the treatment they received. Scholars routinely read palimpsests by applying chemicals to them. In 1919 English novelist and manuscript scholar M. R. James wrote that erased text could be

> revived by the dabbing (not painting) upon it of ammonium bisulphide, which, unlike the old-fashioned galls, does not stain the page. Dabbed on the surface with a soft paint-brush, and dried off at once with clean blotting paper, it makes the old record leap to light, sometimes with astonishing clearness, sometimes slowly, so that the letters cannot be read till next day. It is not always successful; it is of no use to apply it to writing in red, and its smell is overpowering, but it is the elixir of palaeographers.

There were other such elixirs. The most powerful was Gioberti's tincture: successively applied coats of hydrochloric acid and potassium cyanide. I'll just repeat that: successively applied coats of hydrochloric acid and potassium cyanide. Needless to say, ammonium bisulphide,

FIGURE 7.1 *The spine of the Palimpsest*

too, has a severely detrimental effect upon parchment. Working in the twenty-first century, Abigail couldn't apply chemicals to reveal text in Mr B's book. There was little that Abigail could do to make the erased text appear: that would be a challenge for the imagers.

But it was not an option for Abigail to do nothing with the Palimpsest. Despite all the lessons of history, Mr B gave the go-ahead for her to perform radical surgery on the manuscript. It was a brave decision, and we hope that history will say that it was the right one. The reasons for it certainly sounded excellent at the time: the only way that the scholars could read the Archimedes text that was now hidden in the book's binding, and the only way that the imagers could take the scientific images that would be needed, was for Abigail to take the entire manuscript apart.

The Path is Blocked

On Monday, 3 April 2000 Mr B, Reviel, Natalie and Mike gathered at the Walters. It was a historic day. Abigail was going to disbind the Palimpsest. All went smoothly to start with. Just before the sale, in order to make the book at all presentable, Scot Husby from Princeton had carefully put a temporary binding on the codex, designed so that it could easily be taken apart. Abigail quickly took this binding off, leaving the parchment text block naked, without its covers. It was a pitiful sight, though it took Abigail some time to make clear that it was also a tragic one. And here begins the worst part of the story of Mr B's book – because if, to Reviel Netz, the Palimpsest was the unique source for the diagrams that Archimedes drew in the sand, to Abigail Quandt it was a conservation disaster zone.

The spine of the book was covered in glue. This was a post-medieval practice, which helped to secure the structure of the codex but which obviously presented problems for Abigail in taking it apart. If you look carefully (see fig. 7.1), you can see that the spine seems to have two separate colours. The darker colour is hide glue, made from animal skin, and Abigail could remove that reasonably easily. This forms the second half of the codex, from folio 97 onwards. The real problem is the light glue, from folios 1 to 96. According to Abigail, 'The other half of the text block has been coated with a transparent adhesive, probably a type of poly(vinyl) acetate (PVAC) emulsion. While PVAC will swell in contact with water and/or alcohol, there is no way to dissolve it once it has formed a dried film on the surface of an object. Attempts to remove this adhesive from the spine folds of the Palimpsest have proved to be extremely risky, since the glue is stronger than the parchment' – in other words, this is stock-in-trade wood glue. Precisely those lines that Heiberg could not read, because they were hidden in the spine of the bound codex, were now coated and stuck together with commercial glue.

This was not the worst problem. Let's look at the unique surviving folio of Archimedes' *Stomachion* (fig. 7.2). Think of it as a cross section of the brain of a great man. It is, quite literally, in pieces, and large parts of it are simply missing. The rest of it is covered in an awful purple colour. Now, up until this point I have insisted that parchment is tough. Its basic constituent, after all, is the stuff that your shoes are made of. There are only two ways in which you cannot just wear out your shoes but destroy them. One is to burn them. But the Palimpsest had survived fire at St Sabas. Another is to throw them into a bucket

FIGURE 7.2 *Archimedes'* Stomachion!

of water and then expose them to air. Pretty soon they will get mouldy. And that is, more or less, what happened to this folio and, in varying degrees, to the entire Palimpsest. If you immediately take care of your wet shoes, then you can brush them up reasonably well. But that's not what happened to the Palimpsest. Far from it. The Palimpsest was left to stew and the mould was left to grow. And you know what? Mould grows by eating what it is growing on. The mould has actually digested the parchment. All the folios of the Palimpsest have suffered in some degree from the mould. Normally, the side of the parchment that was on the inside of the animal is in a worse state than the side that the animal presented to the outside world, because skin has evolved – or been intelligently designed – to resist microbe attack from the environment. But in the face of the mould attack that the Palimpsest was subjected to even the hair side was frequently heavily damaged. Sometimes it doesn't look so bad, and the folios seem strong enough. But Abigail showed them to me backlit over a light box, and light shines through them like stars in the night sky.

So the leaves were stuck together, and they were extremely fragile. And then, of course, four of them were painted over with forged portraits of the Evangelists. Worse, the forger did not just scrape off the prayer-book text and paint on top of it. He also 'distressed' the folio – he made incisions into it, and took nicks out of it – to make the picture look older after he had finished it. And you know what: it's always tempting to display pictures in manuscripts independently of the codex itself. Perhaps this is why there is a nice curved rust stain at the top of the folio – Abigail says it was made by a paper clip. Not formal enough for you? Maybe. Then why not take a piece of Blu-tack (a blue putty-like substance) and stick it to its backing that way. There's plenty of Blu-tack on the back of this folio. Try reading through that. What a way to treat a book. Any book. What a tragedy that it was this book.

The disbinding of the book, upon which all depended, came to a virtual standstill. The Archimedes Project took what can best be described as a duck dive. Reviel went back to Stanford, Natalie to Cambridge. The lights went out in the studio that had been especially prepared to image the book, and Mr B went home. Abigail spent days just looking at the book, thinking, and documenting. The days turned into weeks and the weeks into months. I dodged press enquiries with breezy comments about the importance of the book and some small conservation issues. Abigail and I stopped talking – always a bad sign. Then she asked for what seemed to me to be an extravagant amount of money to employ her colleagues at the Canadian Conservation Institute to begin a whole battery of tests. To my surprise, and somewhat to my annoyance, Mr B wrote the cheque. Mike Toth sent me dark emails warning of slippage in the schedule so early in the project and the dangers of pure research taking us away from our well-defined and limited objective. There was nothing I could do about it. At the Walters, as in many American museums, curators cannot tell conservators what to do. This is ultimately a very good thing, but also occasionally an incredibly frustrating one. It just didn't seem that much of a problem to me, and yet it brought my whole system to a standstill. Never mind about me. Picture, if you will, Assistant Professor Netz, newly installed in the Department of Classics at Stanford, trying to get tenure. The one manuscript that he needed had almost miraculously appeared. He had seen it; he had even touched it; he knew better than anyone the secrets that it contained. But now he was reduced to begging for glimpses of parts of it. Noel was out of leaves; Netz was out of luck.

The world was watching, the scholars were poised to read and the scientists were ready to image. But everybody was waiting for Abigail – not all of them patiently.

The Heiberg Photographs

Reviel made himself busy, stirring every bush he could about the Palimpsest and digging into its history. He studied Heiberg's work over and over again. He read it cover to cover. And then, in the introduction, he noticed that Heiberg had said that he took photographs of the manuscript when he was in Constantinople. Since the manuscript itself had disappeared into private hands for most of the twentieth century, the photographs would have proved extremely useful to anyone who could find them. The trouble was that no one had been able to. There is a large archive of Heiberg material in the Royal Library of Denmark, but repeated searches in this archive had not revealed the photographs. Reviel, however, thought he would give it another shot, so he wrote an email to a colleague of his, a Danish historian of ancient science, Karin Tybjerg. Karin prevailed upon the Keeper of Manuscripts at the Royal Library, Erik Petersen, to have another look, and Erik had an idea. The Heiberg archive had been deposited at the Royal Library after Heiberg had died. But what if Heiberg had given the photographs to the library *before* he had died? Heiberg would have understood the importance of the photographs and, as a good humanist, might well have wanted to make them publicly accessible. If so, where would they be? In among the photography collection, of course. And Erik found them. They are Ms. Phot 38 in the Royal Library. In June of 2000 Reviel and I visited Copenhagen to see the photographs. We were warmly welcomed by Erik and we were handed a plain album full of photographs of a manuscript. There were sixty-five in all, and they were a smoking gun.

The photographs give a clear picture of what the manuscript looked like in 1906. If you compare the leaf containing Archimedes' *Stomachion* now with its condition then, you see that they are barely recognisable as the same folio. The *Stomachion* page was whole in 1906. It is a mouldy fragment now. Of course, some folios in the Palimpsest are worse than others. The tragedy is that their condition is almost in an inverse relationship to the importance of the texts that they contain. Archimedes has been extremely unlucky: the folios containing the *Method* and the *Stomachion* are in the worst condition of all. When I tell you that Abigail marked the *Stomachion* folio as 'very poor', you will understand that she is a master of the understatement. That's not my style. I tell you: the body of Archimedes may have died by the sword at the hands of a Roman soldier in the third century BC, but the genius of Archimedes was eaten by mould over two thousand years later.

There is, of course, no sign of the forgeries in Heiberg's photographs. On the photograph of folio 57r Heiberg had written 'M16' – it was the sixteenth folio of the *Method*. Now, a picture was on this page. A balding man with a white beard, and wearing a green robe, sits down in a chair with a high, curved back, his feet resting on a blue stool. In his right hand he holds a pen, and in his left a scroll upon which he is writing. In front of him is a desk with the instruments of his trade, and before him at eye level upon a lectern is the book from which he is copying. He is set within an archway, and the whole picture is framed with a border. The background is gold. There is hardly even the faintest trace of the prayer-book text, let alone the writings of Archimedes.

The Heiberg photographs are dramatic and unequivocal evidence that most of the damage to the book occurred in the twentieth century, after it had been revealed as the unique source of treatises by Archimedes. Abigail was stuck with an old book, but one that had only recently sustained such serious damage. Who was responsible for it?

The Forged Miniatures

In early March of 1999 I had popped in to see John Lowden in his rather cramped office on the top floor of the Courtauld Institute, where he is the Professor of Medieval Art. I showed him a picture of one of the forgeries. To my astonishment, he immediately cried out 'Snap', and pulled out a publication that he had written on a manuscript in Duke University Library, North Carolina. The codex at Duke contained four Evangelist portraits very similar to the ones in the Palimpsest, and John had demonstrated conclusively that they were modern forgeries.

He told me to go downstairs into the library and pull out a publication by Henri Omont, published in 1929, of Greek manuscripts in the Bibliothèque Nationale in Paris. I quickly found what he knew I would – that the figures of the Evangelists in the Palimpsest, like those from the Duke manuscript, were copied from illustrations in that book. They were not exact copies; their backgrounds were much simpler than the backgrounds of the pictures in Omont's publication.

But the figures of the Evangelists themselves, their chairs and their writing desks were the same. Abigail established that the drawings were actually traced on a scale of 1:1 from the publication.

Following the Christie's catalogue, I had been cursing the scribe of the prayer book and the greedy and careless monks at the Metochion for the appalling state of the book. The Duke codex, too, had belonged to the Metochion. Since both books had paintings by the same forger, I was more sure than ever who was to blame for the books' condition.

But I was wrong. In May 2001 Abigail received back a monumental work of research and scholarship: the Canadian Conservation Institute delivered their report on the Archimedes Palimpsest. It's an impressive but depressing read. It is also full of useful information about the appalling condition of the book. Among a whole range of pigments that they chemically identified in the forgeries, one was particularly revealing: phthalocyanine green. This colour only became commercially available in Germany in 1938. As we have seen, by 1938 there were no manuscripts at the Metochion. In fact, the forgeries were made at least fifteen years after Marie Louis Sirieix was supposed to have acquired the codex.

The realisation that I had entirely misunderstood the story of the Palimpsest made me angry and I wanted to set the record straight. I wanted in particular to know who had been responsible for the catastrophic treatment of the book after it left the Metochion. Now it seemed likely that Marie Louis Sirieix was to blame. But the story told by Robert Guersan was short on particulars. Perhaps Sirieix had not even known that the book contained the unique letters of Archimedes; Anne Guersan seems to have had to recover this information. Without further documentation it would be impossible to be sure.

The Willoughby Letter

In May 2006 I walked into work and found placed upon my desk, without ceremony, a copy of a letter. It had been left there as an early-

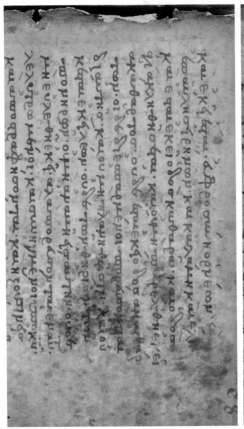
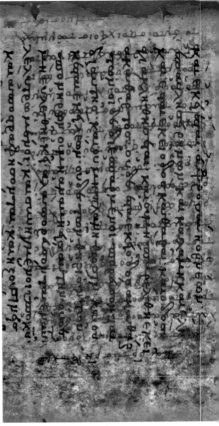

A detail of the Palimpsest in normal light. The Archimedes text is difficult to see.

The same page in the pseudocolour process that Keith Knox developed by combining an image taken in natural light with an image taken in ultraviolet light.

(Previous page) The gorgeous luminous quality of ultraviolet fluorescent light can make the Archimedes Palimpsest look beautiful. Here is the diagram to Archimedes' *Spiral Lines,* proposition 21 (see Chapter 4). It is obscured by the text and decoration of the prayer book. The hand drawn in the initial letter to one of the prayers seems to use the straight lines of the diagram as a sleeve.

Q TO
A Q:
IS TEAR
POSSIBLY
ORIGINAL?

GUESS

Reviel Netz has annotated this ultraviolet image identifying some characters and guessing at others. The note in the margin is Reviel asking Abigail Quandt whether the small hole in the centre of the parchment was an original blemish in the skin, or made later.

Nigel Wilson works from printed reproductions of the images, mainly in the summer months, when the light is good.

Will Noel and Reviel Netz study a leaf of the Archimedes Palimpsest in the conservation laboratory at the Walters.

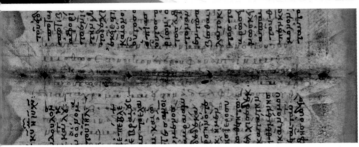

(Left) A pseudo-colour image of the Hyperides text in the Palimpsest. Note that the Hyperides text is written out in one column, while the Archimedes text is written out in two.

(Middle left) A detail of the third unique text in the manuscript, a philosophical commentary, in natural light.

(Lower left) A pseudocolour image of the same detail as above, with the word 'Aristotle' circled.

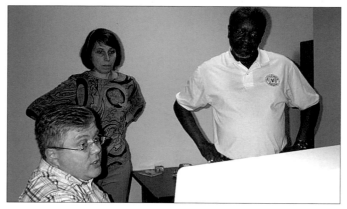

Bob Morton, Abigail Quandt, and Gene Hall watch
as an EDAX X-ray image of a forged page emerges, agonisingly
slowly, on the computer screen.

After 15 hours of imaging at
EDAX a scan was made that
had read through gold.

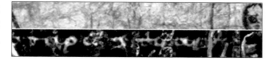

Outside Beamline 6-2 at the Stanford Linear Accelerator Center: Uwe Bergmann,
Abigail Quandt, Keith Knox, Mike Toth, Reviel Netz, Will Noel.

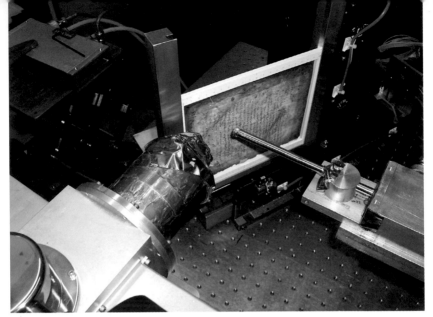

A leaf of the Archimedes Palimpsest in the beam at SLAC. The leaf moves on a stage in front of the X-ray beam, which is a hair's width in diameter. The detector, wrapped in silver foil, is on the left, at 90 degrees to the beam.

Uwe Bergmann is delighted as Reviel Netz announces to Will Noel that he can improve upon Heiberg's reading of the manuscript with an image scanned at SLAC.

Abigail Quandt inserts one of the forgeries into the beam at SLAC.

(Left) A regular image of one half of a forged page.
(Right) An 'iron map' of the same page, taken at SLAC, revealing the text underneath.

13 March 2006 was the day that the new *On Floating Bodies* text appeared at SLAC. Reviel rushed up to the Beamline to play with the images. Everybody helped. From left to right: Uwe Bergmann, Abigail Quandt, Keith Knox, Reviel Netz, Roger Easton.

A detail of folio 1v of the Palimpsest, taken in normal light.

An 'iron map' revealing the colophon of the scribe of the prayer book: + [This] was written by the hand of presbyter Ioannes Myronas on the 14th day of the month of April, a Saturday, of the year 6737, indiction 2.

morning gift by my good friend Georgi Parpulov, a Bulgarian scholar of Greek manuscripts with a wry smile and an extraordinary ability to uncover the deeply buried. Georgi had dug this letter out of an archive of photographs, the Harold R. Willoughby Corpus of New Testament Iconography, at the University of Chicago. The letterhead made clear that it was from an antiquities dealer living in Paris. It read: Salomon Guerson, Rare Carpets, Antique Tapestries, 169 Boulevard Haussmann, Paris, and it was addressed to Professor Harold R. Willoughby at the University of Chicago, Illinois:

February 10, 1934

Dear Professor Willoughby

Pursuant to our correspondence of 1932 with regard to a manuscript that I had shown to you and a folio which was identified through your mediation by the curator of the Huntington library as being the manuscript of Archimedes described by J. L. Heiberg in *Hermes* vol. 42, page 248, I would like to let you know that I wish to sell this manuscript.

I have shown it to M. Omont of the Bibliothèque Nationale as well as to the Bodleian Library and both have made me offers that I found insufficient. You would greatly oblige me if you would let me know whether this manuscript interests you or at any rate if you would write to me to whom I could offer it with a chance of selling it. I am asking $6,000.

In expectation of receiving news from you, I ask you, dear professor, to be assured of my highest respect for you.

S. Guerson

The evidence of this one letter meant that the twentieth-century history of the Palimpsest needed to be rewritten: not only were the forgeries painted after the manuscript left the Metochion, but the manuscript was identified in 1932 as the Palimpsest, and Sirieix had not owned the manuscript until after 1934. How had the manuscript got from Constantinople to Paris, and who was responsible for the forgeries?

A New History

For a start, it seems very likely that the first trip of the Archimedes Palimpsest to the United States was in 1932, not 1998. And the person who first recognised it for what it was after it left the Metochion was the curator of the Huntington Library in Los Angeles, in 1932. I wrote to my colleague Mary Robertson, curator of manuscripts at the Huntington Library, and although she could not come up with definite proof, she thought it most likely that the curator in question had been Captain Reginald Berti Haselden. Between 1931 and 1937 Haselden had been in correspondence with Professor Edgar Goodspeed of the Department of New Testament Studies in Chicago over some palimpsested material. He was particularly interested in ultraviolet photography and wrote a book in 1935 entitled *Scientific Aids for the Study of Manuscripts*. This was exactly his cup of tea.

It seems that Haselden only had the opportunity to identify one folio of the manuscript, not the entire codex, and that this one folio had been transcribed by Heiberg on page 248 of his article in *Hermes*. This is folio 57. How it was that Haselden identified this folio alone is something of a mystery. Maybe he saw a photograph of just this page. But just possibly it had already been separated from the manuscript – as it is now – and Haselden merely studied this single leaf. Be that as it may, it is further proof, if such is needed, that the forgeries were added after Salomon Guerson wrote his letter, and therefore after the book had been identified as Heiberg's Codex C: folio 57 is now covered with a forgery. Not even Haselden, with his interest in scientific aids, could have identified the Archimedes text through the forgery. The forgeries were indeed done after 1932, and after Salomon Guerson had acquired the manuscript.

Even before Georgi had unearthed the Willoughby letter, John Lowden had already suspected that the Guerson business was involved in the history of the Palimpsest, because he had his own very good reason for suspecting that they were indeed responsible for the forgeries. He discovered that the Guersons owned a leaf from a Byzantine manuscript that was exhibited in a famous exhibition of Byzantine art in Paris in 1931. The unusual way in which the figures in the Palimpsest forgeries were framed was exactly like the leaf that the Guersons owned and that was exhibited in the 1931 exhibition. The Willoughby letter was an extraordinary confirmation of John's insight. It demonstrated not only that the Guersons had owned the manuscript, but also that they had known Henri Omont, from whose publication the Evangelists in the forgeries had been traced.

John also had made substantial progress in determining how the Palimpsest might have travelled from the Metochion to Paris. Salomon Guerson certainly knew one of the most famous dealers of the twentieth century, Dikran Kelekian, and it might well have been through Kelekian that they had acquired some of their manuscripts. In 1931 Kelekian had owned two miniatures taken from the same book as the miniature that the Guerson business had displayed in Paris in the same year. The manuscript from which they all came is known to have been perfectly intact in a convent in Constantinople as late as 1922. By 1931 Kelekian had inserted his two miniatures into yet another manuscript, which came from – guess where – the Metochion. The Guersons had had good access to manuscripts from the Metochion. The circumstantial evidence that the Guerson business was responsible for the forgeries in the Duke manuscript, as well as the Archimedes Palimpsest, is compelling.

But one small thing doesn't add up. The Guerson business was a respectable and successful one on the Boulevard Haussmann. The Willoughby letter shows that Salomon Guerson knew what he had, and he knew it was worth a lot of money. $6,000 is, conservatively, $70,000 today, which was a lot of money for a medieval manuscript in those days. Salomon Guerson thought the book was valuable precisely because he knew it contained the writings of Archimedes. The Canadians, for their part, had demonstrated in their report that the forgeries could not have been done until after 1938. So we are left with the situation that they hung on to the book for at least seven years, waiting patiently for someone to pay the appropriate price for Archimedes, before suddenly making forgeries out of the mathematician's letter to Eratosthenes after 1938. Salomon Guerson may have been a little unscrupulous in his treatment of Byzantine manuscripts, but he didn't have sufficient motive for this particular crime. We need to find one.

The Casablanca *Hypothesis*

On Friday, 14 June 1940 the Germans entered Paris. They wore grey; the Norwegian Ilse Lund wore blue. Czech resistance hero Victor László was sick in a freight car on the outskirts of Paris. American freedom fighter Rick Blaine stood on a station platform in the rain with a comical look on his face because he'd been stood up by a girl. Rick got on the train and left Paris, along with three and a half million others. He eventually made it to Casablanca, where he made a handsome profit in his Café Americain, which was mainly populated by once-wealthy Europeans, most of whom were selling family treasures for a song in order to bribe their way to safety. This is the plot of a movie starring Humphrey Bogart and Ingrid Bergman. Reviel and I have a similar plot to account for what happened to Archimedes. It is just as short on hard facts as the movie, and should be similarly understood as fiction. It has a much darker plot than *Casablanca*. Here is the summary:

On Friday, 14 June 1940 the Germans entered Paris. Salomon Guerson and Archimedes do not leave town, at least not on the same day as Rick Blaine. Salomon thinks that he can stick it out in Paris. Forty-eight hours later he isn't so sure: all Jews are ordered to register at a police station. But he is still there on Wednesday the twenty-sixth when Hitler arrives. Salomon is thankful that Hitler heads down the Champs-Elysées from the Arc de Triomphe rather than up the Boulevard Haussmann, but he can hear the noise down the street from his shop, which he has closed for the day. Salomon never reopens his shop. Its contents are plundered by the Nazis. They take any artwork of value to the Jeu de Paume to be sorted, and then ship it back to the motherland. Salomon goes into hiding, with just a few of his possessions. One of these is the Palimpsest. It is small, portable, inconspicuous and, he thinks, valuable. As time goes on, Salomon gets increasingly desperate. On Wednesday, 16 July 1942 the Vichy police begin deporting Parisian Jews, rounding them up at the Winter Velodrome. Their more permanent deportation camp is at Drancy, from which, in the next two years, 70,000 people, including many of his friends, are shipped to Auschwitz and disappear. Salomon is struggling to stay alive. He looks at his remaining assets; he is reluctant to part with the Palimpsest, but eventually he has to. He cannot sell it himself, of course; if he tries, the book will simply be confiscated. He decides to give it to a friend to sell on his behalf. But Salomon finds himself short of friends, and these friends find the book a hard sell, at any price. Finally Salomon turns to Marie Louis Sirieix. He is hopeful of a good reception: Sirieix is a Resistance hero and his daughter, Anne, is married to someone with an extraordinarily similar surname — Guersan. Sirieix is sympathetic, and he even believes Salomon when Salomon tells him that it is the unique key to the mind of Archimedes. But Sirieix also says that no German will believe that it is Archimedes, and anyway, the Nazis are not interested in ugly books; they are interested in art. The Germans have been systematically looting art from Jews in Paris for months. Sirieix is a freedom fighter, not an intellectual, and he takes the pragmatic approach that if only the book had pictures in it, then that would have real currency. Indeed, it would be more valuable than gold.

Salomon Guerson leaves with a seed planted. The screen goes black for a moment, and resumes with Salomon, a few days later, returning to Sirieix. He says that he hadn't noticed before, but there are several pictures in his book. Sirieix is suspicious but generous. He is much more impressed with Salomon, and he agrees to buy the book. Archimedes' parchment letter to Eratosthenes becomes Salomon's letter of transit, and it is now covered in pictures. Salomon successfully escapes Paris; Sirieix returns to fighting the Germans, confident of eventual victory. He has never been particularly interested in the Palimpsest and hides it in his damp basement. The credits roll over a backdrop of the Palimpsest slowly gathering dust and being devoured by a purple mould.

A Plea to the Reader

Abigail now had the data she needed to start work. She had all the documentation from the Canadian Conservation Institute, she had undertaken her own researches, and others had helped too. It is clear that once Anne Guersan paid attention to the book that she had inherited, she took steps to have it restored. But she may have only contributed further to Abigail's problems. The PVAC glue that locked the Palimpsest pages together was widely used for the spines of manuscripts in the sixties and seventies. Perhaps this is another example of someone trying to do their best for a book and making the problem worse. Someone also seems to have paid particular attention to the forgeries, keeping them separately and mounting them with Blu-tack, which only came on the market in 1970.

There were, however, several leaves that Abigail could not do any work on. These were the three that I had noticed were missing when Mr B first left the book with me. They were present when Heiberg looked at the codex, and he even took a photograph of one of them. Abigail had found traces of pigment transferred on to the facing folios of these now-lost leaves. It was safe to assume that the forger had painted these folios as well. Some forgeries made from the book might have been successfully sold and they might be decorating the walls of an apartment in Paris, in Germany or, perhaps more likely, in the

United States. Look out for them. If you see them, turn them over. If they have two texts on the back, one much fainter than the other, then please let me know. They are very valuable, and not because they have paintings on them. Remember: value translates into cash. You can contact me through www.archimedespalimpsest.org.

Intensive Care

If caring for Mr B's book now sounds like a daunting job, then I have succeeded only in hinting at the true magnitude of the task facing Abigail Quandt and her colleagues in the book and paper conservation lab at the Walters. Every aspect of the material characteristics of the codex has been investigated. The Canadian Conservation Institute took a microscopic core sample from a folio containing Archimedes text. Analysis of the sample only reinforced the fact that the collagen was breaking down and that the surviving palimpsested text was extremely thin – a mere stain engrained in the parchment. Before any work was done on a folio, a colour-coded map was made recording its condition – the tears, the drops of wax, the mould stains, the rust, the Blu-tack. The manuscript was also comprehensively photo-graphed. Each bifolio of the prayer book had its own written condition report, each its own treatment proposal and each its own treatment log. If the condition reports had been assessing the state of prisoners, then those in power would have been wanted in The Hague; if the treatment proposals had been for patients in hospital, then those patients would have been in the intensive-care unit. And intensive care is exactly what they were given. As she worked, Abigail saved everything. To this day there is a box of carefully bagged fragments of the Palimpsest. Each bag is labelled, telling us which bits of thread, which glue, which wax, which pigments, which bits of paper came from which folio of the prayer book. The myriad tears in the parch-ment were given tiny mends, so that more bits did not fall off when they were imaged.

It was not until Saturday, 8 November 2003 that Abigail started to treat the beginning of Archimedes' letter to Eratosthenes. I have edited her treatment log, which might not be a great read but which does demonstrate the intensity with which she worked on the only surviving copy of the letter.

On that Saturday, Abigail separated it from the bifolio that was wrapped around it. It took all day to do this, because the two bifolios had been stuck together with PVAC. She removed loose debris from the gutter. The next day, Sunday, Abigail relaxed the parchment at the spine, by lightly brushing it with a mixture of isopropanol and water. Then she made a tracing of both sides of the bifolio, showing the damaged areas and those that had been obscured by glue and paint. This took two hours. Among other things that Abigail documented on her tracing was a paper reinforcement that had been attached to the spine-fold with PVAC, and which obscured Archimedes' text. Abigail also plotted on her tracing several small fragments of parchment, and a small deposit of purple paint. She concluded that one of the forgeries had once been stuck in the book next to this leaf. Abigail then comprehensively photographed the bifolio. Then she applied more isopropanol and water to the paper reinforcement. After 15 minutes she began to take it off. By the end of the day, she had removed it completely. Monday was a day of recuperation, not for Abigail, but for the bifolio. On Tuesday, 11 November, Veterans' Day, Abigail looked at the other side. Around the spine-fold, there were large gritty deposits, coloured fibres, white fibres, black accretions that might have been hide glue, and white crystalline particles that she thought might have been silica gel, put there possibly in 1971 by the Etablissement Mallet when they were trying to stop the mould. She also noted further blobs of PVAC on the bifolio. She began cleaning the residual adhesive and accretions from the spine-fold. The fold itself was very cockled and creased; Abigail tried to flatten out these creases. All the

FIGURE 7.3 *A section of the Palimpsest, before treatment, after treatment, and in ultraviolet light. Note Netz's cicled 'kuklos'*

residues and accretions that she removed that day were saved. She did not return to the bifolio again until Sunday, 16 November. In the spine-fold, around the fourth sewing station, Archimedes' text was obscured because the parchment was torn and crushed and a loose flap of it was embedded with the PVC and white paper fibres. Repeated applications of ethanol and water freed the flap, which was realigned. The area was then dried under pressure. The next day Abigail started work on several flaps of parchment that were curled up in a severely degraded and perforated area of the bifolio. She applied tiny amounts of ethanol, the flaps gradually relaxed and Abigail secured them back in place. The area was then dried under pressure. On that day Abigail also worked on areas of parchment that were folded over around the edge of the leaf, and these she reinforced with Japanese paper. Abigail never attempted to remove wax droplets on this leaf: it was simply too fragile. When she had fully prepared the leaf for imaging, she sent a sample of the PVAC for analysis at the Canadian Conservation Institute.

All the other folios of the manuscript got this same level of care. I show you one untypically spectacular example. Abigail mended the gutter of one of the Archimedes folios. Here, a flap of parchment had been scrunched up and broken, and it had to be unfolded so that the text could be read. Abigail performed brain surgery that morning. Later in the day, we took an ultraviolet photograph of the folio, and sent it as a jpeg attachment to Reviel Netz. This is the email I got by return:

From: Reviel Netz
Sent: Sun 4/15/2001 10:14 AM
To: "William Noel"

Dear Will,
The attached is your recent AQ picture, fantastic. Circled is the self-obvious symbol for the Greek word Kuklos, meaning 'circle'. First time I've seen this symbol in the Archimedean manuscript tradition, and this has consequences for working out the relationship between the branches of the tradition, as well as of course for the history of mathematical symbolism. Kudos to AQ.

In his enthusiasm Reviel was actually wrong; Heiberg had noticed the kuklos. Luckily Reviel only told me this a lot later. Thank goodness. It was one day where our spirits rose, and these days were rare and precious. Because, basically, preparing the Archimedes leaves for imaging was a time-consuming nightmare.

Most of Abigail's work occurred under the microscope and most of it is now not apparent to the naked eye. The flash of a camera and a clever algorithm, as we shall see, can transform a page. A brilliant scholarly insight can transform our understanding of Archimedes. But Abigail and her colleagues always knew that this was not what their work was about. Except to the very careful observer, other than the fact that they were now disbound, the folios of the Palimpsest look little different after Abigail's treatment from how they looked before she started work.

I had originally hoped to see a dramatic change in the forgery pages. In fact, I wanted her to scrape the forgeries off. But other people had very different views. John Lowden, for example, considered that they were an important part of the history of the codex. What was for me merely incidental graffiti that obscured the writings of a genius was to John a record of twentieth-century attitudes to the Byzantine past. This was a view that Abigail shared. And she brought two more observations to the table. First, if she tried to take off the images, she might well destroy the Archimedes text underneath. Second, even if we did not have the technology now to read through the forgeries, that technology might exist in the future. We could always wait. After all, Heiberg had waited: he had not taken the codex apart, and he had not painted it with Gioberti's tincture. He must have been sorely tempted, but, for the good of the codex, he hadn't. Eventually I saw Abigail's point. More importantly, so did Mr B.

Yet it was here, truly, in the emergency room, that the tide of the project almost imperceptibly changed. It was upon Abigail's patient work that the later triumphs of the project were built. For, by hook or by crook, she did do it. She did take the bloody thing apart. The disbinding started on 3 April 2000. The final folios were disassembled on Thursday, 4 November 2004. On average, one palimpsested folio was liberated from the prayer book every fifteen days. After she had prepared them as best she could, the folios were mounted in specially prepared mats so that the scientists could image them.

Discoveries

Of course, the scholars did not wait until the scientists had taken their images of these folios. Their view was that, if they were in good enough shape for the scientists to image, they were in good enough shape for them to try to read. Once Abigail had started to disbind the leaves, Natalie, Reviel and John Lowden did come and study them.

The first discovery came on 3 April 2000. On the very day that Abigail took the book apart Reviel and Natalie were scrutinising parts of the Palimpsest with ultraviolet lamps. They sat next to each other conferring. Understandably, the first folio came under their gaze quickly. I have explained already that this page is in very bad condition. But as Reviel stared at it under UV, he thought he saw underwriting, and he thought it was underwriting by the Archimedes scribe. He discussed it with Natalie. Natalie, too, studied the leaf. 'Yes,' she said. They had just discovered a new page of Codex C. The very first page of the codex contained *Floating Bodies* text in Greek that Heiberg simply hadn't noticed. On the first day of disbinding, on the first day of reading and on the first page of the codex we had discovered a whole new page of *Floating Bodies* in Greek. It was a major triumph for the project.

It was slowly becoming apparent that Heiberg had not known the manuscript quite as well as people had thought. This became even clearer when Reviel and I went to see the Heiberg photographs. There were sixty-five photographs in all, and they were marked up with notes, by Heiberg, who identified folios of Archimedes text as he went along. Naturally, all the photos were of folios that contained Archimedes text. We could see the way he worked. He labelled those folios containing the *Method* 'M', the *Stomachion* 'St', and the rest he labelled by reference to his own previous edition, which he had published in 1880. However, there were only sixty-five photographs. Of these, thirty-eight were openings, the rest were single folios. Heiberg had photographs of only 103 rectos and versos of folios out of a codex that contained, in his time, 354. One photograph in particular caught Reviel's eye. It was of the right-hand side of an opening. But I noticed that Reviel was not looking at this folio; rather he was looking at the little bit of the preceding folio, on the left-hand side of the original opening, that was by chance included in the photograph. It contained a mere three lines of Archimedes text. Reviel looked, and looked again. 'This is *Floating Bodies*,' he said. Reviel knew instantly that he was reading a section of *Floating Bodies* in Greek, and for the first time. Heiberg had overlooked the folio on the left: he had not got a photo of it, and he had not transcribed it. Looking at the photographs now, one can only admire Heiberg's skill: it is extraordinarily difficult to read the Archimedes text from the photographs, and he had read them. Nonetheless, there were whole sections of *Method* and *Floating Bodies* for which he hadn't had photographs, and which he had left largely unread.

The best day for Abigail and me in this difficult period was Saturday, 13 April 2002. John Lowden was in Baltimore to look at the Palimpsest. I knew that he had to fly to London at 3 p.m., so I went down to the conservation laboratory at about midday to see how he was getting on. He popped his head out of a black curtain to tell me that the Palimpsest had been presented to a church 773 years ago . . . exactly. With the help of an ultraviolet lamp John had looked at the very first folio of the Palimpsest. The first folio of any codex is normally in worse shape than those that follow, but the first folio of the Palimpsest is a wreck. Bookworms don't actually like parchment folios, they like the wooden covers in which the folios are bound; but they don't have a very good sense of direction. The first folio of the Palimpsest is covered in worm holes. Also, the outside two inches of the folio have been stained very dark by the oils in the leather of an old binding. John gave it another look. In the bottom margin, right in the stained area, he had discovered an inscription, technically called a colophon. He could not decipher it completely, but it was clear that the prayer book had been given to a church by the scribe on 14 April 6737. But this is in Greek Orthodox time. In the thirteenth century this was not calculated from the birth of Christ, but from the origin of the world. As we all know, the world was formed on 1 September 5509 BC. To get the modern date for 14 April 6737 one must therefore subtract 5,508. The answer is 14 April 1229. Seven hundred and seventy-three years later, we knew when the Palimpsest was made.

Reflections

As this story unfolded, a picture of the history of the Archimedes Palimpsest was emerging in my mind that was at odds with the one I had previously recounted. The roles of those who had played their part in the history of the book now seemed extraordinarily different. I began to question my hasty condemnation of the scribe who had erased the Archimedes text, to rethink my description of St Sabas as a tomb for Archimedes, and to feel shame for my slander of the monks of the Metochion. It was because the monks of the Metochion had their manuscripts documented that the Archimedes texts were rediscovered; St Sabas is better characterised as a safe house for Archimedes than as a tomb. If the price for that safety was the Christian disguise that the scribe of the prayer book provided, it was a price well worth paying. And if it was love of mathematics that had ensured the survival of Archimedes' letter to Eratosthenes for the first thousand years, it was love of God that ensured its survival to the twentieth century.

The scribe was the unwitting saviour of Archimedes and not his nemesis. The Palimpsest was the creation of religion, not its victim. It was the victim, rather, of two world wars and the art market. It was the damage sustained in the twentieth century that had led most to believe that the Palimpsest was now a battered relic of little research interest. Reviel was convinced that this was a false assumption and the break-throughs that we made only increased his insistence that he be allowed to see the book. Once a few leaves were disbound he arranged a trip to Baltimore together with his friend Ken Saito. They were going to come over the first weekend in January 2001, the sixth and the seventh. This was the moment of truth. Could Reviel and Ken really get more Archimedes text out of the book than Heiberg? Every time I spoke to the press I said, 'Yes'; every time I looked at the wrecked folios of the book I thought, 'No.' In the end it didn't matter what I said, or what I thought. It merely mattered that the book now had its chance, and that Reviel was flying in from California to pass judgement.

8

Archimedes' *Method*, 2001
or Infinity Unveiled

I t was nearing the end of 2000. The Palimpsest had been available for research for almost two years now, and yet there was very little to show for it. I was driven back to the traditional routines of library work: visiting the manuscript, holding a magnifying glass in one hand and a UV lamp in the other, looking at the manuscript intently, one character after the other. I envisaged myself doing just this – slowly and painfully going through the manuscript, though, to be honest, I wasn't sure I would be able to read much more, this way, than Heiberg did. Would it all be just a waste of time?

Will insisted that we had to make priorities. Only a few pages could be made available for my next trip, in January 2001, so, which were the ones I really would like to have? – only a handful of these were from the *Method* and of these only one had a substantial gap left by Heiberg's own transcription.

I therefore asked for the bifolio 105–110 to be ready for our visit. I wouldn't be alone: I had a guest with me, a tourist or, more precisely, a pilgrim. For, now that the Palimpsest was there, this was how historians of mathematics would think of a trip to Baltimore – as a pilgrimage. I knew Ken would value the experience and, besides, I like talking to him. Who knows? We might even get to find out something about Archimedes.

Professor Ken Saito teaches at the University of Osaka and he is one of the best historians of mathematics at work today. I have always admired his early study of the way in which Euclid's results were used in the theory of conic sections. He is a master of the logic of Greek mathematics: when he reads a text, he sees precisely where it comes from and where it leads to. If anyone could work with me on the Palimpsest, this was the man.

Saito first came to visit me at Stanford. It was his first time in America and I thought he would like to see my advanced Greek class. I set my students a translation of Euclid and Archimedes – here at Stanford, most of our Greek language students can easily handle the mathematics and I enjoyed showing those students off. We also had a day in San Francisco, which Ken enjoyed a lot, though I think he just couldn't wait to travel, at long last, to Baltimore.

We had a long flight ahead of us – enough time to prepare for our visit. As we were flying out to Baltimore, Ken and I were discussing some of the perennial questions of the history of mathematics. To what extent did Archimedes anticipate the calculus? How much did he know about its conceptual difficulties?

Here, in outline, was the history of mathematics as it was known, back then, in January 2001. The Greeks invented mathematics as a precise, rigorous science. They avoided paradox and mistakes. In doing so, they also avoided the pitfall of infinity. Their science was based on numbers that can be as big as you wish, or as small as you wish, but never *infinitely* big or small. Numbers that are as big or small as you wish are known as 'potentially infinite', instead of actually infinite. The Greeks did not use actual infinity.

In the scientific revolution of the sixteenth and seventeenth centuries, scientists such as Galileo and Newton brought new techniques into mathematics by bringing in actual infinity. They brought in magnitudes that were in fact infinitely small or infinitely big. This allowed many important breakthroughs, but there was a price to pay: infinity brought in the paradoxes and errors that follow upon it. Mathematics became more powerful but less precise.

In the nineteenth century mathematicians built up new techniques for dealing with infinity. Gradually, a new mathematics evolved where infinity was brought in and tamed, so to speak: one could deal with infinity, without any paradoxes or errors. The precision of Greek mathematics was regained, on a new level – now, with infinity itself being used as a precise mathematical tool. This allowed the great explosion of mathematical discoveries – and therefore of scientific discoveries – in the nineteenth and twentieth centuries.

In a nutshell, then: the Greeks had precision without infinity. The scientific revolution had infinity without precision. Modern science, since the nineteenth century, has had both precision *and* infinity.

What was the potential infinity used by Archimedes? Recall the imaginary dialogue. Archimedes packs a curved object so that a certain area has been left out, an area greater than the size of a grain of sand. A critic comes along and says: 'There is still a difference greater than the size of a grain of sand.' 'Is that right?' exclaims Archimedes. 'All right then, I shall apply my mechanism successively several more times,' and then the area left out is smaller than the grain of sand. 'Wait a minute,' says the critic, 'the area left out is still greater than a hair's width.' Archimedes goes on – and so on, and on and on it goes. The difference always becomes smaller than any given magnitude mentioned by the critic. This dialogue goes on *indefinitely*. This is *potential infinity*.

Let us take another example. First consider the collection of whole numbers using only the principle of potential infinity. Then say that, for each whole number, no matter how large, we can think of another one bigger than it. This is another imaginary dialogue, a kind of auction: you say a million, I say two million; you say a billion, I say a trillion. This bidding sale has no end. But no one is allowed to bring in infinity itself; there is no such number allowed.

But then we may bring in actual infinity. Suppose someone comes in and says, 'I have a number which is even bigger than all the numbers you have mentioned. This is the number of all whole numbers. It says how many whole numbers there are.' The auction ends with a bang: actual infinity has brought it to an end.

There are clearly more whole numbers than a million, a billion or a trillion. The number of all whole numbers is infinity. And it gives rise to all the paradoxes of infinity.

Suppose, for instance, you wish to compare the number of whole numbers to the number of even numbers. We may put them side by side, as two rows.

1	2	3	4	5	...
2	4	6	8	10	...

For each number in the top row there is a number in the bottom row (its double). The bottom row does not get exhausted, ever. For each whole number there is an even number, and vice versa. The number of whole numbers is the same as the number of even numbers. In the case of whole and even numbers, we find that they are the same size even though there are clearly, in some sense, twice as many whole numbers than there are even ones. In infinity, 'normal' concepts collapse: a collection may be equal to its half. And so we cannot count on ordinary rules of addition and summation. Infinity gives rise to too many paradoxes. This is why it is such a difficult tool to handle.

In the nineteenth century mathematicians found the techniques to calculate with infinity. (The main insight came from Archimedes' imaginary dialogues.) The Greeks never made this step (it is a big one). They had collections that were 'as big as you wish', but never collections that were actually infinite.

Even in the *Method* – so we thought, back in January 2001 – Archimedes did not break this rule. He played, dangerously, with infinity. But he did not speak of 'the collection of all the parallel lines in the triangle'. All he said was that, since each parallel line balanced its paired section with a certain fulcrum, so would the entire triangle. Whether this was true or not depended on techniques of summing up infinitely many objects. But Archimedes never explained what he was relying upon for his summation. Even here – in his most radical experiment – actual infinity was avoided. It was left for Galileo and Newton to uncover it.

So went our conversation. In breaks in it Ken Saito would go back to the book he had brought with him: a copy of Heiberg's edition of Archimedes' *Method*. True to form, Saito was immersing himself in the ancient text. We were about to read a hitherto unknown piece of the text. For some reason – we didn't know why – Heiberg had a gap in his edition. What could Archimedes have written there? To make sure that we got to the bottom of it, Saito wanted to know everything about the context.

Here is the overall structure of the *Method*. Archimedes begins with his introduction addressed to Eratosthenes. It is a very flattering introduction: 'You are such a mathematician that you are capable of passing a real judgement on my method.' As we were talking, I suggested to Saito one of my hobby horses. Wouldn't it be like Archimedes, I said, to be *ironical* in this introduction? That is, did Archimedes not intend, perhaps, to unmask Eratosthenes? I suggested that we should think of the *Method* as a puzzle sent for Eratosthenes – and intended to defeat him. It is, after all, a very puzzling text – could it be intentionally so?

Perhaps, nodded Saito, and returned to the text.

The *Method* is indeed a puzzle. We have followed the first proposition with its remarkable combination of physics, mathematics and infinity. Proposition 1 has two striking properties: the application of physics to mathematics and the summation of infinitely many lines. The same combination is repeated through the first thirteen propositions of the *Method*.

Archimedes promises in his introduction that, at the end of the treatise, he will repeat the proofs for some of the results, deriving them now in an 'orthodox', standard way. Most of this disappeared either when the palimpsester discarded parts of the original manuscript, in the year 1229, or at some later time, when a few of the prayers, for reasons we do not understand, got cut out of the prayer book. Either way, much of the end of the *Method* was lost. But proposition 15 survives in part, and it is indeed an orthodox, standard proof, based on the imaginary dialogue of: 'I shall find you an even smaller magnitude.'

Proposition 14 is different. It is neither an orthodox proof, nor is it like the first thirteen propositions of the *Method*. It does not rely on the combination of the application of physics to mathematics as well as infinite summation. Instead, it is based on infinite summation alone. Not that people have paid much attention to it, through the twentieth century. Propositions such as proposition 1 appeared to be puzzling enough. Why bother with this one as well? – especially seeing that this proposition survived in fragmentary form only: Heiberg could read its beginning and its end, but not its middle. The writing was too faint. Could it be read now?

Which was precisely what Saito was preparing himself for. We were going to look at the middle of proposition 14, the part that Heiberg had not read. Abigail had just unwrapped it, and the scientists were about to produce a digital image.

This would be the first major trial for the project. Either we made readings where Heiberg had failed – or we gave up, content with Heiberg's edition. Perhaps he had done as much as could be done. This would be a pity in terms of the Greek edition (where every word counted). But I doubted how much of interest could be revealed for the history of mathematics. In truth, I thought I could use the Palimpsest to further the understanding of the cognitive history of mathematics – looking at such questions as the nature of diagrams and abbreviations, which I have mentioned above; but in terms of the traditional concerns of the history of mathematics – in those terms, I doubted the Palimpsest could teach us much that was new. Perhaps we would be able to read something, perhaps not. But it should not be of much consequence for the history of mathematics.

After all, the general outlines of Archimedes' principles of summation were clear enough from the first thirteen propositions of the *Method*. Heiberg had not read the middle of proposition 14, but he had read enough of other propositions to develop a clear enough guess of how Archimedes would proceed here. The object of this proof was clear, from its beginning and end. Archimedes was measuring the volume of a cylindrical cut. That is: we take a cube (see fig. 8.1). We enclose a cylinder in it. We cut the cylinder (and the cube) by an oblique plane passing through the middle of the base of the cube and

FIGURE 8.1

an edge of its top. What is the volume of the cylinder that has been sliced off by this cut – the fingernail-like shape that is shaded in figure 8.2? This is a very strange figure, framed by a combination of a semi-circle, a semi-ellipse and the contours of a cylindrical surface – which is the entire point for Archimedes: a very strange and unwieldy figure is going to be measured, very precisely, in terms of a rectilinear figure. Let us see how Heiberg understood this measurement. (For the more geometrically inclined readers, please note now that I treat the enclosing figure as a cube. Archimedes himself approaches the problem in the more general terms of any parallelepiped, but we gain a lot in simplicity by considering the case of the cube alone – which is then very easy to transfer to the general case treated by Archimedes.)

Once again, then, we witness the measurement of a curvilinear object. And once again – as everywhere else in the *Method* – Archi-medes uses some kind of slicing by parallels. Heiberg was capable of reading this: a random plane is drawn, parallel to the vertical edge of the cube (see fig. 8.3). This results in various cuts being sliced off

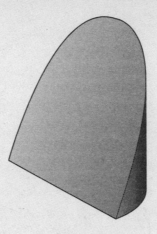

FIGURE 8.2

from the original cube and the original cylinder, as well as from the bases of those figures. Archimedes considers certain planes and lines and derives certain proportions (we will look at these in more detail). Heiberg followed all of this. And then — the gap in the argument. Heiberg could read no further for a long stretch and then, when he picked up the text again, he was already near the end of the proposition. There Heiberg found Archimedes' conclusion, which was that the cylindrical cut was exactly one sixth of the entire enclosing cube.

How had Archimedes got there? Had he actually proved his result? Heiberg couldn't read the relevant passage. Everyone since Heiberg has assumed that it involved the same kind of implicit summation used in proposition 1. That is, having obtained a proportion for the randomly chosen slice, Archimedes had implicitly transferred that result to the entire cylindrical cut — the way Archimedes moved, in proposition 1, from the randomly chosen parallel line to the triangle and parabola taken as a whole. This was everyone's guess; and my guess, too, was that nothing new would come out of this proposition. Saito, meanwhile, was immersing himself in his text: perhaps we were wrong after all?

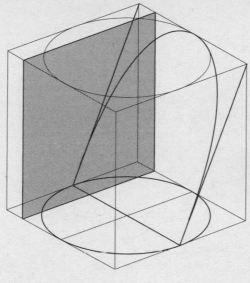

FIGURE 8.3

The Volume of a Cylindrical Cut

Saito and I finally sat there, in front of the bifolio 105–110. We turned quickly to the area that Heiberg had left as white lines, remarking in a footnote: '*quid in tanta lacuna fuerit dictum, non exputo*' – 'I shall not speculate as to what could have been written in such a large gap.'

In order to follow the mathematical argument in more detail, let us concentrate on just the object that interests us. In figure 8.4, we 'slide out', as it were, a section of the cube – the triangular prism cut off by the inclined plane. From now on we shall concentrate on this triangular prism alone. We now draw three further diagrams, reconstructing the text as far as the lacuna. These diagrams – figures 8.5–7 – are simply three different views of this triangular prism. It is so difficult that one needs to view it from certain angles, simultaneously, to gain a sense of it. (Archimedes, however, visualised the object clearly enough on the basis of figure 8.7 alone!)

FIGURE 8.4

In figure 8.5 we see the entire complicated triangular prism with a randomly chosen plane running parallel to the upright edge of the cube.

Figure 8.6 shows the randomly chosen plane *from the side*. The randomly chosen plane cuts off a triangle from the original triangular prism. It also cuts off a smaller triangle from the original cylinder. Thus figure 8.6 shows two triangles, one enclosed within the other: the bigger triangle, from the triangular prism, and the smaller triangle, from the cylinder. The smaller triangle is especially important, because the strange figure that we are about to measure – the fingernail-like figure cut off the cylinder – is made up of the collection of all such triangles cut off from the cylinder. (Those triangles get bigger and bigger – as the randomly chosen plane gets removed further away from the edges of the cube.)

Figure 8.7, finally, offers a bottom view. The randomly chosen plane creates not only triangles from the triangular prism and the

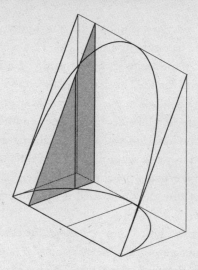

FIGURE 8.5

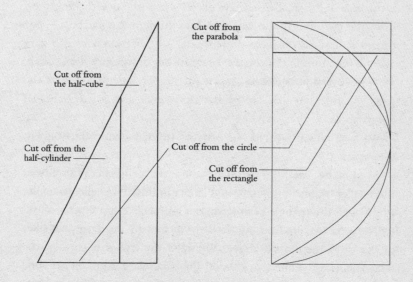

Cut off from
the parabola

Cut off from
the half-cube

Cut off from the
half-cylinder

Cut off from the circle

Cut off from
the rectangle

FIGURE 8.6 AND 8.7

cylinder but also line segments on the bottom of the cube. The bottom of the half-cube is a rectangle. This rectangle is, as it were, the footprint of the entire triangular prism. Within this rectangle we find also a semi-circle. This semi-circle is the footprint of half the cylinder – the half whose slice we are about to measure. To really spice things up, Archimedes then drew another curve inside this rectangle, and – what do you know – this figure happened to be a parabola! And so we have, in figure 8.7, a rectangle, inside it a semi-circle and inside that a parabola. And then, a straight line passes through them all – the line which is the footprint of the randomly chosen plane.

The randomly chosen plane creates a line through the rectangle – this line is the base of the greater triangle of figure 8.6, the one that is cut off from the triangular prism. The randomly chosen plane also creates a line through the semi-circle within the rectangle – this line is the base of the smaller triangle of figure 8.6, the one that is cut off from the cylinder. It also creates a line through the parabola – this time, the line has no three-dimensional meaning in terms of figure 8.6 and functions in the context of figure 8.7 only. Once again, then, we have several lines encased inside each other: one that cuts off the rectangle, then one that cuts off the semi-circle, and one that cuts off the parabola.

We have now presented our cast and we may concentrate on just four actors.

The first two are from figure 8.6: these are the greater triangle and the smaller triangle of figure 8.6. Let us call them 'the triangle of the prism' and 'the triangle of the cylinder', respectively.

The next two are from figure 8.7. We actually need only two out of the three mentioned above. We need the line that cuts off the rectangle, and the line that cuts off the parabola. Call them 'the line of the rectangle' and 'the line of the parabola', respectively.

These four cast members will now participate in a four-part arrangement of *proportion*.

What Heiberg managed to read, prior to the gap in his reading, was already a magnificent result. Archimedes, through tremendous geometrical ingenuity, has succeeded in proving that, in such an arrangement:

- The area of the triangle of the prism is to the triangle of the cylinder as the line of the rectangle is to the line of the parabola.

A triangle is to a triangle, as a line is to a line: two dimensions, as one dimension.

Here came the long gap in the text. The text picked up again with Heiberg reading the following:

- The volume of the triangular prism is to the volume of the cylindrical cut as the area of the entire rectangle is to the area of the entire parabolic segment.

The triangular prism is to the cylinder as the rectangle is to the parabolic segment: three-dimensional figures are to each other as two-dimensional figures are to each other.

Archimedes' geometrical discovery was that the triangles in figure 8.6 related to each other as certain lines do in figures 8.7. This, in other words, is a statement about a random slice, exactly the same type of statement as we saw in the first proposition of the *Method*. It appears, therefore, that Archimedes was once again making the move, implicitly, from a statement about random slices to a statement about the entire objects from which the slices were taken. The first triangle is a random slice of the triangular prism, the second triangle is a random slice of the cylinder; the first line is a random slice of the rectangle, the second line is a random slice of the parabola. And since, in each random slice, the first triangle is to the second triangle as the first line is to the second line, with the entire objects the triangular prism will be to the cylinder as the rectangle is to the parabola.

So the text states, with Archimedes appearing to make an implicit move. But the thing is, there was after all a gap — a space for Archimedes to make his argument explicit.

What could that explicit argument have been?

We could see why Heiberg had not made much progress. The page was largely illegible – indeed, once again we found ourselves admiring Heiberg for what he had been able to read. Even with the UV light the gap seemed hopeless, and we turned instead to the passages Heiberg had read already, trying to verify them. But even those we could hardly read. How had Heiberg ever made it?

We looked again at the conclusion to the proposition. Having shown that the half-cube was to the cylindrical cut as the rectangle was to the parabola, Archimedes went on with a quick calculation. We remember from the first proposition of the *Method* that a parabolic segment is four-thirds the triangle it encloses. Everyone knows that the rectangle is twice the triangle it encloses. So how much is the rectangle to the parabolic segment? It is as 'two' is to 'four-thirds' which (to simplify a bit) is as 'six-thirds' is to 'four-thirds'. It is as six to four or as three to two. The rectangle is therefore to the parabolic segment as three to two or, more comfortably put: the parabolic segment is two-thirds the enclosing rectangle. We've got it! The cylindrical cut is two-thirds the triangular prism that encloses it or, better put for our purposes, it is four-sixths of the triangular prism that encloses it. It will take a while to show the following result: the triangular prism enclosing the cylindrical cut is exactly *one-fourth* the original cube as a whole. The cylindrical cut is *four*-sixths the triangular prism; so it is *one*-sixth of the original cube as a whole. The strange, fingernail-like object is exactly one-sixth the cube. We've got it! – yet another curvilinear object successfully measured using a rectilinear object.

Another elegant result by Archimedes, then. No application of physics, it appears, this time. The triangles and lines are not put on an imaginary balance. They are simply summed up: infinitely many proportions being summed up into a single proportion. How does Archimedes do this? Does he simply ignore the paradoxes, the errors of infinity?

We would not give up. We went back to the gap in the text. We swapped positions, first Ken looking at the page, then me. I was the more trained and quickly it became clear that I should be doing the looking, Ken writing down what I saw.

Will left the room, counting now on our good behaviour. After many minutes of frustration I did something I shouldn't have done. I slipped the bifolio out of its plastic encasing. Unprotected by the plastic, the reflection from the ultraviolet lamp was clearer. I stared hard into that area of the page – those white lines left by Heiberg – trying to find some traces of Greek characters.

I thought I did see something. At first I discarded it, because it did not make sense in the context. There was no reason for Archimedes to be using such a word. But I did think I saw those three characters, in sequence: epsilon–gamma–epsilon: εγε.

'I think I see "ege",' I finally told Ken. 'Probably something to do with megethos, the Greek word for "magnitude". This does not make much sense.'

Because, you see, Archimedes was talking about certain concrete geometrical objects: a cylinder, a triangle, a parabola. In such a context a Greek mathematician would not make the transition to speak about magnitudes, in general terms. The word 'magnitude', with its generality, is appropriate not in a concrete, geometrical context, but in a more abstract context such as a study in the theory of proportions as such, of magnitudes as such. It was as if, in the middle of a calculation with concrete numbers, the text moved to a discussion of the principles of calculation as such.

'Oh, that's very interesting,' said Ken. I should explain that Ken is a well-behaved Japanese scholar. That was an expression of extraordinary agitation. I know he wanted to ask me whether I was sure, but probably he thought such a question might be impolite.

'I am quite sure,' I said, looking at it again. Indeed there was less and less doubt the more I looked at it. In fact, I began to see the traces of a theta, immediately following the epsilon–gamma–epsilon. This was epsilon–gamma–epsilon–theta. No doubt Archimedes was talking about a megethos. He was talking about abstract magnitudes.

This process of gradual certainty is so typical of the reading of the Palimpsest. By getting acquainted with the page you gradually learn how to discard the noise; you learn to concentrate on the signal. It's a little bit like tuning through the airwaves: the radio signal is at first noisy, but then you settle on it and it begins to transmit. I now actually saw this 'magnitude'. I stared at it, dumbstruck.

'Archimedes must be applying result 11,' said Ken.

At first I didn't quite hear, looking as I was – closely – at the page. And then I began to be even a bit annoyed. How could Ken be telling me what was happening through the lacuna, based on a single word? I was still looking for more words. Ken went on.

'In the introduction to the *Method*, Archimedes mentions that he will use certain basic results. One of these results is proved elsewhere, in the treatise on *Conoids and Spheroids*. It deals with general magnitudes. I always thought Archimedes meant this result to be used only in the later parts of the *Method*, where he uses orthodox, geometrical methods. But apparently he uses it in proposition 14 as well.'

Now this got me interested. I put the page back into its plastic casing and picked up the copy of Heiberg's edition that Ken had been reading all the time. By God, what he said did make sense!

We were both now going feverishly through the possible argument, drawing figures, sketching proportions, seeing for ourselves how this result could be used for bridging the gap from the random slices to the entire objects. The result had to do with the summation of proportions. It did make sense. Archimedes could be summing up proportions. So it was not an implicit move after all: Archimedes must have had an argument.

'But wait, Ken; there's a problem' – I stopped, tearing myself away from the figure we had drawn. 'If this is right, then Archimedes must be summing up a collection made of infinitely many magnitudes. This does not sum up. It becomes infinite; you can no longer calculate with it.'

Ken agreed. Something was still missing. The basic result used by Archimedes was based on a proposition proved in *Conoids and Spheroids*, and there it was clear that it could be proven only for sums involving a finite number of magnitudes, because otherwise you would have to speak about an object made of infinitely many magnitudes, which made no sense. That was actual infinity – and how would Archimedes even go about talking about it?

'If one thing is clear, it is that the Greeks did not use actual infinity. There is something wrong here. Or else, something very new.'

This was clear, indeed. It was January 2001, and we knew that we had hit on a major discovery for the history of mathematics. Just what, though?

And could we be simply mistaken? I trusted Ken's insight into Greek mathematics. It all made sense. And I was sure I did see that word, those four letters epsilon–gamma–epsilon–theta (well, at least the first three were certain . . .). But could we base a new interpretation of Greek mathematics on this evidence alone? – a new twist to the entire trajectory of Western mathematics?

That evening Ken and I explained to Will that we really, really wanted to see digital images of this page. An entire chapter in the history of science was waiting to be written, based on those images.

The Method, *March 2001*

I kept going in and out of my office, checking my mailbox. When would it arrive? It took the imagers just over a month and then, early in March, the CD-ROM got there. I knew this CD-ROM contained some high-resolution, sharp digital images, made with UV, of a single piece of the Palimpsest. It was a small piece of the Palimpsest, no more. But this piece included one side of the bifolio 105–110 – the side I truly needed to read.

For the rest of the day I put all other work aside, looking at a jungle of digital traces, enlarging them so that the pixels blew up and then reducing them again to see the entire picture – getting my mind tuned off the noise, tuned in to the signal.

I could easily pick up again the εγε, now clear as daylight in the digital image. Indeed the theta was very clear as well, and, looking for it, I could quickly pick up several other appearances of the word 'magnitude'. Undoubtedly this was what Archimedes was talking about. A few further words became visible as well, referring to certain geometrical objects: a cylinder here, a rectangle there. Probably Archimedes was applying the general principles of summation of proportion to the concrete, geometrical terms of the figure at hand. And there was no doubt: the digital images made a world of difference.

After making those first inroads, the reading stalled. This was once again a typical part of the cycle of reading: once you had gained your first, easy conquests, there would come a pause. There were no longer any 'easy' words to read, even with the digital images. One needed to do some work, now – looking and thinking: what could those traces mean?

I looked in this manner for a couple of hours, making little further progress. I needed to clear my head a little, so I went out for a walk, after which I took another look and, just out of curiosity, stared not at the line of writing itself but a little bit above it. Something there arrested my attention – this was not just a smudge of digital noise; it had the texture and consistency of real ink. Blowing up the pixels, I saw it – the kind of trace I would normally skip as being too inconsequential but one that, in such a fragmentary text, could be meaningful. This was an accent mark, an acute sign above the line, like this: ´. And, with my acquaintance with this scribe, I could say more: it was the type of acute sign the scribe would use on top of an iota. It was rather like reading the dot of an 'i' and identifying the 'i' on this basis.

More than this: I knew which 'i' this was: it was an iota with an acute accent, i.e. it could belong only in a handful of words where an iota is stressed this way. One likely candidate, in a mathematical context, would be the word *ísos* . . . Archimedes could well be speaking of this being equal to that, right? And indeed I could see a sigma, now that I was looking for it.

What kind of 'equal', then? Looking ahead, I thought I saw another one of those general words of proportion theory – only this time it wasn't 'magnitude' but 'multitude'. The couple of words fell into place: 'equal in multitude'. *Isos plethei*. This was good mathematical Greek. This was 'equal in multitude' to that. I looked further and further. The text was peppered with 'equal in multitude'. It appeared that this was what Archimedes was doing throughout this passage – he was showing how the result pointed out by Ken applied to the case at hand, by showing how this was equal in multitude to that. It was all about such-and-such magnitudes being equal in multitude to other magnitudes.

How I wished Ken was with me then! Because this would be just too good to be true. The expression 'equal in multitude' is used in Greek mathematics when discussing the numbers of objects in two separate sets. Suppose I have a set of three triangles here, and a set of three lines there – then a Greek mathematician would say that the two sets are 'equal in multitude', meaning that they are each made up of three objects.

Now this is what Archimedes was doing here: he was saying that, with the infinitely many slices produced in the cube – once all the random slices were made, the cube cut everywhere – then the triangles produced in this way (i.e. all the various triangles produced in the cube by all the possible random cuts) were 'equal in multitude' to the lines in the rectangle. You see? In each random slice there was a triangle in the cube, standing on top of a line in the rectangle. And Archimedes pointed out that the number of triangles of which the prism was made was the same as the number of lines of which the rectangle was made. Surely he meant this to be verified by the fact that there was a one-to-one relationship: each triangle stood on an individually separate line, and, vice versa, each line was at the bottom of an individually separate triangle.

Archimedes repeated this type of statement three times: he went through the various configurations produced by the slices, showing which set was equal in multitude to which. And indeed, once those equalities of multitude were secured, the result pointed out by Ken did apply. This was typical of Archimedes. He did not actually refer, explicitly, to his result; he did not even quote it. But he set up the conditions under which the result could apply; and this he did by showing, in detail, which equalities of number applied in the configuration at hand.

Only, of course, those equalities of number were like nothing else we ever knew from Greek mathematics. The objects Archimedes counted here – the sets of triangles and lines – were all infinite. Here was Archimedes, explicitly calculating with infinitely great numbers.

More than this: Archimedes was making his calculations based on a sound principle. He apparently was stating that this infinite set was equal to that infinite set, because there was a one-to-one relationship between the two sets. He did not say so in so many words, but Archimedes was never an explicit author. He always left much work for the reader.

Note the following fact. Archimedes could have assumed, in principle, that just because the two sets were infinite, they were also equal. This would have been a very natural assumption to make – that all infinities are equal. But the very fact that Archimedes found it necessary to state that particular sets of infinitely many objects are equal, shows that he avoided this naïve assumption. Instead, he must have assumed that infinite sets could be said to be equal only where a special argument could be made for their equality. And this then leaves only one possible argument for this equality – the argument of one-to-one correspondence.

It so happens that the tool of one-to-one correspondence is the one with which the concept of infinity was finally structured in the late nineteenth century. This is no less than the cornerstone for modern Set Theory. And so we can sum up the lessons learned from pages 105–110 of the *Method*.

First, we find that Archimedes did not merely make an 'implicit' move from a random slice to the object made of those random slices. He relied instead on certain principles of summation. This means that he was already making a step towards the modern calculus, and was not merely anticipating it in some naïve way.

Second, we find that Archimedes calculated with actual infinities – in direct opposition to everything historians of mathematics have always believed about their discipline. Actual infinities were known already to the ancient Greeks.

Third, we see that with this concept of infinity – as with so many others – the genius of Archimedes pointed the way towards the achievements of modern science itself. Back in the third century BC, at Syracuse, Archimedes foresaw a glimpse of Set Theory, the product of the mature mathematics of the late nineteenth century.

Mathematics, Physics, Infinity – and Beyond

It appears that there is some kind of complementary structure in the *Method*: thirteen propositions apply both physics and the implicit summation of infinitely many objects. In proposition 14 physics is no longer applied – but there the summation of infinitely many objects is not implicit, but explicit, based on a rule of infinite summations. It therefore appears that, for Archimedes, the application of physics could act as some sort of short cut. When this short cut was not available, one needed instead an explicit, mathematical rule for infinity. It is as if Archimedes thought that, in the physical world, the summation of infinitely many objects was not such a problem – after all, physical objects *are* made of infinitely many parts. But when one moved to abstract, mathematical objects, there was also a need for a special, mathematical principle for doing such a summation.

Archimedes, after all, did not produce the science of the physical world that Galileo and Newton would later produce. This is even though he had assembled – as we have just seen – the tool kit for the making of such science. I think I understand why. The reason was that, for Archimedes, the combination of physics and mathematics was important not for the sake of physics but for the sake of mathematics itself. Archimedes' great desire was not to find out about the motions of planets but to measure curvilinear objects. It so happens that, in our universe, mathematics, physics and infinity are so closely tied together that, looking to advance pure mathematics, Archimedes also laid the foundation for modern science.

Whichever interpretation we take of this, it is clear that our understanding of the historical relationship between mathematics, physics and infinity will now have to be drastically revised in light of proposition 14. But more than this. We will need to revise our understanding of the Greek treatment of infinity. I like to sum this up with the phrase 'it's not that they couldn't'. They could very well envisage actual infinity, they could even operate with it. For various reasons, in most contexts they preferred to avoid it. But this avoidance was a conscious decision, not some kind of reflection of shortcoming on the Greeks' part. They were ahead of the infinity game. And so the same goes, in my view, for science. I think Archimedes was capable of producing the kind of science of physics that Galileo and Newton produced. He made the decision not to: other things occupied his mind.

So much for the broad picture of the history of science and mathematics. Another thing, also, became clear now – of great interest to everyone involved with the Archimedes Project. The work *mattered*. There were important passages yet to be read. Already, with 105–110, my reading had managed to get substantially beyond Heiberg's. Other pages appeared to be even more difficult, but now it became even more crucial to make them visible. The pressure was now on the imagers to produce a completely new kind of product – an image to make the invisible come to light. Would that be possible?

9

The Digital Palimpsest

Abigail had disbound the Palimpsest, and Reviel and Ken Saito had rewarded her work with an insight that blew apart the boundaries of Greek mathematical thought. But it was clear from the start that Abigail's work was merely a step on the way towards a more radical transformation of Mr B's book. As she was taking the prayer book apart, I was asking the scientists to put all the palimpsested codices that it contained back together again as they had been before the year 1229.

I did not want the scientists to reproduce the Palimpsest; I wanted them to replace it. I wanted them to make something that was so much better than the codex that scholars would not need to make the pilgrimage to Baltimore. I asked them to make the invisible visible, to make it available on desk-top computers around the world and to make it appear in its correct order. Archimedes first, of course, but then the palimpsested texts from the other codices. This was a utopian fantasy. After all, we didn't even know how many other codices there were, let alone what was in them! Yet the result, in 2005, exceeded everybody's expectations: scholars now read texts that they literally had not dreamed of reading in 1998; and they had not been able to read these texts from the manuscript, they had had to read them on a computer. But this success was hard won, and it was a long time coming.

It was clear from the beginning that both teams – the one from Johns Hopkins headed by Bill Christens-Barry, and Roger Easton and Keith Knox from the Rochester Institute of Technology, would be putting most of their efforts, and most of their faith, into a technique called 'multi-spectral imaging'. I needed to understand what 'multi-spectral imaging' involved, and my guide was the only teacher among them, Roger Easton, Professor of Imaging Science at RIT. I thought of images as shapes produced by artists. Roger thought of images as numbers produced by light. Not surprisingly, it took him a little time to explain his view of things to me.

Light

Light, Roger told me, be it from the sun or from light bulbs, comes in waves of electromagnetism, which themselves consist of tiny energy bundles called photons. The photons can be characterised by the distance between their peaks – their wavelength. Some photons come in long wavelengths – such as radio waves, microwaves, and infrared waves, and some in much shorter ones, such as ultraviolet waves, X-rays and gamma rays. Visible light forms a very small part of the entire electromagnetic spectrum, between infrared and ultraviolet. The shorter the wavelength of a photon, the greater its energy; but all photons travel at exactly the same speed in a vacuum – the well-known speed of light: 186,282 miles per second.

Photons interact with matter, which is made up of atoms. More specifically, they interact with electrons that take their places at various distances from an atom's nucleus. Not all photons interact with all electrons: crucially, the interaction depends upon their respective energies; they have to resonate with each other. If they do, a photon will change the energy state of an electron, and in response the electron will itself emit a photon. The photon emitted by any given electron will have a precise wavelength, a precise energy, and this wavelength will depend upon the energy it needs to shed, which in turn depends upon its place in the composition of an atom.

The human eye uses photons to make all the colours of the rainbow. This is how it does it. With its lens, the eye focuses photons emitted by the electrons on to the photosensitive cells of the retina. The photons induce chemical changes in these receptor cells. The changes in the cells depend upon the wavelengths of the received photons: when your cells receive photons with a wavelength of about 400 nanometres they will change in such a way that they generate an electric current that will travel via the optic nerve to the visual centre of the brain, which will interpret the current as a colour: blue. When your cells receive photons with a wavelength of about 700 nanometres, the same process will occur, but the chemical change will be slightly different, so will the resulting current, and so will the colour. In this case, you will see red. We read by recognising patterns of intensity and colour generated in the visual centre of our brain as letters. The problem is that many of the letters in the undertext of the Palimpsest cannot be read, even in bright sunlight.

'What could be a better light source than the Sun?' I asked Roger, 'and what could be a better receptor than the eye?' The trouble with the Sun as a light source is that it gives off photons at all sorts of different wavelengths. The image that your eye sees under sunlight is the sum of images created at all of the visible wavelengths. If you can create a source that emits light over a relatively narrow band of the spectrum, then the resulting image will just carry the information from that one wavelength, which will not be overwhelmed by light at the others.

Consider, for example, images created using ultraviolet lamps. Although photons from these lamps have wavelengths shorter than those that the eye can detect, they have a remarkable effect on the parchment that they hit. They energise the atoms and molecules in the parchment, which absorb some of the energy and re-emit the rest as photons with a wavelength that happens to be in the blue section of the spectrum visible to humans. While the parchment re-emits visible photons, the ink on the parchment obscures them. As a result, the ink is effectively 'backlit' by the soft blue light from this 'fluorescence', the contrast of the faint undertext increases and thus the text becomes more readable. Ultraviolet fluorescent light has long been used by scholars reading palimpsests, and with great success. Reviel and Ken used it to read *Method* proposition 14. But you cannot use an ultraviolet lamp effectively except in a dark room; photons at other frequencies completely obscure what they do.

The eye itself is such an amazing piece of machinery that it is hard to imagine how a man-made version can be better. But the eye has plenty of limitations that we normally do not notice because it has evolved to suit our everyday needs. Its limitations become more apparent when you try to do something extraordinary, though. Looking at planets is difficult, explained Roger, because the size of the image on the retina is so small that it covers only a few of the eye's sensors. Since each sensor 'sees' a large part of the planet, the eye cannot see ('resolve') the fine detail. Here, telescopes come in handy. Or try another problem: I find it difficult to see my cat Gracie after dark because the cells of the human retina do not respond to the wavelengths emitted by warm-blooded animals; these infrared wavelengths are much longer than the light we can see. The human eye is responsive to only a tiny part of the electromagnetic spectrum. But modern cameras can detect infrared wavelengths and can find warm-blooded animals in the dark. This is the basic reason why we use cameras rather than eyes to read the Palimpsest. Unlike the human eye, modern cameras are sensitive to light outside the visible spectrum, and thus can 'see' information to which your eye is 'blind'.

In short, you can get very different results using narrowband illumination captured by a camera from those you get when you look at an object under the sun. The successes of imagers around the world in revealing hidden text by using cameras under different narrowband lighting conditions are remarkable. For example, a team at Brigham Young University has attained extraordinary results by imaging the carbonised rolls of a library that was buried in Herculaneum under the volcanic ash of Vesuvius in the early afternoon of Tuesday, 24 August AD 79. When viewed in normal light, you cannot see any text written on many of these rolls at all. But when imaged at a specific wavelength, the text 'pops out' in the most remarkable way. We did not think that imaging Archimedes would produce such clear-cut results, primarily because the Palimpsest is, physically and chemically speaking, a much more complicated object. The text in the rolls had not been scraped off, it had not been overwritten, and its support hadn't suffered the mould damage that the Palimpsest had. The rolls had been subject to just one catastrophic incident that had changed the chemical composition of the rolls themselves and the text on them. We were right, too; there is no one wavelength at which the Archimedes text pops out. But this is where multi-spectral imaging comes into its own.

Numbers

Roger told me that multi-spectral imaging was a relatively new technique that had become widely available only since the arrival of computers and digital-imaging technology. Computers turn all the information they receive into numerical values – digits. Actually just two 'binary digits' ('bits') are used – 0 and 1 – but they are combined in a great variety of ways. For example, your laptop computer converts your taps on the keyboard into different combinations of 0 and 1, which it can store and use as instructions to make certain patterns on your screen. When you digitally record music on your computer, the loudness of sound at each time interval is again interpreted as a number. When you take a picture with a digital camera, the light that hits the camera sensor is turned into numerical values. Each 'piece' of the image, each so-called 'picture element' or 'pixel', is given a number made out of 1s and 0s. Many images are '8-bit' images, and the numbers attached to these pixels are made out of eight-figure combinations of 1s and 0s. So, for example, the number 10101010 actually has a value of 170. The number 11111111 has a value of 255 – and this is the highest value that an 8-bit number can have because, including 00000000, there are only 256 ways in which 0s and 1s can be combined in an eight-figure series. To extract this numerical information you need a software package – a series of instructions to your processor that sorts the numbers and presents the information in useful ways. And you had better have the appropriate software package: Beethoven's Ninth would not make a pretty picture; and the Archimedes Palimpsest is unlikely to sound any better than it looks.

One of the great advantages of digital technology is that it is possible to combine the numbers from images in different ways. You can instruct the computer to adjust the numerical values in the image – to suppress numbers that are too high or too low, and to amplify small differences if you decide that they are important. This is how computers get rid of red-eye due to the flash in your family photos. But another advantage of digital technology is that you can overlay one set of numbers with another. You can, for example, add a backbeat behind the voice of a rock star. More importantly for our purposes, you can combine an image taken at one wavelength of light with an image taken at another one to make some feature in that scene more visible. If you take images at many different wavelengths and stack all these different images in order of wavelength, one upon the other in a computer, you produce a 'data-cube' of digital information, in which each is seen in different wavelengths of light. Do not imagine this data-cube as a hologram; imagine it as a sea of numbers containing patterns – or curves – that reflect the characteristics of the area imaged. By writing computer algorithms (recipes for retrieving data in a certain way), scientists can carve up the data-cube to manipulate the values of the numbers, accentuate certain curves and extract the information they want. Much more information can be extracted from a digital data-cube created using narrow bands of light than can be retrieved from the Palimpsest under any single lighting condition.

The most basic procedure to extract information from a data-cube, Roger explained, was 'principal components analysis'. You ask the computer to make a set of pictures from weighted combinations of the numerical values of images taken at each wavelength. The images in this new set are based on the amount of difference between numerical values of pixels that are close to each other. As a result they do not show patterns of colour, but patterns of contrast. The first image in the new set highlights those areas where contrast between different features is greatest; the second image shows the next greatest contrast, the third image the next, etc. By this process, you start out with a set of images of the same area in different wavelengths of light and end up with a set of images that combine the wavelengths of light to show the different objects of the image. Obviously, in the Palimpsest the first principal component shows the image feature with the most contrast, which is the prayer-book text, with its nice dark ink outlined against the light-brown parchment around it. But the second principal component is indeed, in large part, the Archimedes undertext. Yet another principal component image might show the mould. Once you have separated out the components, you can make them as bright or as dark as you like by manipulating the numbers.

Modern science has turned light into numbers, and modern scientists can change the numbers. But the skill is in how you change the numbers, and this is as much an art as it is a science.

Digital Cooking

The two teams of imagers started their competition in June 2000, and they worked with five leaves that were already detached from the binding of the codex when it arrived at the Walters.

Bill Christens-Barry took his images with a Kodak digital camera. This is a standard type of camera, used by professional journalists the world over. It couldn't make a very big data-cube, but it could create images with a high spatial resolution. Bill and his colleague Joanna Bernstein imaged at 600 dots per inch. Bill called his best shot at manipulating his data his 'cookie-cutter' technique. He chose a set of images from the ultraviolet range of the spectrum, in which he could see both the prayer-book text and the Archimedes text reasonably well. Then he separated out the principal components of the images he took in normal light and selected one that just showed the prayer-book text. He then played with these two pictures in the computer; he subtracted the image of the prayer-book text from the ultraviolet images that showed both texts well, and so was left with just the Archimedes text.

Keith and Roger's camera made Bill's look like Fred Flintstone's. To select their wavelengths of light they didn't use glass filters placed in front of the lens; they used the latest technology, a 'liquid-crystal tunable filter' (LCTF), by which they could select the wavelength of the incoming photons by turning an electronic knob. The camera even had a tiny electrical refrigerator to keep its sensor cool. With this camera Keith and Roger built data-cubes at thirty-five different wavelengths across the spectrum – a much bigger data-cube than Bill's camera could make. The only disadvantage was that this camera could only image at 200 dots per inch. It had much greater spectral resolution, but less spatial resolution than Bill's camera.

Keith and Roger processed very differently from Bill. They examined each folio that they were looking at and determined pixels that belonged to three different classes of object: pixels that were definitely parchment, those that were definitely prayer book, and yet another class – the important one – pixels that were definitely Archimedes. They then located the corresponding pixels in the images that they took – all thirty-five of them – and made a computer evaluate the vital statistics for each of the pixels. Then, the computer calculated the degree of likelihood that any given pixel was a prayer-book pixel, an Archimedes pixel or a parchment pixel. If the computer was sure that a pixel was Archimedes, it would be very bright; if it was less sure, it would be dimmer. The computer then combined the results from the different wavelengths. This technique is called 'matched spectral filtering'.

It looked as if Bill had come to a gunfight with a knife, or at least with a point-and-shoot camera. But, actually, I looked at the images from both teams and thought that they were marvellous: Bill's images were quite as good, in my eyes, as Roger and Keith's. In the image showing the Archimedes text I could see diagrams where previously I had seen nothing. I could see Archimedes text appear from nowhere. And I couldn't see the prayer-book text. It had all but disappeared into the parchment background. I thought that we had cracked it already. I held out the hope that with these pictures we could recreate the Archimedes manuscript as it had been even before it was palimpsested. This would be the Jurassic Park of medieval manuscript studies, and the Resurrection of Archimedes. If you looked at one of these pictures, you would understand my excitement. I thought that both teams of imagers had done the job that we had asked, and that the only real problem we had was how to choose between them.

On Friday, 20 October 2000 a segment on the Palimpsest was broadcast on ABC's news programme *The World Tonight*, with the late Peter Jennings. It detailed the remarkable efforts of imaging scientists to uncover the erased texts of Archimedes in an ancient manuscript in Baltimore. Suddenly the imagers were stars. Three days later, on the Monday, they were to present their results to Natalie and Reviel. We were all in for a shock.

Bad Recipes

Reviel could not make the review meeting; he had pneumonia. Natalie Tchernetska voiced complaints for both of them. In her words, the photographs of both teams, but particularly Keith and Roger's, were 'out of focus'. They had all sorts of unexplained white spots on them. They were not of sufficient resolution. Getting rid of the prayer-book text had not helped at all in reading the Archimedes text. Plain old high-resolution photographs and photographs just taken in ultraviolet light were much better than these processed images. What had gone wrong? As it turns out, it is not easy for imaging scientists and medieval palaeographers to understand each other. So let us, like the imagers, take each of Natalie's complaints in turn.

Her first complaint was that the images were out of focus. Actually they were not out of focus. The problem was one that all multi-spectral imagers face. To get images of different wavelengths of light they had had to change the filters on their camera. Because the light going through different filters refracted at slightly different angles, the resulting images were of very slightly different sizes. Since they had taken images at many different wavelengths, and these images had not 'registered' properly, the result indeed was that the processed images looked blurred. Now, this doesn't matter much when you are imaging large tracts of ground from space, and trying to find a coca field in the Amazon rainforest, which is the type of thing that this technique is normally used for. But it does matter – very much – when you are trying to read the niceties of tiny Greek script from the tenth century. Clearly, Roger, Keith and Bill were going to have to use fewer wavelengths, or find another way to get around this 'registration' problem.

Her second complaint was that the images had lots of white spots on them, that looked as if they were supposed to be Archimedes text but which were not. Imaging scientists call these spots 'artefacts'. The imagers had in fact found imaging Mr B's book to be extremely difficult. As a result, they had had to write very complicated algorithms to extract the Archimedes text. Now, every time you manipulate an image you are playing with data. You might be bringing out the text that you want, but you are also, inevitably, adding noise, just by stirring the ingredients. Again, in most applications of multi-spectral imagery this doesn't matter – at least not very much. But in trying to read the Archimedes text, it does matter, very much. The scientists had to come up with simpler algorithms.

Roger and Keith took images at 200 dots per inch – about 8 pixels per millimetre. This was a perfectly sensible thing to do. It is, more or less, the resolution of the rods and cones of the eye if the page is viewed at normal viewing distances, and it allowed a complete single folio of the Palimpsest to be imaged in two sections with the available digital camera. They did not make enlarged images of the folios, which would have required a much higher resolution. We simply did not know that Reviel and Natalie wanted to read magnified images to see all of the critical features in the text. If possible, Reviel would have wanted a single Archimedes character to fill up his entire computer screen and still not appear pixillated; he would have loved to see the image as though through a microscope. In reading palimpsest texts, size matters after all. This was another lesson that the scientists had to learn, and another way in which the camera could potentially improve upon the eye.

But the most revealing and unexpected complaint that Natalie and Reviel had was that the imagers had taken away the prayer-book text. They wanted it back again. What on earth had we been doing, and why? The scientists had actually succeeded in separating the Archimedes text from the prayer-book text and eliminating the prayer-book text, and now the scholars were saying that this didn't help. The reason that it didn't help is actually quite straightforward. The scientists had made the prayer-book text disappear by making it exactly the same colour as the parchment. The trouble was that now, when the Archimedes characters disappeared beneath a bit of prayer-book text, the scholars didn't know why: it was no longer clear to them whether the Archimedes letters were invisible because they in fact did not exist, or because they were actually hiding underneath the letters of the prayer book. The scientists had created images with characteristics that the scholars simply did not value, however cool I thought them to be.

The whole day was a litany of complaint. I was as confident in the afternoon that the results were useless as I had been in the morning that they were a triumph. Mike Toth, the project's programme manager, Abigail and I met in closed session at the end of the day. And then, to my amazement, Mike insisted that nothing at all had gone wrong. In fact, he explained, this was how experimental imaging projects worked.

If you ask scientists to come up with a solution to a difficult problem, you will make errors in defining that problem and they more likely than not will fail to get the best solution first time. Really difficult problems, said Mike, get resolved in incremental steps. These steps begin with criticism and end with understanding. Mike said that it was quite normal in such imaging projects for scientists to produce a misconceived product. We were just at the beginning of a long process by which the imagers might come to understand fully what the scholars needed and through which they could refine their techniques. Furthermore, Mike insisted, the imagers had done well: they had succeeded in separating the Archimedes text from the rest of the manuscript, and there were signs that they were pulling out Archimedes text that could not be seen at all under normal light conditions. Actually, he went on, instead of firing the imagers, we should make them join forces and hire them all. In other words, Mike thought that Mr B should pay for all three of them to work on the project; we could combine Bill Christen-Barry's experimental approach with the processing skills of Keith and Roger.

I didn't actually think that Mike was nuts, because I knew that he had a vast amount of experience in judging the results of technical projects. But I could not see the way forward and I dreaded to think what the reaction of the 'source selection authority' would be when I emailed him. His reply was, typically, far briefer than my wordy missive. His verdict: 'OK.'

The First Words

Throughout the taxing period to March 2001 Reviel and Natalie had been trying to transcribe the Archimedes texts from the scientists' images. I was copied in on emails that reveal like nothing else the difficulty of their task. Here is a typical one from Reviel to Natalie:

Natalie, I'm making progress!

Take a look at 48v col. 1 line 6, after the easily readable word perile/psomen. Heiberg is surely wrong to get the rho immediately after without a gap – there is surely a one character gap; furthermore his undotted eta is a very bad eta. This scribe tends to have a small foot of the eta flexed inside a little bit, like a knee reacting in a knee-jerk, but this foot is very smooth, a continuous parabolic curve; in fact, this is more like the scribe's kappa than like his eta. Now, the character just preceding the rho is faint, but does suggest an alpha. Heiberg's concluding to/s seems likely, and so we may have ark[2-3 characters]to/s. How about arkounto/s? Then the immediate couple of words is perile/psomen arkounto/s – 'we shall include', 'sufficiently'. The entire passage could be made to read, e.g., kai allo/n pleiono/n (homoio/n touotois) theo/roumeno/n ta (pleista) ou perile/psomen, arkounto/s gar ho tropos hupodedeiktai dia to/n proeire/meno/n. I bracket words that are truly speculative, though there is some trace of a lambda for pleista, and the famous 'moi' at the beginning of line 5.

This transcription was one that Reviel made from one of the trial images. The transcription might have been helpful to Natalie, but it was of absolutely no use to the imagers. In the Proof of Concept, Reviel found his own way to show what text he could decipher, and what still needed work. He drew pictures.

Working mainly from the ultraviolet images, Reviel would write in green what he could read and in red what he could only guess. There are alarming amounts of red in these pictures. Sometimes he would send images with questions on them. One particularly import-ant passage seemed to be on folio 105. Reviel writes in what he sees but frankly admits to total guesses on the folio. It seems like an extraordinary struggle. And indeed it was. It was worth it, of course: eventually we discovered that Archimedes knew about actual infinity. But we couldn't go on like this indefinitely.

Making Light Work

Roger, Bill and Keith had a lot to prove. But they not only learned from the criticism of their efforts; they came up with a new concept for the imaging of the Palimpsest based on their early results. They would address the resolution problem and image not at 200 dpi but at 600. To address the registration problem they were not going to filter the light at all. Instead, the images would be collected under three different lighting conditions, with low-wattage tungsten lights (which give off a very 'reddish' light), with Xenon strobe lights (which give off short flashes of bright, white light), and with 'long-wave' ultraviolet lamps that emit most of their light at 365 nanometres, which is just barely shorter than the short-wavelength limit of the human eye. They would also take the images with a professional colour digital camera, the type now used by every professional photo-journalist in the country. There is no point in using the latest technology if the latest technology doesn't help you. Although Bill's Kodak camera didn't have the spectral precision of Roger and Keith's, it could get the spatial resolution that the scholars were looking for, it meant that the registration problems would be less severe, and Bill had demonstrated in his experiments that more processing was not needed to separate the prayer-book text from the Archimedes text. So, the knife won out over the gun after all. The Proof of Concept imaging took place in early 2001. I had to wait several months for the imagers to come up with a processed product.

Success was achieved by trial and through error, but this time the imagers had good data and a much better idea of what the scholars wanted. The imagers were, of course, playing with numbers. But in what follows I explain their solution visually, in terms of colours. It is, quite literally, easier to visualise this way.

Up until this point, the scholars had found the UV images to be the most useful. The scientists therefore looked at what it was that the scholars didn't like about the UV images. They had two serious deficiencies. Firstly, they were rather 'soft'; they seemed to lack defin- ition. Secondly, they were essentially monochromatic – they were shades of blue: the parchment was bright blue, and the ink was dark blue. And although the texts stood out better than they did in natural light, it was harder than ever to distinguish between the prayer-book text and the Archimedes text. Keith Knox took the UV images as his starting point. He wanted to make it clear which text was Archimedes, which text was prayer book, and with a minimum of image processing. Also he had to restore the sharpness that the UV image lacked.

In the Proof of Concept imaging the imagers noticed that there was a big difference in the appearance of the manuscript when it was imaged using white strobe lights from when normal tungsten lights were used. Low-wattage tungsten light is, as I mentioned, very red compared to strobe light, and in tungsten light the Archimedes text was much fainter. The image consisted of red, green and blue 'chan- nels', and he saw that in the red channel the Archimedes text almost disappeared completely. To me this was a bad thing, but not to the imagers: they had two simple, unprocessed images of a page, and these images were completely different. By combining them they could come up with a different, synthetic image.

So Keith made a new picture altogether. He started with a blank 'digital canvas'. On to this canvas he could insert his images, and he had three digital channels in which to do this – red, green and blue. In the red channel he put the tungsten-red image. In the blue channel he put the ultraviolet-blue image (and in the green channel he simply put the ultraviolet-blue image again). The important point for Keith was not that the Archimedes text disappeared in the tungsten-red image; the important point was that both the parchment and the Archimedes text were red. So in the red channel of his picture he had bright Archimedes, bright parchment and dark prayers. In the blue and green channels he had dark Archimedes, bright parchment and dark prayers. By combining these elements into one picture, he got bright parchment, dark prayers and dark Archimedes with a red tint.

This was very neat. It involved far less processing than images produced in the initial trials, it clearly differentiated the prayers from the Archimedes text by colour, and it gave the Archimedes text a greater clarity than the UV image. The images were really just what Reviel was looking for. They had a resolution of more than 600 dpi, they made a clear colour difference between the parchment, the Archimedes text and the prayer-book text, they had few artefacts and they were not blurry. The process had another great advantage: it worked well over relatively large areas of the palimpsested texts, and little local processing was necessary; in fact, the processing could be automated. An entire day's worth of images could be processed overnight on Keith's laptop computer as it ran on the desk in his hotel room. We called them 'pseudocolour images', the method that produced them 'pushbutton processing', and Keith's package of software code for making them 'Archie 1.1'. By September 2001 we had the key to unlock the secrets of the Palimpsest. No one had done any serious transcription work from the Palimpsest itself since Reviel and Ken had come on 6 January 2001.

A New Box for the Brain

Writing books in the Middle Ages was a laborious business. A scribe named Raoul working in the Monastery of St Aignan, in France, wrote: 'You do not know what it is to write. It is excessive drudgery; it crooks your back, dims your sight, twists your stomach and sides. Pray, then, my brother, you who read this book, pray for poor Raoul, God's servant, who has copied it entirely with his own hand in the cloister of St Aignan.'

Roger, Keith and Bill became twenty-first-century Raouls, and we should spare a thought for them. They created text just as surely as Raoul did, and although their procedures were very different, they had exactly the same feelings about the process. From 2001 onwards they would visit the Walters every six months or so and, for ten days at a stretch, image the fifteen folios of Mr B's book that Abigail and her team had most recently liberated. And while Abigail had liberated the leaves, I placed the scientists in their very own cell – a bare white-painted cinder-block room with no windows that cannot have been much bigger than the average medieval monk's living quarters. And I had to lock them in it. Frequently they were working after hours in a museum containing thousands of priceless treasures, and they would have to call me to let them out if they so much as wanted to use the restroom.

Each time they came, the imagers filled their cell chock-a-block with equipment, which Roger drove down from Rochester. Roger had made a special gantry for the imaging of the codex: the cameras were mounted above a motorised X-Y stage, upon which each bifolio was placed and imaged. The imagers to this day have not touched the Palimpsest. Each folio was wheeled in by a conservator from the conservation studio about fifty feet away. Each one was mounted in its own bespoke mat. A conservator would place it carefully on the X-Y stage. Once it was on the stage, everything was moved by computer. To turn the leaf, the imagers had to make a phone call to the conservation studio and someone would turn the leaf for them.

Roger was in the driving seat, literally. He drove the X-Y stage, and he took the pictures with a click of the mouse. Each side of each leaf was photographed thirty times: to get a resolution of 600 dpi, ten separate pictures of each folio had to be taken, and in three different lighting conditions. Keith was 'the lights': he flicked the switch that turned on and off the strobe lights, the tungsten lights and the ultraviolet lights. Bill recorded every move on spreadsheets. We now have over 15,000 records. For each image we record which folio, which side of that folio, which position on that side of that folio, the date that the image was created, the camera make, the camera serial number, the lens brand, the lens serial number, the lens size, the wavelength of the illumination and whether it is fluorescent or reflect-ive, the make, serial number and wattage of the illumination source, the size of the aperture on the camera, the shutter speed, resolution, the pixel X count, the pixel Y count, the camera incident angle and the distance of the camera from the folio. There are more columns than this, and some of them, even today, I do not understand. But the scientists needed to document everything thoroughly, not just for their own records but for posterity. There is always the possibility that someone might use this data to make better images with more effective processing algorithms in the future.

If you think this is boring, you are not alone. Ten days sitting in a cell-like room, taking pictures in the bright light and then in total darkness – Bill C.-B. called it 'trained-monkey work'. It was unbelievably boring. It was also frustrating: things broke and they had to be fixed; there were long pauses for leaves to be delivered; and the worst thing was the 'whirr' of the X-Y stage as it moved from one section to the next. But they couldn't oil the cogs. And for Keith it didn't stop. Each night he would take the data collected that day back to his hotel room and make his marvellous creations: entirely new images using the ultraviolet and the low-wattage-tungsten images as ingredients. And it is an important conceptual point: these things are not images of the Palimpsest; they are synthetic creations made from images of the Palimpsest. They are works of art. Well, they work, anyway. And that's the point.

Still, at this stage, we have no product. All the images had to be assembled so that scholars could access them. First, the ten individual shots of each folio had to be 'stitched' together, and this had to be done for strobe, ultraviolet, and pseudocolour images. Roger Easton and his graduate students at RIT had to perform 5,520 stitching operations. They then had to devise a way by which scholars could access the images easily. The browser that Roger and his students designed is the mechanism by which the scholars access the texts in the Palimpsest. It is infinitely more flexible than the Palimpsest itself. If they want to, they can read the prayer book, with the leaves falling in the right order. At the click of a mouse, though, the images magically reorder themselves so that they appear in their Archimedes order, as they were before they were palimpsested. The scholars can also choose whether they want to see these pages in normal light, ultraviolet light or in synthetic pseudocolour. And they can see the Archimedes pages in more detail than the eye can see the original: you can zoom in on a section of a page and 'blow it up' without losing resolution.

Of course, the imagers did not understand the text they were creating. It was up to Nigel Wilson and Reviel to read the Archimedes text. He and Reviel are now working on completely new editions of *Method*, *Stomachion* and *Floating Bodies*. Theirs is, in many ways, an ideal collaboration. Nigel has greater familiarity with the transcription and decipherment of tenth-century Greek cursive than Reviel. On the other hand, Reviel understands Archimedes' mathematics so well that he can guess words that are no longer visible in the codex. When you make a scholarly transcription of a text, you need to note what it is that you can see and what it is that you can guess. For a word to be really solid in our transcription, therefore, both Nigel and Reviel have to see it. Reviel and Nigel work independently of each other, the one in Stanford, California, the other in Oxford, England. They confer when they have completed a passage, and then they compare notes. Here is a typical example, from folio 105v, which contains *Method*, proposition 14. Nigel writes:

Dear Reviel,

In col.2 line 4 I think the reading PhANERON hWS EIRHTAI does not fit the spaces as exactly as we should like, and my suggestion, based on staring a long time at the image, is that we read PhANEROI TO SKhHMA. This introduces a verb which A. does not use much if at all elsewhere, but it is good enough as Greek. Have another look and see what you think.

To which Reviel replies:

I definitely see now your Chi, which makes SKhHMA a very attractive reading. Looking at it further, I wonder whether I do not see a nu after all at the end of PhANERON. How about TOUTO GAR PhANERON TWi SKhHMATI, with the scribe substituting, as he does so often, omicron for omega, and then, following upon those two neuter accusatives, he can find no fault in SKhHMA? I am not sure TOUTO GAR PhANERON TWi SKhHMATI is very good Greek, but it is less radically deviant than TOUTO GAR PhANEROI TO SKhHMA (which, if correct, would be rather exciting). Perhaps, if we ask for a super-high-resolution Xray of this particular point, this may serve to clarify the possible value of the technology.

Occasionally Reviel writes to me when he is excited. The first folio of Archimedes' letter to Eratosthenes was imaged on Thursday, 20 November 2003, four days after Abigail had finished preparing it; but it wasn't until Wednesday, 12 October 2005 that Reviel transcribed it. He left the most difficult pages to the end, because by then he could read faint traces of script with much more fluency:

> I'm making some progress here. Was a funny sensation to transcribe the introduction to the *Method*, rather like a Shakespeare scholar transcribing the manuscript text for 'To be or not to be'. Surprisingly many subtle changes, of some significance (e.g. Eudoxus was the first not to 'discover' a result, but to 'publish' it, etc.). It will help morale to notify everyone that reading of the forgery pages 57–64 is absolutely crucial. And I so want this border paper to be removed by Abigail. Talk to you – Reviel.

I already own two printed results of the digital Archimedes. The first is a beautiful book, printed by Nigel. Like Archimedes' letters, this book is private, for Nigel's friends. It exists in only fifty copies. It is his transcription, made from the pseudocolour images, of *On Floating Bodies*, propositions 1 and 2, including the diagrams. It includes a transcription of folio 81v, which Heiberg overlooked and which is now on the back of a page containing a forgery, covered in glue. There are no gaps in Nigel's transcription that I can see. However, some of it is in Latin, based on Moerbeke's text, because Nigel printed this book in 2004 and at this stage he didn't have a pseudocolour image of folio 88r.

The second is the monumental first volume of three by Reviel entitled *The Works of Archimedes*, and published by Cambridge University Press. This is the first proper translation into English of Archimedes' *Sphere and Cylinder* and Eutocius' commentary on the same. It is peppered with diagrams. These, I have no doubt, more accurately recreate the designs manufactured by Archimedes on the sands of Syracuse than any yet made. That's why Reviel's first words to me were: 'Yes, I need to see the diagrams, especially of *Sphere and Cylinder*.' Clearly, we gave him what he wanted, and we gave the world a better understanding of the most important scientist who ever lived.

The digital Palimpsest is encased in a silver box − a 300-gigabite external hard disk drive that you can plug into your computer. Scholars no longer read Archimedes by looking at iron marks made with a feather on animal skin. Archimedes' treatises are now digitally stored as 1s and 0s in a computer. Archimedes has received his latest IT upgrade. Only Nigel Wilson does not use this computer disk. To the amazement of the imagers, Nigel prefers to use hard-copy prints of the pictures. Nigel is an end-user − he gets what he wants. Even now, he does most of his transcription work from these prints, in the summer months, when the light is good, using a magnifying glass.

A New Voice

A great codex that had already revealed most of its secrets − as you will recall, that's what most of the experts thought when the Palimpsest was auctioned at Christie's. Given the reputation of Heiberg as a philologist of ancient texts, and given the treatment that the Palimpsest had received since Heiberg's time, this scepticism seemed well founded. Even Reviel thought that his work would actually be mainly about the diagrams. The discovery of two unknown folios of *Floating Bodies* and the new reading of *Method* proposition 14 changed Reviel's view of things. It didn't take long for the rest of the world to be convinced. On Wednesday, 6 December 2000 I got a call from Will Peakin: he wanted to write an article on Mr B's book for the colour magazine of the *Sunday Times* of London. The cover of the magazine of 17 June 2001 has an image of the Palimpsest, and the words 'EUREKA: It's just a few lines of scrawled Greek text, but new technology has identified the hand of Archimedes – and the results are rewriting history.' But we hadn't seen anything yet. This was just the start.

Up until the summer of 2002 we had all been working for Archimedes. But that was about to change. About thirty folios of the Palimpsest do not contain Archimedes' treatises. They come from other palimpsest texts. It was Natalie Tchernetska's task to look into them. She started with one particular page on which Heiberg had read just a little phrase that no one subsequently had been able to identify. When she received pseudocolour images of this page, she painstakingly transcribed just a few more lines. Then she tried to find a match for these lines in Byzantine texts. One particularly rich source for Byzantine texts is called the Suda – it is a massive tenth-century encyclopedia of authors ancient and modern. Eventually Natalie found a close match: it was a quotation of a lost speech by an ancient author named Hyperides. A few days later, on Saturday, 19 October 2002, Natalie sent me the following email.

Dear Will, In the course of further exploration of the non-Archimedes folios, I recently deciphered the text of a Greek orator, unknown otherwise. I could identify parts of lost speeches by Hyperides: ff. 135–138 contain a fragment of his lawsuit speech 'Against Timandros'; ff. 136–137 a fragment of a political speech, possibly 'Against Diondas'; ff. 174–175 possibly a fragment of the same political speech. Kind regards, Natalie

Natalie had never heard of Hyperides; nor had I. He sounded like a character out of Asterix, perhaps a close cousin of Ekonomikrisis, the shrewd Phoenecian merchant in *Asterix the Gladiator*. But no: it dawned on us quite soon that this was truly a sensational discovery. Hyperides is, in fact, one of the ten canonical orators of antiquity. He was born in 389 BC, five years before Aristotle. Like Aristotle, Hyperides lived in Athens, and he was a politician in the world's most influential democracy.

In the ancient world, seventy-seven speeches were attributed to Hyperides, who was celebrated for his style and his wit. His most famous speech is lost. It concerns Phryne, a prostitute famous for her beauty. In fact, legend has it that her body was the model for Praxiteles' famous statue of the goddess Aphrodite at Cnidus. But Phryne was also Hyperides' mistress, and when she was accused of offending the Eleusian mysteries, Hyperides defended her. He wasn't doing so well, so he ripped open her robe and exposed her breasts to the jury. Neat trick. It worked, and she was acquitted. But despite the style and subject matter of Hyperides, his speeches suffered particularly badly from the transition from roll to codex. In 1998, László Horváth, from Budapest, valiantly searched for a codex that was mentioned as containing Hyperides' speeches in the sixteenth century, but he never found it, and its contents were never properly known. Indeed, until the nineteenth century, Hyperides was only known through quotations from later authors. Then, in 1847, papyri containing his texts were discovered in a tomb in Thebes, in Egypt. The last big discovery was in 1891. But now, in 2002, Natalie had discovered new Hyperides text, and what's more she had found it in a codex. And if we can read all these folios, we will have added more than 20 per cent to the surviving work of this great figure from the golden age of Athenian history.

Hyperides was outspoken in his support of resistance to the military might of Philip of Macedon and his son Alexander the Great. When Alexander died, in 323 BC, he advocated full-scale rebellion. The rebellion failed; Hyperides had his tongue cut out to make a mockery of his oratory and then was executed. Plutarch, in his *Lives of the Orators*, writes of Hyperides: 'His monument is now altogether unknown and lost, being thrown down with age and long standing.' Not so. Natalie was to go on to find ten folios of the Palimpsest that contain his speeches. But retrieving the literary legacy of this great figure is appallingly difficult. The pages of the Palimpsest containing his speeches are even more difficult to read than the Archimedes pages. As I write, an international team of scholars, including Natalie herself, Pat Easterling, Eric Handley, Jud Hermann, László Horváth and Chris Carey are working collaboratively to provide a critical edition of the texts.

One of the speeches that Natalie identified mentioned some of the great historical figures from antiquity – Demosthenes, the well-known orator; Philip of Macedon and his son, Alexander the Great. It also mentions a figure far less well known – a certain Diondas. Natalie boldly suggested the circumstances in which this speech might have been delivered. Philip of Macedon's military might had been growing, and Athens needed to react. Demosthenes was particularly hostile to Philip, calling him 'the pestilent knave from Macedonia', and he successfully negotiated an alliance with the city state of Thebes. Hyperides was delighted and supported a proposal that Demosthenes receive an honorific crown for his diplomatic triumph. But in 338, despite their alliance, the Athenians and the Thebans lost disastrously to Philip's forces at the Battle of Chaeronea. At this point, Diondas indicted Hyperides, because, he argued, Hyperides' support for Demosthenes was unconstitutional. It seems to have been a blatant and cynical political move to damage both Demosthenes and Hyperides – who spearheaded that anti-Macedonian sentiment in Athens. We know that Hyperides wrote a speech in his own defence and that he was acquitted. This, deduced Natalie, was Hyperides' lost speech. It not only sheds light on Athenian politics in the grim days after Chaeronea, but it also provides new context for one of the greatest speeches of antiquity – Demosthenes' own speech 'On the Crown'. These pages will be studied for years, but already great progress is being made. One of the most difficult of the Hyperides leaves is being deciphered by László Horváth, from Budapest. He emailed me to tell me that on his page, when Hyperides discusses previous alliances between Athens and other Greek city states, he differs from the great historian Herodotus on the number of ships that Athens contributed to the Greek fleet at the great Battle of Salamis, when the Greeks, led by Themistocles of Athens, triumphed over the Persians, who threatened to overrun them under Xerxes, in 480 BC. Hyperides gives the total as 220 ships, while Herodotus says that the Athenians provided 180. Since Herodotus' total for the number of ships provided by all the city states does not tally with the figures that he gives for individual cities, László thinks that Hyperides' speech might be crucial in assessing the details of one of the most important battles of Western civilisation.

There seems to be no end to the secrets of the Palimpsest. On Monday, 11 June 2005 I received an email from Nigel Wilson, in which he wrote that he had identified several further leaves of a philosophical text, on one of which he 'read the name Aristotle clearly enough'. There are seven folios of this text in the Palimpsest, and this text has yet to be transcribed and identified. I passed this information on to Reviel, who transcribed many more words. He could not match them in any search engine for Greek texts. This sounds familiar. Perhaps this is an as yet unknown commentary on Aristotle. Since Nigel thinks this manuscript was written in the late ninth century, this would have to be a commentary from the ancient world. It is not difficult to come up with suggestions. Perhaps the most convincing so far is the suggestion of Marwan Rashed, a French scholar whom Reviel contacted. He suggests that it might be a text by an early Christian author criticising various Greek philosophies, including the Pythagoreans, for their failure to take account of the possibility of Creation out of nothing. As such, we might well have, uniquely preserved in the Archimedes Palimpsest, the views of an early Christian author on the inadequacies of the pre-Christian world view.

We now know that Mr B's book is not really the 'Archimedes Palimpsest' at all; the Archimedes codex is but one of the important manuscripts wrapped up in it. Mr B's prayer book houses a small library of unique ancient texts. As well as the Archimedes manuscript, it contains five leaves that uniquely preserve speeches by one of Athens' greatest orators, and seven leaves that uniquely preserve ancient views on Aristotle. It also contains some Byzantine texts: four leaves from a late tenth-century book of hymns, partly in honour of St John Psichaites, an abbot in Constantinople who rebuilt his monastery after it was destroyed in 813 by the Krum, the Bulgarian Khan with the curious wine cup, and two leaves from a saint's life. Seven leaves, from at least two separate manuscripts, have not been identified at the time of writing.

The Palimpsest might not ever reveal all its secrets, but I will make one prediction. I think it is very likely that Reviel and Ken Saito will be the last people to discover new text from the Palimpsest itself, because since then the texts in the Palimpsest have undergone another transformation. In the twenty-first century, if you want to read what Archimedes had to say to Eratosthenes in the third century BC, and what Hyperides said to the Athenians in the century before that, you should not make the pilgrimage to the codex in Baltimore. You can't read it there. You need one of Roger Easton's little silver boxes.

Parenti's Twin

The scribe of the prayer book – exactly whose library was he recycling? It must have been extraordinary. John Lowden once said to me, in jest, that it was the library of Photius himself. It cannot have been that, of course: with the possible exception of the Aristotle commentary, the palimpsested texts were written long after Photius died. Still, Hyperides was one of the authors mentioned by Photius. No modern scholar believed that Photius had actually read Hyperides, but now it seems that Photius has been telling us the truth for a thousand years. Nonetheless, like Photius' library, these texts must have been collected together in Constantinople. But this does not mean that they stayed in Constantinople. Books travelled with their owners. So where were these texts when they were turned into a prayer book?

Understandably perhaps, in assembling the scholars to work on the book I had concentrated on those who could help with the palimpsested texts. It was not until the legendary liturgist Robert Taft got in touch with me that I paid much attention to the texts of the prayer book. He suggested that I gave photos to an Italian scholar, Stefano Parenti. Stefano noted that the prayer book contained certain very rare texts, including one for the purification of a polluted container and another for the storing of grain. These prayers, and others, Stefano also found in a manuscript that can almost be described as the twin of the prayer book. It is in St Catherine's monastery in Sinai, the same place as that in which Tischendorf found the Codex Sinaiticus, and it is written by a priest named Auksentios in 1152–3. Some of the prayers are in the very same order. Others, such as a group of prayers at the elevation of the host and a prayer for the consumption of the leftover gifts of the presanctified liturgy, Stefano knew to be specific to Jerusalem in the Middle Ages. Finally, Stefano noted that there were frequent references to prayers 'for this city' in our prayer book. It seems unlikely, therefore, that the prayer book was made at St Sabas, even though it ended up there in the sixteenth century. But it is eminently likely that it was finished in Jerusalem, just fifteen miles away, and on 14 April 1229 . . .

We do not yet know how the palimpsested texts made it to the Holy Land, and perhaps we never will. The problem is not that it is so unlikely, but rather that there are so many ways by which books could travel there from Constantinople in the thirteenth century. The reason for this is that the Holy Land at this time was a destination of choice for Christians from Europe – for pilgrimage, and for crusade. Jerusalem was a particularly interesting place to be in 1229. Frederick II, the Holy Roman Emperor, the King of Sicily, of Cyprus and

Jerusalem, and of Germany, the wonder of the world for his energy, learning and religious scepticism, had finally fulfilled his vow to go on crusade. On Sunday, 18 February 1229, less than two months before the date in our book, he liberated from Muslim control all of Jerusalem except the Dome of the Rock, and other cities, including Nazareth, where Jesus grew up, and Bethlehem, where Jesus was born. This indeed was something for Christians to celebrate. The scribe of the book had joy in his heart as he wrote out his prayers. Now that I knew that we could recover the texts in the Palimpsest, I had nothing but understanding for the scribe and thanks for the fact that he had used such treasures to write his book. Indeed I wanted to thank him personally. The trouble was, I didn't know his name.

IO

The *Stomachion*, 2003
or Archimedes at Play

A Package from Mr Marasco

It was September 2003 and I was just back from my summer vacation; and a Mr Joe Marasco had sent me a present. There was a funny-looking package waiting for me together with the rest of my mail. Its sender described himself as a fan of Archimedes, which, to be honest, was rather worrying. I got fewer nuts calling me than Will did; but I did get my share of them. (And no, I didn't discover Rasputin in the Palimpsest either.)

I opened it up, cautiously, to find a truly gorgeous toy: large pieces of red glass, cut in all sorts of shapes, fitted together to make a square. Nice, I thought. A pity, of course, that the pieces were fragile and sharp (we were expecting our first child, and I was tending to shop for toys); but I could keep it at my office and show it off, an example of the funny things you get for being an Archimedes scholar.

I understood what Mr Marasco's point was: he was sending me a replica of the Stomachion. But this just about summed up my knowledge of this strange thing. I realised that there was an obscure fragment by Archimedes dealing with the Stomachion. This, I vaguely remembered, was an ancient game, where the point was to take fourteen pieces and put them together in some form. I certainly knew that no one had really studied this fragment. The standard view was that Archimedes was using this game as some kind of starting point motivating a geometrical discussion of some kind – though what this geometrical discussion could have been no one even guessed. I knew where the difficulty lay: our knowledge rested on a small fragment, preserved in mutilated form.

And I also knew that this fragment was right here, standing next to me in my office: the new hard drive, recently arrived from Roger Easton, contained – among other things – the new digitally processed images of folios 172–7. Well, I thought, Mr Marasco made a nice gesture. The least I could do now as recompense was try to see if I could read anything from the *Stomachion*.

Which would be tough. Some time in the sixteenth century, or even before, the Euchologion manuscript had lost its final folios, from 178 to 185. (Right now these are replaced by a paper supplement, inserted into the manuscript in the sixteenth century.) Folio 177 became the last, i.e. the one least protected from mould and other damage.

I did, of course, ask to look at this folio when I visited Baltimore, but it became immediately clear that nothing could be gained by the naked eye. The parchment was so worn down that, in places, it literally disintegrated. There were literally holes in the parchment – Greek words gone for ever. It was now not even a well-defined piece of rectangular parchment. It was made of precarious, unwieldy pieces, an eaten surface that only barely held together.

But this was just part of the problem. Even where the parchment existed, the writing was so faint, so thoroughly mixed with mould stains, that nothing could be made of it. To the naked eye, it was as if this was no palimpsest at all. The first thing that struck the eye was large blobs of an ugly, blackish substance – the remains of the mould. Other than this, you could see – with difficulty – the top text, but the underlying text had disappeared completely. I approached this folio very gingerly. This was not anything I was going to extract out of the plastic coating. I did light it with the UV lamp, but nothing much came up.

Well, that's it, I thought at the time. We are not going to make any progress with the *Stomachion*. A pity but, then again, it is not such an important treatise anyway – and, even if we were to make any more readings, would that help at all? The text is just too fragmentary: we'll never understand the *Stomachion*, and I should better invest my time more profitably elsewhere.

In all of this, I was merely following the traditional response. Heiberg was able to read only some fragments of this text and did not venture any interpretation of it. Dijksterhuis, a great Archimedes scholar, wrote a careful commentary on each of Archimedes' treatises, but on the *Stomachion* he had practically nothing to say; indeed, we can see his growing impatience. He began with some kind of speculation, namely that '[the treatise] may indicate that [Archimedes] studied the game from a mathematical point of view ... [he] discussed some of the properties of the so-called Stomachion'; but then Dijksterhuis loses his confidence: 'In the Greek fragment, however, we do not find much about this investigation.' Dijksterhuis's conclusion is: 'It can no longer be ascertained whether this result was the object aimed at or whether it played a part (and if so, what part) in the investigation as originally announced.'

For the fundamental point is that this single bifolio of the Palimpsest is nearly all we have got to go by. On this bifolio Archimedes concludes his treatise on the *Measurement of the Circle*. Then he begins a new treatise, whose title (very hard to read) may be something such as the *'Stomachic'* or the *'Stomachion'*. There are some words of introduction, then a single simple proposition and the beginning of another one. Both, obviously, are mere preludes to the real action of the treatise. We do not have any of the substantial mathematics left. Essentially, when the maker of the Palimpsest chose which folios to use out of the original Archimedes book, he threw away all of the *Stomachion* except for this one single bifolio. And it is easy to see why: the *Stomachion* was the final treatise in the original Archimedes book, and we have just seen an example of this important rule of manuscripts: *the end is always in the worst shape.* The parchment on which the *Stomachion* was written was probably already in rather bad shape in the thirteenth century, and thus this treatise was simply thrown away –

not good enough to serve even as recycled parchment. The maker of the Palimpsest probably reasoned that this particular piece of animal skin would not survive another round of re-scraping.

There are some further pieces of evidence, without which our position would be even more precarious. We have some evidence from antiquity referring to a game, called the Stomachion, or 'Belly-ache' – the game was supposed to be so difficult that it made your belly turn. (The difficulty of putting pieces together would be a constant theme of the *Stomachion*, throughout its history.) It involved fourteen pieces, put together. They made a square. So much was implied by the ancient testimony on the game itself. The evidence suggested that the game was not invented by Archimedes himself but that he made some mathematical reflections upon it. (In the same manner, contemporary mathematicians nowadays may use Rubik's cube in order to introduce ideas from Group Theory.) Those mathematical reflections became sufficiently well known in antiquity, so that some people came to call this game 'Archimedes' Box'. But very few people ever looked into Archimedes' actual treatise. The only Greek manuscript to survive, in the year 1229, containing the text of the *Stomachion* was the one in front of us – the original Archimedes book serving as foundation for the Palimpsest. And so, in the year 1229, as the maker of the Palimpsest threw away the bulk of the *Stomachion*, he was throwing away the only evidence the world still had in Greek.

There was one further piece to the puzzle. Just like the Palimpsest itself, this evidence was ignored for years. In this case, obscurity was the outcome not of the ravages of fortune – as with the Palimpsest – but of scholarly neglect. The manuscript in question was in plain sight for all to read, but it remained unread for generations simply because *too few scholars read Arabic.* Only in 1899 did Suter – a German scholar – come across an Arabic manuscript from the seventeenth century that mentions the 'Stumashiun of Archimedes'.

Indeed, much of the Greek heritage survives in Arabic only (and much of it is still unpublished, because of the same scholarly neglect; quite possibly, there are more works by Archimedes extant, still remaining to be retrieved from unnoticed Arabic manuscripts). Such translations into Arabic were originally made at the Arabic centres of learning, such as Baghdad, from the ninth century onwards. Typically, however, the Arabic versions are very distant from the original. The Arabic mathematicians were very good scientists. They added a great deal that is original and not present in Greek science itself. For this reason they would often rewrite their sources, abridge them, rephrase them, etc. This clearly was the case here, with the *Stomachion*. The manuscript found by Suter is unfortunately no more than an Arabic abridgement of a small part of the original Archimedean text. The Arabic manuscript is a very brief text indeed – a couple of folios long – which once again furnishes us with very little information. But it does one crucial thing: it discusses the construction of the Stomachion, as a square divided into fourteen pieces. Based on the Arabic text, therefore, we can reconstruct the precise shape of the Stomachion puzzle (see fig. 10.1). This is a famous diagram: everyone who knows anything about the Stomachion is familiar with this figure of a square divided into fourteen pieces, the canonical form of the Stomachion puzzle. This is what Archimedes was playing with. So, Marasco's model was essentially meant to be a copy of a diagram contained in a seventeenth-century Arabic manuscript (with a certain proviso – of which more later).

This, then, was the sum of our knowledge: there was a treatise by Archimedes dealing with a certain game, whose object was to construct some shapes from certain fourteen given forms. This was all we knew.

And then again, no one even bothered very much with extending this any further. When the sale of the Palimpsest was made, everyone was repeating with excitement that we might be getting new readings of the *Method*. But literally no one was suggesting that we might be getting new readings of the *Stomachion*. This treatise was the poor relation, the one everyone kept forgetting about – partly, because so little was left to work with; but more importantly, because the thinking was that, after all, this was *just a game*. This could not possibly rank with the significance of Archimedes dealing with such major issues as

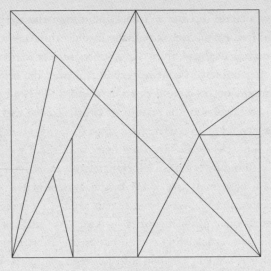

FIGURE 10.1

infinity and the application of mathematics to the physical world. Here was Archimedes at play, an Archimedean pastime. A pity we knew no more about this – but at the end of the day, we could survive without it.

Such was the feeling – my feeling, too – when the Palimpsest resurfaced. And so it was only with reluctance that I turned on my external hard drive, trying to see what the pseudocolour images might teach me. It would be hard, grinding work, probably for little gain. But let us try nonetheless: at one point or another, so I reasoned, I must look at this, and if I did it now I should have something interesting to tell Mr Marasco when I wrote back to him with my thank-you note.

Making Sense of the Stomachion

One would, in principle, have hoped that the text we did have would furnish us with enough clues. We had no more than a single Greek bifolio, but after all this was a crucial one: the first in the treatise, so it included the *introduction*. Surely the introduction ought to give a sense of the goal of the work. And yet what Heiberg had managed to read was tantalisingly fragmentary and obscure. He had the first paragraph more or less complete, and it read as follows:

> As the so-called Stomachion has a variegated theory of the transposition of the figures from which it is set up, I deemed it necessary: first, to set out in my investigation of the magnitude of the whole figure each of the figures into which it is divided, by which [number] it is measured; and further also, which are the angles, taken by combinations and added together; all of the above said for the sake of finding out of the fitting together of the arising figures, whether the resulting sides in the figures are on a line or whether they are slightly short of that but so as to be unnoticed by sight. For such consideration as these are intellectually challenging; and, if it is a little short of being on a line while being unnoticed by vision, the figures that are composed are not for that reason to be rejected.

This paragraph may be obscure, but it does tell us something. Archimedes will look at the measurements of the various pieces out of which the Stomachion is composed. And he will also look at angles, to see which pieces, put together, fit in combination (to make a straight line, i.e. add up together to 180 degrees). So that the treatise is some kind of study of the ways in which the figures of the Stomachion can be fitted together.

Now, here comes an important consideration. The people who did most to influence Heiberg's interpretation of the *Stomachion* were the Roman grammarians of the late Imperial period, writing many centuries after Archimedes' death. It so happens that this group of authors became fond of a certain cliché: to compare the many expressions one can form with just a few words to the many ways in which one can make different figures with just a few basic shapes. Thus, they said, one could take the Stomachion pieces and fit them together so

FIGURE 10.2

as to make an elephant, or a warrior, or a bird: the possibilities were unlimited (see fig. 10.2).

So here is one sense of variety: the pieces can be fitted together in a free game of creativity. What must be stressed straight away is that there is *no limit* to the number of shapes one can make in this way. This is because, to make an elephant or a warrior, one must be allowed to put together pieces in a free manner, not necessarily setting a vertex next to a vertex. In figure 10.3 we get a close-up of the 'elephant', and we see how several of the pieces are placed 'loosely' next to each other and do not meet exactly vertex to vertex. Now, if this is the rule – that pieces are allowed to be placed 'loosely' next to each other – then the logic of infinity kicks in. For it means they are allowed to be placed *continuously* along any edge. One is allowed to

FIGURE 10.3

attach piece X at one-half the way from the end of the edge, or at one-third the way from the end, or at one-fourth, or at one-fifth ... There are literally endless ways of positioning one piece next to another. The number of different elephants one can make with fourteen pieces is literally infinite. We are reminded, once again, of how ubiquitous infinity is in mathematics.

Heiberg, with his huge learning, was aware of this Roman grammarian cliché. And so, as he was turning from the first paragraph to the second, he thought he had an idea of what Archimedes meant: he thought Archimedes was talking about the boundless plurality of the elephants. Now there was very little Heiberg could read at this point – the writing becomes much more difficult – but he thought he could reconstruct some traces of meaning: 'So it is possible ... many ... with the same shapes ... moved around ...' So Archimedes was saying, Heiberg thought, that there were both elephants and warriors to be made, and many of them too.

What's the point of that? Heiberg did not know, and nor did we, following him. For if the point is that there are many elephants to be put together, then there can be no interesting mathematical question to ask regarding them. How many are there of those elephants and warriors? Infinitely many or, better put, as many as you wish. What on earth can Archimedes be looking for? Perhaps, so we thought, he was just making some random comments on the geometry of the fourteen shapes. Not an important treatise, for sure.

So I still reasoned. I was in good spirits, though, studying the images in my hard drive. The pseudocolour did work. Indeed, it worked incredibly well. The manuscript has deteriorated terribly since Heiberg was looking at it and still, with the pseudocolour technology, I could go through the lines and occasionally read them as if they were written in plain ink. In places, this was like waving a magic wand: you looked at the naked-eye image and saw nothing at all and then, turning on the pseudocolour, Archimedes' Greek was plain to see on the screen. I quickly confirmed Heiberg's readings and made a few completions, to make better sense of the first paragraph. Heiberg did not read everything there, but he certainly got the drift, and I could now prove this based on Archimedes' Greek.

Still, I could not see Archimedes' point in all of this. To make some better sense of it, I decided to take a step back and read Heiberg's text again for whatever it was worth. This is a standard move in such research: before making a plunge into the deciphering of the text, it is good to try and gain some kind of understanding, however imprecise, so as to guide the reading. And so I turned off the computer and picked up Heiberg, reading first through the little he could make of the Greek, and then through Suter's text.

Just to make sure I was following this text, I compared the diagram Heiberg provided – the canonical diagram of the Arabic manuscript – with the model I now had from Marasco. Anyway, it would be more fun working with the model than with the diagram!

At this point I became furious with Marasco. His model did not directly match the diagram. There was something wrong – was he after all a true crank, someone who couldn't even read a diagram correctly? Or had I misread the diagram? I looked at it again, and I began to wonder if perhaps something had gone wrong by accident. Perhaps Marasco had prepared the model from the correct diagram and then his shapes had got mixed up through some error?

But wait, I wondered: is it at all possible to fit the pieces together in a square by placing them in some other arrangement from that of the original diagram? I mean, surely there is no more than one way of fitting all those fourteen complex shapes together? This seemed quite a complicated arrangement . . . But then again, perhaps there is more than one way of fitting those pieces together?

Well, this had to be clarified. I certainly became *curious* now. I checked through the figure, piece by piece. Marasco's model *was*, indeed, the original diagram, with the pieces of the square arranged differently. Of course, I saw it now: there were some ways in which one could rearrange the diagram. There was certainly more than one way of fitting the fourteen pieces together into a square.

And then, all of a sudden, my throat went dry.

Could this be Archimedes' point, then? – that there were many different ways by which *the same square could be fitted together with the same pieces*? This would be too exciting . . . Let me explain why.

Improbable Combinations

The significance of my new thought – that the goal of the *Stomachion* may have been to calculate the number of ways by which one could form the square, given the same pieces – was that here, finally, one came to a meaningful problem. No longer are we dealing with the continuously changing, infinitely many arrangements of elephants and warriors. There must be a certain finite number of ways by which the square can be fitted together with the given figures. I always imagined the number to be 1 – that is, my intuition was that the accepted diagram represented the *only* way by which the square could be fitted together. Now, thanks to Marasco, I saw this intuition of mine was plain wrong. I still had to show that there were *many* ways (if there were only a handful of ways of arranging the square, then this would not be an interesting problem for Archimedes to solve). One also had to show that the number could in principle be calculated, that it did not involve a huge calculation beyond Archimedes' means. And so we should now study, in pure mathematical terms, the problem of the Stomachion square: how many ways are there of fitting together the given pieces into a square? Also, of course, I should now go back to the hard drive, read more of the second paragraph of the introduction, and see if it fitted in with the new hypothesis. There was lots of work to be done. We were going to uncover the prehistory of combinatorics.

Combinatorics is essentially a simple science: as its name suggests, it is the study of combinations. Suppose, say, you wish to make a choice: you have three candidates for the presidency. How many combinations have you got? Obviously, three. Now, make it slightly more difficult: imagine that you are choosing not a president but a Roman-style pair of consuls of equal powers. We need, therefore, to choose two consuls out of three candidates. How many options have we got? This may appear tricky at first sight, but actually the reply, once again, is three: to choose two out of three is really the same as choosing one out of three, for, after, all each time we are choosing a single candidate *to leave out*. To choose A and B is the same as to leave out C; to choose A and C is the same as to leave out B, and to choose B and C is the same as to leave out A – and this exhausts, once again, our options.

Now imagine that we are selecting not consuls of equal power but, instead, a president and a vice-president. How many options have we got? Now this is somewhat more complicated. Essentially, each of the choices we made above for consuls bifurcates: each of them can be turned into two choices of president and vice-president. If we choose, as consuls, A and B, then we have two president and vice-president pairs to form out of this selection – A as president and B as his deputy, or vice versa. In short, for each choice of consuls we have two choices of a president-and-vice-president pair – in other words, the number of options now becomes $3 \times 2 = 6$. There are six ways of choosing a president-and-vice-president pair out of three candidates.

This is all suggestive of the nature of combinatorics. In some ways, indeed, this is a simple science: many of its questions, even the more interesting ones, can be approached without any complicated tools. This is related, however, to the main drawback in combinatorics: there are very few short cuts. There is no surprising theory on the basis of which we can solve everything, easily. Rather, it is almost as if, for each new problem, we need to invent a new, ingenious approach. Combinatorics is a science of endless ingenuity, of endless puzzles and games.

Where did this science come from? This in itself has always been something of a puzzle. Most scholars think it emerged out of games. And this was, also, how it gave rise to the science of probability. This was in the seventeenth century, after card games were introduced into Europe. Quickly enough, Europeans everywhere were busy playing card games. Everyone was betting: which hand is dealt next? Now, when you bet fortunes on hands, it does focus your mind on some very well-defined questions. How likely am I to get an ace? How likely to get a joker? The answers to such questions essentially involve combinatorics. You need to calculate how many combinations of cards are possible, and then how many of them contain an ace. Say there are a million possible combinations, and a hundred thousand of them contain an ace. This then means that the odds are one-in-ten for being dealt an ace. Worth betting, if the return is over one-to-ten, not worth it otherwise.

Now this is very useful to know. In the long run, the card player who has combinatorics up his sleeve is bound to win. He is no more likely to win each individual bet, but he is certain to place his bets in such a way that, in the long run, he will end up the winner. Which is precisely why casinos in Las Vegas are prosperous: they apply the science of combinatorics against people who fail to apply it. Science wins.

Fermat – better known for his Last Theorem – and Pascal – better known for his deep theological observations – were among the first to apply this science. They did not make a fortune with their bets. (Historical evidence suggests that mathematicians – unlike casinos in

Las Vegas – are not very good about following through with their scientific knowledge.) Instead of making a fortune, they created the science of combinatorics, quickly using it to calculate the probabilities of events not only in card games but in many other domains as well. The calculations of combinations are much more than a trifling game, it turns out: they serve as the foundation for the science of probability.

Probabilities now serve among the cornerstones of science. And that's the reason why combinatorics is so important. Indeed, physicists today believe that the universe is governed by quantum mechanics – which is essentially probabilistic in character. There are no rules saying that this or that must happen; physics merely asserts a certain *probability* of events happening. Einstein, famously, differed. He passionately refused to concede to 'God plays with dice.' The evidence, so far, seems to suggest that on this Einstein was, for once, wrong.

Ancient Combinatorics?

There is a certain puzzling, intangible quality to combinatorics. It's often a very abstract science. There are often no diagrams to be drawn. You just go through the problem in your head, considering the various options and possibilities. This is a fun subject – but, generally speaking, not a visual one.

Now this non-visual character of combinatorics makes a world of difference. We have already seen many diverse problems discussed by Archimedes, but with all their diversity, we can also see that the great majority of those problems have to do with *geometry*. After all, the diagram was the key tool of Greek mathematics. Even though Greek mathematicians made interesting discoveries in, say, number theory (for instance, showing that there are infinitely many prime numbers), their main field was that of visual, concrete science – that of geometry. To calculate how many ways there might be of making certain selections and combinations? This would be just too abstract, too non-visual. And for this reason we did not think of combinatorics as a field Greek mathematicians were likely to tackle. The standard opinion was that problems of pure calculation were not made an important part of mathematics before the seventeenth century.

It was in the summer of 2002, at Delphi, at the most recent international meeting of historians of Greek mathematics, that this view changed, following a talk by Fabio Acerbi. Fabio studied physics all the way up to a PhD, but then decided this was not his field after all, settling to become a high-school teacher so as to concentrate on his love of the ancient world. (He is the graduate of an Italian public high school, where one studies not only the sciences but also Greek and Latin.) He quickly produced a series of articles, combining his mathematical and linguistic gifts in original, inspired studies of ancient mathematics. The first of them to make a real splash was the one he was presenting to us at Delphi. Its topic was Hipparchus' numbers.

Here, again, was a question to which few paid any attention at all. Plutarch mentions (in the course of an otherwise unrelated philosophical discussion) an ancient quarrel between a philosopher and a mathematician. The philosopher – the Stoic Chrysippus – once said that by the rules of Stoic logic, one can combine ten assertions in more than a million ways. The mathematician Hipparchus then countered, stating that the correct number was either 103,049 or 310,954, depending on how the number was to be defined – so that, either way, Chrysippus was wrong. Now Hipparchus was a great mathematician and astronomer. (Among other things, he was the first to produce a catalogue of all the stars visible to the naked eye – a remarkable achievement by any standard.) But this reads like some kind of private joke to which there is no need to pay any special attention. And indeed, historians of mathematics have never tried to make any sense of those numbers.

From 2002 at Delphi, let me now move back to the year 1994 – when David Hough, a graduate student of mathematics at George Washington University, leafed through a textbook of combinatorics. He came across Hipparchus' numbers, mentioned as a kind of curiosity. He also happened to consult at the same time a handbook of important mathematical numbers. This handbook contained, among other things, what are known as 'Schröder numbers'. The tenth Schröder number was 103,049 – i.e. the same as the smaller Hipparchus number.

Now this is some coincidence, thought Hough. He consulted with the author of the combinatorics textbook, Richard P. Stanley, an MIT professor of mathematics, and in 1997 they published a small notice in the *American Mathematical Monthly*, suggesting that Hipparchus could have produced some genuine combinatorics. Lucio Russo, an Italian historian of mathematics, came across this notice and suggested to Fabio Acerbi that he should look this up. And by the summer of 2002 Fabio was ready with a theory of how Hipparchus' problem could be defined, and how the two numbers – 103,049 and 310,954 – could be seen as the correct solutions to this problem. More than this: he could show, by means available to an ancient mathematician, how this was obtained.

In essence, one of the possible interpretations of a Schröder number is the number of ways a sequence of characters can be put inside brackets: e.g. the four characters abcd can be put inside brackets in various ways:

(a(bcd)), (ab(cd)), ((a)(b)(cd)) etc. . . .

The fourth Schröder number is 11, i.e. there are 11 different ways in which the four characters abcd may be put inside brackets. (This is surprisingly high – as is so often the case with combinatoric problems.) Acerbi showed that, according to Stoic logic, the problem of combining ten assertions could be seen as analogous to that of putting ten characters inside brackets. And he then developed a method for solving this problem within Hipparchus' means. He showed, finally, that with one extra condition (that is, when it is allowed not only to 'assert' claims, but also to 'negate' them), the number becomes 310,954, confirming the second number reported by Plutarch.

At Delphi, we were at first sceptical. All of this went against our hard-won intuitions. But the more we looked at Acerbi's evidence, the more we became convinced. Once again: the numbers can be no coincidence. You are not going to hit upon the tenth Schröder number by sheer accident. The only way Hipparchus could have come up with his numbers was the way Acerbi did – by doing the maths. And so, even though the brief mention by Plutarch tells us almost nothing – even so, it is sufficient to prove, beyond doubt, that ancient combinatorics existed.

This was a stunning discovery: the study of pure calculation – of counting the number of possible combinations – was invented already by the Greeks, and it was brought to a high level of sophistication by at least the time of Hipparchus.

Hipparchus lived in the second century, which makes him perhaps fifty years or more younger than Archimedes. But there was now nothing unlikely in assuming that Archimedes himself was engaged in combinatorics. This would make him the first person – as far as we can judge – who ever produced a study of combinatorics. Indeed, this would now make perfect historical sense: Archimedes would be at the inception of a tradition whose culmination would then be the work of Hipparchus. The pieces fit together. My interpretation of the *Stomachion* could fly. Just to be sure, I sent a quick email to Acerbi – was he familiar with anyone ever suggesting the *Stomachion* could be a study in combinatorics? – and then went on to work, feverishly, on the transcription. Another email went to Nigel Wilson, alerting him to the significance of folios 172–7 and asking him to make as much progress as he could with the reading of those folios. I knew I needed his expertise to confirm my own guesses.

I also sent another email, to my colleague Persi Diaconis in the Mathematics Department at Stanford. Persi is a magician-turned-mathematician. He still likes to perform tricks and one of his favourite pursuits is the application of mathematics to games. He is famous for his proof that one must shuffle a deck of cards *at least seven times* to make it thoroughly remixed. More recently, he studied the flip of a coin (showing that it is not truly random after all: about 51 per cent of the time coins actually end up landing *on the same side as they started with*). He likes all sorts of surprising combinations. I knew he would like my problem – and I also knew that he was a distinguished combinatoricist. Most important, he was a friend: he would not laugh at me for asking him such a trivial question. And so I put the question to him: how many ways are there of fitting together the Stomachion square?

Fitting the Pieces Together

The first reply I got was from Fabio. He was quite sure no one had ever considered the possibility that the *Stomachion* was a combinatoric study, pointing out (quite rightly) that, until recently, no one had considered the possibility that *any* ancient treatise could be dedicated to combinatorics. I replied quickly, sharing with him the few readings I had and suggesting that he join me and Nigel Wilson in producing an article on the *Stomachion*. I liked the spirit of teamwork we had had with the publication concerning infinity and the *Method*, and I relished the prospect of another one – though, in this case, the collaboration would be based on email alone. To this day Fabio has still never laid eyes on the physical manuscript bifolio of the *Stomachion*.

The team would expand further. I did not hear back from Persi for quite a while: it turns out he does not use computers. Eventually I left him a note and the next day he showed up at my office, telling me they were working on it. He had given the problem to his students. His wife, Susan Holmes – a distinguished statistician – had also got hooked on the problem. A number of colleagues, hearing what I was working on, were sending me emails with calculations. Everyone was trying out combinations with the fourteen pieces and a square. And no two solutions were alike. Clearly the precise calculation was much more difficult than it had appeared at first sight. We were all coming to terms with the mathematics of the Stomachion.

The easiest way of visualising the various possible combinations of the Stomachion puzzle is by thinking of them as the results of sub-stitutions and rotations. That is: suppose you take the original arrange-ment of the Arabic manuscript (see fig. 10.4). Then you could take,

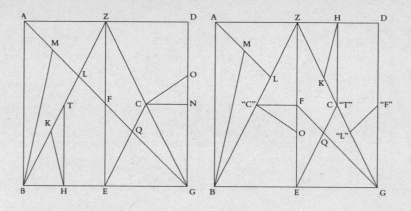

FIGURE 10.4

say, the triangle BZE (composed of the four pieces ZLF, LFEHT, TKH, KHB) and substitute it for the triangle ZDG (composed of the three pieces ZDOC, ONC, NCG). The result would be a new arrangement. This would be an example of a substitution. Call this substitution S (above right).

Or, alternatively, you could take the triangle AGB (composed of the seven pieces AMB, MLB, KHB, TKH, LFEHT, FQE, QEG) and rotate it around an imaginary axis passing through the points F and B. The result would be a new arrangement, as in figure 10.5. This would be an example of a rotation. Call this rotation R.

It would be easiest if we could just count all the substitutions and rotations possible and then multiply them to get the number of possible arrangements. This indeed was the approach everyone was basically taking at the outset. But this will not do. This is because there are very complex ways by which the various substitutions and rotations interact. To give an immediate example: once you've applied substitution S, you can no longer apply rotation R. Substitution S destroys the line AG in the triangle ABG. There is no longer a triangle there to rotate. And vice versa: once you've applied rotation R, you can no longer apply substitution S, because rotation R ends up destroying the triangle ZBE: there is no longer a triangle there

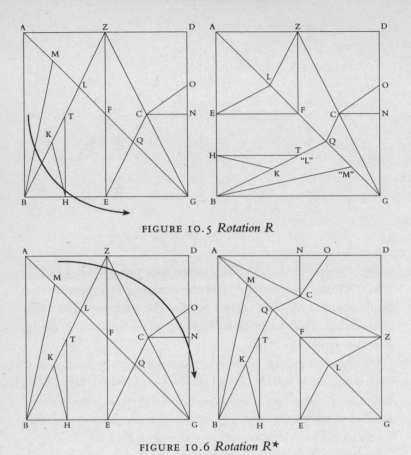

FIGURE 10.5 *Rotation R*

FIGURE 10.6 *Rotation R★*

congruent with the one at ZDG. In short: there is a very complex pattern of which substitutions and rotations can combine, and which cannot. This becomes a kind of second-order combinatoric problem, over and above fitting the fourteen pieces together: the problem of fitting the substitutions and rotations together. This kind of complexity, with combinations and then combinations-of-combinations, very often arises in discrete mathematics.

There is yet a further complication. We saw that some substitutions and rotations rule each other out; but others *cancel* each other out. To see this, let us consider a very simple case. One possible rotation, as we

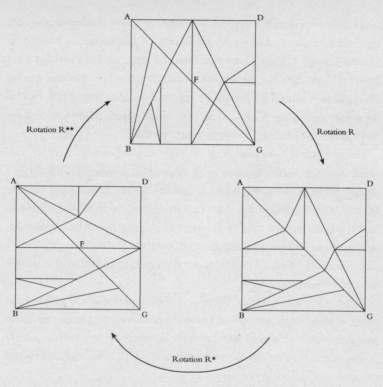

FIGURE 10.7 *The three rotations R, R* and R**, combined, end up cancelling each other: we're back to the original square.*

saw, is rotation R: turning the triangle ABG around the imaginary axis FB. Another possible rotation, of course, is what we may call rotation R★: turning the triangle AGD around the imaginary axis FD (see fig. 10.6). What happens if we apply both rotations R and R★? We end up having rotated the entire square. Nothing in the internal arrangement has changed. In this sense, the two rotations cancel each other out. Worse still: if we add in another allowed rotation, call it R★★, where we indeed rotate the *entire* square around the imaginary axis DFB, then the effect of the combination of the three rotations R, R★ and R★★ is to cancel each other out: having applied them all, we return to exactly the starting position (see fig. 10.7).

This is once again a typical situation in finite mathematics, of a type studied most directly by a branch of mathematics known as Group Theory. Group Theory is, essentially, the study of various ways by which permutations add up and cancel each other. It is this theory that is demonstrated by Rubik's cube, and we find that it can also be demonstrated by the Stomachion. The simple game proved to contain in itself an introduction to finite mathematics.

For our immediate purposes, though, the following is what mattered. A simple multiplication of all allowed substitutions and rotations would provide us with what is known as an 'overcount' of the Stomachion solutions, for two reasons: some of these substitutions and rotations in fact rule each other out, and cannot be combined; while other combinations are allowed, but then end up being cancelled out. There are fewer Stomachion solutions allowed than the simple multiplication suggests.

How many solutions are there? I was on tenterhooks. I needed the number to be high enough: if I ended up with some twenty or thirty solutions, then it would just be such an obvious anticlimax. Surely Archimedes wouldn't have bothered with such a treatise unless the number had been big enough.

The weeks passed: the mathematicians were still working at it. Meanwhile, I kept going back to my hard drive, adding to the transcription, each time a few characters. Gradually, word by word, it came to make more and more sense. In a way, it was the mathematicians who helped me most in the reading. For this is how readings take place: you can make a reading only once you have formed some kind of guess as to the possible meanings of the text to be read. This, above all, was why Heiberg had not succeeded in reading the infinity passage in the *Method* – or in reading the *Stomachion*. He had expected neither actual infinity nor combinatorics.

I began to make sense of the small theorem we had, right after the introduction. The mathematicians made clear that a major simplification resulted from the fact that certain pieces were 'glued together'. It could be proved, geometrically, that no substitution or rotation could ever separate, for instance, the two pieces AMB, MLB. There is no legitimate way the two can fit inside the square unless they are glued to each other along the side MB. In effect, then, it is as if we had just one piece – ALB – with the line MB forming a kind of decorative pattern, no more. Applying such reasoning in two other places, it could be shown that the problem amounts to a puzzle with eleven effective pieces, not fourteen. This, indeed, was a major simplification. And it became clear that the first small theorem was likely to make a contribution towards this kind of geometrical analysis.

Better still, the analysis of the structure of substitutions and rotations seemed to make sense of the second, and last, paragraph of the introduction – the one that Heiberg had been unable to read. I could now, finally, offer a reading – one that was even supported by Nigel Wilson. This was crucial: Nigel was not privy to the mathematical discussions. While those discussions were indeed requisite for my *own* formulation of the text, it was important to see that the reading was there even without any knowledge of the mathematics. And so the text that we put together went like this:

> So then, there is not a small number of figures made of them, because of it being possible to rotate them into another place of an equal and equiangular figure, transposed to hold another position; and again also with two figures, taken together, being equal and similar to a single figure, and two figures taken together being equal and similar to two figures taken together – then, out of the transposition, many figures are put together.

It does appear as if Archimedes is discussing precisely this phenomenon of rotations and substitutions.

But at an even more elementary level, the most crucial thing for scholars, at this point, was that the new reading was inconsistent with the 'elephant and warrior' interpretation. This treatise was *not* about how many *different* figures could be composed. We know this, now, because of the repeated insistence on *congruity* of different pieces and piece-combinations. For the sake of moving pieces about – as you do when putting together a warrior or an elephant – such insistence is irrelevant. But it is absolutely to the point, if the goal is to compose different combinations *within the same square*. Those different combinations arise precisely from the fact that one may substitute one piece for another (or one combination of pieces for another) because *the two are congruent*.

We were thus confident that Archimedes' treatise dealt with the problem of the combinations for constructing the square from the given fourteen pieces. We could say even more: the clear emphasis of the introduction was on one small statement – to which the first paragraph led, and from which the second paragraph took off. It appeared that this statement asserted the very point of the treatise. So here is what Heiberg could not read: '. . .There is not a small number of figures made of them . . .'

This is what Archimedes was doing in this treatise: *counting a big number*. The operative word – 'number' – is in fact the very same word, *plethos*, that was so crucial in the reading of the infinity passage in the *Method* (in the context of abstract proportion theory, *plethos* is usually translated as 'multitude', but in this counting-based context the best translation is 'number'). In both cases we see Archimedes, surprisingly, looking at big numbers: those of infinity, in the infinity passage, and those of combinatorics, in the *Stomachion*.

But was the number really that big? This we still did not know. I knew that the various back-of-the-envelope calculations people were producing at first all involved an overcount, because of the problems just mentioned. How many remained then? I just did not know. And as the days passed, I began also to worry that my problem – which at first I thought might have been too trivial – might in fact be too complicated. If modern mathematicians couldn't solve this straight away, perhaps I was wrong in believing Archimedes would have tackled it?

I did finally scribble that thank-you note to Marasco, mentioning that the Stomachion might be even more interesting than it appeared at first sight. He promptly showed up at Stanford. It turned out that

Marasco was a retired businessman from the computer industry, with a PhD in physics. He understood very well what the mathematical issues were; and he also had the business experience, and the contacts, to suggest one further avenue for progress: to spread the word among computer scientists, offering a small reward for the one who first came up with a solution to the Stomachion puzzle. He worked out that $100 would be enough, which he then put up. This became the informal Marasco Stomachion Award.

My mathematical friends had now decided that they must get their minds around this, too. Persi Diaconis and Susan Holmes had already brought in another renowned combinatorics couple, Ron Graham and Fan Chung from UC, San Diego. They had been conversing by phone and email for a few weeks already, but at some point they decided they must take a more hands-on approach. Persi and Susan went down to San Diego and for a long weekend all four of them did nothing but draw diagrams and study the combinatoric principles underlying the Stomachion puzzle. At the end of it, they came up with what they were quite sure was the final count.

At the same time Bill Cutler, a computer scientist from Illinois, had found a way of defining the problem in computer algorithm terms. That is: he described to the computer how to put together a Stomachion square, and then produced software that went systematically through all potential arrangements. Many of them aborted. The software then counted all potential arrangements that *did* work – in this way counting all the actual solutions to the Stomachion. This software came in first: Bill Cutler won the Marasco award!

The answer was 17,152. That is: there were 17,152 different ways of arranging the pieces and still getting a square. In figure 10.8, you can see part of the printout produced by Cutler's software. And to think that I had been surprised to find there was more than a single solution!

Mercifully, the group of mathematicians also found the same number. And while they could not claim priority, they did something extra that was crucial for our understanding of the problem. Cutler's

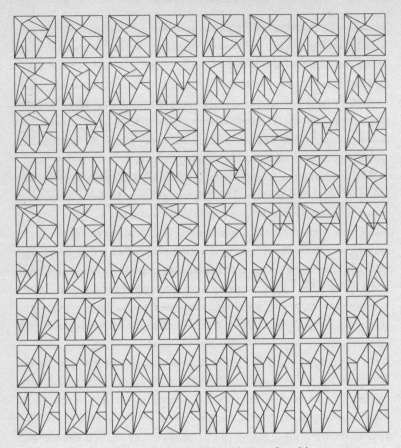

FIGURE 10.8 *Some of the solutions found by*
Bill Cutler's software

software was based on counting all the possibilities one by one – a
process that, in principle, is doable by machine only. Archimedes
certainly did not do it that way. But the mathematicians found their
number with 'pencil and paper', which would have been Archimedes'
method also (only he would have used papyrus and reed pen). They
literally did not use any computers for their work. Nor did they
rely on any high-powered mathematics not available to Archimedes.
Instead, what they did was produce an ingenious 'map' of the poss-

ibilities. The various solutions to the puzzle were arranged into twenty-four basic 'families', depending on a certain arrangement of the main constituents. Inside each of those twenty-four families a list of basic possible solutions was drawn, with lines connecting any two solutions that could be transformed into each other by simple substitutions and rotations. At this stage the study had produced 536 basic solutions. Finally, certain simple rotations, which do not involve any substitutions at all, could be applied independently of all the rest, so that one could generate, from each basic solution, thirty-two rotations. This finally gave rise to the 17,152 solutions found by the mathematicians.

We now had everything in place. We had the historical context, thanks mainly to Fabio Acerbi's pioneering work. We had the reading, confirmed by Nigel Wilson. We had the mathematical solution, produced by a distinguished group of mathematicians and confirmed by computer software. We also knew that this solution was well within the means available to Archimedes himself. The pieces fitted together: we had a watertight argument showing that, with the *Stomachion*, we have the earliest evidence anywhere for the science of combinatorics.

This was early December 2003. I announced our new discoveries at a conference at snowbound Princeton. Gina Kolata, science correspondent to the *New York Times*, was there, and two weeks later we all found ourselves on the front page of the *Sunday New York Times*. 'In Archimedes Puzzle, a New Eureka Moment', read the title. Which, indeed, it was. We had now gained a completely new understanding of Archimedes, as well as of the process of the making of Western science. Once again, we had rewritten the history books. And we had done something extra, more precious than everything else: we had, quite by accident, stumbled upon Archimedes at play.

New Light on an Old Subject

The autumn of 2003 might have been a high point for Reviel, but it was a low point for everybody else. The new interpretation of *Stomachion* was thrilling, but you could look at the Palimpsest 17,152 ways and, even after three and a half years, it was still not completely disbound. And however many ways you looked at the images, they just were not good enough – at least not good enough for Mr B. He was not satisfied with our progress, and he told me so – in no uncertain terms. Worse than that, Reviel agreed with him. There were passages on folios already imaged that he still could not read. And they were important passages. The very first folio of the Palimpsest, for example, was *Floating Bodies*. Heiberg had not read it; it had never been transcribed, and Reviel and Nigel were making very little headway with it. Most challenging, of course, were the folios containing the forgeries. The pseudocolour and ultraviolet were of almost no use on these folios. And very little progress was being made on the pages of the Palimpsest that contained texts from other palimpsested manuscripts. The pressure to decipher these grew to a new pitch after Hyperides was discovered, but we were having little success.

I told them I was happy to look for other solutions. I was lying. I was exhausted, and I really didn't think we could do any better. Mike Toth told me that there was no point in sending out a new Request for Proposals across the country. Since 11 September 2001 most imagers, he said, had been on lucrative government contracts developing systems to locate and identify terrorists. He should know, I thought. Mike and I have a 'don't ask, can't tell' policy. I don't ask, because he can't tell. Just staying the course was a daunting prospect for me, for Abigail and for Roger. The forgeries, in particular, seemed entirely beyond us. I had no idea what to do.

A Meeting of Minds

Inevitably it was Mike – leading me by the hand at this point – who came up with ways forward. His first idea was to get us to the heart of the intelligence effort at the CIA – to the wizards of Langley. Mike even got me, a foreigner, into CIA HQ – quite a feat so soon after the attacks of 9/11. We toured the CIA museum with its curator, and met Charlie the Catfish. Charlie really looks like a catfish and he swims like a catfish. He's actually a mechanical gadget and his mission is still classified. Not sure he will be of much use in Afghanistan or Iraq. I also saw a bug, literally and figuratively: a remotely controlled dragonfly that could steal sound. Unlike Charlie, she had never been operational: she was too easily blown off course by the wind. After leaving the museum we went into the elevator and up several floors. I was introduced to Dr Don Kerr, who was the Deputy Director of the CIA for Science and Technology. I presented him with images of Archimedes' *Floating Bodies* to hang on his wall. It was, after all, the government that had invented multi-spectral imaging. And then the imagers spent two hours in briefings and conversation with experts at the CIA who clearly knew far more than they were allowed to say. It was cool, but we did not come away with the radically new approach to our problem that we so clearly needed.

Programme managers sometimes take a bad rap as unimaginative bean counters. Not mine. Turning 180 degrees from his secret resources, Mike decided to take full advantage of the press. Archimedes had always found his friends through the press. It was because of the *Washington Post* that Mike had got in touch with us and, in fact, because of it that Keith, Roger and Bill had known the manuscript was at the Walters. The subsequent success of the project had secured more air time. Within a few days of the publication of Will Peakin's article in the *Sunday Times* I was meeting with John Lynch of the BBC at Washington Union Station for a chat and a quick bite. There John told me that he had produced a science programme that recounted the story of Andrew Wiles's single-handed effort to prove Fermat's Last Theorem. I had seen, and marvelled at, this programme. I agreed to make the documentary with the BBC's flagship science series *Horizon*. In the event, the director of 'Archimedes' Secret', as the programme on the Palimpsest was called, was Liz Tucker. It aired on 14 March 2002 and attracted 2.9 million viewers – over 13 per cent of the UK viewing audience that evening. The project to retrieve the unique texts of Archimedes was now world famous. Surely, ambitious and cutting-edge imaging scientists would want to be in on this act? Let's cut to the chase, Mike said, and have these guys thrash out solutions to the most difficult imaging problem in the history of science.

Mike told me that I should not waste anybody's time – least of all mine. I didn't have to bother with a full scale RFP – I just had to send out a short summary of our problem: we needed to read text that had been written on animal skin in about AD 970, erased shortly before 14 April 1229 and written over, and scraped off again, and covered in paintings. Anyone who responded to the challenge would not have to write thorough, wordy proposals – just a brief summary of 500 words. To any credible proposal I would give a good sample of our data, information on how we had collected and processed it, and tell them that they were welcome to improve upon it. Mike told me to make clear that I was not looking for science experiments, but rather practical propositions that could be made to work within six months. And then he told me to invite the best ten suggestions to a summit at the Walters. This was, Mike insisted, an efficient way to explore a variety of new approaches, and quickly. It would also be inexpensive. And Mike insisted on this point – that we did not pay these people anything. The best of them, he said, would not come for money; they would come for Archimedes.

And come they did. This was thanks in no small part to Keith, Roger and Bill, who searched for anyone who might help. Kirk Martinez, whom Bill and Keith had been to see in London a year earlier, came from the University of Southampton. From the University of Rutgers Bill conscripted the delightful Professor of Chemistry, Gene Hall, and from Bartlesville, Oklahoma, he pulled Bob Morton and Jason Gislason, who work for ConocoPhillips. Andy Johnston, who worked on the Archimedes database, brought in John Hillman from the University of Maryland and his colleague Bill Blass from the University of Tennessee. They had recently imaged the 'Star-Spangled Banner'. Abigail found Emanuele Salerno. Emanuele came from Pisa and represented the Easyreadit consortium, a European advanced image-processing collaboration with representatives in the Netherlands, Italy, the United Kingdom and France. She also contacted Mike Attas and Doug Golz from the University of Winnipeg, Canada. Finally Uwe Bergmann came from Stanford. His mother Ingrid, who lives in Karlsruhe, Germany, subscribes to *GEO* magazine. Uwe was visiting from California, where he is a scientist at the Stanford Linear Accelerator Center. Although Ingrid did not know much about his work, she had thought he might be interested in an article on the placebo effect in the magazine. So she had left it on his bedside table. He had picked it up, read it, and looked at the next one too. This was by Katja Trippel, and it was an excellent piece on the Archimedes Palimpsest. This had caught Uwe's imagination. He thought he could help. He emailed us at exactly the right time.

The summit started on Thursday, 1 April 2004, which I thought most appropriate. In my undying scepticism I had asked Mr B to come. I did not want to try to convince him of something I almost certainly would not believe in and probably would not understand. If he decided to go for anything that a scientist suggested, he needed to know precisely what he was getting into, both in terms of time and money. He came, and saw the conference unfold. Everybody played their part. Mine was to pass the drinks. It was intense. We didn't have the time to be genteel; we wanted clarity, and we wanted proposals to run with, and we wanted them fast. Tempers flared as eminent scientists advocated their own proposals and criticised their opponents – their equipment and their competence. Under these circumstances passing the drinks actually became quite important. As ever, I had a generous hospitality budget, and discussions went on well into the night. On Sunday morning Mr B, Abigail, Roger, Mike and I met in closed session. Then and there Mr B approved the funding of three new approaches to the task.

New Approaches

DEREK

On Saturday, 10 February 1996, Deep Blue, an IBM supercomputer programmed by Feng-Hsiung Hsu and Murray Campbell, had defeated World Champion Gary Kasparov at a game of chess. It was a very public humiliation for mankind: computers could not only calculate faster than humans; they could outwit the best of them – and at their own game. Could a computer guess characters better than Reviel Netz and Nigel Wilson? Mr B thought that it would be an interesting experiment to try. So did Reviel; I think, like Kasparov, he wanted a computer to beat. I kept my thoughts to myself. But what the hell! – it couldn't hurt. Any computer processing would interfere minimally with the campaign as a whole: none of it would involve the manuscript itself, as the computer would work best from the pseudocolour images that we had already generated. In terms of work flow, Mike assured me, Optical Character Recognition by a computer was a breeze.

There were three impressive proposals, but they all seemed a long way from implementation in the time period required. Mike, once again, came up with an idea to get a result. We would hold a competition. The goal of the competition would be for the imaging scientists to produce something that could help Reviel read the text. The machine that got closest to Reviel's transcription of two designated pseudocolour folia would triumph, and Mr B would pay $10,000 to the winner. Now whether or not you think $10,000 is a lot of money or not depends upon who you are. To design a machine for Reviel, a professor might not think it is a lot of money. Clearly they didn't, and we didn't get machines from them. But Derek Walvoord was a graduate student of Roger Easton's at RIT, and $10,000 seemed like a lot of cash to him. Six months later, he delivered his product.

Derek set himself the task of identifying characters by comparing them to a known alphabet. His machine is effective and very simple to operate. It works on any PC. You pull up a pseudocolour image of the folio you want to work on and select a 'Region of Interest', normally a partially obscured character. Then you run the software and sit back as you see the machine do its number crunching. It produces a list of characters in order of likelihood. It works too. You can click on a partially obscured theta, and the machine will display a theta as the closest matching character. Amazing. The only problem is, of course, that you knew it was a theta anyway. The letters you want it to recognise are precisely the ones that are so obscured that the human eye cannot recognise them.

Derek's machine was affectionately called DEREK. DEREK was impressive. But it wasn't Deep Blue, and it couldn't beat the ten giga-neurone computer inside Reviel's skull. But it showed enough promise for Mr B to give the go ahead for DEREK II. DEREK II is much more powerful, because it combines optical recognition of the characters with a statistical approach to the Greek alphabet, and to Archimedes' vocabulary. This will be useful in helping the scholars see possible combinations of letters and words for those parts of the text that have now been completely eaten away by the mould. It is being tested as this book goes to the press.

EL GRECO

There were several multi-spectral-imaging proposals at the conference. We could, in theory, have invited any of these contributors to image the Palimpsest. Emanuele Salerno had worked extremely hard with the data that we had sent him, but he concluded that no better results could be achieved with that data. Like other participants, he wanted to collect more data. There is virtually no limit to the amount of slices that you can add to your data-cube: image with enough wavelengths and you are called a hyper-spectral imager. But Mr B concluded that it was not worth the investment to essentially revisit techniques that we had already tried.

Bill Christens-Barry was on the inside track, of course. He knew that Mr B was not seriously invested in multi-spectral imaging any more. But Bill came to the conference with a *very* inexpensive method to address all the problems that the scholars had found in the early trials, yet which could give a far more finely sliced data-cube than was possible with the push-button processing Keith had used to process the pseudocolour images. So he put his idea forward. A year or two earlier, he and Keith had been to the National Gallery in London to see a multi-spectral imaging apparatus called VASARI. Giorgio Vasari was a sixteenth-century Italian painter, but VASARI is an acronym standing for Visual Arts System for Archiving and Retrieval of Images. VASARI interested Bill and Keith because it did not filter the light in front of the camera. Rather, it used light sources of very particular wavelengths, and thus avoided filters altogether. This very largely avoided the registration problems that had so beset Keith and Roger when they compiled their dense data-cubes. The problem then was that narrowband light sources of sufficient intensity were very expensive. But technology is always on the move and by 2004 Bill realised he had an extraordinarily cheap way to generate light at specific wavelengths. He could use Light Emitting Diodes, or LEDs. LEDs are the lights that you can find all over the dashboard of your car, and have been able to for some time. But only in recent years have they become available at many different wavelengths. LEDs are so cheap that they are almost throwaways. Bill's thought was to attach them to fibre-optic cables and illuminate the parchment in various wavelengths of light.

Mr B agreed to fund Bill's proposal, so Bill put his machine together and we tagged the experiment on to our last production-imaging session, at the end of 2004. Roger brought down the monochrome scientific camera from RIT that he had used with Keith in his initial experiments. To achieve the same resolution as the Kodak camera, forty images needed to be taken of each folio. Bill's machine looked like a wonderful gadget, and Bill had automated the controls so that it could take a great many images quickly. LEDs are easy to build into electronic circuitry and have no moving parts, so the automation of the system was very simple. This was effective hyper-spectral imaging on the cheap. Although the idea stemmed from VASARI, Bill's imaging machine looked nothing like it, and a different technology was used, so we christened it EL GRECO, the nickname of the great painter Domenico Theotokopoulos, as a nod to the Greek text that it was designed to capture.

Using EL GRECO Bill avoided the registration issues that had plagued the initial trials, and he had the narrowband light that he needed to slice his data-cube more finely. Bill found that the most effective post-processing technique for the EL GRECO data was the algorithm that Keith had written for the push-button processing. In fact, time and again during this experimental phase, we realised quite how effective the push-button processing was at retrieving Archimedes' text. The EL GRECO images of the Archimedes text were slightly better than the standard images that we had been distributing to the scholars. More importantly, EL GRECO gave us the chance to tailor-make our wavelengths for the different texts in the manuscript. The standard pseudocolour worked better for the Archimedes text than it did for the Hyperides and the Aristotle commentary. By using different LED sources for the various palimpsested codices we hope in the future to make significant strides.

EL GRECO was an improvement, but it was no better at reading through gold than the standard techniques that we had been using. To do this we needed a very different technology.

X-RAYS

Gene Hall, Professor of Chemistry at Rutgers University, calls himself the 'Paper Detective', and he specialises in identifying and dating forgeries of all sorts, but particularly letters and banknotes, by examining their chemical composition using X-ray fluorescence. X-rays, just like visible light, consist of photons, but the photons of X-rays have a much shorter wavelength (hundredths of nanometres, rather than the hundreds of nanometres in visible light), and a very much greater energy. The human eye cannot see them but other detectors can, and these detectors can convert the information into a form that we can see. We are all familiar with X-rays because of the dentist. But the X-ray images of our teeth are generated by transmitted X-rays. That is, X-rays are zapped through our jaw and received by an emulsion plate on the other side. Gene wasn't interested in the transmitted X-rays. He was interested in the X-rays that do not get through. These interact with the material that stops them, and they cause this material to send out other X-rays at very particular wavelengths. And these emitted X-rays contain crucial information – if you can get it.

Now here is the important bit. While the photons of visible light give you colour information, X-ray photons give you elemental information. This is because they interact with atoms differently. In the early 1920s Niels Bohr and his colleagues thought of the atom as containing a nucleus of protons and neutrons, and electrons were to be found around this nucleus, orbiting in shells at various distances from the nucleus. This may well be how you think of an atom; it is one of the very last creations of classical physics, and it will serve our purposes. Bohr labelled each shell with a letter, the one closest to the nucleus being letter 'K'. (The reason that these distances have been designated with letters from the middle of the alphabet is simply that when scientists first probed the make-up of the atom, they were not sure how many shells they would find, so they left room at either end of the sequence.) Photons of visible light interact with electrons found in Bohr's outer shells: since they are further from the nucleus, less energy is needed to change the state of these electrons. Higher-energy, shorter-wavelength X-ray photons interact with electrons found on Bohr's inner shell, K, where much more energy is needed to change the state of the electron. And when I say that X-ray photons change the state of electrons on the inner shell, I actually mean that they knock them from the shell entirely. However, at the same moment that the electron 'on' shell K is displaced, it is replaced by an electron from the next shell, L. The electron on shell L makes a quantum leap to the inner shell. As it does so, it has to lose a lot of energy, and hence emits an X-ray photon. Now, since the atoms of each element have their own distinctive arrangement of electrons, the precise wavelength of this emitted X-ray corresponds to the energy difference of the electrons involved. Hence it will be specific to the element of the atom hit by the incident X-ray. If you can detect this emitted X-ray, you can determine which element it came from.

Gene's thought was that his instrument should be able to detect the X-ray photons given off by the iron in the ink of the palimpsested texts. It was a neat idea, and it was the idea that Gene had very briefly put into practice in his lab with a forged leaf from the Palimpsest before the conference; but the results had not been conclusive.

Another participant in the conference was convinced that Gene's idea was a good one. His name was Bob Morton, and he was a research scientist at the petroleum company ConocoPhillips. Bob is not normal. Certainly his child psychologist didn't think so. He doesn't have an IQ because she reported that he does not belong to the population for which the test was devised. He is one of the most alarming, funny and inventive people I have ever met, and I say this without ever having been to one of his fabled Fourth of July parties in Bartlesville, Oklahoma. He came to the conference with his minder,

Jason Gislason, who interpreted Bob for the rest of us until we got used to him. Bob's presentation was, frankly, amazing. It wasn't about Archimedes at all; it was about fossils. Using the same machine as Gene, Bob had looked at fossils from the famous Burgess Shale. He had mapped the distribution of elements in the fossils. More than this, he had mapped the elemental composition of the stone beside the fossilised bones, so that he could determine the chemical make-up of the soft tissue of the fossil. He called the results EXAMS – 'Elemental X-ray Area Maps'. His images of these fossils were far clearer than normal photographs. His final image stole the show. He called it a SEXI – a 'Stereo Elemental X-ray Image'. It was a 3-D image of the fossil *Marrella splendens*, made out of various EXAMs, in silicon, iron and potassium. He had made this by taking two EXAMs of the same fossil at a slightly different angle – actually 7.5 degrees, which is the difference in angle at which your two eyes see the same object at a distance of 4.2 feet. He then overlaid the two images on top of one another and colour-coded them so they would be seen separately by your eyes when wearing 3-D glasses. The result was truly amazing. Not only did you see the fossil in startling 3-D clarity, you also saw its elemental composition. Not surprisingly, I wanted Bob and Jason on my X-ray imaging team, and so did Mr B.

Both Gene and Bob used an EDAX Eagle II Micro X-ray Fluorescence imaging instrument. Inside a chamber is an X-Y stage (a calibrated moving platform), controlled by a computer. The stage moves the sample beneath an X-ray generating tube and an X-ray detector. The software on the EDAX machine is very clever. The detector actually picks up a wide range of X-rays. The result is a data-cube of information analogous to the data-cube collected by the multi-spectral imagers. However, since this is a data-cube of X-rays, it contains elemental information rather than colour information. As the sample is scanned, the computer automatically produces EXAMs extracted from the data-cube, each of which displays the distribution of a particular element across the area of the scan. EDAX probes cost the low hundreds of thousands of dollars. Mr B was all for buying one, but we thought we had better try it out more vigorously first. So we got in touch with EDAX, specifically Tara Nylese and Bruce Scruggs. We asked if we could come up to their offices in New Jersey for a week and try out their machine with two folios of the Palimpsest. So Abigail, Bob Morton, Gene Hall and I went up to their office in New Jersey and occupied it for a week. Tara, Bruce and the entire EDAX team opened their doors.

We had brought one of the toughest of all challenges, folio 81, and we intended to image the recto. It was not a particularly important part of the Palimpsest: it contained part of Archimedes' *Equilibrium of Planes*, the text of which was well known through Codex A. It was also in good physical shape. But it was almost entirely covered by a forgery. Our first scans were not very successful. But with Bruce, Bob and Gene in conversation, we refined our parameters: we doubled our dwell-time (that is, the amount of time that the detector stayed over a particular area), so that we could pick up a bigger signal; we increased our resolution (that is, the granularity of the recorded image in dots per inch) and we reduced further the area that we would scan: we concentrated on just one line where we thought Archimedes text could be. Fifteen hours later, we had a whole bundle of maps. We had a large number of maps that contained elements from the forgeries. We had a gold map – blank across the folio – a zinc map, a barium map and a copper map, all of which brought out parts of the forgery. But we also had an iron map. I emailed the iron map to Reviel; he could read the words: *para eutheian*. We had read through the gold.

There was only one fly in the ointment. In fifteen hours we had scanned half a line of Archimedes text. There were approximately thirty-five lines of text on any forged folio. If we worked on all four forgeries, it would take us 4,200 hours. Bob had always warned me that time was the biggest factor in X-ray imaging. If we went ahead with this procedure, I would be retired by the time we had finished imaging the Palimpsest.

Beamtime

The conclusion was clear: since we didn't have the time, we needed a more energetic source for our X-rays. This was where Uwe Bergmann showed his stuff. He also gave a presentation at the conference suggesting that X-rays could be used to retrieve Archimedes text. But while Gene and Bob proposed to do their work on an EDAX Eagle machine, which is the size of a small refrigerator, Uwe Bergmann proposed to use a machine the size of a football pitch – the SPEAR (Stanford Positron Electron Accelerating Ring), which is part of the Stanford Linear Accelerator Center, or SLAC, in California. SPEAR was built as an atom smasher – more technically, a synchrotron, which is an oval particle accelerator. The particles, electrons and their positively charged equivalents, positrons, are accelerated to very, very, very nearly the speed of light. The electrons travel in one direction around the ring, and the positrons in the opposite direction. When they collide they create new particles and particle physicists analyse the results. It was at SPEAR that Burton Richter discovered the charm quark in 1974 and Martin Perl the Tau lepton in 1976. This is very cool. It is, in fact, so very cool that I was rather determined to get Archimedes there, even if it meant transporting him across the United States.

The SPEAR is not used as an atom smasher any more, and anyway, we didn't want to hit Archimedes with particles travelling at 99.999999986 per cent of the speed of light. Rather, we wanted to hit it with light itself, and now SPEAR is used as the world's greatest light bulb. To explain this, I take you back to two of Isaac Newton's famous Laws of Motion. The first states that every object in a state of uniform motion tends to remain in that state of motion unless an external force is applied to it. Now, even though the electrons in the synchrotron are travelling at a uniform (extremely high) speed, their state of motion is not uniform; they are not travelling in a straight line. Actually, they are bent by very powerful magnets. The third law states that for every action there is an equal and opposite reaction. So what happens when the highly energetic electrons are swerved? – what's the reaction? Well, electromagnetic radiation – lots and lots of it, spun off the ring like tomatoes off the back of a truck turning a corner at high speed.

To the particle physicists this synchrotron radiation was wasted energy, an inconvenient by-product of the atom-smashing process. But one day in the mid-1970s someone summoned up the courage to ask the particle physicists if they could literally 'tap' the ring and capture the synchrotron radiation that it was emitting. For several years at SPEAR, X-ray scientists, like parasites, harnessed the synchrotron radiation provided by the ring that was primarily there to serve the atom smashers. But eventually the high-energy physicists moved on to yet bigger machines, and from 1990 SPEAR has been dedicated to the generation of synchrotron radiation. A synchrotron X-ray beam is intense (that is, there are an awful lot of photons), collimated (that is, all the photons point in the same direction) and polarised (that is, the electromagnetic field of all the photons swings in a well-defined plane). In other words, you have a colossal army of X-rays, all marching to the same drum, and the experimenter can call the tune. The Stanford Synchrotron Radiation Laboratory (SSRL) is one of the most advanced light sources in the world. Today, more than fifty synchrotrons are operated around the world and many more are under construction. They have names like BESSY, Boomerang, Diamond, Soleil, SPring-8 and SPEAR3 – the newest upgrade of the ring at the Stanford Synchrotron Radiation Laboratory.

A number of 'beam lines' run off the synchrotron to little independent labs. We were designated beam line 6-2. Many beam lines have two hutches, so that while one experiment is being run, another can be set up: there is no downtime for beams at SSRL, because 'beamtime' is a precious commodity. The hutches are lead-lined, and while the experiment is running, no one can enter the hutch. It is not a good idea to be zapped by that beam. And that is what you get when you get beamtime at SSRL: a beam line and a hutch.

While the EDAX Eagle probe is a commercial machine, designed for a wide variety of applications, with an awful lot of software attached, the synchrotron is just a light source. Uwe had to build the machine.

Unlike the EDAX machine, which sends out X-rays at many different wavelengths, Uwe could tune his beam precisely to the best wavelength in order to look at iron or any other element. Uwe and Abigail got Greg Young of the Canadian Conservation Institute to do exhaustive tests on an old parchment document of Abigail's to make sure that his experiment would not damage the parchment. Having conducted these tests, Uwe realised that he could raise the intensity of his beam at the wavelength that responded to iron. Uwe attenuated his beam, using especially designed filters. He fine-tuned it with a filter of Reynolds Wrap (or Bacofoil), which, he assured me, was quite as good for the job. He designed his X-Y stage, and carefully calculated the distance between the sample and the detector. He constructed a humidity chamber, so that the humidity would remain constant and the folio of the Palimpsest would not change shape while the scan was running. All the computers and work stations were positioned outside the hutch. Each of the several computers did different things: one recorded the position of the beam; another recorded the position of the sample on the X-Y stage – and if the stage stopped moving, the experiment would automatically shut down so as not to damage the parchment. Another computer recorded the data in the scan, and a final computer was used to convert the files into a format that we could use in the post-processing software and which we could distribute to the scholars.

To help him, Uwe had Martin George to write the software for the computers, which had to meet two very different criteria: it had to be advanced enough to precisely capture the data, and it had to be simple enough for me to use. Abigail, Mike and I would have to take turns with Uwe in running scans, keeping an eye on the Palimpsest and even fine-tuning the beam. If it was simple enough for me, then Mike and Abigail would handle it just fine. But believe me, this means simple. The reason we had to use it was that the experiment would run for seven days, it would run twenty-four hours a day, and we would have to do shifts.

It didn't look like a professional set-up. Inside the hutch the guts of the machinery were scattered all over the place; outside the hutch looked like an electronics junk yard. But I soon realised that this is precisely what serious professional operations look like, because looks don't matter and, essentially, new machines were tailor-made for very different operations every day in this extraordinary place.

Uwe estimated that the scanning of one of the two columns of folio 81r, the forged page, would take thirty hours – approximately seventeen times faster than at the EDAX machine. Abigail put the folio on to the X-Y stage, and the scanning started. It was utterly mesmerising. Back and forth the scan would go, and slowly the iron map would appear that brought out the Archimedes text. We had to be constantly watchful for a fading signal, as the position and strength of the beam changed over time (the electrons got topped up three times a day). If it did change, we had to 'nudge' the beam. We couldn't scan large sections because the resulting files would get too big. So Mike wrote down the idiot's guide to the synchrotron for me and stuck it on a computer. It's the nearest I've come to computer code: 'Press STOP; Open hutch; Turn on light; Check humidity; check ARCHIE; Turn off light; Close hutch; flick SAFETY switch; press EXIT PLOTTER; Press EXIT RASTER; Check FILE save in Dir/*.*; Select RASTER; press RETURN; Change XY coordinates; press APPLY; flick SHUTTER 3 switch; select RASPLOT; choose pixel 1; press START.'

Thirty hours later we had a column of text to show Reviel. And Reviel read it: we had achieved our objective. We assured Uwe that we would be back, and when we came we would bring the most important pages of text, containing the most difficult challenges.

March 2006

We returned to SLAC for two weeks in March 2006. This time we took more people out. We needed more people to staff the beam, but we also needed the talent: Uwe could spend all his time optimising the experiment that only he understood; Bob lent his years of experience on imaging with X-ray fluorescence; Keith and Roger were there to process the images; Abigail was joined by Jennifer Giaccai, the conservation scientist at the Walters. And Mike and I were both there to lend a hand when we could.

This time, also, we brought out the very first page of the manuscript. This was the page that Reviel and Natalie had first recognised as *On Floating Bodies* in April 2001, and the one that also contained the inscription by the scribe of the prayer book containing the date 14 April 1229. The page really was a wreck and the pseudocolour images had revealed nothing.

From the moment the scanning started it was clear that something extraordinary was happening. The charred, stained, and worm-eaten parchment in the hutch appeared on the screen as a dense lattice of Greek characters. I knew that we were seeing, pixel by pixel, line by line, here at the Stanford syncrotron, a map of the iron on the page that would give us the previously unknown Greek version of Archimedes' *On Floating Bodies*. Keith Knox sent the first images to Reviel by email. He received this reply:

From: Reviel Netz
Sent: Mon 3/13/2006 12:32 AM
To: Keith Knox
Cc: Nigel Wilson; Mike Toth; Uwe Bergmann; Roger Easton;
William Noel
Subject: folio 1v col. 1

Thanks Keith for the images.
XRF for 1v col. 1 is sensational. I attach the transcription of

iv col. i lines 2-11. Previously, with very hard work, I squeezed some 3.5 lines out of the old pseudocolor, but now I fairly easily read effectively the entire text, noting a couple of errors, too, in my old pseudocolor based reading.

 Reviel.

This leaf comes from the very long final proposition of *On Floating Bodies*, which is, by common consent, the most complex proposition ever written by Archimedes. It concerns the conditions under which a conic section, somewhat similar to the hull of a boat in appearance, will or will not be stable when immersed in water. It is significantly different from the Latin text that Heiberg derived from Moerbeke, and a group of diagrams appears where none was suspected. This unique surviving text of Archimedes' *On Floating Bodies* in Greek was revealed on 13 March 2006, 777 years after it had been erased and overwritten.

The Gift-giver

The colophon from which John Lowden had so painstakingly extracted the date on which the scribe of the prayer book had dated his work as 14 April 1229 was also on this same page. I sent out the following email:

> All: We attach two images of the lower section of fol. iv. 'Before' was taken when the Palimpsest arrived at WAM. 'After' was taken today: it's an X-ray fluorescence image taken at SLAC; after Abigail Quandt conserved it. It contains some text written on April 14, 1229. But can anyone now give us any more details?

My friend Georgi Parpulov was the first to reply:

> **From:** Georgi Parpulov
> **Sent:** Tue 3/14/2006 4:39 AM

To: William Noel
Subject: colophon

Hi, Will,
+[This] was written by the hand of presbyter John Pogonatos (?)
on the 14th day of the month of April, a Saturday, of the year 6737, indiction 2.
Wait till you hear from Nigel Wilson: he will be able to read it with much greater precision.

Before we heard from Nigel, we heard from John Lowden:

From: Lowden, John
Sent: Thu 3/16/2006 10:31 AM
To: William Noel; Georgi Parpulov; Nigel Wilson, Reviel Netz
Subject: RE: colophon

Have just received this on return from Dublin. The improved legibility is astonishing.
First impression is that the name (refining GP) is Iw(annou) iere(os) tou Murwna
I would check Ioannes Myronas iereus as scribe.
But maybe I should check first and communicate after!
Yours (too hastily?)
    John

And then finally, on the Sunday, we got confirmation from Nigel:

From: Nigel Wilson
Sent: Sun 3/19/2006 7:32 AM
To: William Noel; Georgi Parpulov; John Lowden; Reviel Netz
Subject: Re: colophon

Dear Will, John, Reviel et al.,

I agree with John's suggestion and that Myronas is probably the name; the last letter could be alpha and has an accent. I have asked a Greek student of mine to check in the telephone directories to see if it is still a name in Greece. (Mylonas is well attested.)

Best wishes,

Nigel

There we are then. The case is nearly closed. Finally we know who preserved the texts of Archimedes, Hyperides and the rest. The priest Ioannes (John) Myronas finished his work on 14 April 1229. As in all detective stories, we need a motive. In that year 14 April was the day before Easter Sunday. Traditionally, it was a day upon which people made gifts to religious institutions for the good of their souls. What an extraordinary gift this was. Ioannes did not just redeem himself. On the anniversary of Christ's Resurrection Ioannes Myronas gave the world its greatest palimpsest and saved the secrets of Archimedes.

'The Vast Book of the Universe'

Moonlighting for Archimedes

This is not typical university work. The Archimedes Palimpsest seems to insist on being unique, and the project of its decipherment has few parallels. Remarkably much has been achieved in less than ten years; and, remarkably, nearly all of this was achieved by week-end warriors, summoned by the thrill and glory of working for Archimedes. We all had our day jobs: Will Noel was curating manuscript exhibitions at the Walters, I was teaching Greek science at Stanford, while Roger Easton was teaching imaging science at Rochester, and Nigel Wilson was editing the works of Aristophanes for the Oxford Classical Texts series. I am not sure what Mike Toth was doing. In fact, only one individual got the Archimedes Palimpsest itself as a day job – and this underlines the priorities of manuscript studies. Abigail Quandt put aside most of her other obligations to concentrate, day after day, on the disbinding and conservation of the manuscript. Her hands were the busiest.

And all of us did this for one simple reason: that we are in awe of one individual who lived, some 2,250 years ago, on a triangular island in the middle of the Mediterranean. That we succeeded in doing so much for him is, in my view, due to three individuals. They deserve our thanks.

The Patron

That so much has been accomplished so quickly is, primarily, a tribute to the owner of the Palimpsest. The team of scholars and scientists working on the project have something which is, today, very rare: our work is led by *a rich patron*. There was a time when this was standard. Science in Alexandria – as well as in Syracuse – was pursued under the patronage of Hellenistic kings. No doubt a rich patron commissioned the Archimedes manuscript in the tenth century. Most Renaissance artists and scholars worked for rich patrons. However, since at least the Middle Ages, scholarship has often been pursued within public institutions. The Church is the most obvious example, and it is due to her that most manuscripts survive. Today most manuscripts are held by a different kind of public institution – the state or its universities. Almost all the important manuscripts of the world can now be found in such institutions and, at first, everyone's feeling was that the manuscript should belong to the public. We were proved wrong. In retrospect, it was a stroke of luck that the manuscript found itself in private hands. No public institution could have acted so flexibly, with such generous and well-thought application of resources. Think of it: the owner did something rather outrageous. He entrusted it to Will Noel, who is by now a world expert on the Archimedes Palimpsest but eight years ago could not tell Archimedes from Pythagoras. The owner then more or less told Will Noel to do with the manuscript as he pleased. The owner implicitly promised to pay along the way as would be necessary. (I say 'implicitly' because, I am told, the owner is not a man of many words.) It turns out this was the clever thing to do. Had the manuscript been housed at a university, the academic politics of its research would have been much more difficult, and each expense along the way would have had to be accounted for in a much more tedious, haphazard and time-consuming fashion. In short, the owner saved us the disadvantages of public institutions. Not that private owners are to be preferred in principle. In my own view, private owners are, in general, not the best custodians of world treasures. After all, it was the Greek Church that saved the manuscript for a millennium – and then it was private owners that, through the course of the twentieth century, very nearly destroyed it. With the current owner we have been lucky. He has not merely done well by Archimedes; he did all he could.

The Philologist

I do not know the owner of the Palimpsest all that well. Will Noel does: almost daily, he is in email correspondence with him, discussing the way forward with the Palimpsest Project. My own daily correspondence is even more virtual. It is all in my head. And it is with another great benefactor of the project – without whom, once again, all of this would have been impossible. In my thoughts, I always converse with Johan Ludvig Heiberg.

We have been critical towards him throughout the book, right down to those last pages – those gaps he left, those false guesses, these diagrams he never bothered with. Now is the time to admit the truth: without Heiberg, we could never have made it. We look at the text, and see at first just a jumble of meaningless traces. We interpret a few of them. We conjecture a sense. We get to a dead end. And then we check Heiberg and, lo and behold, he has already made sense of it; he read even further than that! Only then, looking back at the page, we see those traces that provided Heiberg with his reading. And then, finally, based on Heiberg's foundations, we can go further and add to his readings.

The transcription project was rather like an expedition to a lost island. You believe you face what no one has ever witnessed. And then, time and again, the same uncanny experience: you suddenly realise that *the previous explorer – Heiberg – has been here already*. I had been excited as I saw symbols for circles emerging out of Abigail's treatment of the Palimpsest. As they came out of a conservator's treatment of the manuscript, I took it for granted they were new. But no: Heiberg had seen them as well and noted upon them in his critical edition. Again and again, Heiberg took me by surprise.

Let us put it this way. There is a long tradition of readers of Archimedes, from such scholars as Hero of Alexandria, Eutocius of Ascalon and Leo the Geometer from Byzantium, coming all the way up to the present day. No one in this tradition will ever rival the authority of Heiberg. We are extraordinarily lucky that it was he, and no one else, who was there in Istanbul in 1906, to study this manuscript for that brief historical moment. For no one else could have made out so much of the manuscript. Heiberg has, very nearly single-handedly, saved the text of Archimedes. It is only thanks to the most modern technology that we may now be going even beyond him. And for this, I suggest, our gratitude should go to Archimedes himself.

The Founder's Tools

I started out by saying that Archimedes was the most important scientist who ever lived. We can now see how: in the tools he created – and in the way in which later science was shaped by Archimedes' blueprint for science. Archimedes, more than anyone else, shaped the history of the calculus – the essential study for the measurement of curves – and he was also, incredibly, the founder of combinatorics, the science underlying our own theory of probability. These two – the calculus, and the theory of probability – underlie contemporary imaging science. The imaging scientists working on the Archimedes Palimpsest applied a science that was fundamentally Archimedean.

To illustrate this, I now concentrate on a relatively standard tool used by imaging scientists: the equalisation of probability curves. While standard, it is a useful introduction, because it brings into focus the main concept of imaging science, namely that of *information*.

We have often mentioned the term 'information' in this book. We have discussed the way in which books move from one information storage to another, how changes in information technologies impact on the transmission of knowledge. It is time to come clean and explain that 'information' is not some kind of vague, metaphorical concept. Information is a technical term, possessing a clear, if subtle, mathematical definition. Most important, in contemporary science, information can be *measured*.

The fundamental intuition can be articulated as follows. We look at an array of numbers and we ask, 'How predictable is it?' Suppose the array of numbers goes something like this:

255, 255, 255 ... 255

that is, all the numbers are exactly 255. There is a clear intuition that this is very predictable and so also very uninformative. On the other hand, an array that goes something like this:

127, 45, 254, 11, 6, 189 ... 39

is much less predictable and so contains more 'information'.

Now let us look back at the arrays of numbers:

255, 255, 255 ... 255   127, 45, 254, 11, 6, 189 ... 39

What do they mean in terms of image science? As Will Noel has explained already, imaging scientists do not think of images as faces or flowers. They think of images as two-dimensional (sometimes many-dimensional) arrays of integer values. Each of the integers in the array represents the properties of a pixel; most typically they consider the grey level of a pixel in a black-and-white picture. In a black-and-white picture each pixel is assigned a level of grey, usually ranging from 0 (least light – that is, black) to 255 (most light – that is, white). The 255, 255, 255 ... 255 array, therefore, is correlated with a perfectly blank image – one which is totally white. The 127, 45, 254, 11, 6, 189 ... 39 array, on the other hand, is associated with a complex pattern of light and shade. The perfectly blank image is completely predictable (totally white), therefore totally uninformative; the complex pattern of light and shade is much less predictable and therefore also much more informative.

At this point, it can be mathematically shown that: the most informative image is the one in which all levels of grey are equally probable.

That is: in the perfectly blank image, a single level of grey was the most probable – the totally white one; all the rest had no probability at all of occurring. In the complex pattern of light and shade, however, all levels of grey were equally probable. And this is the underlying mathematical reason why the complex pattern of light and grey is the more informative.

The goal of imaging science is to make images as informative as possible – so that, for instance, scholars can then use them to read the words of Archimedes. The above mathematical result implicitly suggests a certain possible technological application: in order to make an image more informative, let us equalise its distribution of probabilities. We should try to make all levels of grey equally probable.

How do we do this? We need a new mathematical conceptualisation. We go back to the image and consider it not merely as an array of numbers but, instead, as a curve. We draw a two-dimensional matrix with the familiar x and y axes; x goes horizontally, y vertically. We make the x axis stand for the possible grey levels – going from 0, the perfect black, up to 255, the perfect white. For each of the 256 levels of grey, we draw on the y vector the number of times it occurs. So, for instance, the perfectly blank image has a very simple appearance in such a matrix: it is empty everywhere except for a single, tall column standing on the 255, at the rightmost end of the x axis (see fig. 12.1). A complex pattern of light and shade, on the other hand, has a more complex appearance (see fig. 12.2).

To simplify a bit: most images appear as a kind of bell-curve, with most pixels somewhere in the middle between black and white, and the rest somewhat less probable (more black or white) as we move away from the centre.

Now recall: our aim – to make the image as informative as possible – is to make the distribution of probabilities *as equal as possible*. That is to say that, since the most informative image appears as a 'flat' curve, or rather like a rectangle – one where all levels of grey occur equally often (see fig. 12.3) – we wish to take a curve such as the bell-curve in the figure and turn it into a flat, rectangular shape.

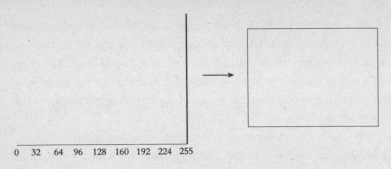

FIGURE 12.1 *A distribution of pixels where all pixels have 255 level of light corresponds to the perfectly blank image.*

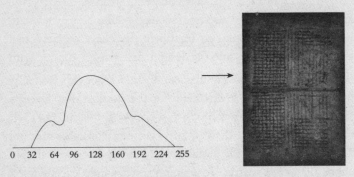

FIGURE 12.2 *A normal image has associated with it a curve that has a roughly bell-like shape.*

Now Archimedean science kicks in again. For this operation – the transformation of a bell-curve into a rectangle – is simply the measurement of a curvilinear object by a rectilinear one. When Archimedes was measuring his parabolas, showing how they were equal to two-thirds a given rectangle, he was doing *precisely* the kind of operation we need to do right now. (Indeed, some of the curves we need to measure may take the form of a parabola.) And what contemporary scientists do, at this stage, is apply the tools of the calculus – i.e. of the science arising out of Archimedes' measurement of curvilinear objects – in order to 'flatten' the curve correctly.

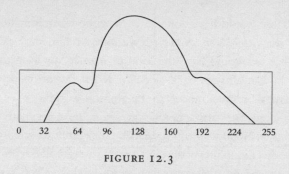

FIGURE 12.3

We applied the theory of probability to develop the notion of 'information' and to discover that the most informative image is the one associated with an equal distribution of probabilities of grey levels. We then applied the calculus to transform the curve of the actual distribution of probabilities into the desired 'flat' shape associated with the equal distribution of probabilities. The end result was no more and no less than the simultaneous application of probability and the calculus. This is just an example of what imaging scientists do, but also a representative one (if you wish, an *informative* one) – though, of course, to develop the images used for reading the Palimpsest, much more than this was required. But this is precisely the type of mathematical technique applied. Probability and the calculus are what imaging science is made of. And so, without Archimedes, we would not have the science to read him.

Archimedes' Blueprint for Science

Even more important than the contents of Archimedes' science was his spirit – his blueprint for science. After all, his combinatorics has been lost – when, in 1229, Ioannes Myronas decided not to use all of the parchment in front of him and to use but a single leaf of the *Stomachion*. It remained for seventeenth-century mathematicians to reinvent the science of combinatorics, and therefore to create probability. They would have done so even without Archimedes having written the *Stomachion*. And yet: without Archimedes' example, I doubt that we would have the kind of science we have today. We can see how it all goes back to Archimedes' invention of applying mathematical, abstract models to the physical world.

Let us take as our starting point, once again, the mathematical notion of *information*. Not only imaging science – the computer sciences as well as many other disciplines of the digital revolution are all essentially based on this concept. As mathematical concepts go, this is a very recent one: it was introduced in the year 1948 by a mathematician working at Bell Laboratories named Claude Shannon. He was working on making telephone lines function better, and it occurred to him that there could be a mathematical theory associated with the amount of information travelling through such lines. His inspiration came directly out of physics, and the concept of information, as found by Shannon, is inherently a concept of mathematical physics.

What Shannon did was to take the concept of *entropy*, defined in mathematical physics, and to apply it to the flow of information in (say) telephone lines. What is entropy? It is a measure of how 'probable' a given physical state is. A physical state can be very likely, in which case its entropy is high; or it can be very unlikely, in which case its entropy is low. We can therefore see where Shannon took his inspiration: information is (to simplify a bit) *reverse entropy*.

One of the deepest observations ever made by science is that – hold your breath – *probable things happen more often*. So that, more often than not, physical systems would move from unlikely states – with low entropy – to more likely states – with high entropy. Wait long enough, and *the amount of entropy in the universe must increase* (or, as we may put this after Shannon, *the amount of information in the universe must decrease* – which is also the reason why reception on our cellphones is so bad). I am completely serious about saying that this is one of the deepest observations ever made by science. It is a beautiful example of how, by the power of pure thought, we can work out how the universe *must* behave. It is a tautology, that probable things happen more often; and because of this tautology – which we came to by pure thought alone – we can see also that *the amount of entropy in the universe must increase*. This is known as the second law of thermodynamics, and it ranks as one of the most fundamental discoveries of physics.

This becomes especially significant the moment we can calculate which physical systems have more entropy and which have less. This was the reason the concept of entropy was introduced in the first place, in 1872, by a German physicist called Boltzmann. He produced a mathematical approach for measuring the amount of entropy in a physical state. In particular, he could show the following. Suppose we take as our physical system a certain gas, composed of many gas molecules. Then Boltzmann could show that the more rapidly, on average, the gas molecules were moving about, the less entropy the system had; or that the slower, on average, those molecules moved about, the more entropy the system had. In short, Boltzmann could show that higher entropy is associated with the slower motion of molecules. Based on the second law of thermodynamics – showing that entropy must increase – Boltzmann could also show that gases must eventually move from faster states to slower states.

Now, it is also established that what we call 'heat' is really a measurement of the speed of molecules in the physical system. A 'warm' system is really one where the molecules move faster, a 'cool' one is where they move more slowly. And so Boltzmann shows, based on the second law of thermodynamics, that all systems must, eventually, became *colder*.

This is magic – belonging right up there in the pantheon next to Archimedes. Applying pure thought alone, Boltzmann proved, in 1872, that *everything must, eventually, become colder*. But the comparison with Archimedes can be sustained further.

Why did Boltzmann produce his mathematical theory in 1872? Because the behaviour of heat was the urgent scientific problem of his time. So much else in science was already understood in mathematical terms – but not heat. In the two centuries prior to Boltzmann, scientists were working hard on extending Newton's achievement.

Newton determined, on purely mathematical grounds, how the planets must behave. The universe was made of points – centres of gravity – exerting the force of gravity on each other. This was a unified theory of motion, where everything was reduced to basic tools of geometry and calculation. The theory was published in 1687, in Newton's *Principia*. And from 1687 onwards, all scientists tried to emulate Newton's achievement – to produce mathematical theories to which one could reduce various physical phenomena. In the early nineteenth century electricity followed gravity, analysed by mathematical techniques somewhat comparable to those of Newton himself. By 1872 the central physical phenomenon still resisting mathematical treatment was heat. Boltzmann, in his study, made a fundamental contribution to the mathematisation of physical science. He was essentially completing Newton's programme.

Only that it wasn't Newton's – it was Archimedes', as Newton would be the first to admit. Newton, in 1687, was himself heir to a long tradition. His great predecessor was Galileo; both Newton and Galileo aspired, above all, to return science to its Archimedean heights. They wished to take Archimedes' mathematical tools and to make such tools deduce as much of physics as one could. The Newtonian programme of reducing physical systems to geometrical representations obeying mathematical laws was all taken from the Archimedean blueprint for science. And so, without Archimedes, there would be neither Galileo nor Newton. Nor, for that matter, Boltzmann nor Shannon. Nor, for that matter, contemporary imaging science.

The 'Vast Book'

'Philosophy is written in this vast book, which lies continuously open before our eyes (I mean the universe). But it cannot be understood unless you have first learned to understand the language and recognise the characters in which it is written. It is written in the language of mathematics, and the characters are triangles, circles and other geometrical figures. Without such means it is impossible for us humans to understand a word of it, and to be without them is to wander around in vain through a dark labyrinth.'

So Galileo wrote, in 1623, recovering the spirit of the science of Archimedes. This metaphor of the vast book of the universe is still with us. We do think of the universe as a 'book' whose secrets we try to uncover; and we still use mathematics to do so. The importance of Archimedes to the history of science is in his having shown how this metaphor could literally work. The book of the universe was first deciphered by him – and it was found to be written in the language of mathematics.

In 1623, when Galileo came to write down these words, all the manuscripts of Archimedes were already gone. Codex B was lost some time in the fourteenth century; Codex A some time in the sixteenth century, probably when Galileo was still a child. Only one copy remained – but this was hidden from sight. The monks who used it never did learn to read its triangles, circles and other geometrical figures.

In 1687, when Isaac Newton's *Principia* was published, this codex – that is, the Archimedes Palimpsest – was still in the Holy Land, still hidden from sight. It was worlds away from the British scientist cloistered in his lodgings at Trinity College, Cambridge.

In 1872, when Ludwig Boltzmann published his study on the second law of thermodynamics, the Archimedes Palimpsest was already in Istanbul. It was about to be discovered, however briefly, by Heiberg. But by 1948 it was lost again. When Shannon produced his mathematical definition of information, the manuscript was probably already lying mutilated in some Paris apartment.

Fifty years later it walked on stage. And now, science was ready. The science inspired by Archimedes came full circle to be able to recover nearly all of his words. And now, finally, we do get something of the full measure of the man.

A final word of caution should be added. Once again, we have not yet got everything. There are still gaps in our reading. But we remain optimistic. Even now, as I write, I am studying the latest SLAC images of the forgery pages, and I see that Heiberg's transcription even of *Method* proposition 1 needs significant revision. The science inspired by Archimedes never stands still. This process extends without end: science steps back from physical reality to consider its mathematical underpinnings and, this way, more and more is always found. Archimedean science keeps making progress; in time, it will catch up with Archimedes.

ACKNOWLEDGEMENTS

Reading the Archimedes Palimpsest was a far more complicated undertaking than the narrative encompassed in these pages might indicate. Indeed we do not know all the people who helped. Choosing just a few may alienate many, but the contributions of some have been so substantial that we cannot conclude this book without listing them below. Knowing that this list is incomplete, we nonetheless extend our thanks to all who have so generously contributed to the project. A lot of the work was done at nights and week-ends, and on vacation, and we have also to thank the project's many widows and orphans, particularly Carol Christens-Barry, Dale Stewart, Daniel and Donald Potter, Elisabetta Gaiani and Sofia Bergmann, Hanneke Wilson, and Lucretia Toth. Deep gratitude is owed to Uwe Bergmann, Serafina Cuomo, Patricia Easterling, Roger Easton, Jr, László Horváth, Geoffrey Lloyd, Abigail Quandt, Ken Saito, and Nigel Wilson for their expert assistance in the writing of this book. All mistakes of fact and interpretation are our own. Many friends helped us make ourselves clear, including Richard Ash, Christopher Collison, Charlie Duff, Susan Elderkin, Guy Deutscher, Richard Leson, Amanda Mann, and Jean-François Vilain. Success depends upon a good editor, and we had the wonderful Francine Brody at Weidenfeld and Nicolson.

MANAGEMENT AND ADMINISTRATION

Ken Dean
Barbara Fegley
Kirstin Lavin
Richard Leson
Griffith Mann
Amy Mannarino
Joan Elisabeth Reid
Harold Stevens
Mike Toth
Gary Vikan
Lynn Wolfe

CONSERVATION AND HANDLING

Kevin Auer
George Chang
Jane Down
Gil Furoy
Jennifer Giaccai
Paul Hepworth
Erin Loftus
Amy Lubick
Maureen McDonald
Mike McKee
Elizabeth Moffatt
Elissa O'Loughlin
Abigail Quandt
Jane Sirois
Scott Williams
Gregory Young
Anthea Zeltzman

SCIENCE AND IMAGING

Allyson Aranda
Mike Attas
Uwe Bergmann
Bill Christens-Barry
David Day
Charles Dickinson
Roger Easton, Jr
Alex Garchtchenko
Martin George
Jason Gislason
Douglas Golz
Gene Hall
Tom Hostetler
Keith Knox
Matthew Latimer
Bob Morton
Nick Morton
Tara Nylese
Emanuele Salerno
Bruce Scruggs
Derek Walvoord

DATA AND INFORMATION TECHNOLOGY

Martina Bagnoli
Diane Bockrath
Doug Emery
Cathleen Fleck
Andy Johnston
Joe McCourt
Carl Malamud

SCHOLARSHIP

Fabio Acerbi
Colin Austin
Chris Carey
Persi Diaconis
Patricia Easterling
Mike Edwards
Zoltán Farkas
Eric Handley
Jud Herrman
Susan Holmes
László Horváth
John Lowden
Gyula Mayer
Henry Mendell
Stephen Menn
Tamás Mészáros
Stefano Parenti
Georgi Parpulov
Erik Petersen
Marwan Rashed
Peter Rhodes
Ken Saito
Robert Sharples
Richard Sorabji
Natalie Tchernetska
Stephen Todd
Nigel Wilson
David Whitehead

FURTHER READING

Those interested in finding out more about the Archimedes Palimpsest, its imaging, conservation, and scholarly study, should visit the website www.archimedespalimpsest.org, and follow the links. It is our hope to present all our data on the web at www.archimedespalimpsest.net, and we have already made a start at this. Other than this, readers might like to consult the following publications.

ENCYCLOPEDIAS

Gillispie, C. C. (ed.), *Dictionary of Scientific Biography* (New York, 1975).

Hornblower, S. and A. Spawforth (eds.), *Oxford Classical Dictionary* (Oxford, 1996).

The Catholic Encyclopedia, at www.newadvent.org.

ANCIENT MATHEMATICS

Those interested in learning more about ancient Greek science would best start with these very readable books:

Lloyd, G. E. R., *Early Greek Science: Thales to Aristotle* (London, 1970).

————, *Greek Science after Aristotle* (London, 1973).

Those interested more specifically in the achievements of Greek geometry should start with:

Knorr, W. R., *The Ancient Tradition of Geometric Problems* (New York, 1986).

ARCHIMEDES

The best general book on Archimedes' scientific achievement is likely to remain for many years to come:

Dijksterhuis, E. J., *Archimedes* (1956; revised edn, Princeton, 1987).

The following is a three-volume publication, written in Greek, with Latin translation and introduction. It may be difficult to read. Still, we thought we should mention this; we have referred to its two authors quite frequently:

Heiberg, J. L., *Archimedes, Opera Omnia* (Leipzig, 1910–15).

Those interested in the early history of the calculus and its concepts should still read:

Boyer, C. B., *The History of the Calculus and its Conceptual Development* (New York, 1959).

HYPERIDES

The speeches of Hyperides known before their discovery in the Archimedes Palimpsest are edited with a translation in the Loeb Classical Library:

Burtt, J. O., *Minor Attic Orators*, vol. II (Cambridge, MA, 1954).

MANUSCRIPT TRANSMISSION OF THE CLASSICS

For the transition from roll to codex:

Roberts, C. H. and T. C. Skeat, *The Birth of the Codex* (London, 1983).

For those interested in Greek scripts, the following are good introductions:

Barbour, R., *Greek Literary Hands* AD *400–1600* (Oxford, 1981).

Easterling, P. and C. Handley (eds.), *Greek Scripts: An Illustrated Introduction* (London, 2001).

Metzger, B. M., *Manuscripts of the Greek Bible: An Introduction to Greek Palaeography* (New York, 1981).

★

For a broad survey of the history of writing, readers might try:

Sirat, C., *Writing as Handwork: A History of Handwriting in Mediterranean and Western Culture* (Turnhout, 2006).

There are many technical studies on the making of manuscripts. A useful basic text, with bibliography, is:

Brown, M. P., *Understanding Medieval Manuscripts: A Guide to Technical Terms* (Malibu, CA, 1994).

Not at all relevant to Archimedes, but for readers who would like to know more about the wonderful world of medieval manuscripts, the best general introduction available is:

De Hamel, C., *A History of Illuminated Manuscripts* (London, 1987).

For those interested in the transmission of ancient texts through to the age of printing, the following are indispensable:

Reynolds, L. D. and N. G. Wilson, *Scribes and Scholars*, 3rd edn (Oxford, 1991).

Wilson, N. G., *Scholars of Byzantium* (London, 1983).

A major scholarly feat, focused on the history of the text of Archimedes in Latin-speaking Europe, is:

Clagett, M., *Archimedes in the Middle Ages* (Madison, WI, 1964–84).

IMAGING AND IMAGING PROCESSING

Roger Easton recommends:

Baxes, G. A., *Digital Image Processing: Principles and Applications* (New York, 1994).

Falk, D. R., D. R. Brill and D. G. Stork, *Seeing the Light: Optics in Nature, Photography, Color, Vision, and Holography* (New York, 1986).

For advanced light sources, such as the Stanford Linear Accelerator Center, check out http://www.lightsources.org.

THE PALIMPSEST

The main publications on the Archimedes Palimpsest since September 1998 are listed below, alphabetically by author:

Christens-Barry, W. A., J. R. Bernstein and M. Blackburn, 'Imaging the Third Dimension of the Archimedes Palimpsest', *Proceedings of IS & T PICS Conference* (Montreal, 2001), pp. 202–5.

Christie's, New York, 'The Archimedes Palimpsest', sale catalogue 9058, Thursday, 29 October 1998.

Down, J. L., G. S. Young, R. S. Williams and M. A. MacDonald, 'Analysis of the Archimedes Palimpsest', in V. Daniels, A. Donnithorne and P. Smith (eds.), *Works of Art on Paper, Books, Documents and Photographs*, The International Institute for Conservation, Contributions to the Baltimore Congress, 2–6 September 2002 (London, 2002), pp. 52–8.

Easton, R. L., Jr, and W. Noel, 'The Multispectral Imaging of the Archimedes Palimpsest', *Gazette du Livre Médiévale*, 45, 2004, pp. 39–49.

Handley, E., 'Eureka? The conservation, imaging and study of the Archimedes Palimpsest', exhibition pamphlet, Trinity College, Cambridge, 21–2 and 25–9 July 2005.

Knox, K., C. Dickinson, L. Wei, R. L. Easton, Jr, and R. Johnston, 'Multispectral Imaging of the Archimedes Palimpsest', *Proceedings of IS & T PICS Conference* (Montreal, 2001), pp. 206–10.

Lowden, J., 'Archimedes into Icon: Forging an Image of Byzantium', in A. Eastmond and L. James (eds.), *Icon and Word: The Power of Images in Byzantium* (London, 2003), pp. 233–60.

Netz, R., *Archimedes: Translation and Commentary, with a Critical Edition of the Diagrams and a Translation of Eutocius' Commentaries*, vol. I: 'The Sphere and the Cylinder' (Cambridge, 2004).

———, *Archimedes: Translation and Commentary, with a Critical Edition of the Diagrams and a Translation of Eutocius' Commentaries*, vol. II: 'Advanced Geometrical Works' (Cambridge [forthcoming]).

———, *Archimedes: Translation and Commentary, with a Critical Edition of the Diagrams and a Translation of Eutocius' Commentaries*, vol. III:

'The Mathematical-Physical Works' (Cambridge [forthcoming]).

————, 'Archimedes and Mar Saba: a Preliminary Notice', in J. Patrich (ed.), *The Sabaite Heritage: The Sabaite Factor in the Orthodox Church: Monastic Life, Liturgy, Theology, Literature, Art and Archaeology* (2002), pp. 195–9.

————, 'The Origin of Mathematical Physics: New Light on an Old Question', *Physics Today*, June 2000, pp. 31–6.

Netz, R., F. Acerbi and N. Wilson, 'Towards a Reconstruction of Archimedes' Stomachion', *Sciamus*, 5, 2004, pp. 67–99.

Netz, R., K. Saito and N. Tchernetska, 'A New Reading of Method Proposition 14: Preliminary Evidence from the Archimedes Palimpsest (Part 1)', *Sciamus*, 2, 2001, pp. 9–29.

————, 'A New Reading of Method Proposition 14: Preliminary Evidence from the Archimedes Palimpsest (Part 2)', *Sciamus*, 3, 2002, pp. 109–25.

Noel, W., 'The Archimedes Palimpsest, Old Science Meets New Science', *Proceedings of IS & T PICS Conference* (Montreal, 2001), pp. 199–201.

Parenti, S., 'The Liturgical Tradition of the Euchologion "of Archimedes"', *Bollettino della Badia Greca di Grottaferrata*, IIIs. 2 (2005) [but actually 2006], pp. 69–87.

Quandt, A., 'The Archimedes Palimpsest: Conservation Treatment, Digital Imaging and Transcription of a Rare Mediaeval Manuscript', in V. Daniels, A. Donnithorne and P. Smith (eds.), *Works of Art on Paper: Books, Documents and Photographs*, The International Institute for Conservation, Contributions to the Baltimore Congress, 2–6 September 2002 (London, 2002), pp. 165–70.

Tchernetska, N., 'New Fragments of Hyperides from the Archimedes Palimpsest', *Zeitschrift für Papyrologie und Epigraphik*, vol. 154, 2005, pp. 1–6.

Wilson, Nigel, 'Archimedes: the Palimpsest and the Tradition', *Byzantinische Zeitschrift*, 92, 1999, pp. 89–101.

————, 'The Archimedes Palimpsest: A Progress Report', in 'A Catalogue of Greek Manuscripts at the Walters Art Museum and

Essays in Honor of Gary Vikan', *Journal of the Walters Art Museum*, 62, 2004, pp. 61–8.

———, 'The Secrets of Palimpsests', *L'Erasmo*, 25, 2005, pp. 70–5.

———, *Archimedes' 'On Floating Bodies' I.1–2*, edited with an English translation (Oxford, 2004).

Young, G., 'Quantitative Image Analysis in Microscopical Thermal Stability Measurements', Canadian Conservation Institute Newsletter, 31 June 2003, pp. 10–11.

INDEX

Note: *italic* page numbers denote references to Figures.

saltiness. This means – among other things – that we are to be active in the world as his representatives. We are to get out of the saltshaker and into life itself – not to be trodden down but to be zestful witnesses to Jesus as Lord and Saviour, as the one who alone gives life and meaning to a dying world.

I owe debts to many people for their contribution to this book. My mother Sue and my recently deceased father Bob, my brother Bobby and my sister Cathy gave me a joy and zest for life that were perhaps the greatest foundation I could have ever received for reaching out to others. They taught me how to celebrate.

It was Mrs Ethel Renwick who first introduced me to Christ by reflecting both the love of God and the truth of the gospel. In March 1999, at eighty-nine years of age, she went to be with the Lord. Her life illustrated at its best what this book is all about.

My experiences as an undergraduate student in Spain were also critical to my growth and understanding of evangelism. There I met Ruth Siemens. She demonstrated Christ's love to me and to all of my friends, whom I would drag over for a meal. But it was the way she lived that taught me more than anything else about lifestyle evangelism. I respect her profoundly.

In the mid-1970s and early 1980s I worked with the student ministry of InterVarsity Christian Fellowship. I am so grateful for their quality of leadership, their commitment to the integration of faith and thought, and the substantial and stimulating teaching I absorbed in those years, not to mention the fun of batting around ideas with fellow staff. That experience shaped and moulded my life in significant ways. I am also grateful that I never had the slightest restraint put upon me because I am a woman. Rather, I was constantly encouraged to use and develop my gifts.

I am also thankful for the churches where I have been privileged to teach and train over the past twenty years. One great source of encouragement to me over the years has been meeting so many faithful and committed Christians, be they pastors, church staff or laity. Thank you for allowing me to be a part of your church families.

My thanks go as well to dear friends for their help and

prayers as I prepared this new manuscript: Jim and Ruth Nyquist, to whom this book is dedicated, Fred and Elizabeth Catherwood, Bob and Martha Molenhouse, Doug and Adele Calhoon, Nancy Bergner, Kay York, Leanne Payne, Susan Yates, Sally Nevius, Jody McCain, Char Sandberg, Margaret Philbrick, David and Felicity Bentley-Taylor, and David and Pam Bock. I also appreciated the stimulating conversations I had on evangelism with IVCF staff Rick Richardson, Debbie Abbs, Mark Ashton, Jim Sire and Doug Schaupp.

Most of all, I thank my husband, Dick, for his love, his enthusiastic encouragement and his sacrificial assistance that really made it possible for me to write. I thank God for you every day. And my thanks go out as well to my wonderful children, Elizabeth and David, for your support, your love and your prayers.

A note about other people whose names appear in the book is also in order. Except for Mary (in chapter 1), Stephanie (in chapter 1) and Pat (in chapter 11), and my family, the names of all of those whom I mention by only a first name have been changed to preserve their privacy.

What I wrote in 1979 still holds true today. I have a deep-seated conviction that much of our evangelism is ineffective because we depend too much on technique and strategy. Evangelism has slipped into the sales department. I am convinced that we must look at Jesus, and the quality of life he calls us to, as a model for what to believe and how to reach out to others. This basic assumption underlies both the content and the structure of this book.

It is my hope and prayer that those who read it will indeed be freed to live as salt and light, so that they will be Christ's agents of healing and hope in a broken world.

1

Sleepless in Spain

Christians and non-Christians have something in common: we're both uptight about evangelism. Our fear as Christians seems to be *How many people have I offended this week?* We think that we must be a little obnoxious in order to be good evangelists. A tension builds inside: *Should I be sensitive to people and forget about evangelism, or should I blast them with the gospel and forget about their dignity as human beings?* Many Christians choose to be aware of the person but then feel defensive and guilty for not evangelizing.

A year abroad

I certainly felt that way during a year I spent studying at the University of Barcelona, Spain. Of course I wanted my friends to know God, but every time I got up courage to be vocal about Jesus, an image leaped into my mind of an aggressive Christian buttonholing an unwitting victim. As a non-believer, I had thought many Christians were weird, spreading leaflets on street corners and nabbing strangers. I was terrified that if I said anything at all about Christ, my friends would consider me just as strange. And I would agree with them. There was a part of me that secretly felt evangelism was something you shouldn't do to your dog, let alone a friend.

To evangelize, it seemed, required insensitivity and an inclination to blurt out a memorized gospel outline, without inhaling, to every stranger you met. It never occurred to me that my pre-Christian, unredeemed, almost common-sense understanding about how to relate warmly to people might be valid. For instance, I knew how offended I had been as an

11

agnostic when someone tried to push religion on me without even bothering to discover who I was or what I believed. That was a proper response, I see now, for I should be offended when I'm being treated as someone's evangelistic project instead of as a person.

Yet when I became a Christian I thought I was supposed to throw out my common-sense perceptions in order to be spiritual. I thought I was called to 'offend for Jesus' sake'. The way I thought I was supposed to share my faith went against my very grain. But, I thought, with a somewhat twisted logic, *Is it really so much to ask that I turn people off as soon as I meet them, when you think of all that Christ has done for me?*

Still, I knew Christians were called on to do hard things. And because it was so hard to do, I thought such evangelism had to be spiritual. The result was that I would put off witnessing as long as possible. Whenever the guilt became too great to bear, I would overpower the nearest unsuspecting sceptic with a nonstop running monologue and then dash away thinking, *Whew! Well, I did it. It's spring and hopefully the guilt won't overcome me again till Christmas.* (And I'm sure my sceptic friends hoped the same!)

I witnessed like a Pavlovian dog. The bell would ring; I would get ready, activated, juices running; and then – *BAM!* – I'd spit it out.

Paradoxically, I also knew that unless I really cared for my friends, they would never be interested in the gospel. I was deeply moved by the way Jesus demonstrated compassion to the people he met. I wanted to do the same, although it didn't occur to me that this had much to do with evangelism. So I tried to reach out and care for the people God had placed around me. But I felt guilty for not outlining the gospel to every non-believer I met.

It wasn't that I never spoke about my faith; in retrospect, however, I was far too paranoid about people's responses to me and consequently too silent. But one thing hindered me from speaking: I felt that unless I gave a person the whole thing, all at once, then I wasn't 'evangelizing'. So when my friends at the University of Barcelona said they were curious about my faith and began asking questions, I thought, *Isn't that amazing! And I wasn't even evangelizing!*

And so I approached my year abroad in Spain, seeking to establish caring relationships with students and asking God to touch their lives. I also asked him to teach me how to share my faith and to free me from fear.

During this time I shared a flat with Ruth Siemens, who was working for a student outreach organization called the International Fellowship of Evangelical Students. She is a remarkable woman, abounding in gifts, intelligence, zest and vision. Every time we talked about my desire to do Christian work, she suggested I start a Bible discussion for my friends who were seekers. I acted as though it was an interesting idea, but to myself I thought, *Well, that's what happens when you've been in the Spanish sun for too long. You sort of lose touch with reality.*

But Ruth was persistent, and at last I decided to go ahead with it even though I thought it was ridiculous. She helped by coaching me on what to say as I asked my friends to a study on the life of Christ. Assuming I was having a conversation that related to spiritual things, I could say, 'How would you like to come to a study on the biographies of Jesus Christ?' or 'Wouldn't it be fascinating to examine the primary source documents to see for ourselves what Jesus has to say and who he claims to be?' or 'Why don't we see for ourselves how Jesus views the role of women?'

When the actual moment arrived, my fear was so great that it reduced me to a rather catatonic state, and I mumbled, 'You don't want to come to a Bible discussion, do you?' To my amazement and alarm, they all said that it was a great idea and that they were eager to come. The study was to begin the following Wednesday evening at my flat.

One of the surprises was the kind of people who wanted to come. Without realizing it, I had formed a mental picture of the people God would lead me to. I expected it to be the 'likely' ones: those who seemed a bit passive or lonely or vulnerable. But it wasn't at all the anaemic types that God brought into my life. They all seemed terribly normal. They were vital, opinionated, interesting people who had strong questions about the existence of God as well as about everything else. They were stimulating to be around, but I would never have thought of them as being open to spiritual things.

Then I met Mary. She was a young Irishwoman taking a

year's study in Spain. She was bright and funny, with a ready quip for everything. I invited her over for a meal to meet my flatmates. I wondered if she would be interested in coming to the Bible discussion. Suddenly, not knowing yet that I was a Christian, she said, 'This has been the best month I've had all year! Do you know that I've talked three people out of being Christians this month!'

I gulped and thought, *Thank goodness I didn't ask her to the Bible discussion! I would die if someone like that ever came.*

The next day I ran into her after lectures and she smirked. 'See you next Wednesday at seven. What a lark that will be! I wouldn't miss it for the world!'

I smiled blankly and said it would be great, but nothing registered in my mind. What was I doing next Wednesday? Wednesday! Oh, no – it wasn't possible. How did she find out? Who told her? Nothing could possibly be worse than Mary coming to the Bible discussion.

I raced to my flat to tell Ruth and my other flatmate, Kathy Lang, the terrible news. Then I noticed a sly expression on their faces. 'OK,' I demanded, 'which one of you did it? Who betrayed me?'

They laughed but refused to confess. They said simply that God was answering my prayer by bringing spiritually open students to the Bible discussion. I moaned and wondered who else God would bring who would be as open and receptive as Mary.

One thing was clear: God and I had drastically different opinions about who was spiritually open. He seemed to have a special attraction to hard-core cases. And I felt he wanted to give them all to me.

I had Christians all over Barcelona praying. It was almost my first experience in leading a Bible discussion, and to do it with a group made up mostly of non-believers terrified me. Then Wednesday came. The study was to begin at 7:00. It was 7:15 when the doorbell finally rang. I opened the door, expecting to see the crowd, but there stood Mary, alone. She sauntered in, took a quick look around and said, 'My, looks like you're really packing them in tonight.'

'Ah, well, you know how busy everyone is, and it's early yet. Listen, make yourself at home and I'll be right back,' I said as I dashed to the bathroom, closed the door and burst into tears. I felt so ridiculous. Everyone was praying for me and would ask how the Bible discussion went. And then of all people to turn up, it had to be Mary.

I returned and decided to make polite conversation, thinking she would leave soon. Instead, she abruptly asked, 'Why are you a Christian? How can you be a thinking person and reject your mind? It's intellectual suicide to believe something without any evidence to support it.'

'Mary,' I said with unexpected courage, 'I couldn't agree with you more. I've always been amazed by people who can accept Christ blindly. But you know what else mystifies me? How anyone can reject Christianity blindly without bothering to investigate the evidence.' And so began a two-hour conversation. We discussed such issues as the historicity of the New Testament documents, the uniqueness of Jesus and the evidence for the resurrection. It seemed largely an intellectual exercise to me.

Then as she was leaving I popped John Stott's book *Basic Christianity* into her hands. 'Read it sometime in the next couple of years,' I said as she walked out of the door. No-one could ever have accused me of using pressure tactics.

The next day the others who were supposed to come to the study apologized and said they had completely forgotten. But they promised they would be there next Wednesday. And next Wednesday came. I felt reassured. God wouldn't let me go through another experience like that. And once more I asked several Christians in Barcelona to pray.

So 7:00 came. Then 7:10, 7:15, 7:20, and finally the doorbell rang. I rushed to the door, eager to see my friends. I threw open the door, but only one person was standing there – Mary.

Once more she took a look around and said, 'This Bible discussion is really dynamite, isn't it? Never seen such crowds.'

That did it. This was the closest thing to martyrdom I'd ever experienced. 'Mary, would you excuse me for a minute. I'll be right back,' I said and rushed into the bathroom again. I couldn't believe it. This was the second week I had prepared the same passage. I had prayed every day. And the only 'faithful' member was Mary!

I didn't understand, but I returned to Mary, hoping she

would leave quickly so I could cry later. Instead, she said, 'I read that book you gave me. I came to that chapter on sin and I wanted to hide under the bed.'

It never occurred to me as she spoke that the Holy Spirit was convicting her of sin. I merely thought it was a strange but interesting response. She plied me with questions and told me a great deal about her life and her family. I began to glimpse for the first time who she was – a sensitive young woman who covered her questions and wounds effectively. I was moved as she shared her life, and I genuinely cared for her.

Still, her initial disdain and negativity toward Christianity intimidated me. I thought that perhaps God was seeking her. What I didn't see was that her badgering me with questions, her coming to the study, even her hostility and anger were signs that she was grappling with God.

Then came the bomb. She suddenly looked straight at me and said, 'I feel like God is over there,' as she gestured with her hand, 'and I am over here. I've really wanted to know God all of my life. But how do I bridge the gap? What would I do if I wanted to become a Christian?'

I stared at her in disbelief. No-one had ever asked me that question. I felt not only inept but terrified that at this crucial moment God wouldn't come through. I had wondered what I would do if this ever happened, but the same scenario had always plagued me: The person would ask me how to become a Christian. I would say, 'Fine. Let's just pray together and ask God to come into your life.' We would pray and then she would say, 'Er, Becky, I hate to say this, but … um … I don't feel any different. I mean I feel just exactly the way I did before we prayed.' I would secretly think, *Oh, how embarrassing!* but I would say, 'Well, listen. Why don't we just try it again.' We would pray again, but then she would tell me she still felt the same. Then I would say, 'Well, look, it's Saturday. Maybe weekends are a busy time. Let's try it again next week.' And I would escape as fast as I could.

Just the thought of facing such an episode made me quake. And here was Mary, asking me to help her, immediately, directly and now.

'Well, what should I do?' Mary asked me.

'Er, well, I guess you could, um, pray,' I answered weakly.

'I don't know how. What should I say?' she persisted.

'Well, uh, you could tell God what you told me,' I stammered.

'OK. When should I tell him?' she asked.

For the first time I brightened. 'You can tell him the minute you get home,' I replied, leaping from my chair and ushering her quickly out of the room. 'As soon as you get home, just tell him everything,' I said as I pushed her through the front door. 'And read the last chapter of Stott's book on how to become a Christian,' I shouted as she walked down the steps looking a bit bewildered.

I felt miserable. God wasn't asking John Stott to lead Mary to faith; he was asking me. And I felt I had failed. I had been ashamed and embarrassed. I felt inadequate and unqualified to help Mary. But most of all, I lacked the faith and the guts to believe that God would actually come through and that he could use me. So I tried to forget the entire incident. After all, maybe Mary had just had a bad day. She was probably feeling emotional and would have been terribly embarrassed later if I had done anything anyway.

The next day Ruth returned from a trip. As I recounted my experience with Mary to her, she became more and more excited. Before I could even finish, she interrupted, her eyes shining, and she said, 'Oh, Becky, then you led her to Christ, right?'

And I answered, a bit subdued, 'No, actually I led her out of the door.'

It was the only time I ever saw Ruth unable to cover her disappointment. 'Becky! Why not? You've led other friends to Christ, haven't you?'

'Er, well, let's see now. It's sort of hard to remember. I suppose, er ... actually, er ... no.'

Mary returned to my flat a few days later. I was amazed to hear her account of what happened after she left me and amused by how she described it. She told Ruth in a somewhat exasperated tone, 'Well, I asked Becky what to do and she told me to go home. But at least she said to read the last chapter of that book. Now listen, I really do believe this stuff and I prayed that prayer at the end of the book. Does that mean I'm "in"?'

Ruth assured her that she was indeed a child of God. But I

remained somewhat sceptical and waited to see the results. The results, by the way, were that Mary grew steadily and is a Christian to this day. It was apparent that God had been working on her a long time before I ever met her.

Being yourself

Two feelings came from this experience. One was a feeling of failure. I think we could safely say that, by most standards, I had failed. I felt sadness over my lack of faith and courage – but not despair. In fact, my other feeling was hope. That experience made me realize that when God is seeking a person, he will not allow my fear, my feeling of intimidation or my lack of knowledge or experience to prevent that person from finding him. With all the mistakes, I still had seen the power of God at work overcoming my clumsiness and helping me speak to Mary.

The more I reflected, the more I realized that I couldn't have done it worse. And yet Mary had survived me! Even with all my mistakes, God had used me. Granted, I wasn't much more than a warm body sitting in front of her. But I had guided her to the right book. At least I had tried to answer her questions, and I genuinely cared for her.

This experience forced me to reflect seriously about my problems in evangelism. I had thought that only with a slick presentation, a polished formula and memorized verses could anyone be successful in evangelism. But I discovered that God was indeed glorified in my weakness.

If anyone had told me then that I would eventually be writing a book on evangelism, I would have laughed uproariously. The incongruity simply would have been too great. It has been a long pilgrimage with many failures from my experience with Mary to where I am today. And even now, when I speak on the subject of evangelism, I often sense people are breathlessly waiting for the same thing that I was: a new argument-proof, set approach, the magic formula that works on one and all or your money back. But even if I had such a formula to sell, it still wouldn't work.

Our problem in evangelism is not that we don't have enough information – it is that we don't know how to be ourselves. We forget we are called to be witnesses to what we have seen and know, not to what we don't know. The key on our part is authenticity and obedience, not a doctorate in theology. We haven't grasped that it really is OK for us to be who we are when we are with seekers, even if we don't have all the answers to their questions or if our knowledge of Scripture is limited.

But there is a deeper problem here. Our uneasiness with non-Christians reflects our uneasiness with our own humanity. Because we are not certain about what it means to be human (or spiritual, for that matter), we struggle in relating naturally, humanly, to the world. For example, many of us avoid evangelism for fear that we will offend someone. Yet how often have we told our sceptical friends that that's why we are hesitating?

I met a student one afternoon while visiting her university campus. Our conversation moved to whether we believed in God. It was an easy, almost casual talk. I began telling her about my faith in Christ, and she seemed interested. But as I became more enthusiastic about what it meant to be a Christian, she seemed to withdraw emotionally. Still, I kept on talking about Jesus – for want of knowing what else to do. But even though my mouth kept moving, I was very aware that I was turning her off. So there I was, having a private conversation with myself, trying to figure out how to stop, while I could hear myself talking to her about Christ.

Suddenly I realized how ridiculous all this was, so I said, 'Look, I feel really bad. I am very excited about who God is and what he's done in my life. But I hate it when people push "religion" on me. So if I'm coming on too strong, will you just tell me?'

She looked at me in disbelief. 'I can't believe you just said that. I mean, I cannot believe you honestly said that,' she answered.

'Why?' I asked.

'Well, I never knew Christians were aware that we hate being recipients of a running monologue,' she answered. (So much for my evangelistic skill.)

'Listen,' I responded, 'most Christians I know are very hesitant to share their faith *precisely* because they're afraid they'll offend.'

'But as long as you let people know that you're aware of

where they're coming from, you can say anything you want!' she responded immediately. 'And you just tell Christians that I said so.'

Her response was perceptive. What she was saying was that when I told her I hated to be someone's evangelistic project, I was also establishing that we had a great deal in common: I didn't want to dump the gospel and she didn't want to be dumped on. That is a natural response, a human response and a shared response. What surprised her was that I was human, too, not some superdisciple whose feet never touch the ground. In fact, I am offended by the same tactics as she is. So on the basis of our strong, common human bond, I was freed to communicate my faith.

God has given me increasing freedom to talk about him to others. But my experience with Mary made me realize that, although some of my friends had become open to God through my influence, no-one had ever become a Christian in my presence. Even if they wanted to, I wouldn't let them! As I pondered my discomfort about evangelism, I discovered several things about myself.

For one thing, I was so afraid of being identified as a religious fanatic or a Bible-basher that I often remained silent when the topic of God came up. How people saw me mattered more than how God saw me. Ironically, most people respect and respond to a person who has definite ideas and who communicates them clearly rather than to someone who seems apologetic and wishy-washy. My experience in Spain confirmed that.

When I was a student in Spain, I was amazed to see how 'evangelistic' and bold the Marxists on campus were. Their style wasn't obnoxious, but they were convinced and it showed. They communicated their beliefs articulately and with zeal. As I watched students respond to them, I was surprised to see how open they were and how much respect they had for someone who really believed in something and was willing to stand up for it.

All of my paranoia about how I thought people would respond if I were bold about Christ had made me defensive. If I had gone to a religious conference, I would stammer when asked, 'How was your weekend?' Or I would tend to hide my

Bible under other books so my agnostic flatmates wouldn't think I was strange. (As if that kind of behaviour would keep people from thinking I was strange!)

I was behaving this way, I told myself, in order to be sensitive to seeking friends. But to them I looked weird and the Marxists seemed confident and convinced. I finally had to agree with the apostle Paul that if we fear God first, then we will try to - persuade people (2 Cor. 5:11). Whatever you fear (or supremely respect) the most you will serve. Fearing what people thought of me, I served them and it backfired. When I began to fear and respect God the most and then serve him, I felt a new freedom to share my faith, whether I won a popularity contest or not. I didn't feel called to be offensive, just more bold. And the irony was that, since I wasn't trying to please them first but God, people listened and wanted to know more.

I found out something else: I didn't understand other people's genuine desire. Although I saw the needs and emptiness in the lives of my friends, I couldn't imagine that it was Jesus Christ they were really searching for. Jesus was for 'religious folk', not for my pagan friends. So because I never really expected them to respond to the gospel, they didn't.

This feeling was associated with my own self-doubt. I feared that Jesus was just 'my thing'. Wasn't it arrogant to suggest that my view was the only way? But as I grew to understand the nature of Christianity, I saw that our faith stands on historical data as well as subjective experience. Truth was the ultimate issue, not a feeling in my heart. God was asking me to stand not on my own ideas or emotions but rather on the person and work of Jesus Christ. If anyone was guilty of being offensive, it was Jesus – not me. Realizing this freed me from cowering when accused of being narrow. I could answer, 'I know, and isn't it amazing that Jesus actually said so many scandalous things? People of his day were as offended by his claims as we are. Wouldn't it be intriguing to study him to discover why he felt justified in saying what he said?'

Still, I was paralysed by the fear of offending people and for ever ruining their chance of entering the kingdom. So I thought, 'I'll just be nice and smile and hope they catch on.' Well, Girl Guides smile too, so that can't be all there is to witnessing for Christ. Furthermore, I realized that I was giving myself too much credit. What I was saying was that if I made one mistake or couldn't answer one of their questions, then it was all over. They were doomed. Their eternal destiny rested on my ability to know every answer. God might be eternal and powerful, but he could never again reach the person I had offended or the one whose question I could not answer.

It's odd. If you are sensitive enough to realize that you could offend someone, then offending others is probably not your problem. What I often see is this: sensitive people who run around saying, 'I'm just so afraid of being insensitive.' So they remain silent when what they need to be is more bold. Or instead of finding creative ways of expressing faith, they spend their time proudly pronouncing what they don't do. 'I have never used gimmicks or buttonholed people like those others.' It's easy to agree about how evangelism is done poorly. But how pleased is God going to be when he asks us what we have done with our lives and we reel off everything that we *didn't* do?

Finally, I saw that I had a problem talking about God naturally. I was fine until the topic of religion came up. Suddenly I felt as if I needed to sound spiritual, and instead of listening I would panic because I couldn't remember any Scripture verses. My hands would get clammy; my eyes would dart from side to side in the hope that no-one else was listening; the tone of my voice would change and I would begin to talk 'religiously'. Then I would wonder why they looked so uncomfortable when we talked about spiritual things.

The truth is, *I* was the one whose tone had changed. My problem was that I didn't think God could be a natural, integrated part of an ongoing discussion about films, raising children, studying or gardening. When speaking to sceptics, I kept my discussion of God too compartmentalized and separated from 'normal' living.

The strength of weakness

These new insights began to free me. Mary's growth and flourishing as a young Christian affected my faith and my ability to witness. But it was the conversion of another atheist friend of mine eight months later that brought fresh discoveries and permanent change into my life. I will tell that story later in chapter 10. But it was what Stephanie told me the night she became a Christian that startled me.

'At first I thought, *Fine, let Becky have her religion – that's her thing,*' she said. *I'm not the least bit interested, but if that's her thing, then it's all right with me.* Then you invited me to dinner and before we ate you asked if we could thank God for the food. I thought, *Oh, how quaint.* Only you didn't just thank him for the food – you thanked him for me and our friendship. It touched me profoundly and unexpectedly. I'd never heard anyone pray so personally before, much less thanking God for *me.* I never thought you felt our relationship had anything to do with God. But then I caught myself and thought, *That's ridiculous – thanking someone who doesn't exist for me.*

'Then we went to the Bergman film and afterward you said you'd studied the very same concept that was in the film in the Bible that day. I never dreamed an ancient faith would have anything remotely in common with cinema! Another day you invited me to an objective, no-strings-attached study of the person of Jesus in the Bible. Fine. Only the trouble was – I was truly drawn to this figure called Jesus! He seemed so real as we would read about him each week. I found myself wondering what Jesus would say about different situations I'd find myself in during the week.

'But you know what affected me most? All my life I used to think, *How arrogant for someone to call himself a Christian, to think he's that good.* But then I got to know you – and Becky, you are far from perfect, yet you call yourself a Christian. So my first shock was to discover you "blow it" like I do. But the biggest shock was that you admitted it, where I couldn't. Suddenly I saw that being a Christian didn't mean never failing, but admitting when you've failed. I wanted to keep Christ in a box and let you be religious during Bible studies, but the more you let me inside your life, the more impossible it became to keep the lid on Christianity. Even your admission of weaknesses drove me to him!'

That confession changed my life. What astonished me was that she had seen me in all kinds of circumstances – she had seen the real me – and it gave the gospel more power, not less. I had always thought I should cover up my doubts and problems because if she knew me she wouldn't become a Christian.

But the more open and transparent I was (even with my weaknesses), the more real Jesus became to her.

Please get this straight. In saying we must be human with each other, I am not condoning sin. God calls us to obedience. I am not suggesting we share our weaknesses as if we were in a 'competitive sinning' match in order to prove we are real. Sin isn't God's desire for humanity; loving obedience to him is. But so is humble confession when we fail. So our goal must be to live within the balance of aiming for full obedience and humble openness. The paradox I constantly experience is that as I allow people inside – to see who I am with the pain and problems as well as the successes – they tell me they see God. It's when I cover up (ironically, for 'God's reputation') and try to appear 'together', with no problems, that they can see only Becky.

I had to learn from experience what Scripture teaches in 1 Thessalonians 2:8: to share the gospel we must share our life, our very selves. If we don't grasp that Christ has freed us to be authentic, we will see evangelism as a project instead of a lifestyle. And we will tend to see non-Christians more as objects of our evangelistic efforts than as authentic persons.

I once asked a woman if she felt comfortable about evangelism. 'Oh, yes!' she responded. 'I do it twice a week.' (Somehow it sounded more like taking multivitamins.) Evangelism isn't just something you 'do' – out there – and then get back to normal living. Evangelism involves taking people seriously, getting across to their island of concerns and needs, and then sharing Christ as Lord in the context of our natural living situations.

The problem stems from our great difficulty in believing that God is glorified in our utter humanity rather than in our spiritually programmed responses. Most of us fear that who we are inside just isn't enough. So we cover up our honest questions and doubts, thinking we won't sound spiritual. But in doing this we forfeit our most important asset in evangelism – our real person. Not to accept our humanness means we lose our point of authentic contact with the world. We, of all people, should be offering the world a picture of what it means to be truly human. Yet it is often Christians who fear their humanity more than anyone else. When we get a good look at Jesus, we will see that it is not our humanity we need to fear.

2

Jesus – the most human of us all

Our humanity is not our problem in evangelism. In fact, if we could learn how to be authentically human as God designed us to be, we would discover that our humanity is not a liability – it's an asset! The most human of all human beings had no difficulty with who he was.

Though Jesus shared God's divine nature, he also came to us as the first whole person since Adam and Eve before the Fall. It is Jesus then who provides for us the model of what it means to be human. By following his lead, we will not only take on more of God's character but also find ourselves becoming more comfortable with our humanity. As God frees us to be authentically human in the way he designed us, we'll discover that evangelism will begin to flow naturally from who we are.

Jesus, one of us

Jesus told us that as the Father sent him into the world, so he is sending us (John 17:18). How then did the Father send him? Essentially Jesus became one of us. The Word became flesh (John 1:14). God became human. The implications of the incarnation are vast, but one area that greatly affects evangelism is this: Jesus gives us permission to be human. Yet we struggle to believe that God intends us to be truly human. We think we must get dressed up in our Sunday best to talk with God. We're afraid that being made of flesh and blood meets with divine disapproval. The fact that we love to laugh, go for a walk with a friend, sip tea and read a good book for the sheer pleasure of it is probably regarded from on high, we fear, with a cosmic frown. We forget that it was God's idea, not ours, to make us human. He did not fashion us as angels who operate only in the realm of the spirit, nor did he make us animals without will or reason. God made us *human*. How do we discover what it means to be authentically human? We look to Jesus.

The fact that God became human also affects the style in which we share our faith. God didn't send a telegram or shower evangelistic books from heaven or drop a million bumper stickers from the sky saying, 'Smile, Jesus loves you.' He sent a man, his Son, to communicate the message. His strategy hasn't changed. He still sends men and women – before he sends tracts and techniques – to change the world. You may think his strategy is risky, but that is God's problem, not yours.

In Jesus, then, we have our model for how to relate to the world, and it is a model of openness and identification. Jesus was a remarkably open man. He didn't think it was unspiritual for him (fully realizing he was the Son of God) to share his physical needs (John 4:7). He didn't fear losing his testimony by revealing to his disciples the depths of his emotional stress in the Garden of Gethsemane (Mark 14:32–52). Here is our model for genuine godliness. We see him asking for support and desiring others to minister to him. We must learn, then, to relate transparently and genuinely to others because that is God's style of relating to us.

Jesus commands us to go and then preach, not to preach and then leave. We are not to shout the gospel from a safe and respectable distance and remain detached. We must open our lives enough to let people see that we too laugh and hurt and cry. If Jesus left all of heaven and glory to become one of us, shouldn't we at least be willing to leave our circle of church friends or Bible discussion group to reach out to a friend?

There is also confusion about what it means to be spiritual. We feel it is more spiritual to take our seeker friends to a Bible discussion or to church than to a play or a pizza restaurant. Just as we do not understand our natural points of contact with the world, so we don't understand our natural points of contact with God himself. Again, he made us human. He is therefore interested in every aspect of our humanness. It is the stuff of our humanity – the everyday grit and glory that we all encounter simply by walking out of the door each morning – that God uses to shape a holy life within us. We dare not limit him, then, to Bible studies and discussions with Christians. He created life and he desires to be glorified in the totality of all that adds up to life. And his power and presence will come crashing through to the world as we let him live fully in every aspect of our lives.

How can we relate to people in a way that will change the world? Jesus did it in two ways: by his radical identification with men and women, and by his radical difference. Jesus seemed to respond to people by noticing first what he had in common with them (John 4:7). But it was often in the context of their similarities that Jesus' difference came crashing through (verse 10).

As people discovered Jesus' profound humanness, they began to recognize his deity. God's holiness became shattering and penetrating as Jesus confronted people on their own level of humanity. But the point is that it took both his radical identification and his radical difference to change the world. So it will be for us.

Jesus the delightful

One of the more fascinating aspects I've witnessed in recent years is the emerging phenomenon of white, middle-class, reasonably well-educated adults thirty-five to fifty years old who are returning to the fold, or at least are willing to reconsider traditional Christianity. In the past they considered Christianity unenlightened, narrow and a retreat from postmodernism's complex reality. But with mature careers and young children and aging parents, they are slowly, quietly, privately searching for the deeper significance of life and the possibility that faith may offer hope to people like themselves with real lives and real burdens.

If I have learned anything over the past twenty years, it's that, besides demonstrating the love of God to seekers, there is nothing more important than drawing them to consider Jesus. People simply don't know who Jesus is or what he is really like. When seekers look beyond their Sunday-school stereotypes and are willing to take a fresh look at Jesus, the scales begin to fall from their eyes. I've never seen a person yet who hasn't been fascinated to encounter the Jesus of the Gospels.

Even we who know him need to be refreshed and reminded. I reread the Gospels a while back out of a desire to 'rediscover Jesus'. I was a bit alarmed by several attitudes that I sensed increasingly among believers. One was that the Gospels are light reading for the spiritually young whereas the Epistles are the real meat and potatoes for the mature. Another was an attitude that focused only on the Gospels but manipulated Jesus into being the Lord of their particular cause – the environment, women's rights, religious tolerance or the like. These can all be valid causes, but they sometimes revealed more about the person advocating the cause than they did about Jesus.

If a disciple must first master the life of the Master, then we need to grapple in radical, accurate and penetrating ways with the Gospels as they reveal the person of Jesus. As I reread the Gospels, I was struck by how vastly different Jesus is from the common stereotypes that many people have about Christians.

For example, isn't one common stereotype that Christians are dour, with a holier-than-thou attitude toward anyone who doesn't share their beliefs? And we'd be their last choice to invite to a fun party! Yet look at Jesus. He liked to go to parties and to weddings. He was the kind of man people invited for dinner. And he came. He went to where people were.

Jesus was utterly delightful. He enjoyed people. When two men first approached him, they became tongue-tied and unsure of what to say (John 1:35–39). When Jesus asked them what they wanted, they responded, 'Er, well ... we were sort of wondering where your house is.' Now Jesus knew that how he decorated his house was not the burning issue in their hearts. But instead of delivering a sermon, he took them home with him, and they became his disciples. Later some of their relatives were among the first people he healed. But Jesus was more than merely charming; he cared about building a sense of family.

Jesus established intimacy with people quickly. It was partly because he was open but also because he understood people and wanted to establish rapport with them. He let people know that he had a sense of who they were and that he appreciated them. The first thing he did on meeting Simon was to give him a nickname. The first thing he told Nathanael was that he recognized the basic honesty of his character. Jesus drew people. Some came because Jesus recognized who they were, others because they had glimpsed something of who he was. He was approachable; he wanted people to know it, and they did.

Children loved him. Adults were affected so much by him that some just wanted to touch his clothes. Why? They saw that Jesus loved them. His love was extravagant, almost reckless – never cautious or timid. And he talked of his Father's endless love.

The people of Jesus' day thought holy men were unapproachable. But Jesus' work was in the marketplace. He made people feel welcome and that they had a place. His life was a constant demonstration that there are only two things that really matter in this life: God and people. They are the only things that last for ever.

Isn't another stereotype of Christians that we care far more about following the rules and getting converts than we care about people and their pain? Yet Jesus was profoundly compassionate. He cared deeply and was not afraid to show it. He was profoundly committed to setting people free and making them whole. He touched people at the deepest level. He wanted to heal not only blindness and leprosy but also the things that prevented joy and beauty and freedom and justice.

The Stoics may have been proud of concealing their tears, but Jesus never concealed his. He showed them plainly on his open face, whether he was weeping for a city or for a friend's loss. He healed people because he cared about them, not merely so they would follow him. He saw a woman weeping over the loss of her only son (Luke 7:11–17). No-one asked him to do anything, probably feeling it was hopeless anyway. Moved with compassion, he took the initiative and brought the boy back to life. In fact, he even touched the bier on which the boy lay. As it was the Jewish practice to use the open bier, Jesus' touching it meant pollution according to ceremonial laws. But Jesus responded to human need first.

Once, Jesus was on his way to heal Jairus's daughter, who was at the point of death. A woman who had been haemorrhaging for twelve years and had 'endured much under many physicians' (Mark 5:26) suddenly touched his garment and was healed. Jesus had so much concern for her that he stopped long enough to find out who he had healed and to learn of her story. Can you imagine Jairus's anxiety as the long story unfolded?

But Jesus listened patiently and lovingly.

On another occasion a leper came to Jesus, no doubt full of shame and wounds (Mk 1:40-45). Timid but desperate, he said, 'Well, if you want to, I think you could heal me.' And Jesus, moved with compassion and looking at him steadily, said, 'Oh, I want to,' and healed him.

I was also struck by the practical dimension of Jesus' compassion. His feelings were no deeper than his practical concern. He healed Jairus's daughter, and at the moment of this stupendous miracle, he simply told them to get her something to eat. His care was consistent. Never flashy, sometimes almost quiet. Even after his death, Jesus demonstrated the very same care. If I had been resurrected, I would have rented the Coliseum and hired the London Philharmonic Choir to sing the 'Hallelujah Chorus.' But in one post-resurrection account we find Jesus making the disciples a little breakfast!

Another mistaken idea is that all Christians are judgmental and have little understanding or sympathy for the complexities of the human condition. Yet Jesus was perceptive. He had an extraordinary ability to see beneath the myriad layers of people and know what they longed for, or really believed, but were afraid of revealing. This is why his answers so frequently did not correspond to the questions he was asked. He sensed their unspoken need or question and responded to it instead.

Jesus could have healed lepers in countless ways. To the leper in Mark 1:40-45 he could have shouted, 'Be healed ... but don't get too close. I just hate the sight of lepers.' He did not. Jesus reached over and touched him. Jesus' touch was not necessary for the leper's physical healing, but it was critical for his emotional healing.

Can you imagine what it meant to that man to be touched? A leper was an outcast, quite accustomed to walking down a street and seeing people scatter, shrieking at him, 'Unclean, unclean!' Jesus knew that this man had not only a diseased body but an equally diseased self-concept. He needed to be touched to be fully cured. And so Jesus responded as he always did, with total healing for the whole person.

If someone had asked me in my agnostic days to describe what I thought Jesus was like, I would have readily given an answer. I pictured him as a sweet, kind man, his hair parted down the middle with a kind of halo effect such as one sees in adverts. I thought he probably spent most of his time skipping along the shores of Galilee, humming religious tunes with his disciples – the kind of person everyone would love, especially your mother. I sincerely believed this and did not think it was the least irreverent. Granted, my biblical understanding stemmed largely from a Hollywood film director of the 1920s – Cecil B. De Mille – and Hollywood seems to have a knack for making spirituality and severe anaemia almost synonymous. But even from the few Christians I knew, I sensed that Jesus was something of a weakling, and several of them certainly behaved that way.

Then one day I looked at the New Testament. Instead of a meek, mild Jesus, I found a man of profound passion – an extraordinary being, flinging furniture down the steps of the temple, casting out demons and asking people how they expected to escape the damnation of hell. He said such bland, innocuous things as 'I came to bring fire to the earth' (Luke 12:49). G. K. Chesterton points out that even Jesus' literary style reflects his passion: 'The diction used about Christ has been, and perhaps wisely, sweet and submissive. But the diction used by Christ is quite curiously gigantesque; it is full of camels leaping through needles and mountains hurled into the sea.' Moreover, his style consists of 'an almost furious use of the "a fortiori". His "how much more" is piled one upon another like castle upon castle in the clouds.'[1] After seeing this shattering personality who fills the Gospels, having got even a glimpse of him, I could never, never again say with casual indifference, 'Oh, how interesting.'

Jesus the exasperating

How do the Gospels shatter stereotypes that people have about Jesus himself? For example, take the sentimental notion I mentioned above, the one that believes Jesus was always sweet and smiling, abhorred conflict and would never get angry or say anything that would offend. I've had sceptics willing to study the Bible with me just on the promise that there was a biblical story of Jesus getting so angry he threw furniture down the stairs!

For if my first impression of Jesus was that he was delightful, another equally forceful impression was that he was exasperating. Wherever he went, he produced a crisis. He compelled individuals to decide, to make a choice. In fact, he struck me as the most crisis-producing individual I had ever encountered. Eventually nearly everyone clashed with Jesus, whether they loved him or hated him.

A friend of mine has said that he always discovered a lot about a person when he knew who liked the person and who did not. In Jesus' case we have the story of the holiest man who ever lived, and yet it was the prostitutes and lepers and thieves who adored him, and the religious folk who hated his guts.

Why did he cause so much controversy? I will examine this more closely in later chapters. But partly it was his unabashed claims. In his address at the synagogue in Nazareth he read from Isaiah and then, as the congregants looked straight at him, said, 'Today this scripture has been fulfilled in your hearing' (Luke 4:21). In other words, 'It's become true now because it is fulfilled through me. You are looking at the fulfillment.'

Characteristically, the first response was favourable as they 'wondered' at his 'gracious words'. But on reflection they began to think, *Wait a minute. Isn't this Joseph's boy?* Then Jesus mentioned that prophets have always been rejected by the people. And within moments they became so outraged they tried to kill him. They struggled not only with who Jesus said he was but with who he said they were as well. He made them confront both themselves and him.

Or what about the common misunderstanding that Jesus' followers were drawn from the religious of his day? What a surprise when people discover that many religious leaders were profoundly offended by Jesus' understanding of religion and piety. The religious of his day were particularly incensed that he deliberately healed on the sabbath. But what do you do with a man who is supposed to be the holiest man who has ever lived and yet goes around talking with prostitutes and hugging lepers? What do you do with a man who not only mingles with the most unsavoury people but actually seems to enjoy them? The religious accused him of being a drunkard, a glutton and having tacky taste in friends. It is a profound irony that the Son of God visited this planet and one of the chief complaints against him was that he was not religious enough. Do you realize, just for that quality alone, the appeal Jesus will have to sceptics? He is irresistible!

The religious of his day were offended because he did not follow their rules and traditions. He was bold and outspoken. He favoured extreme change and valued what they felt was insignificant, which was largely the 'unlovely'. Jesus knew the power and prestige of the Pharisees, a key group of Jewish leaders. And he knew they expected people to show deference to them. But he loved the Pharisees and wanted them to see plainly who they were and how far many of them were from God's kingdom.

What did he say to them? Well, I think Jesus would have been my last choice as a speaker for a fundraising drive. To say he was not the master of subtlety would be to put it mildly. Imagine a scene in which you would gather all the powerful leaders and religious elite so they could hear Jesus give a talk. (Matthew 23 describes such a scene.) When they are seated, Jesus comes out and his opening words are: 'You bunch of snakes! You smell bad. You remind me of decomposed bodies walking around. You're hypocrites and blind guides. And I want to thank you very much for coming.' It was not exactly a speech that endeared Jesus to the Pharisees, which was what the disciples pointed out when they told him with a sudden flash of insight, 'We think you might have offended them.'

But for those who loved him he was equally exasperating. He constantly kept smashing some of his own followers' expectations of what the Messiah should do. He simply did not fit their mould. He did not try to. They thought the Messiah would come in power and liberate Jerusalem. But the only power that Jesus demonstrated was the power of servanthood. His disciples wanted to know who would be first in terms of prestige. Jesus told them the first would be the greatest servant, for Jesus' own greatness was seen not in the degree to which he was elevated but in the degree to which he came down and identified.

Eventually even John the Baptist struggled with who Jesus was. He did not feel Jesus behaved as the Anointed One. John had taught that the Messiah would bring an age of judgment – but Jesus brought mercy. John felt the Messiah should separate himself from sinners and tax collectors (like the prophets of the past), not invite them for dinner.

Jesus put people into crisis by compelling them to do something. He commanded Peter to lower his nets for a catch of fish after he had caught nothing all night. He told the rich young ruler to sell all his possessions. He told a Samaritan woman, who he knew was living with another man, to go and call her husband. He insisted that John baptize him when doing so would violate John's understanding of the Messiah. He told the Pharisaical lawyer, who was far more interested in debate and discussion than obedience, to do what he understood and not to talk about it.

Last, there is the popular notion that Jesus was tolerant of all religious positions. Some people foist on him the modern view that all roads lead to God. But while some religious leaders might be self-effacing, Jesus was self-advancing. Other religious leaders often required their followers to obey rules or laws or 'a way'. Jesus said, 'I am the way, and the truth, and the life' (John 14:6). Based on that, we are asked simply to follow him. Jesus was a confident man. He was secure and he knew who he was. Jesus didn't make suggestions; he uttered commands ('come to me,' 'follow me,' 'drop your nets'). I think we can safely say that Jesus was hardly the victim of a poor self-image!

He believed he was the Son of God. All these traits – his delightfulness, his compassion, his sensitivity, his passion, his ability to establish rapport as well as to exasperate –sprang from the fundamental fact of his deity. He said he was the bread of life (John 6:35), the light of the world (8:12), and the resurrection and the life (11:25). He said, 'The Father and I are one' (10:30). He informed people that knowing him was the same as knowing God (8:19), seeing him was the same as seeing God (12:45), believing in him was the same as believing in God (verse 44) and receiving him was the same as receiving God (Mark 9:37).

C. S. Lewis warns in *Mere Christianity* against the claim that Jesus was merely a good teacher but not the Son of God. John Stott also points out that Jesus could hardly have been a good teacher if he was so wrong about the chief subject of his teaching, namely, himself.

Let us suppose that I made the kind of claims that Jesus did, and people began to say, 'Isn't Becky terrific?! I mean, the way she forgives sins – she really has a style all of her own, doesn't she? And her ethics are so brilliant and impeccable! And what a superb teacher, not to mention her perfect, sinless life. There is one little problem. She does seem to be a little confused about her deity. But other than that, she really has it all together!' Now whom do you think they would lock up first, the people saying this or me? No-one is a little confused about his or her own deity and is sane. Yet intelligent, well-meaning people say this about Jesus every day. So let us eliminate the option that Jesus was merely a good teacher. That was never left open to us.

But the continuing question that Jesus faced because of his claims and action was voiced the loudest by the Pharisees. They saw Jesus healing on the sabbath and asked, 'Who do you think you are, healing on the sabbath?' And Jesus answered, 'The Lord of the sabbath.'

Which leads me to my last impression of this towering figure. How did Jesus justify his behaviour and claims that seemed eventually to lead everyone into conflict or crisis? I think it could be stated briefly like this: 'I do what I do because I am the Lord – and you are not. You follow me; I do not follow you.' His answers were most often that simple. He said he was the Lord. He knew it. He lived like it. He acted like it. He wanted people to respond accordingly.

3
Jesus – the Lord of all

Once I was invited to a university as part of a team to teach for a week on evangelism. I stayed in a hall of residence with the students, and on the first day I met Lois. She was bright and sensitive – and sceptical about the existence of God. After we had several talks about God, I told her I was having a Bible study to look at the person of Jesus. She could come and examine the primary source material as critically as she would any historical document.

'OK, I'll come. But the Bible won't have anything relevant to say to me,' she replied.

You have no husband

The next day I discovered Lois was living off campus with her boyfriend, Phil. To my great surprise, he came with her to the Bible discussion. Not knowing her background, I had already decided to lead the study on the woman at the well in John 4. I began introducing the chapter to the group, noticed Phil and Lois sitting there, and suddenly remembered the passage dealt with a woman who had sexual problems. I feared Lois would think I had planned this just for her.

With a step of faith I frantically tried to think of how to avoid the crunch of the passage (though I was sure God had got me into this mess). Lois and Phil were seated close to my left. Thinking it would be better if Lois did not read the passage aloud, I asked each person to read one paragraph aloud in turn as we went around the circle. I called on Sally, who was immediately to my right, to start, calculating we would finish before it was Lois's turn.

To my dismay, a woman three seats away from Lois started reading. (I discovered later it was Sally's twin sister who happened to be sitting next to me.) Then Lois's turn came and she read the portion that says, 'Jesus said to her, "You are right in saying, 'I have no husband'; for ... the [man] you have now is not your husband."' It was her first experience of reading Scripture, and her eyes grew as big as saucers while I hid behind my Bible!

'I must say, this is a bit more relevant than I had expected,' she commented with considerable understatement. And as she saw with what sensitivity and perception Jesus interacted with the lonely woman, Lois's face showed how moved she was.

The next day Lois and I talked again. In fact, she came every day for the entire week to discuss faith and bring her questions. She had been brought up by parents who were prosperous, well educated and morally conservative. She knew her parents would be mortified to know about her living situation. 'Even though I think my parents love me, they never have been able to show it,' she said.

'What drew me to Phil was my desperate need to be loved. He does love me, yet it feels like sand being poured through a sieve. My heart has this unslaked thirst for love that can't ever seem to be filled,' she said sadly.

'Lois,' I responded, 'romantic love can be real and deep, but only if it is not asked to be what it isn't. It is not within Phil's power to give you a sense of being and purpose. No human can fill every inner crevice of our longings.'

'So it's all a sick joke, right?' she replied. 'Why do we carry such a hunger when it can never be met? I told him that I thought our love would give ultimate purpose and meaning to my life. I banked all my need for love in him. He's already told me that he feels an unbearable pressure to be all that I need. And it's odd, but even knowing that he loves me, my heart is still restless and unfulfilled. Can this immense wish to be loved ever be gratified?'

'Lois, your longing for love is very valid. But human love, for all its wonders, will never be able to handle the immensity of the task. It can go away or die or fail us at the precise moment we need it most. And if it is to meet our needs and longings, love must have a base.'

'But what base is there that is big enough and stable enough to build our lives upon?' she asked.

'The only base we can really count on is God's love. That's what Jesus saw in the Samaritan woman. He recognized a woman who was thirsting for a love that would truly satisfy her and never leave her. So he directed her toward himself. Jesus knew that what the soul longs for is a safe home, a place where we are loved and known perfectly – and that can only be found in God.'

Lois sat for a long time, taking in what I had said. Finally I broke the silence and said, 'Lois, would you like to come home now? Would you like to ask Christ to come into your life?'

'Yes. But what do I bring to the equation?' she asked.

'All you bring to God is your faith and your willingness to let him be at the centre of your life. Can you think of anything that would block Christ's rule in your heart?' I asked.

'No,' she said.

'Well, I can think of one,' I said. 'What will you do about Phil? Loving him is not the problem. But desiring to please him over loving and obeying God first, is.' Then we talked about how becoming a Christian isn't merely fire insurance; it's a living relationship that affects every aspect of our lives: values, lifestyle, sexuality.

As we talked, it became clear God had been pursuing her for a long time. There were tears and struggles followed by an utterly sincere prayer asking Christ to come into her life as Lord.

Immediately she said, 'Becky, as a young Christian, I've got problems. I'll have to tell Phil and move out; I have nowhere to go; it's impossible to get a room in hall this late, and now I'll have to pay this month's rent in two places.' So we prayed again, and as she left my room, I agonized over how such a young believer could handle so much.

After dinner the students who had attended the Bible discussion stopped me, saying they were fascinated by the study on Jesus. Then we heard a noise and turned to see what it was. Here came Lois, slowly walking down the corridor, carrying several suitcases and smiling with tears streaming down her cheeks. I silently thanked God. I too felt the tears slip down. Seldom have I seen a more graphic picture of what it means to become a Christian. Everyone began asking her why she had left home.

'Oh, no, I haven't left home. I've finally found my home,' she replied. 'You see, today I became a Christian.'

That one decision had far-reaching effects. That same night three women decided they wanted to become Christians. Another woman who had assumed she was a Christian realized she wanted no part of it if it demanded total commitment. The next day Lois was allocated accommodation on campus (unheard of at such a late date), and she discovered her new flatmate was a dynamic, mature Christian.

Three months later her boyfriend, Phil, became a Christian, and he too grew rapidly. He had been hostile over her conversion and furious with her for moving out. But after he was converted, he told her, 'Lois, if you hadn't been willing to obey Christ, even when you saw I was hurt and angry, I would have been forever dependent on you to meet all my needs – just as you had been dependent on me. Your obedience affected my eternal destiny.'

Lois's conversion was profound for her friends as well as for her. She recognized that becoming a Christian had tremendous implications. She came to see that, if Jesus is Lord, then the only right response to him is surrender and obedience. He is Saviour and he is Lord. We cannot separate his demands from his love. We cannot dissect Jesus and relate only to the parts that we like or need. Christ died so that we could be forgiven for managing our own lives. It would be impossible for Lois to thank Christ for dying for her and yet to continue running her own life.

She also saw that submitting her life to Jesus involved a cost. Jesus discouraged enthusiasts from committing themselves to him until they had weighed the implications. 'Follow me' was his repeated command. 'But there could be no following without a forsaking, a renunciation of competing loyalties, of personal ambition, of material possessions, of family relationships (Luke 14:25-33),' John Stott writes. 'Before a person could follow Jesus, he had to repudiate himself and his right to organize his own life.'[1]

Why Jesus is the Lord God

One may ask: what right does Jesus have to ask for so much? How can he get away with it? The biblical answer is: because he is the Lord. This is what the disciples preached ('We proclaim Jesus Christ as Lord,' 2 Cor. 4:5) and how they told us to live ('In your hearts sanctify Christ as Lord,' 1 Pet. 3:15). He is Lord because of who he is: God incarnate, Lord of creation and Lord of life.

First, Jesus is God incarnate. Colossians 1:15 tells us, 'He is the image of the invisible God, the firstborn of all creation.' Hebrews 1:3 says, 'He is the reflection of God's glory and the exact imprint of God's very being.' And Colossians 2:9 says, 'In him the whole fullness of deity dwells bodily.' Commenting on this last text, Dr Martyn Lloyd-Jones says, 'There is nothing beyond that, He is the sum total of all the Divine attributes and power.'[2]

C. S. Lewis puts it this way: 'Then comes the real shock. Among these Jews there suddenly turns up a man who goes about talking as if He was God. He claims to forgive sin. He says He has always existed. He says He is coming to judge the world at the end of time ... And when you have grasped that, you will see that what this man said was, quite simply, the most shocking thing that has ever been uttered by human lips.'[3]

But how do we see this shocking God side of Jesus' nature? Certainly the events of his birth are a good place to start: the angel announcing to Mary the virgin birth, or the wise men being guided by the star of Bethlehem, or Simeon and Anna identifying the baby Jesus as the Messiah to his astonished parents in the temple. Or think of Mary and Joseph unobtrusively making their way to Bethlehem without any fanfare. But when Jesus is born, all heaven seems to break loose! The heavens part, and angels burst into paeans of praise right in front of shepherds who were merely minding their own business. They're terrified, and who can blame them (Luke 2:8–14)? We also see the God side of Jesus' nature affirmed at his baptism when a voice from heaven is heard saying, 'This is my Son, the Beloved, with whom I am well pleased' (Matt. 3:13–17).

Second, Jesus is Lord because of his relationship to the

universe. He is the Lord of creation. Colossians 1:16–17 says, 'In him all things in heaven and on earth were created, things visible and invisible, whether thrones or dominions or rulers or powers – all things have been created through him and for him. He himself is before all things, and in him all things hold together.' And Hebrews 1:3 teaches that by Christ all things consist. The Son is the agent of creation. He upholds 'all things by his powerful word'.

How do we see Jesus' supremacy in 'things visible and invisible'? We see it when Jesus has a pointed one-to-one conversation with Satan himself. Satan tempts Jesus with everything he's got and is roundly defeated (Matt. 4:1–11). We see Jesus' supremacy when the demons recognize him instantly and bow to his authority fearfully (Mark 1:23–28). We see it when Jesus takes Peter, James and John up to a mountain and, as he prays, his face begins to shine like the sun, his clothes become as white as the light, and Moses and Elijah appear and begin to speak to Jesus. As they discuss his impending death, a cloud envelops them and a voice from heaven is heard again: 'This is my Son, my Chosen; listen to him!' (Luke 9:28–36).

Of course the disciples are terrified. Think of it. Earthlings have just been allowed a peek into that other unseen dimension called eternity. Not only that, but they actually eavesdropped on a conversation among Jesus, Moses and Elijah! They were permitted that opportunity because of who Jesus is. What they heard and saw, but only realized the full implications of later, was that Jesus had existed prior to the prophets, his death had been planned before he ever came to earth, and Jesus was not only the Son of God; he was also ushering in the kingdom of God!

Third, Jesus revealed his God-nature in his authority over nature. The first miracle Jesus ever performed was at a wedding party. The wine had run out, so he turned the water into wine. What kind of label would you put on wine like that? 'Glory!' from the Hallelujah vintage, perhaps. Another time the disciples and Jesus were in a boat headed for the shore. Jesus was sound asleep when suddenly an awful storm arose. The wind and waves were so great that the boat began to sink. Experienced fishermen were alarmed. In desperation (and probably irritation at Jesus for sleeping and for suggesting they set out in the boat in the first place), they woke him up and said, 'Teacher, do you not care that we are perishing?' And in the midst of this vicious storm, Jesus casually got up, looked at the lake and said, 'Peace! Be still!' Then the wind ceased and there was a dead calm. If you think the disciples were feeling overwhelmed by the storm, think how they felt on seeing this! 'They were filled with great awe and said to one another, 'Who then is this, that even the wind and the sea obey him?"' (Mark 4:35–41).

Finally, Jesus' deity is revealed in his authority over life itself. He is the Lord of life. 'I am the good shepherd. I know my own and my own know me' (John 10:14). He created us. He understands human nature. He knows us thoroughly. He loves us and died for us. Not only is he competent to direct our lives but he has the power and authority to be the only true guide.

But how can we be sure that Jesus can be trusted to govern our lives? What would Jesus know, for example, about how to handle a person's hellish bondage to drugs or alcohol? What can Jesus do about the guilt and grief of past sins that haunt us? How can he help the anguish of a mother who aborted her baby years ago and still grieves the loss? What does he know about the complexities of modern relationships? The answer, as it turns out, is plenty.

The Gospels show that Jesus had immense authority over everything that wounds and destroys human beings. Those in deep bondage to evil he delivered; those suffering enormous guilt for their sins he forgave; those suffering illness he healed; and even the dead he raised to life. He did exactly what the text in Isaiah said the Messiah would do: 'The Spirit of the Lord is upon me, because he has anointed me to preach good news to the poor. He has sent me to proclaim release to the captives and recovery of sight to the blind, to let the oppressed go free, to proclaim the year of the Lord's favour' (Luke 4:18–19; compare Is. 61:1–2).

In the New Testament the lordship of Christ is no mere abstract principle. The Gospel writers illustrate as well as teach the principle. Mark does this through the idea of authority. Jesus began to teach, and the people were astonished, 'for he taught them as one having authority, and not as the scribes'

(Mark 1:22). Jesus showed authority over the spirit world as he healed a demon-possessed man. And the people were amazed, saying, 'He commands even the unclean spirits, and they obey him' (verse 27). Jesus demonstrated authority over the physical body as he healed Peter's mother-in-law (verse 31). And Jesus also revealed his authority over death by restoring the daughter of Jairus to life (5:35–43). Jesus is Lord because of who he is.

Jesus also revealed his authority by forgiving sins (Mark 2:1–12). Here he moved into dangerous territory, for the people correctly realized one thing: 'Why does this fellow speak in this way? It is blasphemy! Who can forgive sins but God alone?' Jesus answered, 'But so that you may know that the Son of Man has authority on earth to forgive sins ... I say to you, stand up, take your mat and go to your home.' And the people were all amazed, saying, 'We have never seen anything like this!'

Of course, Lois did not realize the full extent to which Jesus is Lord. But she understood enough to know she could not follow him without obeying him. She either had to live under new management or forget about Jesus. I wish I could say that Lois is the norm. All too often, however, people say they believe in Jesus and their lifestyles betray their beliefs. Cathy, for instance.

Traveller's tale

When I did Christian work among students, I frequently used public transport to visit campuses. Once, on a long coach journey, I found myself sitting next to a rather nervous-looking young woman. As it turned out, Cathy was only seventeen. During our conversation she told me she was a Christian from a Christian home. Yet she looked frightened and lost, and as I began probing, I discovered she was running away from home. She had spent all of her money on the coach fare and planned to hitchhike further. She had no money, she hadn't eaten for a while, and she was afraid.

We discussed her inability to get along with her parents, among other personal problems. When I asked how her faith in Christ affected her decision to leave home, I was disappointed (though not surprised) by her impoverished understanding of what it meant to be a Christian. At no point did she seem cognizant that following Christ involved letting him be the Lord in her life; she just described her faith in Jesus as a 'nice feeling in my heart'. As we talked about who Jesus Christ is and how he is Lord as well as Saviour, she decided she wasn't willing for him to have that much control, though she fully believed he is God.

After arriving at our destination, I persuaded Cathy to let me buy her lunch in the Students Union, and during the next hour as we talked I silently but fervently prayed while she continued to insist on carrying on with her trip. I had previously arranged meetings with students all day, but by merely observing me with her in the Students Union, they sensed the situation and realized I needed prayer. So the Christian students quietly prayed at several tables while I continued to talk with her.

Suddenly Cathy looked at me in surprise and said, 'I can't believe I'm saying this – but I'm going to go home. And not because you want me to, or because I want to, but because I've decided to mean business with God. If Christ is going to be Lord of my life, then he'll have to call the shots and he'll help me work out my family problems.' We rejoiced and thanked God together. We even prayed together in the student cafeteria as she committed her life to Christ in a new and total way.

Then I tried to catch up on my appointments while Cathy phoned her parents. She was certain they wouldn't have seen the farewell note. To her disappointment, her mother answered the telephone weeping because they had found the note and were frantic with worry. They had gone immediately to their knees in prayer asking God to protect her and bring her back. (They began praying, I discovered later, five minutes before her decision to return.) Then Cathy told them she had meant to run away from home, but 'God put this Christian next to me on the coach – it was weird!' I laughed as she described me as 'this woman who goes from one university to the next and just talks about God – all day long – and she even gets paid for it!' It was evident that God wanted her parents to read the note in order to bring healing in their relationships not only to God but to each other as well.

I put Cathy on the coach, and with a radiant face she thanked us all. (By now all of the Christians in the cafeteria were in on this drama!) I thought that would be the end of this episode, but there is an exciting sequel.

One month later Katey Finney, then a colleague of mine in InterVarsity Christian Fellowship, was sitting on a city bus next to an older woman. When this woman discovered that Katey worked with IVCF, she said, 'I love that organization! One of their staff workers sat next to my runaway daughter, and she came back home to us. Consequently we talked and really listened to her. As a result of that crisis, I realized I need to grow more in God. I feel I'm stagnating. Do you think we could meet again?'

The amusing thing is that a coach driver who was a Christian heard the story and shared it at the Christian coach drivers' monthly meeting. (I didn't know such a group existed!) Later I was told that it had been an inspiration to them all, and they were grateful that I chose to travel by coach. Perhaps I should have asked for a 'spiritual discount'!

A question of control

Cathy's story ended marvellously because of God's great grace. However, what is distressing to see as we consider Cathy's story is how little her faith had actually affected the way she lived her life. The truth is, up until the point she decided to pray, it would be hard to see the difference between Cathy and any secular person. Why is that? How is it possible to say we believe in Jesus and yet see it make so little difference in how we live?

Cathy is a classic example of what we see all too often in the 'modern' believer. Her faith operated exclusively in the realm of her personal, subjective, private experience. She said she was a Christian, but the truth is, she behaved like a modernist.[4] For example, she made her decisions essentially as a moral relativist – what was right was dictated by the situation she was in, not from any consideration of whether her behaviour violated any absolute truths. She operated as an autonomous individual in assuming all the moral authority she needed in her decision to leave. That decision came from within herself, not from any revealed truth in the Bible. She exhibited a narcissism that focused on her own desires and personal needs, putting her will ahead of understanding what God's will may be. What made her vulnerable to behaving this way? She was unwittingly reflecting the characteristics of what our modern culture believes.

My point is this: if Christians are this influenced by our modern secular culture, then imagine the impact our culture has on those who don't believe in God. One of our great challenges in evangelism is how to convey the truth of the gospel to people who live in a morally relativistic culture. How do we communicate that what we believe must dramatically affect how we behave and the kind of person we become? Especially how do we do this to people who have little or no appreciation of what it means to say that anything is true? The complete loss of belief in any moral absolutes in our world today makes it difficult to understand that truth has any binding consequences. Our impoverished understanding of truth inevitably affects our understanding of what it means to call Jesus Lord.

Lois, who had been living with her boyfriend Phil, was perhaps unusual in recognizing quickly the tie between belief in Christ and behaviour. But how do we communicate Christ's authority and lordship to those who do not believe as we do, who do not accept Christ's lordship over all of life?

Clearly two things must be avoided. First, we must not be so anxious to get our friends into the kingdom that we fail to present a clear and honest picture of Christianity. Unless seekers have as clear as possible an understanding of the gospel, both its costs and privileges, before they commit themselves to God, our harvest will be poor indeed. We must seek to communicate that salvation is tied to a relationship to the living Christ as Lord as well as Saviour; it is tied to objective truth that demands a total response. Warm feelings and shivers are not enough; they are not even required.

Second, we must avoid the trap of legalism in both tone and content. It is vital that we help seekers see the connection between belief and behaviour. Yet we mustn't communicate God as a distant tut-tutting God who will have nothing to do with seekers until they get their act together. That leads only to despair.

Neither may we put roadblocks in the way of faith, demanding behaviour that is based on our personal views of sanctification. A friend once told me that she felt unable to become a Christian because she loved to swim on Sundays.

That, she was told by her parents, was an unforgivable affront to God. Her husband, who came from a less conservative background, said, 'Oh, I knew Jesus didn't mind if I swam on Sundays; he just didn't want me to dive!'

How do we talk about Christ's rule over human life in a way that draws the seeker? One way to do this is by showing our friends that God's rule for our lives stems from his love for us and his desire for our best. In fact, following his commands helps us avoid heartache and pain.

Recently a friend of our family, a young man who is a gifted guitarist and singer, asked my husband and me to come and hear him sing in an informal setting. His lyrics reflected much of the sentiments of our age: disenchantment, alienation, disappointment and the deep longing to connect. One song dealt with his anger and pain over a recent break-up with his girlfriend. Some of the lines went something like this: 'Someday you'll realize that you need to ask my forgiveness. What you did was so wrong, you'll even have to ask Jesus Christ to forgive you. And even if Jesus never existed, you'd better ask him anyway!'

All right, I wouldn't encourage him to quit his night job to become a systematic theologian. But what was striking were his frequent allusions to religious metaphors. Clearly he was seeking to make meaning out of his life.

The next day he came over to our home and thanked us profusely for coming. Then he said, 'You know, my mum doesn't like that song about my break-up with my girlfriend. She's into New Age stuff and says I shouldn't be putting out all that negative energy.'

'Well,' I responded, 'you're not going to get anywhere by trying to pretend your anger isn't there. First, you have to own it – and it certainly sounded to me as though you've done that! But the next step is being sure you don't get stuck there. It's learning how to forgive – that's the hard part.'

His eyes lit up and he said, 'That's exactly the stage I'm at now. But boy it's hard to do! Sometimes I wonder if it's worth the effort.'

'You know, Jack,' I answered, 'Jesus talks a lot about forgiveness. He tells us it's only reasonable for us to forgive others since we need God's forgiveness. But I think Jesus wants us to forgive so *we* won't be carrying around that smouldering anger inside of us. Forgiving others is also for our benefit.'

'So Jesus was arguing for hedonism in telling us to forgive?'

'Well, actually, his argument is the exact opposite,' I answered. 'Hedonism says that if you feel like hating, then go right ahead. Go with your impulses. Jesus says that if we resist doing what we feel like – to seek revenge – and do what he says – to forgive – we'll end up truly free. Hedonism promises freedom and leaves us in bondage. Jesus promises freedom and delivers.'

'Wow! I'll have to think about that. That would make a fantastic song, though,' he said shortly before he left.

What will happen next? I don't know. But what if he really tries to forgive her and then discovers he doesn't have the power to do so? Maybe he'll learn what most serious seekers eventually come to see – how impoverished human resources are. That insight is what prompted G. K. Chesterton to say, 'Christianity isn't difficult – it's impossible.'[5] In other words, what Christ calls us to do we cannot do apart from his empowerment. Once Jack comes face to face with his own limitations, he'll be more open to hearing about the One who has the power to transform his heart.

How did the opportunity arise to speak to Jack about Jesus? First, I didn't give him a sermon; I just turned up. Going on *his* turf showed him that my husband and I genuinely care about him. Second, listening to his songs enabled us to understand him better. I could hear his questions and struggles through the lyrics of his songs. I saw where he was hurting. There is great wisdom in the old adage 'Scratch where it itches.' Once I knew where his itch was, it was easy to help him see that not only did Jesus care about his struggles but Jesus had something relevant to say on the subject! What I hope will eventually draw Jack to consider Christ is that he saw, even if for only a moment, that Jesus understands the practical struggles of his life and cares about his pain. It was only a small beginning but a promising one.

The last thing Jack said to me was, 'I hate being controlled by my anger.'

'Ah, there's the rub, Jack, because whatever controls us really is our god – even if we hate it.'

'Well, I certainly need to be controlled by a better god than this,' Jack replied as he left.

The person who seeks power is controlled by power. The person who seeks acceptance is controlled by the people he or she wants to please. We do not control ourselves. We are controlled by the lord of our life.

If Jesus is our Lord, then he is the one to whom we submit, for he has the ultimate power. There are no bargains. We cannot manipulate him by saying, 'Let's make a deal.' If he is Lord, the only option open to us is to do his will, to let him have control. Jesus remains Lord whether we accept him or not. His lordship, his essence, is not affected by what we choose. But our lives are drastically changed by our choice.

Jesus' ownership of our lives is not a control that manipulates us or takes away our dignity. Jesus never presumes things or decides things for people. He does not abuse or bully people. In fact, we find Jesus asking as many questions as people asked him. He does not decide what people need and then give it to them. He asked the blind beggar Bartimaeus, 'What do you want me to do for you?' (Mark 10:51). He asked the paralytic, 'Do you want to be made well?' (John 5:6). He asked Peter, 'Who do you say that I am?' (Matt. 16:15), 'Do you love me?' (John 21:15) and 'Do you also wish to go away?' (6:67). And he told his disciples, 'If you love me, you will keep my commandments' (14:15).

Jesus always preserves our freedom. He allows us to choose him over all others. Jesus will not control us in the wrong way. Nor will he control us in the easy way, by making every decision for us. He governs our lives in the right way: by being who he is without compromise and by insisting we become all that we are meant to be. And he tells us this can occur only through following him, obeying him and maintaining a living, passionate kinship to him.

We are to reflect Christ and obey him not only because of who he is but because of who we have become. The very nature of God dwells in us now. As Oswald Chambers has said, 'Jesus is ruthless in His demands and uncompromising because He has put into us the very nature of God.'[6]

Summarizing God's purpose for human beings, the Westminster Shorter Catechism tells us that we are created to glorify God and enjoy him for ever. God created us for himself. If we are living with any centre other than Jesus, we will be living incompletely. So Jesus continually tries to help people see who or what controls them. That is why Jesus is far more interested in people's lives than in their God-talk. Your life, more than your words, will reveal what really controls you.

Jesus aimed for the point of control in his conversations. He knew that faith meant submitting to his authority, not merely getting him to do what we want. Jesus knew people liked him, enjoyed him, thought he was stimulating and really desired him to be on their team. Jesus also knew that those are not the rules of the game.

There are problems in this issue of control. Either we are controlled by the wrong thing or we try to control Jesus by limiting him to our terms. Jesus will accept our faith, but he will never accept our controls.

Is Jesus' desire to be the Lord of our lives some little fetish of his? Why is it so important to him? Why should we want him to have control of our lives? Besides the fact that he deserves it because of who he is, he knows he is the only one in the universe who can control us without destroying us. No-one will ever love you like Jesus. No-one will ever know you better, care more for your wholeness and pull more for you. You don't need fifteen years of analysis to discover you are unrepeatable. The last breath Jesus breathed on this planet was for you. Jesus will meet you wherever you are, and he will help you. He is not intimidated by past failures, broken promises or wounds. He will make sense out of your brokenness. But he can only begin to be the Lord of your life today – not next Monday or next month, but now.

And the great and joyful paradox is that while he totally transforms us, he makes us more ourselves than ever before.

4

A question of love:
being radically identified
with the world

A person who earnestly desired to share Christ's love with his friends told me, 'Don't give me any new formulas to witness naturally. I've tried everything. It just doesn't seem right to use surveys or steps on someone you know.'

This person is typical of many. Christians say they want to communicate their faith naturally instead of seeming artificial or contrived. So in their pursuit of this they investigate every witnessing technique on the spiritual market.

'I'm not going to suggest a new formula,' I said, 'because I feel as you do that techniques aren't the most effective, especially for friends. Have you ever thought about looking more deeply at the life of Jesus? If you live by the same values and priorities he had, you will find evangelism happening naturally. It becomes a lifestyle and not a project.'

When we develop a way of living that places a special emphasis on people, that demonstrates holiness and a dedicated obedience to God, we can't help but be effective witnesses. Evangelism will flow from our lives instead of from memorized techniques.

But this puts the burden on us. What did Jesus value? How important was love and compassion? What was his notion of holiness? What role does obedience play?

We can and will answer these questions in the next three chapters by looking at Jesus. In this chapter we will consider the way Jesus associated openly with notorious sinners and how this love of his can shape our evangelism. In the following chapter we'll examine Jesus' clash with the Jewish leaders of his day due to his very different definition of what it meant to be holy and to stand apart from the world. Then in chapter 6 we will see what difference it makes according to Jesus to know God not in a merely academic way but in a way that leads us to live out the truth we know.

All three of these areas are vital in evangelism. Let's begin then with the emphasis Jesus placed on love.

What Jesus regarded as important

There was a widely accepted notion among the religious people of Jesus' day that religious activity was what was truly pleasing to God. Jesus smashed that notion. Through both his life and his teaching Jesus proclaimed that the primary way to please God was through proper relationships.

Jesus was wholly concerned with God and wholly concerned with people. That is, according to Jesus, the human cause is God's cause. Jesus' lifestyle arose out of the simple truth of loving God, our neighbours and ourselves. His life was a constant celebration of the supreme value, dignity and preciousness of human life.

Malcolm Muggeridge once said in a lecture, 'That there is more joy in heaven over one sinner who repents is an antistatistical proposition.' Jesus had an antistatistical approach to people. He loved sinners. He demonstrated that everyone is someone to God. There were no little people, no hierarchy. He was not impressed with a pecking order (Mark 10:42–45) but with servanthood (John 13:1–20). He identified with the unimportant, the weak and sinful, the poor and powerless. And because he identified with them, to his critics he became one of them. At his resurrection the first to witness his appearance were women, the powerless in his culture.

He once met a blind beggar, Bartimaeus (Mark 10:46–52). To everyone but Jesus, Bartimaeus was an insignificant pauper who wanted to interrupt the schedule of the king. But Jesus stopped everything and asked the people who had shouted at the beggar to get lost, to bring the man to him. Jesus not only served this beggar; he asked those who considered him insignificant to serve him too. What a humiliation for them!

Jesus took time to talk to children and to hold them (Mark 10:13–16). Children seemed to have a habit of bursting in on his meetings with adults. The disciples scolded them and told them to go away. After all, this was Jesus they were trying to see, a very busy and important man. But Jesus scolded the adults and told them their values were wrong. The disciples thought only 'important people' should see Jesus. It took them a long time to understand that, for Jesus, any person was of supreme importance.

The teaching that life is relationships did not begin with Jesus. It is a fundamental biblical principle. To be is to be in relation to someone. The Trinity evidences this. In Genesis we see that God sought relationship with us. Then he gave Adam a mate because 'it is not good that the man should be alone' (Gen. 2:18). It is interesting to note that modern psychology is turning away from seeing mental health in terms of solitary individuals and instead viewing it in terms of the adequacy of human relationships. Since the advent of atomic physics the assumed idea that physical reality was one of particles floating in an empty void has been challenged and changed. At the heart of science itself 'community, not competition, is the metaphor that most deeply informs the work of many biologists. Among physicists, the atom is no longer seen as an independent and isolated entity but as … a set of relationships reaching out to other things.'[1] In other words, what scientists have discovered is that reality at its very core is communal, involving relationships. This new approach that we see in science and other fields is in some ways a return to the ancient Hebrew-Christian understanding of reality in the first place.

Why did Jesus so stress and demonstrate the necessity of a life that bears the stamp of profound love? Jesus said it reveals his Father's essence. Jesus was not loving and kind to others merely because he happened to be warm and considerate and had good role models at home. He loved people the way he did because he was doing his Father's will and demonstrating his character. He taught friends and foes alike that God has an extravagant, endless kind of love for people.

Royalty in rags

In one exchange with the Pharisees (who were very troubled by Jesus' contact with sinners), Jesus painted the bleakest possible picture of their understanding of a sinner. He told the story of a

Jewish boy who insulted and humiliated his father, left home and squandered his inheritance on immoral living. If that was not bad enough, he got so hungry that he found a job tending pigs. (What was a nice, orthodox Jewish boy doing among swine?) But then Jesus went one step further. This boy, no doubt brought up in a kosher kitchen, got so hungry that he wanted to eat the pigs' food! Imagine the orthodox crowd's response to this wretched story. And finally the boy became so hungry that he decided to go back to his father because he was sorry and he knew his father would feed him. Hardly the most abject repentance we have ever read about!

And what was the father's response? Jesus has given us one of the most moving pictures of God in the New Testament. He told the Pharisees that even while the son was a long way off, the father saw him, broke into a run, and with outstretched arms embraced him, kissed him and proceeded to dress him like a king. He did not care about getting his robes dirty. The boy had come home; that was all that mattered. It was time to celebrate and the father threw a party.

Suppose a neighbour were to walk past this scene. Let's imagine this is what happened. He doesn't know that the father has just bestowed clothes and jewellery upon the boy. He sees the father standing with a guest clothed in an ornate robe used only for very special guests, usually royalty. Then as the young man gestures with his hand, the neighbour sees a jewelled ring sparkling in the sunlight. He notices sandals on his feet and a fatted calf being prepared for a feast. Then it hits him. The young man must be a prince! All the details add up: the robe, the ring, the festivity and excitement.

The neighbour wants desperately to go over and say hello, if only he could get up his nerve. But he is only a commoner, a nobody. Yet the father who owns the house seems so kind and generous that the neighbour decides to drop in for a minute and sneak in a hello. Maybe he can even get the guest's autograph. He slowly creeps up behind the two men. The father's arm is still around the shoulders of the younger man as they walk. They talk, but mostly the father listens intently to the young man. His eyes are wise and kind, and occasionally they brim with tears – it seems for joy. The neighbour thinks he has never seen anyone as delighted to see another person.

He decides that if the father is that excited to see this man, then he must be a very important person. So he approaches the two men and speaks hesitantly, asking if he can have the privilege of meeting this most honoured guest. The father nearly bursts with pride and delight. The father would love him to meet his guest. Slowly the beautifully robed young man turns around. But what the neighbour sees frightens him so that he nearly jumps back in disgust. For there in these beautiful robes, exquisite jewellery and sandals is a young man who looks half dead. He is grimy, unshaven and smelly. His face is sunken, and his jaundiced skin seems barely to hang over his bones. He looks diseased. The neighbour begins to feel a bit nauseous and makes a quick excuse to leave. The father is so full of joy that he scarcely notices that his uninvited guest has left abruptly.

Jesus made profound statements in his story. One is that all of us look like that prodigal son when we stand next to the Father. We all look diseased. But when we come to God and become his children, he dresses us in his royal robes of right-eousness. The exciting thing Jesus teaches here is that once we come to him, once we belong to him, we are royalty walking on the earth.

All of us have specks of his royal gold in us. We are all made in his image. That image has been marred, but never so marred that the specks of gold have been obliterated. And never so marred that God by his grace cannot redeem us and adopt us as his own special heirs. When we go out into the world, we ought never to forget that we are interacting with potential royalty. We may be conversing with an heir apparent.

Jesus revealed the nature of God and the tremendous value he places on human life. He also made a powerful statement about the depth and magnitude of God's love for one disease-ridden, sinful person. Jesus reached out to others in love and asks us to do likewise because we are called to mirror the nature of God himself. This is not a call to be affectionate and affable and sweet because it is such a nice thing to do. It is a call to love as God loves.

So deeply did Jesus stress the importance of having a love relationship that he said if we are at the altar and realize we are not at peace with a person, we are to stop doing anything religious. We are to leave the altar and, to the degree it is possible, we are to become reconciled to that person (Matt. 5:23). Jesus went further and said we are to love the unlovely, our enemies (verse 44). We are to love those who do not know the law, not curse them. God's love in us must extend across all boundaries.

A neighbour's love

Jesus also taught about the call to relationship in his conversation with a lawyer in Luke 10:25–37. An intellectual lawyer had come to Jesus with a rather ponderous question: 'What must I do to inherit eternal life?' This reminds me of a particular set of students I worked with over a period of five years: they were brilliant, intense, verbose; they loved spending hour after hour discussing ideas. They were devoted to study. They loved probing the sublime, the esoteric and the metaphysical. The more obscure it was, the better they liked it. Practical questions were considered a bit gauche; direct answers, unfortunate and simplistic. They much preferred to probe for the rare, esoteric pearls. The more I study Pharisaical lawyers, the more I am convinced that the man talking to Jesus was just such a person as those students.

These lawyers insisted on the primacy of learning. They delighted in any abstract discussion of the law. Ancient Galileans were constantly amazed that the Pharisees could spend hours discussing whether it was mint or rue that ought to be tithed. So along came an intellectual lawyer. He was theologically sophisticated and probably thought he would trap this rather naive carpenter into a great theological debate and dazzle him with his brilliance.

'What must I do to inherit eternal life?' the lawyer asked. He had probably anticipated Jesus' every response except the one he actually got. Jesus did the one thing he had not counted on. He did not give him an answer but asked him a question instead (a model in evangelism we could well apply).

'What is written in the law? What do you read there?' Jesus asked.

He answered, 'You shall love the Lord your God with all your heart, and with all your soul, and with all your strength, and with all your mind; and your neighbour as yourself.'

'You have given the right answer; do this, and you will live,' Jesus replied.

Becoming defensive, the lawyer asked, 'Who is my neighbour?'

And so Jesus told him the now familiar parable of the good Samaritan. The dynamics in the story are fascinating.

Imagine the most brilliant person you know approaching Jesus rather smugly with an enormous theological question. Jesus responds with a question that forces him or her to recite an answer that person learned as a child. It is like saying, 'That's a very good question. Now can you remember what you learned in primary school?' He or she answers quickly, feeling somewhat embarrassed and defensive. Now can you think of anything much clearer than the statement 'Love your neighbour'? One would like to think a brilliant theologian might grasp its meaning.

What was this lawyer really reacting to? He wanted a nice, abstract religious discussion. He wanted to parade his knowledge before Jesus. But Jesus called him to act on what he knew. This is not an example of Jesus putting down intellectual thought. On the contrary, Jesus was a supreme intellectual here, for he knew that truth must be evidenced in one's life, not put away in cold storage. But for the lawyer it felt awkward and annoying. He wanted something sublime and esoteric – a rare pearl – not to be told to love some bland and insignificant neighbour!

So when Jesus became specific (as he always does), the lawyer tried to find a way to crawl out. 'Well, what does it really mean to love my neighbour? The whole thing is so complex,' he retorted. 'I don't want to rush into anything. What if I went out and loved someone and he turned out not to be my neighbour? I think we need to study this, have a conference on it.'

Instead, Jesus told the lawyer a story about neighbourliness and asked him to identify the real neighbour. Then he concluded the conversation with these words: 'Go and do likewise.'

Jesus summed up life here in terms of a love relationship to God, to our neighbour and to ourselves. Before any religious activity, our lives are to bear the stamp of profound love. The

priest in the parable of the good Samaritan did not stop to help
the victim, perhaps because he was on the way to the temple. In
other words, he thought more of religion than he did of that
man. His actions reflected his theology.

It is always that way. Our sociology reflects our theology. The
way we treat others reveals what we think God is like. Imagine
the implications this has for evangelism! The way we treat
others is critical. People will understand as much of the love of
God as they see in our own lives. The first Bible many people
will read will be us and how we live.

We are called, therefore, to mirror the love of God – a love
that is so extravagant that we must never keep it to ourselves.
We must spread it around. It is not a mushy love, all sentiment
and no action. Jesus' love drove him deeply into the lives of
people. He cared for their wholeness. When he went out into a
day, he did not ask himself, *Is this my social action day, or do I
give them the salvation message?* Jesus cared for people as he
found them. So must we care for their wholeness – spiritual,
social, psychological, you name it.

And how are we to love and be a neighbour to those whom
we do not know (which constitutes the bulk of the world's
population)? Love must be aggressively translated into simple
justice. The call to a love relationship will involve much more
than emotional empathy. It requires fighting against injustice.
Again, our actions as Christians will reflect how just we believe
God actually is.

But are we really supposed to love the unlovely? Are we
meant to get involved with those whose lives are lived in
opposition to God's standards? Shouldn't we stand apart from
sinners and let our lives testify to God's holiness? Jesus and the
Pharisees clashed over just this issue: does obeying God's laws
require us to have only distant relationships with unbelievers?
To understand this better we first need to examine the
Pharisees, a religious lay movement in Jesus' day.

The Pharisees cared deeply about God and had more in
common with Jesus than any of the other theological schools of
thought of his time, yet some of them were his severest critics.
Thus they have received a lot of bad press. There is a legitimate
and necessary concern in much contemporary scholarship to
portray Judaism (and Pharisaism) fairly and in its own terms.

There is also a difference of opinion among scholars as to whether the conflict stories recorded between Jesus and the Pharisees were really as vociferous as many have portrayed them.[2] Nevertheless, the deep tensions and alternative visions of the destiny and responsibilities of Israel that Jesus and the Pharisees represent cannot escape our attention. Furthermore, as one scholar said, 'The broad picture of the Pharisees in conflict with Jesus seems well rooted in the Gospel tradition. It also seems consistent with, and inevitable in the light of, their different understanding of the divine will.'[3]

The irony of the Pharisees, who cared enormously about obeying the ceremonial laws of purity, is that according to Jesus they did not take the law seriously enough. The basic problem of the Pharisees, it appears, was that most of them were less concerned with the prophets (such as Hosea, Amos, Isaiah, and so on) than they were with the priestly ceremonial laws (found in Deuteronomy, Leviticus, and so on).

What was the result of their exclusive emphasis on obeying the ceremonial laws of purity and their seeming neglect of the moral law – what Jesus called the 'weightier matters of the law, justice and mercy and faith' (Matt. 23:23)? It fed and eagerly encouraged the already existing social hierarchy. Their fervour for ceremonial purity led to an apartheid-type response to almost anyone who was not a part of their exclusive sect. There was strict separation from Gentiles and from Samaritans, and there was even an aloofness from fellow Jews who did not have the leisure to study the law as they did. The Pharisees desired solidarity with the educated, powerful and wise, and utter separation from the rest.

So why should we concern ourselves with an inner-Jewish debate that occurred two thousand years ago between Jesus and the Pharisees? Because their conflicts reveal issues that most religious people wrestle with even today. In particular, how involved should believers be with their unchurched friends? Furthermore, the list of warnings of the temptations faced by the spiritually mature are sobering: hypocrisy (Luke 11:38–41), distorted perspectives (verse 42), ostentation (verses 43–44) and self-righteousness (18:9–14).

Most importantly, just as we must not abandon the law (including all of God's moral law in the Bible as well as the Ten

Commandments) thinking it has meaning only for the people of ancient times, so neither does our obedience to God's law excuse us from having relationships with unchurched people. The call to relationship and the call to honour God's laws actually go well together. Our love for God, others and ourselves, and all the actions that this relationship entails, mirror what the law is all about and what it is preparing us for. We honour God's standards because we have fallen in love with the Lawgiver!

If the Pharisees had properly understood the whole of the law, they would have understood the call to relationship. In fact, one of the best-known passages of Old Testament law highlights this: 'Hear, O Israel: The LORD is our God, the LORD alone. You shall love the LORD your God with all your heart, and with all your soul, and with all your might' (Deut. 6:4–5). Instead, some of the Pharisees denied their relationship, as the young prodigal did to his father and subsequently as the elder brother did to his younger brother. And consequently the Pharisees had no message to the lost.

People or programmes?

I remember being with a Christian student on a beach during an evangelism training week. Bob and I met several religious sceptics and began talking about all sorts of things. Eventually the conversation got around to Christianity, and it was a lively and invigorating discussion. We even exchanged addresses before leaving. I was feeling very good about the conversation, but Bob seemed very quiet.

When I asked him what was wrong, he said, 'I thought it was an absolute failure. There are four major points to the gospel and you only brought in two of them, and they weren't even in the right order!'

I said, 'What were the names of the three people we met this afternoon?'

'Oh, I don't know,' he said. 'Whatever difference does that make? There were two women and a man. Or was it the other way around?'

I stared at him in disbelief and sadness. Here was a young man who genuinely loved God. He was exceedingly religious and sincere. I doubt whether he ever missed his daily quiet times. And yet he had missed the entire point. He was sure his agenda, his four points, were the supreme value. Yet his method was so rigid that real live human beings could not penetrate it. We must beware of this kind of pharisaism, for it is so frequently the disease of the devoted. This student was so busy rehearsing his four points of salvation that he forgot that he was speaking to the very people Christ had come to save.

We must never forget that to be a follower of Jesus is to be dominated by love. We may not be well versed in Scripture or have a theological qualification; we may be timid and unsure of ourselves; but we have arms and hearts that were meant to be used. We must ask ourselves, *Do I treat people as royalty walking the earth, including even my parents, my spouse, my flatmate, the student in my hall that I can't stand? Do I believe that by merely seeing me God would break into a run and embrace me? Does my life reflect only religious activity, or does it bear the mark of profound love?* When our lives are characterized by the love of Christ, we can begin to interest people in the gospel.

It bears repeating: if we are going to arouse seekers' curiosity in Jesus, then we must demonstrate the love of Jesus. One of the challenges in learning how to love people is seeing beyond their emotional baggage and into their hearts.

A few years ago I was returning home after speaking at a conference. It was late and I was exhausted and eager to get home. Initially I didn't notice that there was anything wrong with my car, but once I was on the motorway, I saw smoke coming from my engine. As I pulled over, I saw that the car behind me was pulling over too.

A couple got out of the car and asked what they could do to help. The man said that he was starting to overtake me when he realized that I was having serious car problems. He said, 'I told my girlfriend that if you were my sister I wouldn't want her to be stranded on the motorway at eleven at night.'

I was overwhelmed by their kindness to me. We secured my car and they drove me to the nearby services from where I phoned my breakdown service. They told me that it would be at least one hour before their van could come. (As it turned out, it was two hours.) I thanked the couple for all their trouble and told them to get on with their plans for the evening. But they insisted on staying with me until help arrived. So we got some coffee, sat down and began to talk.

His name was Kurt and he was a lorry driver who drove all over the country. Her name was Carla. Although they lived a long way from each other, they had been seeing each other for a year, and she had just arrived to spend the weekend with him. As we began talking, they told me they were both divorced and both had children. Just by observing them, I realized that they were in love but frightened about making another mistake.

Initially Carla was reserved, but as I began to ask about her life and especially about her children, the tragedy of her life came pouring out. She was heartsick over her daughter Val, whose life experience had been one of unbelievable demonic darkness. Val had been on drugs since she was twelve, married at sixteen, and though she was only twenty-one years old, she had already been married twice and had attempted suicide three times. One of the most bizarre aspects of her daughter's short life was how many deaths she had witnessed. Both of her husbands had been killed, and Val's only child had a deadly disease. I've been told many painful stories in my life, but this truly was one of the worst.

'Carla, how on earth are you coping with so much pain? Where do you get the resources to handle all of this?' I asked.

'I don't think I am handling it well. I can't sleep at night. I smoke five packets a day. I just don't know what to do or how to help her,' she answered in despair, inhaling her cigarette deeply.

'Well, you must begin by caring for yourself. You won't be able to give much to Val unless your own cup is filled,' I answered.

About this time Kurt received a telephone call on his mobile phone and excused himself to answer it.

Carla went on, 'You know, Becky, I've done everything I can think of to help my daughter. Several years ago, when Val was still living at home, I realized that I had to get my own act together if I was going to be able to help her. I decided to change jobs so I could be there for her.'

'What is your job now?' I asked.

'Oh, I run a bar. I just knew I had to have something with more stable hours,' she answered matter-of-factly.

Of course, the obvious question was, What in the world did she do before she decided to clean up her act and pull pints? I didn't have to wait for the answer.

'You know, a lot of my friends thought I was mad to change jobs. You know, since my other job had shorter hours and quite good pay. I dunno, somehow I just didn't feel being a stripper was a good role model for my daughter,' she said in utter seriousness.

It may have been my imagination, but I gulped so hard on my next sip of coffee that I was sure everyone in the restaurant heard it. But by God's utter grace, I don't think my expression changed.

'Well, I can certainly see your point. What you did certainly makes sense to me,' I answered as if I heard this every day.

'I just don't know where to turn. Val was discharged from the hospital last week after trying to take her life again. Oh, Becky, I love her so much and I feel so helpless,' Carla said as tears began flowing down her cheeks.

It was amazing to behold. At first glance Carla had an appearance that was hard, almost cold. Just one look at her and it was obvious that her life had been very difficult. Yet as she began to share her life, with all its catastrophic pain, her entire countenance changed. Her appearance became soft and vulnerable. What did I possibly have in common with a pint-pulling ex-stripper? Carla had a mother's heart. She loved her daughter just as I love mine. That connection alone was a powerful one.

'Listen, Carla, all I can offer you is what has helped me through the most difficult times in my life. Carla, you were never intended to go through this much pain alone. Nobody is expected to handle all of this without help.'

'You mean, I should see a social worker or something?' she said as she wiped the tears from her cheeks.

'First, you need to turn to God. He's there, Carla, and he loves you very much. Before you can offer Val comfort, you need to be comforted by the Lord.'

'You know, I do believe in God even though I don't know him very well. The other day when I got the call that Val had slit her wrists, I asked myself, *Does God ever get involved in the messes we make in our lives?*'

'Oh, Carla, getting involved with our human mess is God's specialty! In fact God *solved* the human mess by sending his Son, Jesus. Jesus got right down into the trenches of life with us. He died for all of our messes, Carla. And he wants you to turn to him and let him carry this horrible burden for you.'

'How would I even start with God? I've made such a complete screw-up of my life.'

'You start by telling God exactly that. Tell him you are sorry for all your sins. Ask him to forgive you. Thank Jesus for dying on the cross for your sins. Then ask him to come into your life. From that point on, you will have God's Spirit living and working through you. You won't be trying to help Val alone; God will be reaching out to her through you. But you can't minister to Val unless you allow God to minister to you first,' I said.

'I can't imagine what God must think of me,' she said sadly.

'Carla, God sees everything about all of us. He sees where you've blown it. But he also sees how much you care and how hard you are trying to help your daughter. He knows that you were willing to change jobs just to help Val. He loves you, Carla. And he wants to come into your life so he can make you the Carla you were intended to be. The Bible says that when we become Christians, he makes us into oaks of righteousness. We become strong and stable and people can come and find rest and comfort in our branches, because we are rooted in the love of Christ.'

'Oh, how I would love to be an oak,' she said wistfully. 'How do I find out more about this? What can I read? And what can I give to Val that will help her?'

'The most important thing you can do for Val is to make your own commitment of faith. But I was thinking about what to send you as a thank-you gift for your enormous kindness to me. May I send you a Bible in a translation that's easy to understand? And I'd like to send you a book of the psalms for Val to read. It's a paraphrased version that I think will speak to Val's heart. Would you like me to send it?' I asked.

'Oh, very much! Let me give you my address. Well, come to think of it, the place where you should send it is to my bar,' she answered, looking sheepish.

'Sure, just give me the address,' I answered as I got out my pen.

'Ah, well, it's not exactly something I'm proud of. But we named the bar something that would get people's attention,' she said. Then she told me its name. Suffice it to say, it verged on the pornographic.

As I was writing it down, Kurt came back to tell us that my help had arrived. As we walked into the cold winter's night, I turned to both of them and thanked them from the bottom of my heart for their generosity and kindness. As I was about to leave, Carla suddenly hugged me with an intensity that almost made me cry. Then she whispered, 'Do you think hotel rooms still have those Gideon Bibles? I thought I might start reading it tonight.'

My continual amazement, as I engage in the task of evangelism, is how profoundly I am blessed. It is not an experience in which I have something to give but nothing to receive. It's not an experience in which they are changed but I remain unchanged. The truth is, I am as affected by my encounter with them as they sometimes are with me. As I engage in evangelism, I find it's not only *their* needs that are met; *mine* are too. God's intention is to bless us both – the giver of the truth and the receiver. I was incredibly moved by the selfless sacrifice that Kurt and Carla made. They helped me in a real time of need. Imagine, they were on their way to a romantic break, and they interrupted it because, as Kurt said, 'What if that stranded woman were my sister?' When we allow others to minister to us, it makes our relationship with seekers more authentic.

That isn't to say that the experience of evangelism is always painless. As I enter into the stories of others and listen to their pain, it is very difficult to hear of lives so torn apart by the destructiveness of sin.

Furthermore, as I listen carefully and try to understand their questions about faith, it sometimes feels threatening and uncomfortable. But there is fruit from such an experience. For it forces me to delve deeper into the Bible to try to understand what the Scripture teaches in light of their questions. It makes me more dependent on God as I ask him to show me the way with the particular person I am talking to. The result is that I almost always come away with a deeper understanding of the richness of the gospel. I am changed by our encounter because now I understand biblical truth in a fresher or deeper way than I did before. There are no two ways about it: evangelism is exciting!

Evangelism is also rewarding because it blesses other believers. The first thing I did the next day was to go to my favourite Christian bookshop and send Carla her gift. There is a marvellous woman working at the shop who truly has the appearance of the quintessential 'little old lady' – but looks are deceiving! She often sends books for me after I've been on a speaking trip, so when she saw me, her face lit up and she said, 'I can't wait to hear the story!'

She loved the story, and as she was about to write up the order, she said, 'Now, where am I sending this to?' I suddenly remembered the name of the bar, and I was horrified at the thought of telling her, especially at her age. 'OK, brace yourself,' I said as I told her. She immediately burst into the most glorious smile and said, 'Can you *imagine* this Bible going to any better place? Praise God!' Then she lifted the Bible in the air, and waving it heavenward, she prayed, 'Lord, let your word go forth and bring light, healing and the saving knowledge of Jesus Christ as it goes to … to … to … well, I'm not going to say where, but you know, Lord!' Now that's my kind of Christian!

5

A question of holiness: being radically different from the world

I recently saw a remarkable film called *The Apostle* whose central character, Sonny, is a Southern, 'Holy Ghost-filled' evangelist and preacher. Sonny is a fiery, vital man whose relationship to Jesus is equally passionate in nature. Sonny loves his church; he loves to preach the gospel, to evangelize and to pray. We see him lead people to Christ, and in one of the most moving scenes in the film, we watch him respond to the greatest crisis of his life by wrestling with God in prayer through the night.

His crisis comes when he discovers that his wife (the church organist) is having an affair with a younger pastor. In an unguarded moment Sonny picks up a baseball bat and hits the young pastor so hard it knocks him unconscious. (Eventually the young pastor dies from the blow.) Knowing he will be arrested and possibly sent to prison, Sonny escapes to a faraway place, leaving his wife and children behind, and becomes a fugitive from the law. There he has a 'dark night of the soul' experience, and though it's unclear exactly why, he emerges feeling cleansed and restored in faith.

He starts a new church in a new town, and it soon becomes evident he has not lost his flair or fire. The church worship scenes are so authentic that it feels as if Robert Duvall, the director, writer of the screenplay and actor who portrays Sonny, simply let the camera roll during genuine praise services. It's that real. Duvall is brilliant in his portrayal; he knows his character, Sonny, from the inside out.

If the film's focus had dealt primarily with the common struggle every believer faces of how to be holy and human, it wouldn't leave the Christian viewer, at least, feeling strangely troubled. Or if the film had ultimately painted Sonny as a blatant hypocrite – which would have been very unsatisfying – it would have at least resolved the questions we are left with. But Sonny is portrayed as a genuine believer. So what's the problem?

First, one can't help but love Sonny. His emotional intimacy with the Lord is irresistible. Neither do his sermons stray from the truth, only his life. What is hard to fathom is how a man with a faith that large doesn't have a commensurate sensitivity to sin and commitment to obedience. Sonny's praise life may have been Davidic in nature, but his confessional life fell far short. Even in the pivotal scene after his escape, in which he prays and fasts, we never hear Sonny struggling with much depth or comprehension about the sins of his life.

For example, Sonny never seems to be very disturbed by the fact that he's been a married womanizer – there's just a wink and nod to his self-acknowledged 'wicked, wicked ways'. There's even a suggestion that he may have been physically abusive to his wife. He starts a romance with a woman in his new community with whom he has a definite spiritual influence. Yet he never tells her that he is actually still married. Nor does he wrestle much with the moral implications of fleeing from the law. He's surely preached sermons on reaping what you sow, yet he's not inclined to pay the consequences. His flight from the law is illegal. Yet Sonny prays from the heart with such warmth and humanity that he makes us want to close our eyes and forget about all the contradictions between his faith and his behaviour.

Part of the power of the film is that, whether intentionally or not, it brings us face to face with the impact of modernity. It's all the more devastating because it's seen through the life of a believer. Modern people just don't grasp that there must be a connection between belief and behaviour. Why isn't Sonny's faith evidenced by more godly behaviour? Therein lies the contradiction: Sonny is a holiness preacher who isn't holy. The unspoken message regarding his private sins is this: 'The rules don't apply to me because I am so sincere in my faith. There are no consequences to my actions because in my heart I didn't mean to hurt anyone. My only responsibility is to do the Lord's work and build a church, not to bear the consequences for past actions.'

It isn't Sonny's faith that is troubling, it's that his beliefs have not been translated into his behaviour. *Holiness* isn't a word used much in modern parlance. It sounds too judgmental and narrow to our ears. Yet, as William Bennett writes in his book *The Death of Outrage*, 'There is a vital link between reasonable judgment and authentic compassion. Without judgment, there can be no common ethic ... No rules to govern behaviour. No wise counsel on how best to live ... We see every day the human cost of "tolerance" and "openness." Moral judgments need to be made, not for the sake of satisfying a "Puritan passion" or a "rigid moralism," but because we human beings live better, more noble, more complete and satisfying lives when we hold ourselves to some common moral understanding.'[1] In Sonny's case his 'common moral understanding' was the Scriptures. Sadly, his love of biblical truth was reflected far more in his preaching than in his lifestyle.

That film represents one side of the problem. If our lives do not give testimony to the radical difference that knowing Christ makes, our evangelism will ultimately be ineffective and hollow. However, there is the other side of the coin. Sometimes we reduce the call of holiness to trite and legalistic behaviours, such as the man I mentioned earlier who said he could swim on Sundays but not dive.

Holiness external and internal

I was on a visit to a university and was trying to get to know the nonbelievers who lived in the hall of residence where I was staying for a few days. One night I learned there was an excellent film on television and, suspecting there would be a large crowd, I went along. The room was packed with students and cans of Coke. During the adverts we laughed and talked, and I said why I was visiting their campus. Friendships began to form between myself and several others. A majority of those students came to hear me when I gave a talk later that week.

While we were watching television, however, a Christian student walked past and looked at us a bit disapprovingly, then saw me and left bewildered. Later she came to me and wondered why I would do such a frivolous thing as watch TV when it wasn't even a religious programme. Didn't I feel it was wrong? Shouldn't I have been upstairs praying for them and my talk rather than living exactly as they did? Was I giving them a worldly model instead of a spiritual one?

This incident raises some very important questions for us in evangelism. For example, what does it mean to be holy? How much are we to identify with the world? When are we in danger of being indistinguishable from the world? Many times I've seen Christians keep themselves at arm's length from their non-Christian friends because they thought they were thereby being spiritual. But when our understanding of spirituality isolates us from people as well as from our culture, then we have misunderstood true holiness. If we grasp Jesus' approach to holiness, we will not be isolated from others, but neither will we be identical. Holiness, in fact, is not merely a concern of Jesus'; it was vitally important in the Hebrew Bible as well.

For example, the Old Testament is a profoundly moral book. Through Moses came the first major expression of the depths of God's concern for morality, for instance, in the Ten Commandments. Nathan boldly rebuked David concerning moral fault with Bathsheba (2 Sam. 12:1–9), and Elijah confronted Ahab concerning Naboth's vineyard (1 Kgs. 21:17–19). But the moral nature of God is chiefly brought home to us through the prophets Amos, Hosea and Isaiah. The Old Testament indeed dealt seriously with the question of inner sin and morality.

Also, it is a common misconception that the law only referred to external conformity and not to a conformity of the heart in regard to holiness. The facts are otherwise. As Gustave Oehler says, 'The law insists on the disposition of the heart, when it says in Exodus 20:17, "Thou shalt not covet"; when it binds men to love God with the whole heart and soul, to be placable toward their fellow men, and the like, Deut. 6:5; Lev. 19:17.'[2] H. W. Robinson adds a similar note, 'Even the Priestly Code, with all its elaborate precautions for ceremonial holiness, is still, in large measure, a moral document, the outcome of a passion for perfection that shall be worthy of Yahweh.'[3]

Finally, the holiness code in Leviticus begins in chapter 19 with, 'You shall be holy, for I the LORD your God am holy' (verse 2). Then toward the end of chapter 20 the Lord says again, 'You shall be holy to me; for I the LORD am holy' (verse

26). Just examining what Leviticus 19 and 20 have to say about what constitutes holy behaviour is enlightening: Revere your parents. Do not steal or lie. Be a good neighbour. Be reasonable with your neighbour. Pay a decent wage. Do no injustice. Be not partial to the poor or defer to the great. Give honest weights and measures.

Holiness, from God's perspective, is intimately connected to how we treat people. Holiness is rooted in relationship.

As we have commented previously, not all of the Pharisees were critical of Jesus. But those who did criticize Jesus for not being a holy man tended to concern themselves with the external, ceremonial manifestations of sin. Even though biblical teaching showed otherwise, they behaved as if evil came only from the outside. When one's concern is only for external evil, then the logical way to avoid being 'contaminated' is to avoid the object altogether, or worse, to blame the object for causing the problem.

Take the problem of lust. Both Jesus and the Pharisees agreed it was wrong. But if one sees evil as externally imposed, then the culprit is not one's desire but the person desired. One very orthodox sect called the 'Bruised and Bleeding' Pharisees thought lust was evil. So they determined they would avoid the source of the problem, namely, women. And whenever they came into the presence of a woman, not only would they avoid talking to her, but they would close their eyes so they could not see her at all. Of course, this caused them to run into walls, and hence their name. Can you imagine the shock of an exceedingly pious member of the 'Bruised and Bleeding' sect walking by and discovering Jesus deeply engaged in conversation with a prostitute? Activity like this made it difficult for them to believe that Jesus was a holy man.

And so the critics of Jesus failed to see the devastating power and effect of such internal sins as pride, jealousy and uncharitableness. We would do well to learn from their lesson.

Jesus' understanding of holiness

Both Jesus and his critics agreed that being holy was of fundamental importance. They agreed that God's historical purpose was to call out a people for himself; that this people would be a holy people, set apart from the world to belong to him and to obey him; and that their holiness or difference would be seen in all their behaviour and outlook. Jesus demonstrated in his Sermon on the Mount how clearly he believed that we were to be different. In Matthew 6:8 we read, 'Do not be like them.' Our character is to be completely distinct from what the world celebrates.

Jesus required a righteousness to exceed even that of the scribes and Pharisees, and to be demonstrated in the totality of his followers' lives – both in ethical behaviour and in their religious devotion. Jesus took holiness seriously, but he and the Pharisees radically differed over the nature of holiness. Let us look at Jesus' understanding of holiness.

Radical identification, radical difference

The Pharisees understood holiness in terms of ceremonial purification and separation from the masses. But Jesus demonstrated what holiness is through his radical identification with and his radical difference from the world. As A. T. Robertson comments, the Pharisees 'were aloof in spirit and built up a hedge around themselves to keep off infection. Jesus plunged into the midst of the disease and sin to root both out.'[4] Jesus walked alongside people. He was approachable. He allowed a prostitute at Simon's banquet to express her love and devotion to him by touching him (Luke 7:36–50). He accepted people as they were.

But we must remember the other side too. Jesus called his disciples to be different as well. He identified, yes, but he was never identical with the world. My fear today is that we may enjoy talking of the Christian's pharisaic problem while we ignore the call to be different. We must never try to escape from the truth that there is a fundamental difference between Christians and non-Christians. If we ignore or minimize this difference, we will be of little use to God or to the world.

Jesus tells us that we are salt and light (Matt. 5:13–16). Jesus does not say that we are to become light. Jesus says, 'You are light.' So we must begin reflecting who we really are and not try to hide it.

Perhaps our mistake is to settle for a far too superficial

difference, one that focuses mostly on externals and personal disciplines. If you asked religious sceptics what they felt made a Christian different, their answer probably would be frightfully inadequate. Once in an evangelistic talk I asked some seekers what they thought the big issues were for Christians, what we truly fight for.

In utter seriousness a male student answered, 'Judging from what I've seen, you stand against swearing, dirty jokes and rowdy parties. Is that right?'

'I think there are larger issues than that for Christians,' I said. 'For example, Christians are against murder.'

Everyone laughed, and he said, 'I hardly think anyone wouldn't be, but that issue doesn't come up very often.'

'Oh? Do you know how Jesus defines murder? He says it's murder when we destroy people with our words. It's murder when we put people down and treat them as insignificant.' I was referring here to Jesus' Sermon on the Mount, especially Matthew 5:21–22.

There was an instant hush in the audience. He said, 'I had no idea that Christianity had to do with how you treat people. I thought it was merely do's and don'ts and being sure you don't swear.'

What a stunning rebuke when the world believes that the only difference between us lies in *their* greater ability to tolerate four-letter expletives. Imagine how powerful our witness would be if unbelievers saw that the real 'language issue' for Christians is that we refuse to gossip and speak judgmentally of others. If only we lived like that! Jim Cymbala said in a magazine interview that what most sapped the Christian's witness and spiritual power was grieving and quenching the Spirit's power through gossip and slander.

How, then, are we to be different? John Stott in his treatment of the Sermon on the Mount summarizes this portion of Matthew and consequently defines our 'difference' this way: (1) a Christian's character (for example, we thirst for righteousness, we are peacemakers, we are pure in heart); (2) a Christian's influence (we are salt and light in our communities); (3) a Christian's righteousness (we are conformed to God's moral teaching); (4) a Christian's piety (which is marked by our sincerity of devotion); (5) a Christian's ambitions (we seek first the glory of God instead of self-centred material wealth and possessions); (6) a Christian's relationships (we do not judge others but we serve them); and (7) a Christian's commitment (we obey Christ as Lord).[5]

I frequently hear that the call to be holy and the call to demonstrate love to sinners are mutually exclusive. (As if love were the antithesis to holiness!) Jesus welcomed and loved sinners; he did not drive them away by too much affectation of righteousness. He showed genuine compassion for people, but he was also direct and uncompromising in denouncing sin. Jesus had compassion, but there was also toughness in his love. He won them without sacrificing the purity of his life.

The paradox of *agapē* love is that we accept our neighbours unconditionally and with open arms and at the same time desire God's very best for their lives. If Jesus is our Lord, our compassion will be shaped by his moral absolutes. Christ both was merciful and made judgments. Some things, he said, were immoral and destructive, but he never ceased to love. Indeed, it was his love that prompted his judgment.

But Jesus could keep that delicate balance of expressing love and truth without crushing people, we say. How can we ever achieve such a thing? How can God use us to bring conviction of sin without our coming off as judgmental and unloving?

The truth is, it is the Spirit of God who convicts a person of sin, not us. Nevertheless, God uses us to mediate both his love and his holiness to others. By our being prisms of his presence, a conviction of sin may come. But how?

I know a Christian woman who has cared deeply for a non-Christian woman who has indulged in more sins than I care to count. Her life is a mess. One day this woman said to the Christian, 'It's funny, my pagan friends tell me they accept me. They say it doesn't matter what I do. I'm free. Yet it's only with you that I feel loved and safe, and I know I could always come to you. But it's also only with you that I feel remorse for what I'm doing, and I long to clean up my act and get my life together.'

That is holiness. Sometimes the very presence of the Holy Spirit within us brings conviction of sin to another, without our ever saying a word. This is especially true when we pray for that person. God's love in us never abandons; it identifies deeply with individual people. But it also brings the reality of God's presence, the purity of his holiness. It is not intimidated by, nor does it flee from, the crisis of sin; neither does it deny the reality of sin's existence.

But sometimes it is the very love of God that demands that we speak painful truth to a friend. For example, a seeker friend of mine was committing adultery. I agonized over what to say to her. I knew how negative her experience with Christians had been. I knew I could easily lose her friendship if she thought I was writing her off because she was sinful. At the same time it was clear to anyone who looked at her that she was miserable. Indeed, she sometimes pondered aloud why she couldn't seem to find happiness. So I prayed and asked the Lord to show me what to say.

The next time she mentioned how depressed she was, I said, 'I know you are unhappy. Yet I wonder if you realize that what you are searching for is exactly right. You want to be loved and cherished, and for the ache and emptiness in your heart to go away. The trouble is, you are looking for answers in the very places that are destroying you. Breaking your marriage vows and getting a quick love-fix is not the answer. It's only adding to the problems you already have. You already know I'm going to say this, but I believe the only thing that will fill that void inside of you is God.'

That was the first time I had ever mentioned what I thought about her affair. But instead of being defensive or angry, she thanked me for loving her enough to tell the truth. We need to be very prayerful about whether to speak and what we say and whether we have gained enough trust to speak frankly. Yet my experience has been that as we ask God to show us what to say, he will help us communicate painful truth in a way that they can hear. They may not receive it, but at least they know that we love them too much to stand by silently and watch them destroy themselves.

There are other ways that God's holy presence in us can be expressed to the world. One of the greatest differences about Christians is that we know we are sinners. Therefore, we have the freedom to admit our sins and weaknesses. We are also free to share how God is helping us overcome our temptations.

Our honesty with seekers about our struggles does several

things. First, it punctures the stereotype that Christians think they are perfect. We don't excuse sin by rationalizing it. Indeed, it's because we take sin so seriously that we try to develop a realistic understanding of who we are, warts and all. Our self-honesty, however, leads us to hope, because we see that God is changing us, not overnight and not without setbacks, but slowly and surely.

Our honesty before others also shatters the stereotype that all Christians are judgmental and critical people. By sharing our weaknesses, we acknowledge that we not only understand the human condition but we, too, must overcome it! We are not 'finished products', yet we rejoice that by God's grace we are being strengthened to change. Owning our sins and temptations can actually lead seekers to experience conviction for their sins.

Jake, who is in recovery from substance and alcohol abuse, told me that when he first became a Christian he tried to cover up his past problems. He particularly feared that his admission of being a recovering alcoholic would lessen the power of his testimony to unbelievers. But slowly he realized that, by hiding his past and the fact that he needed to go to recovery meetings weekly to maintain his sobriety, he was actually neutralizing the power of the gospel. What he was inadvertently communicating was that God wasn't great enough and loving enough to forgive him.

Jake recently made a long car trip with Randy, a sceptic friend who is also in recovery. During the trip Jake told Randy about his pilgrimage with Jesus. Along the way they stopped at Jake's parents' home. 'You have no idea what a big step that was for me, Becky. When I was at school,' Jake told me, 'I would never let my friends drop me off anywhere near my home. My family is so profoundly dysfunctional. I was mortified to think anyone would discover the truth. But since I've been walking with Christ, I've slowly come to accept my roots and not feel that I must cower in shame.'

Amazingly, it was that act that opened his friend's interest in the gospel. Jake's friend also came from a deeply dysfunctional family, but he detested them. Randy was fascinated that Jake's belief in Jesus freed him to own the truth about himself and to love his family.

'Why aren't you ashamed to let me meet your family?' Randy candidly asked.

'Because I've finally learned where my true worth comes from,' said Jake. 'Yes, my parents are very broken people, and I grieve for them, but no human being can tell me who I am. Only God gives true identity and lasting worth.'

The 'holy difference' that Randy saw in Jake was not that Jake never struggled with temptation or that his life was free from suffering. What he saw was that, in knowing Jesus, Jake was finding the strength not only to overcome his addiction but also to accept the most painful elements of his life with love, grace and serenity.

But let's remember that God's holiness in our lives can be expressed in joyful ways too. We do much to further the kingdom of God when people see that we know how to celebrate life. A Christian friend of mine, Jody, told me she has a neighbour who is a devotee of the New Age because, she says, 'they only emphasize the positive. There is none of the negative stuff you get with Christianity.'

One day Jody rang me, laughing and reciting the following story: 'My neighbour called me and she said, "Jody, you have really convicted me of something." Becky, I was alarmed because I knew how defensive she was toward anything she considered negative, especially from Christians! Then she continued, "You have really convicted me," she said, "that I don't know how to have fun."'

'What?' asked Jody, as puzzled as she was stunned.

'Jody, you enjoy life. You know when to stop working and relax. You just have more fun living life than I do. All I do is work and worry. You're going to have to teach me how to lighten up! Do you think it has something to do with your faith?' she asked.

'Becky, I had hoped that my life was a witness to her. But if you asked me to guess how I was influencing her view of Christianity, I would have never dreamed it had anything to do with my "fun quotient",' Jody confided.

So let us remember as we witness to others what Ignatius wrote: 'The glory of God is a person fully alive.'

We must ask ourselves, *Do I identify enough? Do I welcome people, or am I a member of the holy huddle, the local God squad?*

Do I hang around with people of various beliefs and mores? Do I love the unlovely? Or, on the other hand, am I different enough? Am I Christlike? Do I bring this aspect of Christ's holiness, of his moral standards, of the fruit of the Spirit to my relationships? Or, out of my sincere desire to identify and to love, have I become culture-accommodating?

Jesus had the ministry of the towel but he also had the ministry of the whip. Our lives as Christians, if we are to be effective evangelists, should reflect that same dual stance toward the world.

6

A question of obedience:
another way of knowing God

When we listen to someone explain how we get to know God, we hear frequent references to believing in Jesus, opening up our hearts to him or asking him to come into our lives. We are to make a decision for Christ or pray a prayer or walk down an aisle. Of course, these things – believing, deciding, accepting – really are essential.

But how often do we hear references to a genuine change in the direction of our lives? How often do we ourselves, as we tell someone about Jesus, point out that obedience to Christ as Lord is also involved? Cathy, the seventeen-year-old runaway I met on a coach, for instance, could have avoided making fundamental mistakes if she had understood the importance of obedience.

The Pharisees' view of knowing God

The Pharisees studied God. They memorized the Scriptures and knew every word. They even devised games with their scrolls. They would throw a dart into a rolled-up scroll. The word would be read where the dart landed and they would then have to recite the rest of the verse. They felt that through study they could find God and that knowledge was the avenue to transformation. Jesus himself commented to the Pharisees, 'You search the scriptures, because you think that in them you have eternal life' (John 5:39). To know the Scriptures is to know God, they thought.

There are two points to be made about this. First, knowledge is not enough for salvation. The Pharisees considered themselves supremely righteous because of their vast knowledge.

But they misunderstood a vital point. Mere information makes no-one righteous; it only makes us responsible for what we know. It is impotent to effect real and lasting change within us. One may be over-educated and untransformed.

The Hebrews' understanding of knowledge, however, is that the degree to which we know something is the degree to which we have integrated it into our everyday life. It is of no use to say we believe in something when our actions betray our beliefs. To know is not only to verbalize or intellectualize; it is to submit in obedience with our lives as well. The Pharisees are a positive model for us in this regard. They knew that if they spoke of faith in God, there must be evidence or fruit in their lives to demonstrate this faith.

So the Pharisees took obedience seriously. They tried to obey the ceremonial laws. In fact, they could hardly obey enough. They constantly kept adding new laws. But they understood one very important thing: we are responsible for what we know. Knowledge must automatically translate into obedience, be it words or action. And so the Pharisees tried to integrate into their lives the part of Scripture they chose to focus upon.

So the key question is: what does it mean to obey? 'The word "obedience" does not mean slavish, uncritical adherence; it comes from the Latin root *audire*, which means "to listen." Obedience requires the discerning ear, the ear that listens for the reality of the situation, a listening that allows the hearer to respond to that reality, whatever it may be.'[1]

We must learn from the Pharisees' mistakes here. There are three basic issues. The first issue is: what do we obey? Jesus told them they sought life in the wrong place. 'I am the way, and the truth, and the life,' Jesus said. Those who sought truth were invited into a relationship with him. The Scriptures pointed to him, but they were not to be worshipped. That's because to know and obey the truth comes not from a superficial quest for facts but from entering into a relationship of intimate trust and obedience with Jesus. Truth is known in relationship to God through Christ.

Jesus also pointed out the irony that the Pharisees claimed to revere Scripture yet rejected the very person that Scripture proclaimed. If they really believed Scripture, they would have believed in Jesus, and they would have been drawn to worship him. So an attempt merely to obey the laws of the Bible is not enough. We must obey Christ. Indeed, it is our failure to obey God's law that drives us to realize that we need the inner transformation Christ offers.

The second issue is: why must we obey? The motive for our obedience is as important as the act of obedience itself. God requires heart obedience that is motivated by our love and sincerity of devotion to him. Merely to obey rules at a superficial level and not to allow God total access to our person prevents us from having deep contact with God. We do not obey in order to earn our salvation. We must not obey out of pride. Rather, we obey because of who God is and the marvellous work he has done in seeking and saving us. It was something we could never have done on our own.

The third issue is: how broad is the scope of our obedience? The answer is absolute and universal. We are called to obey the whole revelation of God. Jesus tells us to. We must not pick and choose what we will obey. We cannot focus on the aspects of Scripture we find appealing and ignore that which is hard or uncomfortable. That was the heart of Jesus' criticism of the Pharisees.

It is true, of course, that none of us can encompass the depth of all God's desires for us as expressed in Scripture. We are finite. But what we know we must obey. We are called on to meditate on his Word consciously and regularly, to ignore no portion of it by design or planned blindness, to read both Old and New Testaments, both the Law and the Prophets, both the Gospels and Epistles. It is only by such an overview that we can help prevent the sort of blindness evidenced by some of the Pharisees.

Jesus' view of knowing God

How do we find God and grow in him? Jesus was adamant at this point. He said we must do what he says. We must put into practical obedience the knowledge we have. He continually asked people to drop their nets, to sell all they had and to follow him.

We might say that Jesus had a theology of obedience. And the object of this obedience was a living person – not a historical norm, not a code of laws, but himself. He called people to be accountable to God whether they were believers or sceptics who were searching. For example, he told his disciples, 'What is the point of calling me, "Lord, Lord," without doing what I tell you to do?' (Luke 6:46, Phillips).

To the Pharisaic lawyer who came to trap him in debate, Jesus' response was no different (Luke 10:25–37). 'What must I do to inherit eternal life?' the lawyer asked. And Jesus told him to recite what he understood, which was to love God totally as well as his neighbours as himself.

This lawyer was not a follower of Jesus, and his motive in the conversation was 'to put him to the test' (verse 25). So how did Jesus help him understand the true way? Well, by many standards of evangelizing, Jesus did a rotten job. Jesus did not have the lawyer 'pray the prayer'. Nor did Jesus ask him to read a tract on the five points that lead to salvation. He simply said, 'Go and do it.' In other words, 'Begin to put into practical obedience what you understand.' He called him to be responsible to the light he had already received.

Jesus knew that obedience to his and his Father's words yielded faith, that revelation is based upon obedience. Over and over again Jesus called people to faith and obedience. If I had to sum up a person's response to the gospel message, I would say it's 'Paint or get off the ladder.' Jesus approached people exactly like that. He told them to pick up their brush and paint something.

Do you want to discover who Jesus is and deal honestly with your doubts? Jesus' style is not to suggest that you go and ponder the virgin birth for three months but to begin doing what he says. This challenge can mean much to us as we engage in evangelism.

Jesus' emphasis on obedience is greatly needed today. Unfortunately much of western theology is over-intellectualized. Biblical teaching, on the other hand, is intimately connected with action and life; it is associated with the situation we live in. If some of the Pharisees thought that through knowledge and legalistic obedience one could know God, our present generation may be in even worse shape. We tend to think of knowledge only in cerebral terms, as facts to be memorized rather than as truth that demands our transformation.

When I did Christian work among students I used to ask them if they had learned much at a weekend conference. They would often answer, 'Oh, yes. I took masses of notes.'

And my response would be, 'You don't have to show me your notebooks. If you learned anything, I'll see it in your life.'

Jesus was not the originator of the call to obedience. In the Hebrew Bible as well as in the New Testament there is a consensus. Indeed, Yahweh's purpose is that we should learn to say, 'I delight to do your will, O my God' (Ps. 40:8). God seeks our fellowship with him through our moral obedience. H. W. Robinson writes, 'This is salvation in the deeper and more spiritual sense of the Old Testament ... But even in the religion of the Law ... obedience to the revealed will of Yahweh is recognized as the supreme end of man and the supreme glory of God. The attitude of Jesus to the will of God and his emphasis on the absolute worth of obedience as the supreme "value" of human life are the best illustrations of what the Old Testament indicates as the purposes of Yahweh in creation and providence.'[2] Obedience is critical because it reveals a harmony of purpose between the human will and the divine. And Jesus is our supreme example of one who was utterly obedient to the Father's will.

Jesus' emphasis on faith and obedience also helps us to understand the role of repentance in conversion and discipleship. Too many people believe a Christian is a person who has simply 'prayed the prayer' and 'decided for Jesus'. But many such 'Christians' do not live as if they are under new management. They may claim that they once made a decision, but everything else in their life is unchanged. What a superficial understanding of what it means to be a Christian!

Too many people have stopped at the door that leads to conversion. The door (be it a prayer, a decision or whatever) is simply that – a door. It was closed and it has been opened for one express purpose: so we can go through it and get involved in life on the other side. But some see conversion and discipleship as a revolving door that will allow them to stay there without ever actually participating in life on the other side. They have come to glorify their experience of the door when it was meant only as an avenue of passage to a new life. In fact, it is not our 'door experience' but our new life that demonstrates whether we have been converted.

A true disciple of Jesus is one who does what Jesus does – obeys the will of God. When Jesus called people to obedience, he was calling them to be accountable to God, to begin living for him as he desires. To know Jesus doesn't mean we keep the religious compartment of our lives separate and then engage in other forms of knowing as if there were no connection. 'To convert means far more than to experience the psychological, emotional aspects of change through an inner experience,' writes Jim Wallis. 'The biblical accent is clearly on a reversal of direction, a transfer of loyalties, a change in commitment leading to the creation of a new community ... It is a radical change in the whole of one's life and in all of one's relationships to the world ... We have forgotten that a relationship to Christ means a relationship to the purposes of Christ in history.'[3]

Why did Jesus call to obedience even those who were not following him? Perhaps so that their experience of conversion (that is, one of obedience) would teach them what it means to be a disciple. The more I read the Gospels, the more I realize how vital it is for sceptics to understand this. Frequently I meet sceptics who are not ready to pray and ask Christ to be the Lord of their lives. What are we to say to those who want to know if Jesus is the way but still need to 'check Jesus out' before they are guided by the Spirit into conversion?

Based on my understanding of the gospel, I now say to nonbelievers, 'Tell God (or the four walls, if that is what you think you are speaking to) that you want to find out if Jesus is truly God and that, if you could feel more certain, you would follow him. Then begin to read the Gospels every day. Each day, as you read, something will probably hit you and make sense. Whatever that is, do it as soon as you can.' In other words, I call them to act on whatever strikes them as true and to do it if they are sincerely seeking God. Then they learn from the beginning that seeking God is not simply an academic quest for facts that challenges our mind, perhaps, but leaves our inner self detached and uninvolved. They come to see that to know the truth they must practise obedience to the truth. Truth always requires us to submit. Truth transforms us.

The battle of the desk

When I was working among students, a very bright young woman, Sue, came to me. She told me that she was an agnostic but that her best friend, Larry, had become a Christian. He talked to her a lot about his faith and did not neglect her after his conversion. Instead, he brought her to Christian meetings and introduced her to his new Christian friends. He made her feel comfortable and a part of his very different Christian world. He answered as best he could her many intellectual questions about his faith. And most importantly, he loved her.

'I've seen what faith in Christ has done for Larry,' she told me. 'I see the love these Christians have for each other and for me. I've seen what Jesus is like in the Gospels and a lot of my questions have been answered. But I still don't believe. I'd like to find God, but I'm plagued with doubts. Please don't ask me to pray to receive Christ; it'd be dishonest. What should I do?'

I suggested what I mentioned above, read the Scriptures and look for an opportunity to put it into practice. She gulped and said, 'That's radical. But I'll do it.'

So she began having what she called her 'pagan devotions.' And the Christians around her prayed that God would speak to her in the Scriptures and give her concrete situations in which she could obey. Several months later she said she wanted to talk to me. Here is Sue's story:

'One day I read in the Bible, "if someone steals your coat, don't let him have only that, but offer your cloak as well." For whatever reason, that verse hit me between the eyes. So I said to the four walls, "Listen, walls – or God, if you're there – I'm going to do what this verse says, if the opportunity arises today. I want to remind you that I'm trying to do things your way to find out if you exist and if Jesus really is who he says. Amen."

'The day went by and I forgot the verse. Then I headed for the library to continue working on my thesis. Just as I sat down at my designated desk, this guy comes up and starts yelling at me. He told me he hadn't been allocated a desk, so he was going to take mine. I started shouting back, and pretty soon we caused quite a commotion. But it was when he glared at me and said, "Look. I'm taking it from you whether you like it or not," that it suddenly hit me.

'I just looked at him and moaned, "Ohhhhh, no. No. I can't believe it." And to myself I thought, "Look, God, if you're there, I do want to know if Jesus is God. But isn't there some other way of finding out besides obeying that verse? I mean, couldn't I tithe or get baptized or give up something else? But don't take my desk! I mean, with my luck, I'll give up the desk and then discover that you don't exist."

'But I couldn't escape the fact that I had read that verse the very same day someone tried to rob me. Before, I had always been amused to see how Jesus aimed for whatever was controlling the person in his conversations with people in the Bible. But now it didn't feel so funny. I took a deep breath, tried not to swear and said, "OK, let me think about it."

'He looked bewildered. But just at that moment the librarian came up. She said she'd heard the conversation and was angered by his behaviour. But he immediately began swearing at her and intimidated her so much that she told us we would have to see his tutor. So we trotted over to his tutor's office. It was clear to me by now that this guy carried around a lot of rage and was probably a troubled person. The more the guy ranted and raved, the more agitated the adviser became. Finally the adviser said, "Well, what does Sue think we should do?"

'All this time I kept thinking about what I'd seen in these past several months. I'd seen Larry's life changed. I'd seen something beautiful in this Christian fellowship, something so real I could almost touch it. Even though I was not a Christian, I had been loved by these people. And I'd seen Jesus in the Bible. I felt so drawn to him. I realized that, even without a desk, somehow I still had more than this poor, pathetic guy. I told the adviser that he could have the desk, and the meeting was over.

'When we walked out of the door, he grabbed my arm and asked me why in the world I let him have my desk. I told him he would think I had flipped, but I was trying to discover if Jesus was really who he claimed to be. In order to know if Jesus was really the way to God, I was attempting to obey the things he told us to do. "So I've been reading the Gospels. And today I read that if somebody tried to rip me off, I was supposed to let them – and even throw in something extra to boot." All I could see were the whites of his eyes. "So I'm going to give you the desk, but don't press your luck about something extra."

'Then he asked, "Why in the world would Jesus say such a senseless thing?"

'Then I said, "Hey, if there's one thing I've learned from reading about Jesus and meeting these Christians, it's that Jesus wants to give us a whole lot more than a desk if we'd let him. I think the basic idea is that it's knowing Jesus that makes us rich, not owning possessions. So that desk is yours."

'Becky, as I said those words, I just simply *knew* it was all true. I knew it from the inside out. I sort of felt as though God was saying, "Well done. That's the way I want my children to behave."'

There were a lot of things that Sue did not understand about being a Christian when she became one. But there was one thing she did know: to follow Jesus, or to *know* Jesus, we must do what he says. I am not suggesting that we must do this with every sceptic we meet. But this understanding that to know truth will require us to change by submitting to obedience, must permeate more of our evangelism. Obviously we must be sensitive to what the Holy Spirit is doing in a person's life. But we need to call people to as much commitment as they have been prepared for.

Not everyone we meet is ready to accept Christ as Saviour, but everyone is on a continuum in their relationship to Christ. Our task is to draw them closer to the point where they choose to become disciples. One way to do this is to call them to accountability for what they know. We do not need to be belligerent. A gentle suggestion can be devastatingly effective.

The call to repentance

Jesus calls sceptics to obedience for another reason. The call to obey can also be a call to repentance. Jesus told the lawyer in Luke 10:37 to go and be a 'neighbour' like the good Samaritan. Superficially that sounds like sheer humanism. Jesus seemingly forgot to tell the lawyer he was the Son of God, that salvation rests in him alone, indeed that it is only through Jesus that we can truly love our neighbour anyway! But maybe Jesus had a different strategy. Jesus called him to obey the light he had been given.

Suppose the lawyer went out and sincerely tried to love his neighbour in ways he had never tried before. And since his consciousness had been raised, he would be more sensitive to failure than ever before. Suppose he realized he could not cut the mustard. The harder he tried to love, the more he was aware of his inadequacies. Perhaps on a return visit to Jesus he would say, 'I need help. I can't do it. I've tried to do what you said. Where do I go to get help?' I have a hunch Jesus' second conversation would be very different from the first.

To encourage people to reach out to God, to put him to the test, to do what he says (as a means of finding out if God is there) is to communicate that God is alive. We must live by our belief that the kingdom of God is at hand. We believe God is living and at work. Our faith is not in a historical model; it is in a living Lord. This sense of the aliveness and nearness of God must permeate our evangelism. As Chesterton writes, 'Plato has told you a truth; but Plato is dead. Shakespeare has startled you with an image; but Shakespeare will not startle you any more. But imagine what it would be to live with such men still living, to know that Plato might break out with an original lecture tomorrow, or that at any moment Shakespeare might shatter everything with a single song.' The person who lives in contact with the living God is a person 'always expecting to meet Plato or Shakespeare tomorrow at breakfast'.[4]

Our evangelism will be more vital and substantial, and our efforts will be longer lasting, when we help our sceptical friends see that God is alive and present, that they may discover him by putting his commands into practice and that real conviction that Jesus is God is evidenced not by sentimental feelings about God but by obedience to him. Indeed, it is through obedience that we discover who God is as well as deepen our knowledge of him.

A lifestyle of evangelism

In this and the previous two chapters we have looked at Jesus' lifestyle and priorities as demonstrated by his values in three areas. We saw, first, that his life was marked by a deep love for God, his neighbour and himself. Then we noted how his holiness was reflected through his radical identification with the world as well as his radical difference from the world. Finally, we saw how his love and devotion to the Father were evidenced by his obedience to the Father's will.

If we are to be followers of Jesus, his values must permeate our values. We need to be concerned more with how our lives reflect his love, his holiness and his obedience than with the latest witnessing techniques. When we live as Jesus did, in his power and with his presence, seekers will be drawn to us. Evangelism will not be a dreaded task to be ticked off every Wednesday. Rather, sharing Jesus will become a true delight and evangelism will become a lifestyle.

7

Christ with us

It is easy enough to say that when we live our lives by Jesus' values, evangelism will come naturally. But how do we live our lives like Jesus? It seems too much to ask. Jesus, after all, was God incarnate. I am just a human being – frail, frightened and essentially unable to live up to this ideal.

Of course, you alone can't live up to the ideal. Neither can I. But God knows this, and he has not left us to go it alone. Jesus is with us, and by the power of the Holy Spirit, he calls, equips us and motivates us for ministry. This is the first bit of good news. The second is like it. The presence of Christ brings us his power and ability to use our limited resources in his limitless ways.

Third, Jesus is with us, not only by being in us through the indwelling of the Holy Spirit, but by being a part of those to whom we are called to minister. All people have been created in God's image. When we meet them in a real, personal encounter, we are meeting something of Christ. We are indeed not alone. And that's what we want to see more clearly now.

Jesus in us

We may recall that Jesus told the Pharisee lawyer to be 'a neighbour'. So is that all there is to being a disciple of Jesus? Is it merely to be kind and loving to the people next door? Is it simply to begin serving others? Luke apparently did not think so, for he followed this story with the familiar Mary and Martha passage (Luke 10:38–42).

Immediately after reading how Jesus told the lawyer to go and serve others, we find Martha doing exactly what Jesus requested. She was serving others by preparing a meal. But, we are told, she was 'distracted with much serving'. Why was this? Was she not doing all that Jesus required? Why couldn't she serve with peace and joy? Perhaps because she failed to do what Mary did. Mary allowed Jesus to serve her first. And Jesus said Mary had made a better choice.

This passage emphasizes that serving others is not enough. Indeed, our ministry to others is dependent on our being fed by Christ himself. And it is the Holy Spirit who makes Jesus alive to us and nourishes him in us. Therefore, the Spirit of God is an absolute requisite for what we are called to do. We can learn all sorts of counselling skills, acquire techniques and develop razor-sharp programmes in evangelism, but we will have no lasting impact unless God's Spirit is central in our ministry. We must ask for God's Spirit to anoint us and equip us for the ministry he calls us to. We can no more make a person become a Christian than we can make ourselves new people.

That is the frustration of the law. It can show us what to do, but it cannot make us want to do it. Only the Holy Spirit (and our obedient will) can bring about transformation. We must pray, first, for a renewal of the Holy Spirit in our lives as we seek to minister, and then for his activity in the lives of the people we are seeking. And in a mysterious way, prayer frees God's Spirit to move.

Indeed, prayer is another absolute requisite for evangelizing, for through prayer God changes us and our friends into the likeness of Christ. Just as we pray daily that God's Spirit will renew us and equip us for the ministry he has called us to, so must we pray daily for the conversion of our friends. And not only for the long-range goal of conversion but also for the step-by-step process of gradual acceptance that will result in conversion.

It is helpful to have a prayer partner, perhaps one other Christian living near you who wants to love that community through you. We need to be diligent and persistent in praying for those God brings to us.

When I was in Spain and knew I would be going on to study at the University of Illinois, I asked God to bring the most open seekers and seat them next to me. For three months in Spain I prayed for those whom God would put to my right or my left in lectures.

When I arrived home, I phoned Beth Goldhor Domig, a good friend, and asked her if she would pray with me. We dreamed together, prayed together and set goals together. One goal was that after the first month of term we would begin an investigative Bible discussion. One month later we started a study for our sceptic friends. Four of the ones I brought had sat next to me on the first day of lectures. Beth brought those she befriended on her corridor in the first week.

Ask God to show you just one or two people whom he wants to seek through you. Find someone who will pray and share that dream with you as Beth did with me. And remember in all of this prayer and activity that great mystery of the indwelling of Jesus – 'Christ in you, the hope of glory' (Col. 1:27).

Jesus with us

When we begin to realize the reality and power of Jesus' presence in our daily living, our evangelism takes on fresh force. The failure to see how dramatically Jesus' presence affects a situation is, however, a problem his followers have always had.

In Mark 6:30–44 we read how the disciples had just returned from a successful preaching and healing journey. They were tired and Jesus suggested they go away in the boat to find a place to rest. But as they started to dock, they saw five thousand people waiting on shore for Jesus. (I am not so sure the disciples gave the crowd a big smile on their first glimpse of them!) Jesus felt compassion for them since they looked like 'sheep without a shepherd'. So he taught them all day.

When it grew dark and dinner-time came, the disciples told Jesus to send the crowd away. When Jesus asked why they could not feed them, they responded cynically, 'Oh, sure, with the thousands of pounds we just happened to bring along?' But Jesus told them to divide the multitude into groups of hundreds and fifties. He took five loaves and two fish and thanked God for them. (No doubt Jesus was the only one who was grateful for so small an amount!) He touched the food and fed the five thousand.

How did the disciples fail here, and what can we learn from

it? First, they failed to offer their limited resources. They looked at the task and their meagre supplies and concluded it was impossible. They forgot that Jesus could take natural elements and do supernatural things with them.

Jesus did not look at the five loaves and two fish and say, 'This is terrible. Such a tiny amount of food for all these people! I'll just have to do a miracle and whip up some food from nothing.' It is significant that he worked with what the disciples had.

When we find ourselves in situations that seem beyond our limits (actually we should look for such situations!), we must not hesitate because we feel inadequate. We must not complain about our limited resources. God tells us he is glorified in our weakness. God's Spirit will take and multiply what we have.

Second, the disciples failed to see the power of Jesus' presence. Jesus prayed and then touched the food, and there was more than enough for everyone. Because of who he is, when Jesus touches anything, there is blessing.

But what about us? When we follow Jesus, his Spirit abides in us. That means he is a part of what we do. Everything we touch Jesus touches. If he touched the fish and multiplied them, then how does he touch our activities? He is with us when we gather for Bible discussion, when we eat and dance and work. And Jesus reaches out and touches others through us.

Maggie was struck by Jesus' feeding of the multitudes. She decided to reach out to students on her corridor by having an ice-cream party. She bought the ice-cream, borrowed a scoop and said, 'God, I have trouble believing that you can work through this ice-cream party to tell others of your love. But you dwell in me, so this isn't an ordinary ice-cream party. You are here. Love these people tonight.'

I went to the party and the room was packed with hungry students. The atmosphere was lively and fun. To my knowledge, no-one had a spiritual discussion. Afterward she told me, 'Well, it was a failure. I don't think Jesus was working here.'

'Why?' I asked.

'Because no-one even talked about him. All we did was have fun!'

Maggie demonstrated several misconceptions. First, that having fun was a waste of time. She felt every minute had to be used in serious spiritual pursuit. She did not believe that God would approve of lively spontaneity. Second, she believed that spiritual ministry occurs only when one is speaking about God. If that is true, then God has to work with severe limits. But it is not true. God works as powerfully through the non-verbal as he does through the verbal. We, too, must offer both. We need to let Jesus loose! Remember that Jesus is reaching out to everyone you reach. He wants to speak through everything that you do, not just your verbal witness.

The sequel to the ice-cream party shows this. Maggie told me the next day that eight students came to her. One girl said, 'I couldn't believe you spent your money on ice-cream for us! It was good fun. You made our floor feel like a family for the first time. Why did you do it?'

Another said, 'My friend and I had a great time. We decided we're going to have a party next week!'

And another said, 'It was so nice of you to do that. You know, I felt love bouncing off those walls. What are you into?'

Then Maggie said to me, 'I told you Jesus wasn't at work at that party – that he wasn't showing people who he was. I am the Christian and never noticed him there, but my non-Christian friends did. They don't know who he is yet, but they sensed his presence. I wonder how much I've been limiting Jesus all along?'

When, through the power of the Holy Spirit, we let Jesus reach the people among whom we live, he will create a family atmosphere. Jesus will give people a sense of worth. And his love is contagious; people will imitate it. They will be drawn to us at first without knowing why. What we must not forget is that we incarnate Jesus! Whatever our life intersects with, so does Jesus. Whomever we touch Jesus touches. We do not simply give the gospel – we are the gospel.

Jesus in others

We know we are called to reach out and care for people, but some of us feel so painfully shy that we die a slow death in starting a conversation. Some of us do not feel naturally drawn to people. Reaching out to them seems foreign and makes us uncomfortable.

Learning to care for others requires several things. First, it demands practice. The disciples developed compassion very slowly. For most of them it was a long, hard process that required self-denial and work.

Second, it requires us to look outward. To be consumed with shyness or indifference may have emotional roots or it may mean one is consumed with self. Disciples of Jesus must focus their attention outward in servanthood. We do not listen to others or serve others because we happen to feel like it; we do it out of obedience. I usually find that my compassionate feelings follow obedience (if they were not there at the beginning).

Finally, learning to care for others requires sound theology. Nothing should warm our hearts more than remembering what Jesus is like. We cannot love him long without loving what he loves. We must not forget that Jesus was an agent of creation. His image, however marred now, is stamped in each one of us. That means that whomever we touch bears his image.

Mother Teresa discussed this point in a talk she gave in Philadelphia.[1] She said that after Mass one morning she spoke to a group of sisters. 'During the Mass,' she said, 'you saw that the priest touched the body of Christ with great love and tenderness. When you touch the poor today, you too will be touching the body of Christ. Give them that same love and tenderness.'

Several hours later a young nun came to Mother Teresa, her face radiant. 'I have been touching the body of Christ for three hours,' she said. Mother Teresa asked her what she meant. 'Just as we arrived, the sister brought in a man covered with maggots. He had been picked up from a gutter. I have been taking care of him. I have been touching Christ. I knew it was him,' she said.

'That young sister understood what Jesus meant when he said, "I was sick and you comforted me,"' Mother Teresa commented. 'Jesus comes to us as the sick and the homeless, he comes to us in the distressing disguise of the poor.'

We are reminded here of Jesus' own comment to his disciples as he took a child into his arms: 'Whoever welcomes this child in my name welcomes me, and whoever welcomes me welcomes the one who sent me' (Luke 9:48). This is a radical statement. It requires that we treat human life as sacred and precious, not to be manipulated on the basis of our whims or desires. It reflects what we noted above, that there is something of God's image in every person. Furthermore, when God became flesh in Jesus Christ, he showed graphically the value and dignity of all human life. No matter how distressing the disguise, Jesus tells us that when we receive one such as this, we have received him.

C. S. Lewis made the same point when he wrote:

It is a serious thing to live in a society of possible gods and goddesses, to remember that the dullest and most uninteresting person you talk to may one day be a creature which, if you saw it now, you would be strongly tempted to worship or else a horror and a corruption such as you now meet, if at all, only in a nightmare ... There are no ordinary people. You have never met a mere mortal ... But it is immortals whom we joke with, work with, marry, snub, and exploit – immortal horrors or everlasting splendours ... Next to the Blessed Sacrament itself, your neighbour is the holiest object presented to your senses.[2]

We must see in our neighbours their inherent worth and dignity. In a magazine article a young nurse writes of her pilgrimage in learning to see in a patient the image of God beneath a very 'distressing disguise'.[3]

Eileen was one of her first patients, a person who was totally helpless. 'A cerebral aneurysm (broken blood vessels in the brain) had left her with no conscious control over her body,' the nurse writes. As near as the doctors could tell, Eileen was totally unconscious, unable to feel pain and unaware of anything going on around her. It was the job of the hospital staff to turn her every hour to prevent bed sores and to feed her twice a day 'what looked like a thin mush through a stomach tube'.

Caring for her was a thankless task. 'When it's this bad,' an older student nurse told her, 'you have to detach yourself emotionally from the whole situation. Otherwise you'd throw up every time you walked into her room.' As a result, more and more she came to be treated as a thing, a vegetable, and the hospital jokes about her room were gross and dehumanizing.

But the young student nurse decided that she could not treat this person like the others had treated her. She talked to Eileen, sang to her, encouraged her and even brought her little gifts. One day when things were especially difficult and it would have been easy for the young nurse to take out her frustrations on the patient, she was especially kind. It was Thanksgiving Day and the nurse said to the patient, 'I was in a cruddy mood this morning, Eileen, because it was supposed to be my day off. But now that I'm here, I'm glad. I wouldn't have wanted to miss seeing you on Thanksgiving. Do you know this is Thanksgiving?'

Just then the telephone rang, and as the nurse turned to answer it, she looked quickly back at the patient. Suddenly, she writes, Eileen was 'looking at me ... crying. Big damp circles stained her pillow, and she was shaking all over.'

That was the only human emotion that Eileen ever showed any of them, but it was enough to change the attitude of the hospital staff toward her. Not long afterwards Eileen died. The young nurse closes her story, saying, 'I keep thinking about her ... It occurred to me that I owe her an awful lot. Except for Eileen, I might never have known what it's like to give myself to someone who can't give back.'

What struck me about this nurse and about the young nun is that they knew the poor in their midst. I wonder how many of us really know the poor? Mother Teresa asks the hard questions:

> Do we know the poor in our own family? Maybe the members of our family [or church or college fellowship] are not hungry for a piece of bread, maybe they're not naked or homeless, but do any of them feel unwanted or unloved? ... The Missionaries of Charity care for the crippled and the unwanted, the dying and the hungry, the lepers and the alcoholics. But the poor come to all of us in many forms. Let us be sure that we never turn our backs on them, wherever we may find them. For when we turn our backs on the poor, we turn them on Jesus Christ.[4]

8

Practising the presence of Christ

I was walking through an airport one day when my bag slipped and everything tumbled out. As I was stuffing things back inside, a young woman with a baby stopped to ask the time. Then she nervously bit her lip and asked, 'You don't know where I could get a drink, do you?'

I didn't. But as I searched her face, I saw that she was distraught. So I stood up and initiated a conversation.

She quickly interrupted with, 'Do you know how much a drink would cost here?'

I could see that we were getting nowhere, and suddenly I heard myself saying, 'I don't know, but would you like me to go with you to find the bar?'

'Oh, would you? I would really love the company,' she responded.

Off we went. And all the way I was kicking myself for it – going to a bar at noon with a perfect stranger. How unorthodox! Then I thought, years before it became a popular slogan, *I wonder what Jesus would do in a situation like this?*

That is just the point. What would Jesus do? In the previous chapter we saw the power and the perspective that Christ's presence brings into our lives. But what is our responsibility in being good stewards of the gift of Christ's presence? In this chapter we will look at four ways we can practise the presence of Christ: seeing people as Jesus does, loving them as they are, loving them as we are, and being salt and light in the world.

Seeing people as Jesus sees them

Often we are blind. We act as if those around us were not really people like us. If we see them bleed, we pretend they aren't really hurting. If we see them alone, we tell ourselves that they like it that way.

But Jesus wants to heal our sight. He wants us to see that the neighbour next door or the people sitting next to us on a train or plane or where we work or study are not interruptions to our schedule; they are there by divine appointment. Jesus wants us to see their needs, their loneliness, their longings, and he wants to give us the courage to reach out to them. If we are to do that, we need to do two things: we will have to take risks as well as get beneath the surface of people's lives.

To take the initiative opens us up to the risk of rejection. To let people inside our lives is a frightening but essential ingredient in evangelism. It is risky to abandon our security blankets in order to penetrate the lives of others. At the airport I wondered what I should do now that I was in the bar with the nervous woman I had just met. I realized that Jesus would probably be more concerned about why she needed a drink than about going into a tavern. I knew that if I couldn't be at ease around her when she had a drink in her hand and allow God to lead me into what he perceived as a mission field, then I wouldn't be very effective in communicating God's unconditional love.

After we found the bar, it took only minutes before she began sharing that she had decided to leave her husband. Her husband, unaware of her decision, would be meeting her at the other end of her journey. She was petrified at facing his response and felt totally alone. 'Oh, but it's ridiculous telling this to a complete stranger. How boring this must be for you!' she would comment and then talk on.

The saddest part was her obvious inability to believe anyone could care for her. She trusted almost no-one. When she mentioned a problem with which I told her I could identify, she said, 'Oh, so that's why you act as if you care. Listen, aren't you afraid of picking up strangers like me? You really should be more careful.'

As I began to tell her who God was and that he was the one who brought me into situations like this, she seemed to hang on every word. Soon we were walking to her plane, but I felt torn. I wanted to reach out to her and tell her how moved I was by her problems and that God cared deeply for her, but she was so cold and defensive that I feared her rejection. Finally at the gate I took her hand and said, 'Listen, I want you to know that I really care about you, and I'll be praying for you the minute you get off the plane.'

She just stared blankly. Then, turning away, she said, 'Um ... I'm sorry – I just don't know how to handle love,' and walked away.

The encounter wasn't a resounding success, but I felt I had been obedient. Being a Christian means taking risks – risking that our love will be rejected, misunderstood or even ignored. Now I'm not suggesting that you race to your local bar for Jesus. But if you find yourself in a situation in which you believe God has put you, then accept the risk for his sake.

Seeing beneath the crust

A second way to practise the presence of Christ is to see beneath the crust. We must never assume that a person will not be open to Christianity. Again and again I have had to learn that the least likely-looking people have been the most open to God.

Once when I worked among students I was on a coach sitting next to a woman in her late sixties. Her face was hard, she was chain-smoking, she wore thick make-up and her eyes were vacant. I initiated a conversation, but her responses were blunt and cold, so I quickly stopped and began working on a talk I was preparing. I thought I would have plenty of time to do paperwork because she was so spiritually closed.

A few minutes later, to my surprise, she said, 'What in the world are you doing? You look very busy. What are you writing?'

I tried to avoid answering her question directly because I was certain she would not understand. But she said, 'Yes, it's a nice day. But what are you doing?'

I gulped and then told her what I did for a living and that I was preparing a talk for Christian university students.

'You work for God, do you?' she answered cynically.

I knew that was a dead end, so I said, 'Tell me your name. And what do you do?'

She said, 'I'm Betty. I'm really busy too, just like you. I've got lots of friends. I just never have a moment to myself. Of course, I ... er ... well, I live alone. But I have so many hobbies that I never seem to notice.' Her answer was sadly revealing.

'You know, I've never yet lived alone. I suppose I'm a bit afraid I'd get lonely,' I said.

Suddenly she spun around in her seat and looked at me with great intensity. 'Look, girl. You talk about lonely? I'm so lonely I want to die. Half the time I feel I already have. You know what I said about having lots of friends? Well, I don't. Nobody cares. My heart is bad, and when I feel funny, I run outside, 'cause if I die, at least somebody would know.

'You talk about God. I'm going to tell you something. I came here to see a man. I think he sort of liked me. He was lonely like me, and we just got on. I phoned him and he didn't answer. So I phoned his landlord and asked him if Jack was there. He told me to hold on. When he came back on the line, he said, "Oh, Jack is here. But he's dead. Looks like he died a few days ago. That's a shame. I'll see to it. Goodbye." Is that what'll happen to me? I just lie dead on a floor for two days and nobody knows? What's your God say about that?'

As pitiful as Betty's face was, it was the most alive I had seen her during the whole conversation. Pain had forced her out of her deadness and defences. She hurt too much to be complacent; she had to be real. It seemed as if she were coming up just once more for air.

Trying to identify with her feelings, I said, 'Makes you wonder if there really is a God, doesn't it? Makes you wonder where in the world Jack is now.'

She answered, 'I keep asking those questions. But I've never got an answer. I've been asking those questions over and over since it happened.'

'When did you learn that Jack had died, Betty?' I asked.

'Last night,' she said. 'And I've been up all night ... just asking the silence for an answer.'

I wanted to weep. Not only for her tragedy but also for my blindness and for the goodness of God toward her anyway. I had sat next to a woman whom I had dismissed on sight as being spiritually closed, but she had been up all night asking me ultimate questions. I had wanted to ignore her so I could write my talk on evangelism, but she was asking questions from her depths, and God was reaching out to her.

I told her that I grieved for her pain. I shared that someone very close to me was also going through a time of excruciating loneliness. I told her how this person felt God was meeting her in her brokenness. Betty looked hopeful for a few seconds, then wistfully said, 'You are so young, so young.'

The conversation moved on to other things. I tried to think of some way to reveal God's love. It was clear that for Betty words were cheap. Later in the conversation I said, 'Listen, I'm in your part of the world fairly regularly. What if I visit you when I come?'

It was the second time she brightened. Her eyes lit up and she said, 'You don't mean it? Of course, you can come! Listen, I'm a great cook too! And you could meet my dog. We'd have a great time!'

But when we reached our destination she had become tough again. As we got off the coach she said, 'Well, it's been nice to meet you. Bye-bye.' And she walked off. Then, she stopped, turned round, and looking at me in desperation, said, 'Oh, God, Becky. Don't forget to phone. Oh, please, don't forget me.' And she left.

I sat down in the terminal and wept.

I wish there was a happy ending to Betty's story, but there isn't. I visited her. I spent nights with Betty and her dog. I brought students over to meet her, and they loved her far more consistently and faithfully than I. To my knowledge Betty only took; she never gave. Perhaps she was unable to. In fact, she used us. She was so starved for love that she could only gulp it down and grab for more. She came to know about the source of our love. She knew about Jesus. But she never chose to follow him, at least while we knew her. I met her and I left her a woman alone.

Betty was not a waste of our time. She was important to God and important to us. We did not fail God with Betty. But we cannot make anyone become a Christian. We are not judged by our success but by our faithfulness and obedience, though it was a costly and painful obedience for us.

We must never assume that people are as they appear. All of us have needs. Like Betty, most of us have experienced some form of rejection. We long for things we are scared to death to ask for. We long to be touched, to be appreciated, to be told we are special, but we do not know how to ask. When we have been hurt, we have tender areas like open sores that make us deeply fear being touched and exposed. Still, that is what we long for most of all. What we need is for someone to act like Jesus, to put arms around us, to reach out to us and say, 'Come home with me. I care about you. I want to be with you.'

And that is also what we are called to do. We must not wait until we are healed first, loved first, and then reach out. We must serve no matter how little we have our act together. It may well be that one of the first steps toward our own healing will come when we reach out to someone else. When we get beneath the surface of a person, we will usually discover a sea of needs. We must learn how to interpret those needs correctly, as Jesus did. Jesus wasn't turned off by needs, even needs wrongly met, because they revealed something about the person.

The Samaritan woman had had five husbands and was currently living with a sixth man. The disciples took one look at her and thought, *That woman become a follower of Jesus? No way! Why, just look at her lifestyle.* But Jesus looked at her and came to the opposite conclusion. What Jesus saw in her frantic male-hopping wasn't just looseness. It wasn't her human need for tenderness that alarmed him but rather how she sought to meet that need. Even more, Jesus saw that her need indicated hunger for God. He seemed to be saying to the disciples, 'Look at what potential she has for God. See how hard she's trying to find the right thing in all the wrong places.'

That blows the lid right off evangelism for me. How many Samaritan women and men do you know? Everywhere I am, I see people frantically looking for the right things in all the wrong places. The tragedy is that so often my initial response is to withdraw and assume they will never become Christians. We must ask ourselves, *How do I interpret the needs and lifestyles of my friends? Do I look at their messy lives and say 'That's wrong' and walk away? Or do I penetrate their mask and discover why they are in such trouble in the first place? And then do I try to love them where they are?*

We can show people that they are right to want to fill the void, and then they may be surprised by joy to discover that the emptiness inside is a God-shaped vacuum.

Loving people where they are

In order to establish trust with people, we must love them with the baggage they bring with them. We need to accept them where they are without compromising our Christian standards. Jesus accepted the 'gift' from the prostitute at Simon's banquet (Luke 7:36–50). He shattered his 'testimony' by allowing a loose woman to touch him. But he did not ask her to demonstrate her love for him and sense of forgiveness by exegeting Ezekiel. He allowed her to offer a gift that she was comfortable with.

We, too, must live with the tension of being called to identify with others without being identical to them. That may mean that we demonstrate our support by affirming a friend's motive even if we cannot participate in the deed.

In one place I lived, a woman moved into the flat below mine. Every time I saw her, she was on her way to another party. We always exchanged friendly words, and one day she said, 'Becky, I like you. You're all right. Let's get together next week and smoke a joint, OK?'

I replied, 'Thanks! I really like you, too, and I'd love to spend time with you. Actually I can't stand the stuff, but I'd certainly like to do something else.'

Of course, she looked a bit surprised, not so much because I didn't smoke marijuana but because I had expressed delight at the thought of spending time with her. I could have told her, 'I'm a Christian and I never touch the stuff,' but I wanted to affirm whatever I possibly could without selling short Christian standards. Too often we broadcast what we 'don't do' when we should be trying to discover genuine points of contact. Most of us tend either to over-identify and blend in so well that no-one can tell we are Christians or we separate ourselves and play it safe by having little contact with the world. We should recognize what our tendency is and work against it.

There are, of course, some things we should not do. One test is whether the activity violates a scriptural principle. Another is whether we are violating our own sense of purity. Here it is important to know ourselves.

We must be aware of where we are vulnerable. Under most circumstances it is dangerous to talk ourselves into what we know is a real temptation but say we prayed God would give us strength to overcome. Often people tell me they entered perilous situations because they felt they were the only person who could witness. I believe we must take risks as Christians, but God will not call us into situations he knows we cannot handle. He can find someone else to go who does not struggle in that area.

Loving others as we are

Our message is not that we have it all together. Our message is that we know the One who does! That means we have the freedom to fail. It also means we have the freedom to be ourselves – plus.

Let God make you fully you. Rejoice in your God-given temperament and use it for God's purposes. This point cannot be emphasized enough. We must be authentic. If we try to be someone we are not, people will see it instantly. One man I know with a larger-than-life personality talks about God with anyone he meets almost upon immediate contact. He doesn't have to warm up the subject; he simply talks about the Lord's goodness to him and about how grateful he is to be a Christian. It's so effortless that it is a joy to watch. His smile lights up his face, and his manner is so infectious that I've never seen anyone offended. People can sense his authenticity and they enjoy his style because it's so utterly him. Yet if someone else, with a different kind of personality, tried to do the same thing in the same manner, it would fall flat.

Much has been written about various temperaments. Most of it is helpful, even though I personally resist over-simplified categories that put people into slick personality boxes. Of the many personality distinctives that have been drawn by researchers, one of the most obvious is the extrovert–introvert distinction.

God made some of us extroverts. These are the types who get energized by talking and interacting with people. They are usually comfortable relating to the outer world. They can talk about personal issues with relative ease. I am by nature an extrovert, though over the years I have found I need much more alone time to process and make sense out of my inner world.

Nevertheless, my tendency is to figure things out by talking them through. And I love meeting people and discovering their stories.

God made others introverts. These are the ones who get their energy replenished by being alone. They tend to be more comfortable with the inner world than with the outer world. They need to meditate and think things through first before they are comfortable speaking. They are often more private and prefer to share personal information with a select few.

We should praise God for these differences and take them seriously. In regard to evangelism it means we need to express our faith in ways that are consistent with who we are, as well as be sensitive to the person to whom we are speaking. At the same time we must remember that no spiritual growth occurs without our being stretched. Being an introvert isn't an excuse to never share the gospel. Rather, it means finding ways to share the love of Christ in a way that fits who we are. The key is that we don't become so stretched that we violate how God has made us.

For example, I have a friend, Amy, who is an introvert by nature. Being a mature Christian, she takes seriously Jesus' call to share her faith. At the same time she has had to learn how to express her faith in a way she is comfortable with.

Amy told me, 'I'm not a person who can verbalize my deepest thoughts easily. Nor am I very quick on my feet verbally. So I ask the Lord daily to allow the Jesus who lives in me to love those people I come into contact with. I've been amazed by how often a person will say, "I can't believe how much you care about me." Yet I don't feel I've done anything that extraordinary. But as I share who the source of my love is, and as I pray, things happen.'

In that example alone there is much to learn. First, this is an illustration of the power of listening. Knowing my friend, I'm not surprised people feel loved in her presence. She has an unusual capacity to listen with depth and compassion – more than she is even aware of. Listening well is a powerful way to share the love of Christ. Second, this illustrates the power of prayer. When we ask God to let people experience the love of Jesus though us, something happens that can't be quantified or easily explained. That's because prayer involves mysteries that happen to the soul. As you listen and pray for your seeking friends, it will open doors for God to penetrate.

Amy loves to paint and takes art lessons whenever possible. These have provided her with a great opportunity to bring, as she says, 'the aroma of Christ' to others.

'How do you do that?' I asked her.

'Art lessons provide a safe environment for people. As we paint, people talk easily. Part of my influence in the class was that I shared things of a more personal nature. For example, if I was worried about one of my children, I'd say so. But I'd also add, "I pray for them every single day and, boy, does it help!" Or when I discovered I needed an operation, I was honest about my anxieties. But I also felt free to tell them how grateful I was that my church was praying for me.'

'Soon they began to share more of themselves as well. If someone said she was upset over a problem, I would write a note and tell her I was praying for her. Over time they began to see how my relationship to God impacted how I handled the daily concerns all of us share,' Amy said.

'By the end of the course,' Amy continued, 'several felt free to come to me privately with their spiritual questions or personal problems. One woman started going to church, another went out and bought a Bible, another asked me to pray for her. But I don't feel evangelism is my gift by a long shot. I'm not very good at wrapping things up and closing the deal.'

While we can improve on the skills Amy felt weren't her strength, the truth is that some people genuinely are more gifted than others at 'closing the deal'. These are people with the gift of evangelism. That doesn't mean that those who don't have the gift of evangelism are free to remain silent or will never lead a person to Christ. Just look at the fruit of Amy's witness! She shared authentically how Christ made a difference in her life and people were drawn to Christ. Amy did what the apostle Paul wrote to the Thessalonians: 'So deeply do we care for you that we are determined to share with you not only the gospel of God but also our own selves' (1 Thess. 1:8).

But what if you fear the 'stretching process' will be too much for you as you learn to share your faith? A remarkable student told me once that, though she was an extreme introvert, she knew she had to find ways to share her love for God. She was perceptive and realized she shouldn't ask God to suddenly make her a boisterous extrovert. Rather, she asked him for the freedom to look outward, not to look at herself and be paralysed by fear. She told me she got a summer job as a waitress because it would force her to talk with people.

When she returned to the university, she applied some newly learned lessons. When she was eating in the cafeteria, she would ask her table, 'I'm going back for milk. Can I get anyone anything?' Usually a few would reply yes. When she returned with what they requested, it almost immediately opened up a conversation and they asked her questions. She said the fact that they were both focusing on the extra milk she had in her hand reduced her fear of eye contact. Her being able to focus on something else (even if it was a glass of milk!) kept her from focusing on herself. That led her on to discovering other ways to serve.

She had a plant that everyone admired. So when someone said she had a beautiful plant, she would say, 'Thanks! Let me give you a cutting.' That offer opened conversation but kept her focusing initially on the plant, which helped her fears. She also offered to help students preparing for tests if they were in her field or needed a paper typed. Eventually, after much practice and continually raising the stakes, she became more and more at ease around people. It was a learned skill. But what freed her and helped her to love and accept herself and others was learning that she could take initiative in ways that were reasonably comfortable for her and that people responded to her. She was still reserved but not so desperately afraid. She loved people powerfully but quietly.

What struck me about her was the effectiveness of her non-verbal witness. She told her friends about Jesus, but she demonstrated him in beautiful ways too. She worked on overcoming her timidity but discovered eventually that she had the gift of serenity. People were drawn to her because her presence brought a sense of peace. She would never have realized that she possessed this gift if she had not gone through the excruciating process of taking initiative. She worked on some of the 'limits' in her temperament (just as an extrovert would need to learn when to use restraint), but in the process God blossomed in her the gifts of her temperament.

What these last two examples illustrate is that being an extrovert isn't essential to evangelism – obedience and love are. Since I am an extrovert, my personal illustrations already reflect my own style of witnessing. The joy of these various examples, however, is that God needs all of us to reach all of his children. The lesson is that God isn't glorified in our lives if we try to wear our best friend's personality. We must be who we were created to be. And we must reach out to others in a way that is both sensitive to the person with whom we are talking and consistent with our own personalities.

But regardless of our temperaments, we all must become initiators. The mark of a mature Christian is whether she or he chooses to be the 'host' (the initiator) or the 'guest' (the receiver) in relationships where being a host is most appropriate. There are, of course, times when those who are ordinarily hosts should be guests. The point is that the call to love those around us is in part a call to identify their needs. Once we have some understanding of their needs, we must find ways to meet them that are natural for us.

'But,' you may say, 'the fact is that to take initiative in itself is not natural for me. I'm just a shy person.' Actually, the ability to get outside of one's own skin and serve another is not natural for anyone. But sitting back and doing nothing is not an option. We are called to love, to serve, to identify need and to respond. That is not easy for anyone, but it is what the Holy Spirit helps us to do so that we can become more like Jesus. Nevertheless, in the way we exercise our love, the way we choose to demonstrate it, the way we share Christ with others we can choose a style comfortable for us.

The Christian must be the one who loves, cares and listens first. We all can take initiative, whether quietly or openly.

Being salt and light

We must not become, as John Stott puts it, 'rabbit-hole Christians'. When I worked among students, the form it would take was this: A Christian student leaves his Christian roommate in the morning and scurries through the day to lectures, only to search frantically for a Christian to sit by (an odd way to approach a mission field). Thus he proceeds from lecture to lecture. When dinner comes, he sits with other Christians at one huge table and thinks, *What a witness!* From there he goes to his all-Christian Bible study, and he might even take in a prayer meeting where the Christians pray for the non-believers on his floor. (But what luck that he was able to live on the only floor with seventeen Christians!) Then at night he scurries back to his Christian roommate. Safe! He made it through the day, and his only contacts with the world were those mad dashes to and from Christian activities.

If you're not a student, that description may sound ridiculous or irrelevant. But how often do we in the church imitate the same behaviour? The most common objection I hear when I am training churches in evangelism is this: 'All my friends are Christians! With work, parental responsibilities, church activities, there's no time left to form a friendship with a seeker'.

Life does get more complicated with greater responsibilities as we get older. Yet to have no time to be 'the aroma of Christ' to an unbelieving neighbour, friend or colleague means we aren't taking seriously God's command to 'go and make disciples'.

What an insidious reversal of the biblical command to be salt and light to the world! Rabbit-hole Christians remain insulated and isolated from the world when they are commanded to penetrate it. How can we be the salt of the earth if we never get out of the saltshaker?

Christians, however, aren't the only ones to blame. Even the world encourages our isolationism. Have you ever wondered why, on a typical television programme, everyone always 'behaves' when the minister comes to visit? Suddenly their language changes and their behaviour improves. Why? They want to do their part to keep the Reverend feeling holy. They will play the religious game while he is around because he needs to be protected from that cold, real world out there.

Sometimes non-Christians will act oddly around us because they are genuinely convicted by the Holy Spirit in us, and that's good. But all too often they are behaving differently because they feel that is the way they are supposed to act around religious types.

I am often put in a religious box when people discover what

my profession is. During the days when I ministered to students, I had a clergy card that sometimes enabled me to travel at reduced rates. The only problem was that occasionally ticket agents didn't believe I was authorized to use it! A young female just wasn't what they had in mind when they saw a clergy card. More than once I was asked, 'OK, honey, now where did you rip this off?'

Once when I was flying from San Francisco to Portland, I arrived at the counter and was greeted by an exceedingly friendly male ticket agent. 'Well, hello-o-o there!' he said.

'Er ... I'd like to pick up my ticket to Portland, please.'

'I'm sorry. You won't be able to fly there tonight.'

'Why? Is the flight cancelled?'

'No, it's because you're going out with me tonight.'

'What?'

'Listen, I know this great restaurant with a hot band. You'll never regret it.'

'Oh, I'm sorry, I really must get to Portland. Do you have my ticket?'

'Aw, what's the rush? I'll pick you up at eight.'

'Look, I really must go to Portland,' I said.

'Well, OK. Too bad though. Hey, I can't find your ticket.' He paused, then said, 'Looks like it's a date then!'

'Oh, I forgot to tell you, it's a ... special ticket,' I said.

'Oh, is it youth fare?'

'No, um, well, it's ... er, clergy,' I whispered, leaning over the counter.

He froze. 'What did you say?'

'It's clergy.'

'Clergy!' he shouted as the entire airport looked our way. His face went absolutely pale as he was horrified by only one thought: *Oh, no. I've been flirting with a nun!*

When he disappeared behind the counter, I could hear him whisper to the other ticket agent a few feet away, 'Hey, George, get a load of that woman up there. She's clergy.' Suddenly another man rose from behind the counter, smiled and nodded and disappeared again. I never have felt so religious in my entire life.

As I stood there trying to look as secular as possible, my ticket agent reappeared and stood back several feet behind the desk. Looking shaken and sounding like a tape recording, he said, 'Good afternoon. We certainly hope there have been no inconveniences. And on behalf of our airline, we'd like to wish you a very safe and pleasant flight … Sister Manley.'

As humorous as this incident was, I think it shows how difficult it is to maintain our authenticity before the world. The challenge is not to allow ourselves to become more or less than human.

We know, in short, that Christ desires to have a radicalizing impact upon us and our relationships. But that impact is greatly aided when we live as we are called to live: no longer regarding anyone from a human point of view but desiring to see beneath the crust, to love people as they are with the gifts they have to bring, and to care in ways that correspond to who we are as well. We are not insulated and isolated from the world, but neither are we complacent and blind to its agonies and sorrows and the darkness of its heart. We are salt and light. We make a difference because we are different. And when we live before God as we truly are, he will change the world in which we live.

9

Developing conversational skills

Once a lecturer and I were having a stimulating conversation on a plane. The talk was lively and comfortable – until he asked me what I did for a living. When I told him I was in Christian ministry, he looked at me quizzically as if he were thinking, *Funny, and she seemed so intelligent.*

Clearly taken aback, since he assumed he had been talking to someone normal, he began trying to find the right words to say to a religious type. In a stilted manner he finally said, 'I'm sure it must be very ... er ... rewarding.'

'Well,' I said, 'I'm not sure it's as rewarding as it is intriguing.'

Almost in spite of himself he said, 'How do you mean, "intriguing"?'

'I think one of the hardest issues a Christian must face is how in the world we know that what we believe is true. How do we know we are not deluding ourselves and worshipping merely on the basis of need rather than truth? Or that some psychologists are not correct in saying we worship a glorified version of our father figure. To have to deal honestly with those questions is exciting and intriguing.'

He looked at me in surprise and said, 'Well, I have to confess, though I haven't thought much about faith in a long time, those are the very questions I have. OK, how do you know it's true?' For the rest of our flight we discussed the evidences for and the message of the Christian faith.

Frequently, when I'm travelling to speak, I am asked what I do for a living. You might think I'd try to hide the fact that one of the books I've written is on the topic of evangelism. It is quite the opposite. Often I respond by asking, 'Have you ever been offended or buttonholed by Christians trying to share their faith with you?' That's all I have to say. Everyone seems eager to share a war story.

Once they discover I've written a book that examines how to communicate the Christian faith more effectively, I usually ask them, 'How do *you* share your deepest convictions with others, without betraying your beliefs yet without seeming intolerant or arrogant?' That nearly always opens the door to a provocative discussion of faith. People are especially interested to know how Jesus spoke about faith to those who didn't believe. So even the topic of evangelism, if handled sensitively, can be a door that opens a discussion about faith. But what opened that door was my mentioning one of their 'hot buttons' regarding faith before they did.

These examples reveal one kind of conversational skill. It involves being the first to suggest the defences that our unchurched friends may have. Walls are torn down and bridges are built when we suggest their own objections before they do. It's also important to acknowledge that their objection is often quite legitimate.

In this chapter we will look at ways of moving conversations from discussions of ordinary topics to spiritual ones. We will examine a variety of ways of communicating our faith. However, one thing needs to be made clear. Good communication skills cannot convert anyone. It is the power of God and his divine initiative that penetrate and convert the seeker's heart. Jesus said, 'No one can come to me unless drawn by the Father who sent me' (John 6:44).

So why do we bother building our communication skills? Because we want to be sure that our style of communicating the gospel isn't blocking the seeker's ability to hear it! It is one thing when sceptics take offence at the gospel; it is quite another when their offence is over a blundering, aggressive, insensitive or even an apologetic style. The way we communicate must reflect what we communicate. In fact, the two cannot really be separated.

Once I had lunch with a woman named Mary who told me her office colleague was close to accepting Christ. Mary was especially concerned because she was being relocated by her company, and she felt her colleague needed Christian friends.

When Mary introduced me to her, she looked at her office-mate and said, 'Now I'm having Becky meet you because you really need friends. You'll never make it with God unless someone sticks close to you. So I've asked Becky to keep an eye on you when I'm gone.'

I wanted to crawl under her desk. But as I tried to think of some cover, the colleague looked at me, smiled and said, 'You know, she really, really loves me. And it always shows.'

Although love covers a multitude of conversational sins, there are some principles that will help us to be better communicators of our faith.

The importance of attitude

We cannot overestimate the importance of our attitude. Our attitude and style communicate content just as our words do. If we notice that sceptics seem embarrassed, apologetic and defensive, it is probably because they are picking up our attitude. If we assume they will be intrigued to discover the true nature of Christianity, they probably will. If we project enthusiasm and not defensiveness, and if we carefully listen instead of sounding like a recording of 'Answers to questions you didn't happen to ask', seekers will probably become fascinated.

Why are we sometimes embarrassed or apologetic when we share the gospel? Maybe it's because pockets of unbelief still reside in our souls. Sure we believe, we say, but not so much that we are willing to stick our necks out and take a risk. Ironically, the one sure way to build faith in God is to acknowledge our fears and doubts and then be willing to take a risk in spite of them.

Or we assume our friends won't be interested in spiritual matters, so we don't expect a positive response. Granted, there is often a high level of mistrust among sceptics toward the institutional aspects of Christianity. Recently a poll was given asking Americans to rank their level of distrust for various professions. Television evangelists came in next to prostitutes and organized crime! But my experience is that there is a great deal of openness toward any expression of faith they consider to be real.

Last, our discomfort is due to our own stereotypes of the unchurched. In the evangelism training conferences I have given around the world, I never cease to be amazed by how consistent some responses are, regardless of which country I am in. For example, once I was giving evangelism training in India, and a beautiful woman in a sari raised her hand during the question-and-answer session and said, 'One problem, which I believe may be unique to us Indians, is that we fear offending people when we do evangelism.' I assured her that I hear that comment more than any other no matter what country I am in.

There is a role-play exercise I do in evangelism training in which I say, 'Turn to the person on your right and assume that person is a Christian who has just asked you, "How was your weekend? What did you do?" Tell that person about this event, and one thing you have learned from being here so far.' There is always an immediate buzz of conversation as people excitedly share what they have learned.

After a few minutes I say, 'Now reverse the roles so the other person has a chance to answer. Remember to tell what this event was and one thing you've learned from being here. Only this time pretend that the person asking the question is a non-Christian acquaintance.'

The silence following my second set of instructions is equalled in drama only by the 'you've got to be kidding' look on their faces. The feedback after the exercise is always telling. 'How did you feel going from the first exercise to the second?' I ask. The answer is always the same: 'Terribly uncomfortable!' Their reasons are generally the following: 'Because I knew he wouldn't understand a thing I said'; 'She'd think I was mad'; 'He'd think I was pushy'; 'She'd take offence'; 'My church friends would understand me, but I knew he wouldn't'; 'They'd think I was a religious fanatic to use my weekends to go to a Christian conference'; and so on.

To varying degrees and with only one or two exceptions, I have received those responses from all over North America, Latin America, Asia, India, Europe and the Middle East! I have heard these responses from Catholics, Orthodox, Protestants, mainline and evangelical denominations. What's the problem here? First of all, it's small wonder that we feel uncomfortable with evangelism with paranoid preconceptions like that floating around in our heads! Our fear seems to be that if we dare say a word about God, most people would gladly eat us for breakfast! In other words, what cripple our effectiveness are our *own* stereotypes of others.

But Jesus tells us not to judge others. That means we must refuse to assume a person is closed to God. In fact, why not assume the opposite? Sure, this person may have been turned off by a false and distorted picture of the Christian faith – but that's good news, not bad. Has he ever been exposed to true faith? Does he know what Jesus is really like? Why not assume the best and believe this person might be very open to God? And if we can't pull that off, then at least we must remain agnostic. That is, we must remind ourselves that we really have no basis for assuming the negative.

Here is one thing I've found helpful, especially in avoiding an 'us *v.* them' defensive mentality. When you are speaking to a person about the gospel and you begin to feel your fear level start to rise, pretend that you are talking to a Christian. If you thought you were talking to a believer, you would be much more relaxed and you'd be yourself.

Unfortunately, our insecurities and fears are often mis-interpreted by seekers. When we act stilted and awkward, they mistake our sense of inadequacy for arrogance. What they *think* they are hearing is, 'Well, I'll *try* to explain this to you, very slowly – but I'm sure you're too unspiritual to grasp it properly.' It would be far better to acknowledge our fears instead of pretending we don't have any.

No question is unacceptable

Learn to delight in all questions seekers may pose, especially the ones you can't answer. No questions should be regarded as too hostile. I often tell people I'm very grateful that God is using them to sharpen me intellectually when I am stumped by a question. I tell them I don't know the answer but can't wait to investigate it. And usually I do investigate and learn in the process. What we model by this approach is that we love Christ with all of our minds. A question we can't answer is grounds not for abandoning our faith but for further exploration. Our message is that the truth of faith may be above reason but it is not contrary to reason.

We get into trouble when we feel it's up to us to defend God and prove by our own wits and wisdom that we are right and they are wrong. Of course, there is a legitimate place for debate. But if our style with seekers is to always 'argue them down', we may be winning the argument and forgetting the purpose of evangelism: to introduce the gospel to our hearers in the confidence of *God's* power to convert.

Or perhaps our fear is that we must have all the answers. I often meet sincere Christians who honestly believe they can't share their faith because, as they say, 'What if someone asks me a question I can't answer?' Of course people will ask us questions that we can't answer! What has that got to do with evangelism? The gospel does not need our aid in its defence; it is quite capable of defending itself. As Luther said, 'Let us not be anxious, the gospel does not need our help; it is sufficiently strong of itself.'

It is the Spirit's role to convict of sin and convince the seeker of God's truth. Our task is to share the story of Christ and to ask the Spirit of God to make the message of faith credible and knowable. Yes, we take their questions seriously and answer them as best we can. We work hard to relate the gospel to the cultural context of our hearers. We want to make the Christian position intellectually viable to searching persons. But to refrain from sharing the most glorious news ever announced to humanity because we might be asked a question that stumps us is a tragedy.

Exposing and imposing

Next, we can learn to expose our faith, not impose it. As we have seen, we cannot make someone a Christian. Only the Spirit of God can truly change a heart. Consequently, though we are called to let our own faith be known, we are not called to force it on others. In fact, if our evangelism reflects an aggressive style, it could indicate our misunderstanding of the role of the Holy Spirit. We could not convert anyone if our life depended upon it.

Evangelism, then, is not employing a super sales strategy

with shrewd salespeople. Why? Because the gospel is not for sale! It is a free gift of grace for those who will accept it. God's Word, as theologian Karl Barth said, 'does not compete with other commodities which are being offered to men on the bargain counter of life'.[2]

We don't force our faith on others; neither do we manipulate others into listening. Instead, we tell the good news of what God has done for us and the whole world in the life, death and resurrection of Jesus Christ. We simply share our faith in love, hoping that God will act upon their hearts so that they may receive the truth we profess.

I used to worry constantly after witnessing to someone whether I did it properly, if I should have said this or that, and so on. The Scripture calls us to excellence, but it also says the Spirit will give us what we need for tough situations (Mark 13:11). To be anxious about whether we have witnessed in exactly the 'right way' implies there is some outside perfect standard that we are being judged by. There *are* things that are very helpful to understand as we engage in the task of evangelism, and we will examine them in the next several chapters. But there is no magic formula; there is no absolute and correct way to witness every time. We are called to do the very best we can and then trust the Holy Spirit to speak to a person through what we say and do. We witness in the confident expectation that God will move and act upon our hearers in his way and in his time. Donald Bloesch sums it up best when he writes, 'Evangelism is not the imposition of a point of view but the overflow of a thankful heart.'[3]

Taking it easy

There is an inevitable tension in evangelism. On the one hand, we should feel an urgency about sharing the gospel. The more we care about our friends, the more we long for them to know God. We want to share the good news because we care about their total well-being. I agree with Bonhoeffer, who wrote, 'To tell men that the cause is urgent, and that the kingdom of God is at hand, is the most charitable and merciful act we can perform, the most joyous news we can bring.'[4]

At the same time we need to learn to relax. Since it is the

Holy Spirit's job to convert, that should ease some of our anxiety. We are called to be a witness to the truth of God's good news and to share what we have experienced in simple, personal terms. Jesus did not say, 'Go and be theologians'; he said, 'You will be my witnesses.' Being a witness for Jesus Christ involves our words, and it also involves the way we live our lives, but it does not mean that we are called to be flawless philosophers or apologists. We simply trust the power of God to work through our obedient efforts. I am not saying we should not seek to arouse curiosity in the gospel or to relate the gospel to the situation in which seekers find themselves, but we will probably be more effective with an initial, casual reference to God than nervously wondering about whether we are doing it exactly right.

We need to remember that evangelism is a process. Conversion may take place in a moment, but God will use many people, events and experiences to lead a person to himself. People need time to think, watch, listen and talk through their questions. Our witness is invaluable, but it is still just one aspect that God will use to draw a person to Christ.

When I train churches in evangelism, one point of anxiety that is frequently mentioned is the question of timing. When is it appropriate to proclaim the good news? It is a valid concern, for I have met seekers who were turned off by an approach that was too abrupt or too impersonal or in which they felt cornered and manipulated. Our burden for a person's salvation does not excuse insensitivity.

I remember one young man saying, 'I have a friend who works in my office. We play golf together and are becoming friends. I really want to witness to him, but I keep wondering when the right time is. I mean, at what moment should I tell him? How will I know when the exact time finally comes to witness?' By the time he had finished his question, he had me feeling as uptight and intense as he was. And I could not help but sympathize with whomever the recipient of this talk would be. That kind of anxiety and intensity would scare a person to death!

How do we know if we are speaking at the right time and at the right place? In order to know if there is an 'opening' to proclaim the message of Christ, we need to listen carefully both to God and to our friend. We need to ask God, even as we are conversing with our friend, to give us wisdom and a word of knowledge (1 Cor. 12:8). Then we need to test the waters with the person. Have we sensed on his part any interest in the spiritual comments we have made? Did she seem genuinely interested and ready to pay attention? Jesus warns us against not giving what is holy to those who are uninterested in it (Matt. 10:14).

It is far more effective first to toss out a few casual comments about your relationship to God or about how Jesus views a particular subject. There is something very appealing about openness. Say, 'Hey, I'd like you to meet a friend who's in this fantastic Bible discussion I'm in' or even, 'We had an interesting study this week on how Jesus related to women. He certainly was ahead of the culture of his day in his attitude towards women.' And then see what happens. Their responses will guide you in how to proceed.

Getting rid of God-talk

We should talk the same way to non-Christians as we do to Christians. In the past I used to ask my host before I spoke to a crowd, 'Are there many sceptics in the room?' Then one day it dawned on me that, regardless of the answer, it wouldn't change the nature of my talk. Truth is truth, and its appeal is universal. Of course, we need to speak truth in ways that are relevant and arouse the curiosity of our audience, but in most instances we should be able to tell both groups the same stories or experiences or thoughts. We should not assume that our unchurched friends will not be interested in our spiritual side. We need to invite them into our lives, to share what we share, enjoy what we enjoy. We must not act superior because we know God or have more information.

But when we explain the Christian message, we should do so in plain language, preferably in fresh and creative ways. Few things turn off people faster or alienate them more easily than God-talk. Without realizing it, we use words or clichés that have a correct understanding only among Christians.

When I worked with students, I gave many evangelistic talks. I remember one in which a sceptical but seeking student asked me, 'What does it mean to be a Christian?'

A Christian student who really desired the other student to understand replied, 'It means you have to be washed in the blood of the Lamb.' The first student paled and looked confused. The Christian continued, 'That way you will be sanctified and redeemed.'

Another student, seeking to help his Christian brother, said, 'And the fellowship is so great. Praise the Lord! You really get into the Word and get such a blessing.'

By the end of the evening, it was clear from the sceptic student's face that he felt Christians came from another planet!

To the world, religious clichés are often red rags or else the meaning is imprecise. Of course, we must not dispense with biblical words and concepts. Instead, we need to develop fresh and relevant ways to express what they mean. Frequently I will describe what a word means, then say, 'That's what the Bible means when it talks about sin.' If we do it in that sequence, we can arouse curiosity and dismantle defences.

For example, I attended a film with a woman who is a psychologist. She is a genuine seeker, and I had chosen the film because it raised central issues about what it means to be human. Later, as we sipped coffee, I said, 'The film suggests that the human situation is tragic. From all your experience as a therapist, do you agree?'

She responded, 'I think people get into awful messes with their lives, but I'm not sure I'd call it tragic. Would you?'

'Well, the Bible says the human situation is tragic …'

'Oh, I know,' she interrupted with a tone of cynicism. 'You Christians say we are all sinners.'

'But Joan,' I responded, 'do you know why? The Bible says it's because something very, very precious has been broken. If we weren't so significant, if we didn't have so much meaning, then it wouldn't be so sad. It's only when something precious has been broken that we can say, "How tragic!" That broken-ness is what the Bible calls sin. That's why God hates it so much. Sin caused something extremely precious to become dehumanized.'

'What do you think are concrete evidences of sin in a person's life?' she asked.

'Pride, envy, narcissism, self-deception, perfectionism –

anything that makes us less than we were created to be,' I answered.

'What, then, is the source of sin, according to the Bible?' she asked.

'We are control freaks. We seek to live our lives calling all the shots instead of answering to God's rule. We have a "God complex", and judging by all the people that flood your office, I'd say it isn't serving us well. We've been created to be God-centred and we are hopelessly self-centred. Sin has left us addicted to ourselves,' I answered.

Our conversation lasted for hours as we discussed what the Bible says is the true source and the solution to the human problem. As we stood up to leave, she said, 'Becky, I've got a lot to think about. I've just understood for the first time what Christians mean by sin. I know I don't have any psychological explanations for the source of human ailments that come even close to the depth of the biblical analysis. Let's get together soon after I've had time to think. But I want to thank you, not only for speaking to me about spiritual things, but for saying it in English!'

We need first to understand for ourselves the meaning of biblical words, then we need to translate them in ways that people can understand. I read somewhere that Albert Einstein once said, 'You don't really understand something unless you can say it in a really simple way.' Here are some other common Christian terms we should learn to express in fresh ways: *grace, salvation, justification, sanctification, regeneration, redemption, born again*. Your Christian group may well have other phrases meaningful only to the initiated. Learn to translate them.

Asking leading questions

We can learn to ask good questions. Too often we allow ourselves to be put on the defensive. The dynamics are greatly changed when we turn the tables and begin to direct the conversation by asking questions. My friend Dale Hanson Bourke and I once led an investigative Bible discussion for women who wanted to know more about the Christian faith. When I asked one of my most sceptical friends to come, she at first answered, 'It might be interesting to look at the life of

Jesus, but I know I could never be a Christian. My commitment to scholarship makes any consideration of Christianity impossible. It's irrational, and the evidence supporting it is totally insufficient.'

I answered, 'I'm so glad you care so much about truth and that you really want evidence to support your beliefs. You say the evidence for Christianity is terribly insufficient. What was your conclusion after carefully investigating the primary biblical documents?'

'Er, well, you mean the Bible?' she asked.

'Of course,' I said. 'The New Testament accounts of Jesus, for example. Where did you find them lacking?'

'Oh, well, look, I remember Mother reading me those stories when I was ten,' she replied.

'Hmm, but what was your conclusion?' I continued, and as a result discovered she had never investigated the Scriptures critically as an adult. This is all too often the case. But we can arouse curiosity in others to investigate the claims of the gospel when we help them see that their information and understanding about Christianity are lacking. Just her realization that she had based her beliefs on impressions formed as a child made her eager to come to the study.

Another person I invited to the investigative Bible discussion, a woman who was quite hostile to what she perceived was Christianity, told me, 'Why should I come when I can't stand those hypocrites who go to church every Sunday. They make me sick.'

'Yes,' I responded, 'isn't it amazing how far they are from true Christianity? When you think of how vast the difference is between the real thing and what they do, it's like worlds apart. The more you discover what Christianity is really about, the more mystifying it is that anyone could settle for less. That's exactly why I'm inviting you to come, so you can examine for yourself the real thing.'

'Er, the real thing? Well, what do you mean by that?' she asked. We then talked about what basis we must use to evaluate what genuine faith looks like. She, too, came to the study when she saw that to evaluate Christianity fairly she had to be willing to examine the life of Jesus. But her hostility was changed into curiosity because she was asked questions, not preached sermons. God has made us curious, so let's learn to ask questions.

These principles of conversation are applicable to most of our dialogue with seekers. They can be applied at any time and in any place. Now we need to explore the larger picture of the task of evangelism.

10

Three ways to witness

The heart of evangelism is sharing the story of Christ, the good news of how God took upon himself the sin and shame of the human race so that all who believe in him might be saved.

This message is the most liberating news to ever grace this planet. The question is, then, why aren't we more eager to share it? Why don't we race out to share such joyful news? The psalmist tells us, 'O taste and see that the LORD is good' (Ps. 34:8). Once we know that truth from the inside out, we will always have something to tell others.

Motivation shouldn't be a problem. But perhaps one reason we feel gun-shy about proclaiming the gospel is because we have never led a person to Christ before. Leading someone to Christ is an awe-inspiring experience that changes us for ever. It confirms the truthfulness of the gospel and the reality of God's presence as few other things do. In case you feel inadequate, let me tell you about my first experience.

Born Again in Barcelona

After my failure with Mary in Barcelona, which I mentioned in chapter 1, I asked God to help me be more brave the next time around. Ruth Siemens kept telling me that, when the time was right, I should ask my friends if there was any reason they could not become Christians right now. The Bible discussion I had started for seekers was nearing an end for that year, and all of us were studying for finals. After one exam Todd and I went for a cup of coffee in a student bar.

Of all of the students in the discussion, he was the most cynical to the gospel. He made Mary, in her agnostic days, look

126

like Mother Teresa. Initially he came only to disrupt the discussion, but we befriended him, and eventually he came every week. There was only one more discussion left, and I felt I had to ask somebody in that group to become a Christian. I was sure Todd would never become a Christian (I really did not think I would be instrumental in anyone's conversion till I was at least eighty!), so Todd seemed safe.

I said, 'Todd, you've been part of this discussion all term. You've heard a lot about God, but you've never decided what to do with God. One of these days, Todd, you're going to have to decide. Sooner or later God is going to speak to you and say, "Decide now." And what are you going to say?' I was feeling so proud for sounding firm (even though I knew my confidence stemmed only from the fact that he would never respond) that I failed to notice how serious his face became. 'Yes, sooner or later, Todd, God is really going to speak to you. And when he does, in that year, I hope you will say yes.'

I think I was still speaking when Todd said, 'You're right. God is speaking, and I am saying yes.'

But I went right along without pausing for breath, 'That's right, Todd. One of these days God will reach out ... er, w-what did you just say?'

'I said, "God has been speaking to me now. And I said yes,"' he answered.

I paled. 'Oh, Todd,' I answered weakly, 'you have such a sense of humour. But really, you shouldn't scare me like that.'

'Becky, I'm not kidding. I've been thinking about this for a long time. And I'm ready now,' he replied.

'Todd, listen to me. You can't rush into this. I mean it's a huge decision. And it'll change your life so much. You'd better think it over and then go and see Ruth.'

'Look, Becky. This isn't an emotional decision. I know I put up a good front, but I've been thinking about God for a long time. Now, look, I want to become a Christian!' he nearly shouted.

'Right here? In the bar? In front of everybody? Todd, I just, well, I can't.'

'Why not?'

'Well, because I've never done anything like this before.'

'Don't worry, I haven't either,' he answered. 'I tell you what.

Let's close our eyes, then I'll say something to God and then you do. It'll be over in just a few minutes.'

So we did, right there in a bar in Barcelona, Spain. When I opened my eyes, I still thought it was only temporary. But even if his conversion lasted only a few hours, it would have been enough for me. I said, 'Now, Todd, something Ruth always says is that conversion is a matter of your will. It doesn't matter if you don't feel any different,' since I was sure he didn't (talk about the sin of unbelief on my part!). 'It's your will that you've given to God. The emotions will come later. But there is just one thing I wanted to ask you,' I said.

'Sure, what is it?'

'Er, do you feel any different?' I asked.

'You bet I do!' he roared.

I looked at him in utter shock. 'Todd!' I cried. 'Oh, my goodness – *it works!*' So off we went to my flat to tell Ruth and Kathy.

While we were there, Stephanie, another agnostic friend in the Bible discussion, phoned and asked us to do something that night. During the evening I kept thinking how flabbergasted she would be when Todd told her, especially since he was one of her best friends. We were in a restaurant when she looked at Todd and said, 'You know, you've really changed. You just look happier, more peaceful. Spain must really agree with you.'

And Todd responded, 'It isn't Spain, Steph; it's God. I've become a Christian.'

Thinking he was joking, she said, 'Yeah, right. I'm Santa Claus. You shouldn't joke like that in front of Becky.'

'Stephanie, I'm serious. I've given my life to Christ. I intend to follow him.'

She looked incredulous and then terribly anxious. He was the least likely of all of them to turn to God. If Todd could, then what did that mean about the others? She grew quiet and serious as Todd told us of his spiritual pilgrimage, that he always had hid behind his sarcasm and seeming indifference. We took a taxi home. Stephanie decided to stay over with me. We walked into my room and she said, 'I want to know how he did it. What do you do when you become a Christian?'

Now I could have lived off Todd's experience for a good twenty years. But when I saw how seriously she asked me that question, I thought, *Oh, it couldn't be! It couldn't happen again. I just can't handle this.*

So I said, 'Steph, would you excuse me for a few minutes?' I casually walked out and shut the door. Then I panicked. It was 1:30 in the morning, and I needed help. Kathy and Ruth were asleep, but I went into Kathy's room anyway. I burst open the door and couldn't think of anything to say. So I cried out, 'Pray!' and wheeled back out. Kathy told me she awoke with such a start that she prayed for ten minutes before realizing she did not know what she was praying for!

Back in my room Stephanie and I talked quietly for several minutes. Then she said, 'Becky, I've been running away from God for a long time. It's time I start running to him,' and she became a Christian that night.

As reluctant and inept as I was, that night changed my life. Before my eyes I saw the very two who seemed the least likely turn their lives over to Christ. Perhaps even as significant as that experience is the fact that today, all these years later, Stephanie is a mature Christian married to a Christian man. I am the godmother of their now twenty-one-year-old daughter. God is faithful. And little did I realize that a feeble attempt to witness to one woman would produce a family who loves God.

There are people around us whom God longs to touch through us – people whom only we can reach with our particular style and personality, people whom we have been called to. We must begin to ask God, 'Is this the one? Is she the one you are seeking?' It is a fantastic drama, and God wants to use us to accomplish it.

Since my first experience back in Barcelona, I've seen many people give their lives to Christ. Watching people's lives be transformed by God has convinced me of one thing: there simply is no greater service that one human being can render to another. To see people find wholeness, meaning and joy, to be restored to freedom as they walk in the grace and mercy of God, is a privilege beyond the power of language to describe.

In light of such mercy and grace, the only question we can ask is this: how do we communicate the gospel to an unbelieving world?

Once I was in my car waiting at a red light with my window down. A car pulled up next to mine, and just as I put my foot on the accelerator, a piece of paper came rocketing into my window and hit me on the cheek. It didn't hurt, but I was so startled that I pulled my car over immediately. As I unrolled the paper, I discovered it was a gospel tract. I'm sure the person who threw it into my window was well intentioned, but 'torpedo evangelism' is not what I see practised in the Bible!

I shared this story with a friend of mine who said, 'It's clear that person didn't have the gift of evangelism or she would have done it better. She'd be better off practising her own gifts and leave the evangelizing to you!' My friend spoke somewhat in jest, but she uncovered what many believe: if we don't have the gift of evangelism, then it's all right to remain silent. Nevertheless, God commands each and every one of us to 'go and tell'. That is what makes evangelism unique. Not everyone is called to be a prophet or a teacher, for example, yet even prophets and teachers are commanded to go and make disciples (Matt. 28:18-20). In other words, regardless of whether we have the gift of evangelism, we are still called to share the gospel with others.

However, when evangelism is done as poorly as I've just described above, it forces us to ask, what exactly *is* evangelism? Evangelism in its simplest form is introducing our friends to Jesus. Peter brought his brother Andrew to meet Jesus; Philip brought his friend Nathanael. Michael Green, who has written extensively on the subject of evangelism, believes the best description of evangelism is this: 'a presentation of Jesus Christ in the power of the Holy Spirit so that people will put their trust in God through him, accept him as their Saviour, and serve him as their King in the fellowship of his church.'

Another question we must ask is this: is there a 'right' way to do evangelism? Is one approach better than another? Answer: as long as Christ is proclaimed, the integrity of the seeker is honoured and the motive that drives us is the love of God, there is no form of evangelism that can be faulted. However, I believe there are a few things that, if properly understood, will help us to become more effective communicators of the gospel: understanding both the ways and the means of how to evangelize, and understanding the natural stages involved in the communication process. In this chapter we will examine the ways. In the following chapters we will examine the wonderful means that God has given that enable us to share the gospel in power.

There are three primary ways that God has given us to accomplish the task of evangelism. Our evangelism is the most effective when we proclaim the gospel, when we demonstrate Christ's compassion through our words and compassionate service, and when we depend on the Spirit and point to the demonstration of the Spirit's power. These ways are not mutually exclusive, and it is to be hoped that our lives model all three.

Certainly the primary form of evangelism is the proclamation of God's truth through the sharing of the gospel. However, opportunities to explain the gospel often come only when seekers experience Christ's love through us. Loving acts pique their curiosity, for they verify the authenticity of our message. And some seekers are drawn to consider Christ when they observe the Spirit's presence and power in our lives. One seeker, whose brother's conversion was accompanied by being supernaturally released from a ten-year drug addiction, told me, 'I had intellectual answers to refute every argument he proposed for why Christianity was true – except the major one. Who can argue against a completely transformed life?'

Declaring God's truth

The Bible tells us that true faith comes by the preaching and hearing of the Word of God. 'So faith comes from what is heard, and what is heard comes by the preaching of Christ' (Rom. 10:17). How are we to tell others? By drumming up a little message of our own? Fortunately not, for God's message of grace has been given to us through the gospel – his revealed message through his revealed Word.

It is not a story of human invention but a God-authored gospel that has the power to save! We are called to give the unchanging message that God sent his Son, Jesus, who took our sinful, broken humanity into himself and made it his own by dying on the cross. He sacrificed his life for us and overcame our sin. Then he rose from the dead so that by surrendering our lives to him our sins may be forgiven, our lives made whole and our eternal destiny made secure!

We proclaim the good news of what God has done primarily through the telling of the gospel. But the gospel is also proclaimed when we tell our story of salvation, for our conversion story illustrates the power of the gospel. Therefore, our task is to tell 'his' story and 'our' story in the hope that it may one day be 'their' story.

Displaying God's love

Second, Jesus tells us that the world may accurately judge whether Jesus is who he said he is by looking at how we demonstrate Christ's love (John 17:20–23). In other words, the communication of the gospel includes sharing the love of Christ to an ailing and lost world through self-giving service. How has God equipped us to do this? God has imparted his divine characteristics to dwell within us through the fruit of the Spirit: love, joy, peace, patience, kindness, goodness, faithfulness, gentleness and self-control. These characteristics of Christ are revealed as salt and light in a lost and needy world, whether by caring about the moral decay of our society, demonstrating integrity in the workplace, fighting for the dignity of the downtrodden or for those who suffer from discrimination, or simply loving our unchurched friends where we work, study or live. Whether we are identifying with the pain of our neighbour or serving strangers in a soup kitchen, we are engaged in the form of evangelism that demonstrates Christ's love for a lost and needy world.

Acts of kindness are a powerful means of grace. They are even more powerful when we reveal, at the appropriate time, the source of our love. To hide the good news of God's salvation and simply witness through loving presence is not enough, for then we would be depriving seekers of the knowledge of where they can find hope. 'I have not hidden your saving help within my heart, I have spoken of your faithfulness and your salvation; I have not concealed your steadfast love and your faithfulness from the great congregation' (Ps. 40:10).

Demonstrating God's power

Third, we bear witness to Christ by walking in and pointing to the power of God's Spirit. We know that effectual evangelism can be done only by the regenerating and liberating work of the Holy Spirit. We don't simply impart information when we share the gospel; we need the Spirit's power to give our words meaning and effectiveness. The truth must be spoken in the power of the Spirit. How does that happen? God's means of grace is the gift of the Holy Spirit, who indwells every believer. As we learn to walk in sync with the Spirit, he will give us just what we need in the moment we need it. Besides learning how to avail ourselves of all the Spirit offers, we should also point seekers to the manifestations of the Spirit's power.

In Jesus' ministry the proclamation of the good news was accompanied by the demonstration of God's power. Jesus not only preached to the sick – he healed them. He not only proclaimed salvation to those oppressed by evil – he delivered them. The proclamation of the gospel went hand in hand with a demonstration of the Spirit's power (1 Cor. 2:1–5).

'But that was Jesus,' we may say. 'How on earth are *we* supposed to do that?' Of the three approaches, we may feel the most inadequate in this one. But God has equipped us here too. Through the work of the Holy Spirit we are filled with the fruits of the resurrection victory of Christ. For example, what Christian has not seen God intervene at a point in his life when all seemed hopeless? Or been wonderfully surprised by something God has done when her feeble prayer received a resounding answer? Most of all, we have witnessed lives transformed by trusting in Christ – not the least of which is our own! We have far more in this arsenal than we realize. We must freely point seekers to the demonstration of the power of God wherever we see evidence of it.

Putting it all together

So now we know that people who say, 'I just fix people's cars for the sake of the gospel,' or 'I show Jesus' love by listening to their problems' are demonstrating the way and means of evangelism that *displays Christ's love*. This is worthy, for it reveals the character of Christ's compassion. Fantastic! Yet there is more. At the right time and the right place, seekers need to be able to connect our kindness with the source of our love by hearing the message of salvation. To witness by loving presence but never reveal the source of our love is not evangelism. Or when a person says, 'I preach the gospel, but I leave others to love them into the kingdom,' we know this is the aspect of evangelism that *declares God's truth.* Wonderful! But done alone it is insufficient. All Christians are summoned to the practice of love, for it reflects the character of God and authenticates the gospel we preach. Or for the person who says, 'I just pray and trust God to bring people to salvation', this is evangelism that rightfully depends upon and *demonstrates God's power.* But evangelism that never proclaims the gospel or mediates the love of Christ through acts that the seeker can observe is insufficient as well.

Think of all that God provides so that we may share the good news! He gives us his message of truth, he indwells us with his presence so that we may mediate his divine love to our neighbour, and he fills and renews us with his Holy Spirit. Evangelism is something that *God* does in people's lives; we are only the instruments he uses. It is the Spirit of God who convicts others of sin and who changes people's lives. It is so liberating to remember that God's initiative *precedes* our response. He is always there before us. Once we understand what evangelism entails and we see that God has provided all we need to accomplish the task, it frees us to share the good news with joy.

Evangelism, then, is most effective when it declares God's truth, when it displays Christ's love and when it depends on God's Spirit and points to God's power. But how do we start? Is there a process? Or do we dive in and start preaching to people, simply throwing out words without regard to people or the situations they are in? No, for to do that would be to subvert our best efforts.

In the next three chapters we will explore each stage of the communication process as we learn how to cultivate, plant and reap. We will also explore how to declare God's truth effectively, display God's love and depend on God's power so that our evangelism may be as fruitful as possible.

11

Cultivating the soil

I believe there is a process in the communication of the gospel that involves three phases. A Christian organization called Sonlife Ministries[1] has described this communication process quite aptly as (1) cultivating the soil, (2) planting the seed and (3) reaping the harvest. Or to put it another way, we need to learn 'CPR' in order to share the good news effectively. A lifesaving device to save lives eternally!

The first stage of 'cultivating the soil' is learning how to 'prepare the way' as John the Baptist did for Christ. We do this by arousing the curiosity of seekers so they will want to hear the good news. That doesn't mean we blindly engage in stage one with every seeker we meet. We need to pay attention, for perhaps the curiosity of the seeker has already been aroused. If this is the case, then we may have the opportunity of sharing the gospel, which is the second stage, called 'planting the seed'. Yet even announcing the gospel is not enough. At the right time we need to point out sensitively that God desires a response or decision to be made. In other words, the third stage is 'reaping the harvest', which involves an appeal to the will to make a commitment to Christ. Only God can make the human response positive. But evangelism isn't fully understood unless there is the hope to produce a harvest.

In this chapter we will examine the first stage in the process of evangelism: learning how to cultivate the soil of the seeker. In the next two chapters we will consider the other two stages.

A disclaimer

All along we have been talking about evangelism as a lifestyle.

135

We have looked at Jesus' life and examined a few practical conversational skills so that we may become more natural and at ease in sharing our faith. I do not now intend to change my basic approach. Techniques can be helpful to some people in limited ways, but they will not make us natural. So what follows is not a new, never-before-revealed technique of lifestyle evangelism.

In fact, learning how to speak and live God's truth, living in the presence of Christ's love and mediating it to others, and walking in the power of God's Spirit, not only help us in our evangelism but these graces enable us to live a life of faith. In one sense, evangelism training is simply calling believers to live as true Christians. When we live as we are called to be, evangelism can't help but happen.

But the danger of carefully analysing something – evangelism for example – is that we can turn it into a rigid formula. We can lose our spontaneity and start worrying, *Oh, dear. Am I supposed to be cultivating or planting right now? I can never keep it straight.* That would be the very antithesis of what I am intending.

My hope is that by exploring the natural stages of evangelism – cultivating, planting and reaping – and by looking at the means we've been given to accomplish the task, namely, living in God's truth, love and power, it will free us simply *to be* who we truly are in Christ. When we live by grace, we learn how to walk in the joyfulness of God. So what we have to offer others is not a life of rigid self-consciousness but a life of joyful abandonment to God. Life lived this way is the most powerful magnet for evangelism there is.

So, if what I am about to say in this chapter and the next two sounds like technique or makes you feel stilted, then ignore it. I merely want to look at the process of evangelism in the hope that it will clarify your thinking and make sharing the gospel seem less intimidating.

What it means to cultivate the soil

We cannot make people open to the gospel. We cannot coerce them into considering Christianity. So do we just hang around and wait until seekers come to us and say, 'By the way, I've always wanted to be saved, but no-one ever told me how'? Is there anything we can do to open blind eyes?

There is one sense in which our blind eyes are never fully opened until after we receive faith (Is. 35:4–5). But before there is a faith commitment, is there anything we may do as a possible preparation? Eugene Peterson said in a lecture, 'As we become practised in sin, we develop complex defences against grace. Do we penetrate these defences by frontal assault? Sometimes, but more often indirection is called for, slipping past the defences "on the slant".' Jesus, for example, used this method of 'indirection' when he spoke in parables in order to get through to people.

In Acts 26:18 Paul says Jesus first called him to *open the eyes* of unbelievers, then to turn them from darkness to light and to receive Christ in faith. In other words, Jesus is calling us to arouse the curiosity of seekers before we preach the gospel. If their curiosity is aroused, they will want to hear the gospel message. Remember, we are called to be 'fishers' of men and women who throw out bait, not 'hunters' who gun people down.

This first stage of 'cultivating' is called pre-evangelism. It's what comes before we proclaim the message of salvation. Using our agricultural metaphor, the soil must be cultivated before seed can be planted in order for a harvest to be reaped. How is the soil of seekers broken up or tilled? How is the seeker's curiosity aroused?

Let's examine the three resources that we looked at in chapter 10 and see how they can be applied to this first stage of evangelism.

Cultivating the soil by declaring the truth

All truth comes from God. But what aspect of truth is the most helpful to communicate in this 'cultivating' stage? Our goal, of course, is to proclaim the message of Christ. But if we speak prematurely, we may lose our opportunity altogether. What do we do? We first arouse the curiosity of seekers so they will *want* to hear the gospel. How do we do that?

We need to be careful listeners. We need to discover the questions our seeker friends are wrestling with. We also need to discover how much they already believe. We make a mistake when we assume there will be no points where we may connect in mutual belief. I usually try to find as many points of mutual agreement as possible before we explore where we disagree. This is particularly helpful when in dialogue with those of different religions. When we first establish the points of truth upon — which we agree, it not only builds bridges of understanding but also sheds light on the areas where we disagree.

Also, discern what the larger issue of truth is that lies behind whatever issue is being discussed. We need to encourage our friends to ask themselves what truth they base *their* opinion on, — and then to consider whether that truth is big enough to build their lives upon.

It is also helpful to know the questions that our culture is wrestling with. A wonderful way to do this is by seeing and discussing thoughtful films with seekers, as I did with my therapist friend mentioned in chapter 9. One of the most common threads of conversation between people is 'Did you see such-and-such a film? What did you think of it?' But one word of caution: just because we are striving to relate our message to the problems and issues of the day, that doesn't mean we allow the questions of our culture to reign supreme — — because our culture may not be asking the right questions! Yes, we take their questions seriously. We seek to understand what the Bible says in light of their questions. Yet we take far more seriously the questions that God asks of us. —

But how do we help seekers move from the questions of culture to the divine questions? One way is to develop skills that enable us to move a conversation from ordinary topics to spiritual ones. Once we do that, we are closer to sharing the good news.

As I have said before, we all have different temperaments. Some of us are cognitive; others of us, intuitive. Some respond naturally to ideas illustrated through graphs or charts; others are repelled by them. That is what makes communication with any person exciting and at the same time complex. So when examining any technique or model, we need to ask ourselves, *Does this correspond to the way I relate to people, or does it seem artificial and feel awkward? And even if it feels comfortable for me, would it be appropriate for the person to whom I am speaking?*

It is important to realize we are at least halfway responsible for how a conversation goes. We have choices in how we communicate. We should want to make our conversation count in representing Jesus Christ. But that brings us back to Jesus' own example. Jesus directed his conversations – for instance, with the woman at the well. He did not manipulate her, yet neither did he allow red herrings to get him off the track. He was not moulded by her presuppositions; her alternatives did not keep Jesus from his purpose.

So, to have purpose and ultimate desires for a conversation is not wrong. And it is not wrong to learn a few principles of communication to help us get a conversation going as well as to direct it toward spiritual matters. Here are three models that are not to be understood as rigid techniques but which some have found helpful in moving conversations from ordinary topics to spiritual ones.

Conversational model A: investigate, stimulate, relate

Investigate. First we must discover who the person is. This requires a genuine interest and curiosity in that person. Jesus was known as the friend of sinners. He loved all types of people and didn't distance himself from those whose lives weren't tidy. It is the love of Jesus that motivates our interest in others. One way we discover what a person is really like is by asking questions. Our culture does not encourage us to ask each other questions. We can fly from one end of the country to the other and never speak to the passenger next to us. But Christians are not to be moulded by their culture. We must learn to ask questions, draw people out, so that it becomes part of our lifestyle and not a technique.

To do that we need to learn how to be listeners first and proclaimers second. It is like rowing around an island, carefully viewing the shoreline for a spot to go ashore – a shared interest or a shared problem. Look for ways that God has made you alike. The more interests you have, the easier and quicker those mooring points are discovered. For the sake of Jesus Christ we need to be interesting! The more we enjoy God's world and develop our gifts, as well as explore new interests, the easier it will be to establish rapport with others.

If we listen for the nuances, we can draw others out without prying. Many people hesitate about giving direct messages because they are not sure anyone really wants to listen or are afraid that they cannot be trusted. Frequently people give clues about what things are bothering them or where they feel need. For instance, in response to, 'How are you?' someone says, 'After last week things could only go up.' Or as in the case of Betty when she said, 'I live alone, but I have so many hobbies that I never seem to notice,' which was an even more hidden message.

Sometimes people give us direct data but do not elaborate. For example, one person, after I invited her to a Bible discussion, said, 'Thanks for the invitation, but I can't. I went to a funeral last week, and now I'm bogged down with work.' In both cases the ball has fallen into our court. We must find a way to express concern and give them an opportunity to talk if they want to. We must approach with care any message that we think we hear. If we sense need, it is probably because they intended for us to hear it. Sometimes you may hear a need and feel you are not the person to meet it. Then find a person who can.

Even if you are suddenly tongue-tied and walk away feeling you blew it, it is not too late. Go back later and say, 'Listen, I'm so sorry about your grandfather's death. I just couldn't think of what to say to you the other day. But I care and I'm praying for you' (be sure you do actually pray). That may open just as many doors as an initial statement of condolence.

Stimulate. After we have an idea of who we are talking to, we must seek to arouse their curiosity about the gospel. This is one of the most neglected aspects of evangelism. We try to saturate people with information before we have caught their attention. A look at Jesus and Paul to study their fishing techniques will be helpful.

Jesus was often deliberately vague and intriguing with people at first, not giving the whole answer until he had their complete interest. When Jesus met the Samaritan woman (John 4:7–42), he told her that if she only knew who she was talking with, she would ask Jesus to give her some of his 'living water'. He knew that the Samaritan woman wouldn't understand what 'living water' meant, which was evidenced by her very practical retort that Jesus could hardly offer her living water since he had no bucket to draw water with! But Jesus told her that once anyone drank his brand of water they'd never be thirsty again.

Now we see that Jesus' deliberate obscurity was a stimulus and test of her spiritual interest. When she asked to receive this 'living water', he did not automatically give it to her because he knew she didn't yet understand. Instead, he sensitively approached the subject of her personal life, which as it turns out was somewhat sordid – as Jesus certainly knew. All of a sudden, Jesus' discussion about having a thirst that has never been satisfied begins to make a lot of sense. He did not manipulate her; he sought to arouse her curiosity. There's a world of difference between persuasion and manipulation.

Paul aroused the curiosity of the Thessalonian Jews in the synagogue with his fierce logic and rational arguments (Acts 17:1–8). In Athens he captured the interest of the Greeks by citing their poets to affirm his points: 'As some of your own poets have said, "We are his offspring"' (verse 28, New International Version). Also Paul, after walking through the city of Athens and seeing countless altars to various deities, turned to the people and both cleverly and tactfully said, 'Men of Athens! I see that in every way you are very religious. For as I walked around and looked carefully at your objects of worship, I even found an altar with this inscription: TO AN UNKNOWN GOD. Now what you worship as something unknown I am going to proclaim to you' (verses 22–23, NIV). We too need to develop a style of intriguing evangelism that piques interest in the gospel.

Relate. When we have discovered where people are and have aroused their interest in what we have to say, then we are ready to relate the gospel message. Investigating and stimulating are the necessary pre-evangelistic steps that will enable us to communicate Christ more effectively. But it is not enough to take the first two steps without the third. Paul, for example, knew his audience, found where they needed to grapple with commitment and then proclaimed the gospel (Acts 17:16–34).

The story of the lecturer I spoke to on the plane (chapter 9) is a good example of this model. As our conversation began, I 'investigated' by asking him many questions – about his field, his interests, his life. I took a genuine interest in who he was as a person. We don't take an interest in people in order to trick them into a conversation about Christ. We want to know and understand people because God loves them. Period. It is because of God's love that we also desire to share the good news of Christ. If we take the time to get to know people, it makes it much easier to know how to arouse their curiosity.

Once I understood that the lecturer was an intellectual, it wasn't hard to guess his resistance to faith: that there is no rational basis for believing. When I said, 'I don't think my work is rewarding, but it is terribly intriguing,' I was using the second element of this model. I was arousing curiosity just as Jesus did when he used the phrase 'living water' with the woman at the well. When the professor asked me why my work was intriguing, I had learned enough about him to guess pretty accurately what his objections to faith would be. I answered in a way that was truthful but also relevant to him.

After we had discussed the historical evidence for faith, he said, 'I wasn't going to tell you this, but I was brought up in a Christian home. Yet the more we talk, the more I realize that as a child I blindly accepted Christianity, but as an adult I have blindly rejected faith. For the sake of intellectual integrity I need to know what I've rejected. I'm not saying I believe the historical evidence, but I can't refute it either. So I'm going to get a Bible and start reading. But I want to tell you something. I think what strikes me most about you is that you seem to be a woman of hope and not despair. Why?'

I answered, 'Well, you see, the reason I am a woman of hope and not despair is because I have fallen hopelessly in love with Jesus Christ. I am not the same; I have been made new.' At that moment I no longer needed to investigate or stimulate. I was now free to relate the reason for the hope that is within me.

Conversational model B: concentric circles

Another important skill in moving conversations from common interest to spiritual matters is discerning what the underlying issue is that lies beneath the beliefs being expressed. For example, these days we often hear, 'I don't care what a politician does behind closed doors – I just care about his or her policies.' The unspoken greater issue here is the relationship between public and private morality. Is there a connection? Does compromise in one area affect compromise in another? From there we ask, 'Where does our sense of morality come from anyway?' In other words, what began as a belief being expressed moved to the larger issue of the nature of morality and ultimately landed at the theological question of morality's origin.

The model we will examine next has been adapted from one developed by Donald C. Smith. Conversations, he says, can be like an onion. As we peel off the layers in a conversation, we go even deeper into the mindset of a person. Often conversations begin with general-interest questions. (What do you do for a living? How many children do you have? What are you studying?) Then as the conversation develops and greater trust is established, we ask more specific questions. (What do you enjoy about your job? What era of history are you specializing in? What do you think about the present political scandal?) The next layer is the one that we frequently miss, but it is crucial. This is detecting and speaking to what the greater issue or the greater need is that hasn't been expressed. (Do you think the old adage is true that we reap what we sow? How does your art reflect the nature of humanity? Are you satisfied with what psychology is teaching you about people?) And then comes the theological layer. (What is the source of goodness? What do you think God demands of us?)

Here's how the model works out in practice. Once I spoke with a student and asked, 'What is your main subject?' (general-interest question).

'Art,' Peggy answered.

'I really think that's a great field of study. Why did you decide to study it?' (specific-interest question).

'Well, I suppose because I appreciate beauty,' she said.

'I do too. You know, I had a biology teacher once who said we are nothing more than meaningless pieces of protoplasm. Do you think a piece of protoplasm can appreciate beauty?' (underlying issue behind the interest).

'Mmmm, I've never thought of it before. But we must be more than that. The appreciation of beauty runs so deep in us,' she said.

'One thing has always intrigued me. Where do you suppose beauty comes from? I mean, what's its source? And where do we get our ability to appreciate beauty?' (theological issues).

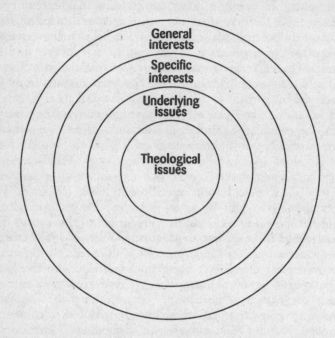

Figure 1. *'Concentric circles' model of conversation*

'You mean like God or something? I don't know, but it's interesting to think about.'

'Well, is there any evidence to support the idea that God is the source of beauty?'

From here on, one can continue this kind of conversation in many ways. The topic is already spiritual, and it can be natural to raise, for example, the question of beautiful people – like Jesus. When we hear people responding to their God-image (such as saying they appreciate beauty), we can help them see that it could be because they were created by a God who enshrines that very quality.

The transitional key in the model is addressing the larger underlying truth issue. It is not stopping at a flat statement of belief but probing deeper. It does not have to be an intellectual, abstract transition. For example, in my earlier conversation with Betty the turning-point was the underlying issue. I had picked up that she was lonely. But instead of asking her directly about it (which probably would have frightened her), I talked about my feelings about loneliness. 'You know,' I said, 'I've never yet lived alone. I guess I'm kind of afraid I'd get lonely.' In other words, I addressed the unspoken emotional issue hidden beneath her words. She responded by opening up her whole lonely life to me.

It could be that this model is not one you will find helpful. Fine. Perhaps you will find the following model more consistent with your style.

Conversational model C: relationships, beliefs, source of authority

This last model deals with the issue of how to keep conversations from degenerating into arguments. What do we say when a person voices an opinion that is in dire contrast to our own, especially an opinion we believe violates God's truth?

I have adapted the following conversational model from Mark Petterson.[2] He says, 'In any conversation the content is controlled to a large extent by the questions. If you want to control what is discussed, then you must take the initiative in asking questions.' He then defines three areas that conversations (and consequently questions) deal with: relationships, beliefs, source of authority.

Relationships. The first area of conversation is how a person stands with respect to a common denominator (work, school, college course, number of children, so on). This is like the 'investigate' part in model A and the 'general interest question' in model B. Conversation in this area is relatively easy and relaxed. We can usually find something of mutual interest.

Beliefs. Everyone has beliefs about politics, love, the meaning of life, God and so on. You might ask, 'What do you think about [a recent news story, an upcoming election, an ongoing social issue or Christianity]?' It is in this area of beliefs that conversation can break down. Meaningful interaction is difficult at this level if the beliefs are not shared. Conversations can soon degenerate into argument, each person solidly maintaining his or her previously conceived dogma and not listening or interacting with the other. For example, someone may say, 'I think church is full of hypocrites!'

You say, 'There may be some who aren't sincere, but I know many whose faith is genuine.'

He returns with, 'Well, I'm convinced that it's just a vast brainwashing conspiracy!' The other person is convinced to the contrary, the battle lines are drawn and fruitful interaction is ended.

How can we avoid the impasse and move into dialogue? The key is to move the conversation to the third area.

Source of authority. What if the Christian had responded by saying, 'Wow, you have some pretty deep feelings about this subject. What was it that led you to have such strong convictions?' In other words, you are asking the person *why* he believes as he does. Asking why makes people disclose their authority. This allows the conversation to continue and very often forces people to admit that what they believe about many important things is mere personal opinion. It may be possible, then, for the Christian to move the discussion on and show how Jesus provides authoritative information. If Christ's claim to be the living God is true, 'then his answers to the meaningful questions of life are of the utmost importance', Petterson writes.[3] By asking the question 'Why?' the Christian can often make any meaningful conversation eventually focus on Jesus Christ, who is the central issue.

It is also in this area that Christians must know not only who their authority is but also why he is reliable. That probably means being able to cite some evidence for the historicity of the gospel. We will take up the use of evidence in our conversations in chapter 15.

Again, these approaches are simply a means to get conversations on to gospel turf. If this isn't your strength, then forget about it. There are other ways to pique the curiosity of seekers. To arouse curiosity by appealing to issues of truth is an appeal to the mind. But how do we appeal to the heart?

Cultivating the soil by displaying God's love

In this chapter we have been considering how to gain a person's initial interest in Jesus. First we considered cultivating the soil by declaring the truth. Now let's look at how we might do this through the second way mentioned in chapter ten – displaying God's love.

Nothing touches the heart of people more than experiencing God's deep care and concern for them. This is especially true in today's world where there is such profound brokenness. It shouldn't surprise us, then, that people are drawn to consider Christ when they can see the love of Christ demonstrated through us. We are called to live a radically different lifestyle so that the loving presence of Christ within us may be seen in all that we do. As Donald Bloesch writes, 'We cannot make people open to the gospel but we can help them to be open to us as persons. In healing and feeding the hungry, Jesus was engaged in pre-evangelism.'[4]

In every stage of evangelism – be it cultivating, planting or reaping – seekers need to see Christ's loving presence in us. But it is especially critical in this first stage. For if seekers do not see the love of Christ in us, then they probably won't be interested in investigating any further. The famous quote from Emerson feels painfully apt: 'Who you are shouts so loudly that I cannot hear what you say.'

It bears repeating that most seekers won't pay attention to our gospel before they have seen our love and care for them as persons. If our hearers do not sense that the motive for our proclaiming the gospel message is love, then all of our efforts will be perceived as 'a noisy gong or a clanging cymbal' (1 Cor. 13:1). Even if we share Christ with virtual strangers, they can tell whether we care about them as persons.

People have amazing radar in this area. They know from our communication whether we regard them as persons to be cared for and enjoyed rather than objects to be manipulated and controlled. They can tell by our style whether they are projects we are working *on* or persons we are working *for.* If we are going to arouse their curiosity about Jesus, then we have to start behaving like Jesus!

I'm frequently asked how to be a witness in the workplace or with family members or flatmates. First, our colleagues must see that we are honest, truthful, reliable, that we don't engage in gossip and that we encourage and praise our colleagues' achievements – even in a very competitive workplace. Then it will be much easier to interest them in the gospel.

Likewise, our family members and those we live with will initially look far more at our behaviour than they will listen to our words. If they see in our behaviour unselfish service, kindness and patience, it will have an impact in drawing them to consider Christ. When I first became a Christian, I made many mistakes in witnessing to my family. But I recall overhearing one family member say, 'I knew Becky was converted when she offered to do the dishes – and it wasn't her turn!'

There are many creative ways to cultivate interest in the gospel by displaying Christ's love. Often the most natural expression flows from doing the things we love.

A friend of mine named Pat is an avid gardener. For the past three years she has organized something she calls a Garden Faire. For two days in early summer she opens her magnificent garden to the public. As friends, neighbours and strangers wander through her riotous poppies, hollyhocks and larkspurs, they can't help but read the thoughtful plaques she has placed throughout her garden. One says: 'All I have seen teaches me to trust the Creator for all I have not seen.' Other plaques have Scripture verses like, 'See! The winter is past; the rains are over and gone, flowers appear on the earth; the singing has come' or 'The whole earth is full of his glory,' or, 'The Lord will guide you always; he will satisfy your needs in a sun-scorched land and will strengthen your frame. You will be like a well-watered garden.' Just the sight of the glorious flowers next to such glorious verses would have made a convert out of me!

As you leave the garden there is a verse that reads, 'The grass withers, and the flowers fall, but the word of our God stands forever.' No-one walking through that garden could have left without knowing that Pat gardens to the glory of God! This is a beautiful example of cultivating evangelism, for it is low-key, sensitive and also a natural reflection of who Pat is.

Pat also volunteered to be the one who welcomes people to her community. When newcomers arrive, she brings them a basket of flowers, freshly baked bread and a list of the neighbourhood activities. One of those activities just happens to be the Bible discussion she leads!

Another way to cultivate friendships and practise the presence of Christ's love is by getting to know our children's friends and the parents of our children's friends. I have followed the example of my dear friend Pamella Bock. Pam held a yearly 'mother and daughter' tea for her daughter, Angela, until she finished school. I have done the same for my daughter, Elizabeth. It's not only a lot of fun, but it enables the mums to get to know their daughters' friends, as well as each other, and it cultivates the soil for future spiritual conversations.

My husband, Dick, says that our workplace and our personal interests should be our target zone for the gospel. As a businessman he says that he was always aware that his employees were watching him. They were observing whether he treated them fairly, seeing if he cared about their safety and well-being, watching how he conducted staff meetings and whether he disciplined employees fairly. Over time they realized that they could absolutely trust him to be fair because they knew he had integrity. They also knew he was a man of deep faith. It didn't take long before his employees began coming in to talk to him about personal problems. Some of his employees' wives even came in to discuss problems at home. It wasn't uncommon to walk past Dick's office and see him praying with his employees and their wives together.

Dick also says that he developed the practice of claiming territory for God. Dick is a great sports lover. So, for example, when he used to play tennis regularly, he would claim the tennis club for Christ every Tuesday and Thursday. And because he walked in expectantly, he often had remarkable conversations about the Lord. He is an avid skier, and he has deliberately taken some ski trips with friends who were not believers. He says that there is something about being in the majesty of God's creation that creates an openness in men to talk about God more easily than they normally would. He's also a racing yachtsman. He says many times he'd find himself crewing side by side with a complete pagan. Yet some of his most powerful conversations about Christ were in the wee hours of the night as they watched an awesome thunderstorm.

Look around you, see where your lives intersect with unchurched people. Claim your territory for God! Whether you are a nursery teacher, a banker, a labourer, a housewife, a student, an executive or an office worker, you have been given your own plot of soil to cultivate for the glory of God.

We've looked at how we can personally arouse curiosity in the gospel through demonstrating Christ's love. How can churches reveal the love of Christ in this stage of 'cultivating'?

Recently I was invited to train a church in evangelism. The pastor told me that his congregation had wanted to demonstrate Christ's love in practical service to their city. They had looked at the needs of their city and responded appropriately. In the past two years they had offered free car washes, free Christmas gift wrapping and free car-mechanic help once a month for single mums. They also gave family and teen workshops and worked among the poor in the inner city. He said most people were amazed to encounter such generosity and many wanted to know why they were doing such kind things.

Some of his congregation had made signs that read, 'Just the outpouring from a thankful heart.' If they were questioned as to its meaning or asked why they were doing these activities, they explained they had encountered the liberating love of Jesus and merely wanted to give something back. The next step, the pastor said, was to be trained in how to be better proclaimers of their faith.

Cultivating the soil by demonstrating God's power

How do we utilize God's power as we seek to 'cultivate'? There are times when we point seekers to the evidence of God's power. But we ourselves must be in constant dependence upon the Spirit of God because our most powerful weapons are those that employ not the wisdom of this world but the power of God: 'The weapons with which we do battle are not those of human nature but they have the power, in God's cause, to demolish fortresses' (2 Cor. 10:4, New Jerusalem Bible).

One example of an indispensable spiritual tool that fortifies us to tell others about the good news is prayer. We pray for blind eyes to be opened! Many people are blinded to the gospel. We need to pray that the Spirit of God will open the eyes of the blind so they can understand the truth about Jesus.

I remember bumping into an old friend I hadn't seen since school days. As we sat looking at a menu, Bob asked me if there had been any significant changes in my life since school. I took a deep breath and began to tell him about my faith in Christ. I remembered him as being intelligent and cynical, and it soon became apparent that in those respects he hadn't changed.

I tried every apologetic approach I could think of, only to be rebuffed with polite but patronizing remarks. Knowing I was getting nowhere fast, I excused myself and went to the ladies. There I prayed a fervent prayer: 'Lord, all Bob is hearing is *blah-blah-blah*. Let my words be spoken in the power of your Spirit. Transmit through me your meaning and speak to his heart. Open his eyes, Lord.'

I returned to the table. A few minutes later, in response to a question he asked me, I began telling Bob my conversion story. Initially he listened with the same scepticism. But suddenly it was as if someone had reached inside his head and turned on a light. Bob's whole countenance changed. In fact, he had a look of astonishment. 'Wait a minute – that makes sense,' he said. He began peppering me with questions about the Bible, about Jesus, about the meaning of the cross. We left the meal several hours later with my challenging him to start reading the Gospels.

The next morning the phone rang. It was Bob saying he'd been up all night and had only the Gospel of John left to read. Soon I introduced him to Christian men who befriended Bob and invited him to a Bible discussion. Six months later Bob gave his life to Christ.

How did it happen? It became clear that God had been pursuing Bob for a long time. Yet I know of no other explanation for what happened in that restaurant other than that the Spirit of God responded to my prayer. Why Bob responded to prayer so quickly, while others I have prayed for have not, is a mystery. But that experience powerfully reinforced for me how vital prayer is to evangelism. We need God's power to do God's work. In this pre-evangelism stage we need to ask God to give us wisdom and effectiveness, but above all we need to ask him to open the eyes and soften the hearts of those we are seeking.

We have looked at the first stage of evangelism and the resources that help us in 'cultivating the soil'. Now we are ready to examine the next stage of evangelism: 'planting the seed'.

12
Planting the seed

The proclamation of the unchanging message of Christ, the second stage, is the very heart of evangelism. 'Faith comes by what is heard and what is heard comes by the preaching of Christ' (Rom. 10:17). What brings people to faith is hearing the story of salvation, seeing the story confirmed in lives that bear the stamp of Christ's presence and love, and experiencing the story for themselves through the power of the Spirit. Our aim in this stage of the process is to communicate the gospel and to share its truth with clarity and confidence and power.

Once we have cultivated the curiosity of our hearers, the first stage, our next task is simply to introduce the gospel in the confidence that the gospel has its own power to persuade. Let's examine how to 'plant' the gospel message, and how, by using the same three ways we discussed earlier (God's truth, God's love and God's power), the seed of the gospel can take root and flourish in the heart of the seeker.

Planting the seed by declaring the truth

There are several ways we proclaim the truth of God's redeeming gospel. Certainly how we live our lives and the evidence of the Holy Spirit's power in us and around us gives testimony to the truth of God's claims. But the principal channel for conveying God's truth is proclaiming the gospel. It is important to remember once again that we did not invent the gospel. The gospel has been handed down to us. It is a message of revelation, not human invention (Gal. 1:16). That is precisely why it is life-transforming! It is *God's* message from start to finish. It is God's personal address, given through his messengers, calling people to repentance and faith.

But the very fact that the gospel has been divinely revealed, not humanly invented, also reminds us of our responsibility. The Bible makes it clear that we are not to tamper with its message (Gal. 1:8). We don't have the freedom to water down the gospel to make it more acceptable to modern trends. Certainly we have a responsibility to make the gospel relevant to the contemporary situation of our hearers. We need to use language that people understand. Our presentation needs to be coherent and understandable. But the essence of the message is unchangeable and timeless. Paul told the Corinthian church, 'We refuse to practise cunning or to falsify God's word; but by the open statement of the truth we commend ourselves to the conscience of everyone in the sight of God' (2 Cor. 4:2).

In other words, we want to make the gospel viable to the world but not palatable. As John Stott once said in a lecture, 'For the gospel to be effective it must remain prickly.' We aren't called to convince the seeker of our own truth and experience. We are simply called to introduce the gospel in the power of the Spirit with confidence and faith in God's power to convert.

Therefore, we need to have a basic understanding of the Christian message so that when we do feel led to give it we can. It doesn't mean that we will always start at the beginning and work systematically through each point. Nor does it mean that we must get all the facts across in a single conversation. Much depends on where seekers are and how much interest they have. But if we have a working knowledge of the essence of the gospel, it will help us enormously. For that reason I have listed in Appendix 1 some gospel outlines that you may find helpful.

'His story'

What is the gospel message? Donald Bloesch states it succinctly: 'The gospel is the surprising movement of God into human history recorded in the Bible culminating in the life, death and resurrection of Jesus Christ and the corresponding movement of God in the personal history of those who believe.'[1] To proclaim the gospel involves telling 'his story' primarily, for it illustrates the truth of what the gospel accomplishes.

Why is the gospel called good news? Because the story of

Christ addresses how God entered human history through Christ, who took upon himself the sin of the human race so that all who believe might be saved from the judgment we rightly deserve. Our message is that Jesus lived, died and rose again for our sin! We are to repent, believe and receive Christ as King. We are to follow Jesus as the Lord of our lives and to live under his rule. Everything about us, every aspect of our being – physical, social, psychological, intellectual, material – is to be lived for God's glory. Our new purpose is to live in partnership with God, whose desire, as Jesus taught in his prayer, is for his kingdom to reign 'on earth as it is in heaven' (Matt. 6:10).

Frequently I am asked, 'How much information should we share in order to communicate the essence of the faith?' It's a fair question. After all, there are entire books written on the subject. It can easily seem overwhelming. In fact, I've never been a person who can easily reduce profound truth to four or five points.

One thing that must be considered is the context. A person giving an evangelistic message to a crowd, for example, will have perhaps only thirty minutes to share the gospel. If you lead an investigative Bible discussion for seekers, you could have as many as seven or eight weeks to explore the life, the claims, the death and resurrection of Jesus. So to a certain extent, the format determines the amount of time available to proclaim the gospel.

But let's say that a friend or acquaintance asks you in private conversation, 'What does it mean to be a Christian? What is it that you believe?' What do you say? Let me share an experience I had recently.

One Sunday evening I came across an article in a magazine that told of a woman who, without having a medical degree, was able to diagnose illness even before it had fully developed. She could sense a tumour, for example, even before it appeared in any test. Some doctors were using her 'expertise' when they couldn't discern what was wrong with their patients. The source of her insight, she said, came from spiritual power – not necessarily God alone, but a whole team of 'spiritual guides'. She described hearing voices that guided her to her diagnoses. 'I love the invisible power. I can totally change people's lives,' she said.

As I read the article, it became clear that what had started as a naïve participation in New Age practices had led this woman into genuine occult practices. I couldn't help but reflect on what amazing times we are living in. Today it is commonplace to find reasonable, intelligent people believe they have been here before in a previous life, visit psychics and read their horoscopes while wearing lucky charms!

I finished the article feeling terribly sad. I turned to the Lord in prayer and asked, 'What do we say to people who are truly searching for you, then read articles like this and get sidetracked into dangerous, even demonic activities? What do we say to those who want an answer for how people like this woman have this kind of prescient knowledge?'

As I prayed, I sensed God was saying, 'Don't get involved in futile conversation about how these people know what they know. Simply ask a true seeker, "What is it that *you* want to know?"'

The very next day, as I entered a lift on my way to a doctor's appointment, an attractive woman in her mid-forties walked in next to me. As we exchanged pleasantries, I noticed she was carrying a book that had the word 'Spirit' in the title. I'm always curious to see what people are reading, so it wasn't unusual for me to ask her what the book was about. She responded by asking me if I had seen the article about a woman who was a 'medical intuitive'. I told her I had read the article carefully. She said that after reading the article she had decided to purchase a copy of this woman's book, and she had done so that very morning.

We had appointments in the same clinic, and as we walked into the empty waiting-room, she introduced herself as Kay. She told me of her astonishment at this woman's apparent ability to discern the physical and emotional ailments of people. How could these 'spirit guides' lead this woman into such knowledge? she mused. Where did such power come from?

After listening to her for a few minutes, I said, 'Is there any particular reason you are drawn to this book?'

'Well, I guess you could describe me as a seeker,' she answered.

I said, 'That's interesting. I would have once described myself in exactly those terms. Kay, we could spend hours pondering how this woman knows what she knows. But I think what interests me more is this: what is it that *you* really want to know?'

Kay sighed and looked out of the window. Then she answered, 'I want to believe there is some force or being out there who has created all of this. I desperately want to believe that this "God" is good. But what I can't get around is this: if God is good, then how can life be this awful? The front page of the newspaper today had a story dealing with moral scandal at the highest political level, another story was about parents who have forced their little daughter to live in a dog cage, and another article was on why children are murdering children. How can it be this bad? How can God be good with this much suffering? Why is life such a mess?' As she asked the questions the pain on her face was wrenching.

'There probably is no greater question than this one, Kay. I too have searched for God, and that question haunted me above all others. I think the issue is this: is the problem metaphysical or is it moral?'

'What do you mean?' Kay asked.

'Is the source of the problem to be found in God's nature or in human nature?'

'That's interesting. What do you think?' Kay asked

'From the different explanations I've seen, I think the Bible gives the most satisfying answer. It says there is a God and he is good. He created us in his image so we could have intimacy with him because he loves us. He also gave us free will because he loves us. Part of our dignity is that he gave us the capacity to choose. But at some point in history human beings chose the human experiment – we chose to be centred in self instead of centred in God. We chose self-rule instead of God's rule. It's what the Bible refers to as the fall, and the results have been catastrophic. Evil became a reality on our planet. So life as we see it now is not the way it was meant to be. It was not God's intention that there be this suffering. All of us now remain in the vicious cycle of self-rule, both by birth and by choice.'

'You know, I wouldn't find it hard to believe that *we* are the source of the problem,' Kay said. 'But the difficulty with that explanation is this: how could God have possibly thought it was worth the risk? How could he, knowing that there would be parents who'd lock up their kids in dog cages, still create us anyway?'

'Well, let's just suppose for a minute that the Christian story is true, that God created us in love. But we rebelled and chose to do it our way. And the effect of our rebellion is that it produced a state of deep separateness – from God, from each other, even within ourselves. In our brokenness we couldn't come to God, so God came to us. God didn't stand apart. He didn't abandon us. He sent his Son, Jesus, who became a man and entered fully into the human crisis and died on the cross for our sins in order to solve it, and to seek and save us. Maybe that doesn't directly answer why God created us, but such dramatic attempts on God's part to rescue us certainly reveal his overwhelming love for his creation.'

'So you're saying Jesus' coming was like God offering people a second chance? But why would he bother? Becky, how could God possibly love people who are so screwed up?'

'Kay, you've hit the nail on the head. The most amazing part of all is watching what divine love really looks like in Jesus. Nothing could turn Jesus' compassion and love into hatred. He was tested to the utmost, but nothing could overwhelm his love. Just *imagine* the implications if the Christian faith is true! Because of love, God created the world. Because of love, Jesus offered himself as a sacrifice on our behalf. Because of love, Jesus defeated and triumphed over everything that assails us – sin, death and evil!'

Kay looked at me for a few seconds and then said, 'What you are saying is profoundly moving. It even makes sense. I don't have any difficulty believing that we are responsible for the human mess. I even understand that we can't resolve the human crisis, even though it's of our own making. God would have to do that too. Perhaps he did by sending Jesus. But then what? Does the Christian just sit back and experience a cosy relationship with God? What about the unbelievable mess of the world around us?'

'You know, Kay, I read a passage in the Bible this morning that may answer your question. It's the very first speech that Jesus gave as he inaugurated his ministry. Obviously a first speech is terribly important because it outlines the mission: it's the person's manifesto statement. In his speech Jesus quoted from a text in Isaiah and said, "The Spirit of the Lord is upon me, because he has anointed me to bring good news to the poor. He has sent me to proclaim release to the captives and recovery of sight to the blind, to let the oppressed go free, to proclaim the year of the Lord's favour." Then he sat down and said, 'Today this scripture has been fulfilled in your hearing."

'Kay, to be in relationship with Jesus isn't finding a convenient way *around* suffering. It's joining Jesus as he works *through* the sufferings of those who are still in bondage to sinful self-rule. As forgiven people, we may then work in partnership with Jesus as he helps the blind to see, the lame to walk, the oppressed to be free.'

Then she asked, 'Where has your search led you, Becky?'

'I am utterly, totally, one hundred per cent convinced that Jesus is who he said he is. I have committed my entire life to him. Surrendering my life to Jesus hasn't insulated me from life's pain and difficulties, but knowing him has brought a joy that none of life's suffering could ever overwhelm.'

'But what do I do? I can't surrender my life to something I'm not convinced yet is true,' Kay said.

'I'd suggest two things. First, pray. Tell God that you aren't sure if he is there, but if he is, tell him you are trying to find him. Ask him to show you if Jesus is the way to God. Second, get a modern translation of the Bible and start reading the Gospels. Determine that you won't stop until you discover who Jesus is. Read and pray every day, and ask God to reveal his truth to you.'

'What if I come to believe that it's true?' Kay asked.

'Then you confess your sins to Jesus and thank him for dying on the cross, accept in faith his forgiveness and ask him to come into your life as King. Then find a church you feel comfortable with and join the family of faith!'

'I can't say I believe yet, but I *will* do what you've suggested. I just wish it were easier, and I didn't feel so vulnerable.'

'Kay, I will pray for you. And I've got wonderful news. As much as it feels like it's all up to you, it's really God who is seeking you! It's God who pursues us, and he promises that he always finds any seeker who is genuinely searching for him. He won't lose you, Kay. You're not going to slip through his fingers. Just look at what's happened in this waiting-room!'

At that exact moment the nurse opened the door and said to me, 'I'm so sorry the doctor has been running late. He's ready to see you now.'

I have prayed for Kay ever since that encounter. I am not sharing this story as an example of how to explain the gospel perfectly. In fact, afterwards I thought of things I should have said, and worried about what I hadn't made clear. But I had to remind myself of what I've already said to you: God is the one who converts, not us. We simply do the best we can in the moment God has given us and trust him for the results.

However, what were some of the elements of the gospel message I communicated to Kay? We touched on four areas that comprise main points of the gospel message: God's nature; the human crisis of sin; Jesus' life, death and resurrection; and the appropriate human responses to such good news, namely, repentance, faith and obedience. Furthermore, because of the nature of Kay's questions, I had the freedom to lay the framework of a biblical worldview. The gospel made greater sense to her because she heard it in the broader context of the stories of the creation and the fall.

What aspects of the gospel we initially emphasize will be determined in part by the seeker we are speaking to. What struck me about Kay was her sensitivity to the sufferings of the world. That is a perspective more typical, perhaps, of someone in her forties than of someone in her twenties. I believe she came to understand that human suffering is rooted in our sin, not God's neglect. She also wanted to know how faith is lived out – how it really works – which is very typical of a modern person. Judging by her responses, it was hearing about the love of God and Jesus' triumph through the resurrection over every evil that attacks humankind that moved her most.

While she intellectually grasped that the source of human suffering is our sinful insistence on self-rule, I didn't sense in Kay a deep realization of her own sin. But such knowledge will come – indeed, it *must* come – if she is to be truly converted. Nobody understands it all in one go. We can trust and ask God to enlighten seekers in their journey, just as he does for us.

Our story

To proclaim the gospel not only involves sharing God's message of salvation; it involves sharing our conversion story as well. However, we need to remember Paul's warning when he said, 'We do not preach ourselves, but Jesus Christ as Lord' (2 Cor. 4:5, New International Version). So what purpose does our conversion story have? Helmut Thielicke helps us to understand: 'The witness not only confesses and declares *his message*, he also confesses and declares *his encounter* with the message.'² When we share our conversion story, it reveals our encounter with God's power and the beauty of his touch upon our lives.

But our story also reveals a terribly important lesson. The only way we ever discover the true nature of Christianity is when we step out and commit ourselves to Jesus. Then we begin to see for ourselves that God is real. There simply is no substitute for direct, personal experience. So long as we remain outside, debating or even believing the truths only in our heads, we can never really embrace the Christian way.

It has often been said that God has only children, no grandchildren. Tradition, in other words, cannot possibly make you a Christian. Only a personal encounter with Jesus as Lord accomplishes that. All of us are required to verify for ourselves what we have been taught on this all-important journey of faith. 'The Creed,' said Metropolitan Philaret of Moscow, 'does not belong to you unless you have lived it.'³

Therefore, if you have trusted Christ but feel your story is unexciting or inadequate because you were brought up in a five-generation Christian home, take heart. Every one of us is absolutely unique. No-one could ever duplicate your journey because it is uniquely your own. You need to take your story seriously. There are truths you were brought up with, traditions you may take for granted (or even be embarrassed by) that your secular neighbour is starving for. There is such brokenness in our society today that many people can't fathom what it would be like to have had parents who prayed every night at their children's bedside.

Besides taking our own story seriously, we need to learn how to communicate it. And as we do so, we need to be honest and real. We don't have to pretend that we are now perfect or that we never struggle in any areas of our lives. To be able to share honestly what some of our difficulties were, or what inner questions and angst led us to seek Christ, can be helpful to others. But that doesn't mean we need to make inappropriate public confessions. Paul's testimony in Acts provides a helpful model (Acts 26:9–23). He first spoke of what he was like before, then what it meant to meet Jesus and what it meant for him since. Follow Paul's example and write down the story of your journey with God. Practise sharing it, first with friends and then with seekers.

Never underestimate the power of *your* story. It is uniquely your own, ordained by God, and it couldn't possibly be duplicated.

Planting the seed by displaying God's love

One of the biggest challenges in communicating the gospel is how to talk about sin. Everyone wants to hear good news, but how do we communicate the 'bad news' without alienating seekers? This is a particular challenge in our happiness-oriented, self-absorbed modern culture. And what exacerbates this problem even more is that we live in an age that believes our problems are rooted either in addiction or in emotional wounding. The point is not that this analysis is entirely wrong. Indeed, many *do* suffer from addictive behaviour; most people *are* emotionally wounded. But neither analysis uncovers our deepest problem – the problem of sin.

I believe one of the critical issues that the church faces is how not to shrink from naming sin and still be the bearers of grace. Christians have tended to deal with the subject of sin in one of two ways: either by being silent or by being judgmental. Either we skip over the uncomfortable bits and wind up conveying a gospel of warm feelings and cheap, sentimental grace, or we behave and speak in ways that appear condescending, judgmental and critical.

How can the whole truth of the gospel be spoken in ways that people can hear? I agree wholeheartedly with Donald Bloesch, who says, 'We can only know our sin when we have first been confronted with the depth of God's love for us revealed in Christ.'[4] But that's impossible, we say. How do we tell seekers about sin and communicate God's love at the same time? We do it in two ways: by our style of communicating and by the substance of our message.

One way our style reflects the love of Christ is when we properly identify with the problems, stresses and hopes of others. That should not be hard to do since we know that we, too, are sinners who have received forgiveness and who constantly depend upon God's strength to conquer sin. Unbelievers need to see God's effectiveness in our lives, but they also need to sense our understanding and sensitivity to the complexities of their problems. Jesus himself modelled this compassionate understanding toward human frailty. 'We do not have a high priest who is unable to sympathize with our weaknesses, but we have one who in every respect has been tested as we are, yet without sin' (Heb. 4:15).

Second, we communicate God's love by our message. Our compassion and sensitivity toward others comes directly from our personal encounter with God's grace through the gospel. We share the cross because it was the means whereby we have been set free, and we know it has the power to set others free too. It is a message that acknowledges the problem of sin while at the same time assures us of the possibility of forgiveness.

We communicate grace and truth, then, by our loving and compassionate style and by the substance of our message of salvation. Let me share an encounter I had that illustrates this.

A year ago I boarded a plane and took my seat next to a man who appeared to be in his late twenties or early thirties. I had just finished speaking to a conference, and all I wanted was to sit quietly and read my book. But my seat-mate soon introduced himself as Rick and seemed eager to talk. As I put my book away I asked him what he did for a living.

He told me he had been a rather famous racing-car driver. In his racing days he thought he had everything: fame, money, all the trappings of success. He felt invulnerable. That all ended when he was in a near-fatal accident while racing. He was in hospital for months, his worst injury being to his legs, which were severely broken. After a long period of therapy and an extended stay in hospital, he was finally released. Remarkably, he was able to walk without a limp, but his doctors told him he could never do motor-racing again.

Without his career or a big income to give him identity, he became terribly depressed. He had been a heavy drinker before, but now he became a fully-fledged alcoholic. Looking back, he said there were four or five years that he couldn't even account for. Then one night, in a drunken stupour, he crashed his car into a wall. For weeks the doctors didn't think he would live, but amazingly he pulled through. When he was fully conscious, he was informed that both legs had been broken again. He was told he would probably never walk. He knew he'd come to the end of his tether.

Rick said, 'I've never been a religious person, but for the first time in my life I cried out to God and asked him to help me. I told him I was sorry I'd made such a mess of my life. I asked God to please let me walk again. I promised that as soon as I was released I would join Alcoholics Anonymous. I also told God that I'd try to find out more about him so we could get to know each other.'

Sure enough, after extensive therapy and to the astonishment of his doctors, his severely broken bones mended, the connective tissues healed and once again he was able to walk. He kept his word, and upon being released from hospital he joined Alcoholic Anonymous. He hadn't had a drop to drink for sixteen months. Not only that, but at the AA meetings he had met a wonderful woman, whom he planned to marry soon.

We talked for a long time about the changes in his life, his goals and dreams for the future and his profound regrets about the people he had hurt during his alcoholic days. What haunted him most was that he had never visited his beloved grandfather while the old man lay dying of cancer in the hospital. His grandfather died while Rick was still in an alcoholic haze; he never got to say goodbye.

Then I said, 'You know, Rick, the pain of facing your regrets, now that you are sober, is tough. It's very tough. But I must tell you how much I admire your courage in facing yourself, for owning your problem and sticking with your recovery. I think owning our problems is the hardest work any of us has to do. It's hard on our pride, but ultimately it is liberating, don't you agree?'

'No question about it. The hardest part was to stop blaming everybody else and accept responsibility for what was my problem alone. But you're right; it was freeing finally to own it. Becky, you really seem to understand, and you don't feel judgmental. Hey, are you in recovery too?' he asked with sudden intensity.

I paused for several seconds before answering. 'Yes, I am in recovery. But not for alcohol. I'm in recovery for a problem far deeper than alcoholism.'

'What do you mean?' Rick asked as his eyes widened.

'I'm in recovery, Rick, from what the Bible calls sin. You know why I don't seem judgmental to you? Because I've learned that the only thing that separates people is their symptoms – but *all* of us suffer from the same underlying disease of sin. It's the one disease everyone needs recovery from.'

'I'm not sure I get it. What's the difference between being a drunk and being a sinner? Isn't it the same thing?' Rick asked.

'Alcoholism is the addictive behaviour. Sin is what lurks behind the behaviour. The *core* of sin isn't so much a set of behaviours as it is having a God-complex. You could never drink a drop of alcohol again, Rick, and still be determined to run your own life rather than let God be in charge. Sin is choosing to be self-ruled instead of God-ruled. And destructive behaviour, in whatever form it takes, is always the inevitable result of refusing to let God be God.'

'Oh, man, I can really identify with what you're saying. I took such pride in being in charge of my life. No-one – not God, not my parents – *no-one* could tell me what to do. And look at where it got me! But if AA is the treatment for alcoholism, then what's the treatment for sin?' Rick asked.

'Let me ask you something, Rick. You said that you cried out to God in the hospital. Now you follow the twelve-step programme, which means you daily acknowledge your powerlessness over your addiction, which you can't conquer without the help of a "Higher Power", right?'

'Absolutely!'

'Have you found the name for this "Higher Power"?'

'No, not yet,' Rick answered. 'But ever since I prayed that night in the hospital, my life has been different. I can just tell God has been looking out for me. I'm still searching, though. I want to know more about who God is.'

'Rick, I know the name of the Higher Power – his name is

Jesus. And the treatment for sin is the cross. All of us have tried to live our lives as if we deserved to be God, and look at the mess we've created! But God sent his Son, Jesus, who took our broken humanity into himself and made it his own. We deserved God's judgment, but Jesus stepped in and took it for us. He sacrificed his life for us and overcame our sin in his own heart so that *our* hearts could be changed. He rose from the dead and he offers to heal our brokenness, to forgive our sins and to make us whole. We just need to surrender our lives to him, to repent and believe.'

'Yes, but I've really screwed up. I mean, I know God is there; otherwise, I'd probably be dead by now. But how could I ever believe that God would forgive me for everything? Especially after all that I've done – it just wouldn't seem fair.'

'That's what the cross is all about, Rick! All of us nailed Jesus to the cross. Alcoholics and teetotallers, church folk and pagans, preachers and prostitutes – all of us are responsible for the death of Jesus. Luther says we carry his very nails in our pockets. But Jesus loved us so much that he voluntarily chose to die for us. Don't you see, Rick, if the cross shows us how serious our sin is, it also shows us that there is nothing we could ever do that cannot be forgiven.

'You think your sins are bad,' I continued, 'but have you ever considered that you've done something worse than being an alcoholic? You are responsible for the death of God's Son. And so am I. Our insistence on playing God is what drove Jesus to the cross. What could be worse than that? And if the cross shows us that God is willing to forgive us for the death of his Son, then why wouldn't he be willing to forgive us for every other sin? That's the amazing love of the cross!'

Rick was a strong, rough-hewn kind of guy. But for the first time in our two-hour flight, he wept. Unbeknown to me, Rick had boarded our plane with the soil of his soul fully cultivated. All he needed was to hear the proclamation of the gospel. He was wide open and ready to receive Jesus as Lord. As our plane touched down, he asked me how to make a confession of faith. Then he bowed his head in silence for several minutes.

Afterward he said, 'Listen, my fiancée will be waiting for me outside. I'd really like her to meet you. I want to share everything we've talked about with her. And I'd like to start our marriage together in faith. Do you have any suggestions?'

'Well, start by sharing with her what has just happened to you. And may I be the first to send you a wedding present? I'd love to give you a family Bible and a devotional book that you can read together. And I'll send a book on the basics of the Christian faith. OK?'

It was a small airport, and as we quickly reached the waiting area, his fiancée was there. Rick introduced me and excitedly began to tell her everything we had talked about. She looked slightly dazed by his overwhelming enthusiasm, but I couldn't stay to help explain. Since I knew someone was waiting to pick me up, I excused myself and started walking across the airport.

Then something happened that has never occurred to me before or since. As I was walking, my heart overflowing with joy by what had just happened to Rick, I suddenly heard the sound of a chorus of praise and another sound that was like the tinkling of chimes. It was unlike anything else I have ever heard in my life. It was so beautiful, so exquisite, so majestic that I stopped dead in my tracks. I turned around to see where it was coming from, and nothing was there. It probably lasted for several seconds, but I stood transfixed in awe.

The sound ebbed away when I realized someone was calling my name. It was Rick's fiancée, calling me from the other side of the waiting area. By the look on her face it was clear that Rick had told her about his new-found faith. With tears streaming down her cheeks, she shouted across a crowded airport, 'Becky, thank you! Thank you! Thank you!'

I cannot imagine a more theologically appropriate bene-diction to that experience. What else can we say in response to a God of such generosity, such love, such grace, who pardons our sins when we deserve death, who transforms us, fills us with his Spirit and delights to call us his own? The longer I live, the more I have come to see that the only language appropriate for such an awesome God is the response of praise overflowing from a grateful heart – praise that says in awe and humility, 'Oh, God, thank you! Thank you! Thank you!'

How was the love of Christ mediated to Rick? How do we communicate God's grace and the tough truth about human sin without alienating people? First, by developing a style of communicating that identifies with the human problem.

Seekers don't need to stand alone in their feelings of guilt and remorse. We can stand right there with them. We can identify with their problem of sin because, even though the sins for which we have been forgiven may be quite different from their sin, we still share the same underlying problem. We, too, sent Jesus to the cross.

Second, we convey grace and truth when we share the message of salvation. Rick felt a great deal of guilt for his alcoholism. Ironically what set him free was looking at the cross and realizing that the core of his problem was much deeper than simply taking another drink. The cross always brings us out of hiding because it makes us see that if Jesus had to die, then we have a problem that is far more serious than we ever imagined. Yet the cross also gives us hope. As I wrote in *Hope Has Its Reasons*, 'The cross breaks our denial, but only *in the very instant* that it shows us the possibility of forgiveness. It shows us our corruption, but in the same breath it tells us the price has been paid … The Christian view of sin is radical but not pessimistic because to see sin in Christian terms is to see that sin can be forgiven. That really is freedom. That really is amazing grace.'[5]

In reflecting upon my experiences with Kay and Rick, I believe they teach us several truths. First, people are drawn to the gospel for many different reasons. Some are drawn to consider Christ because of crisis or pain, others because of guilt over sin, still others because they long for meaning and purpose for their lives. Second, because people vary and their needs are so different, it's not surprising that they respond to different aspects of gospel truth. Nearly everyone responds to the fact that God loves them. But beyond that central truth, what people respond to initially varies enormously. Third, because people's needs are so varied, it may actually affect the way in which we explain the gospel. I know that was true in my experience as I shared Christ's victory over evil with Kay and shared the depth of sin with Rick.

Even theologians, in seeking to define the gospel's essence, and in examining the meaning of the cross, have emphasized different aspects of its glorious truth.[6] To come to true faith in Christ involves confessing our sins, believing in Christ and receiving God's Spirit as we live our lives in full surrender to

Christ as King. But what initially draws a person to consider Christianity will undoubtedly relate to his or her needs and particular situation.

So if you are a person who worries that you never seem to communicate the gospel in exactly the same way, take heart. You are in good company. The New Testament writers were unable to reduce the gospel to a single metaphor. Even Jesus never seemed to repeat himself either. He rarely explained the gospel in the same manner. Sometimes he communicated the gospel using the metaphor of bread; at other times he used the word 'water', because what he said was in the context of the person he was speaking to.

If, however, you are someone who finds great freedom in expressing the gospel in exactly the same way each time, that is fine too. Just be certain you are truly listening to the other person and try to connect the aspects of gospel truth that will be the most relevant to that person. God wants his truth proclaimed. So long as what we say is motivated by God's love and faithful to the truth of the gospel, that is all that matters.

Planting the seed by depending on God's power

We've already said that our communication of the gospel depends not on human strategies or well-polished techniques or even brilliantly reasoned arguments but on divine initiative. It is the hidden work of the Holy Spirit that gives our words meaning and power and that produces changed hearts. God has also given us powerful spiritual resources that serve us in the task of evangelism. For example, the Word of God is filled with the power of the Spirit and brings life and renewal to those who seek him. The great Reformer John Calvin had a similar position: 'God alone is a sufficient witness of himself in his own word.'[7]

Over the years I have been amazed by how powerfully God speaks to seekers through the Scripture. God's Word truly does not return to him empty. J. I. Packer said in an interview, 'You have liberty and authority when you allow the Bible to talk through you, a liberty and authority you don't have if you're offering your own ideas or cherished notions.'[8] I couldn't agree more wholeheartedly.

I have frequently led Bible discussions for seekers in which we examine the life of Jesus. One that stands out in my mind in particular consisted of a group of women who were accomplished and competent professionals. One was a powerful executive who exuded a rather intimidating, no-nonsense air. One week she said, 'I haven't been able to get Jesus out of my mind all week. I keep asking myself, *What would Jesus do with the power I have in my job?* You know, I can spot a person who has complete authority a mile away. And Jesus possesses an authority like no-one I've ever seen. Yet he uses his power so beautifully to serve others. I found myself wanting to talk to him about important decisions I need to make this week. But then I said to myself, *Wait a minute, you don't even know if you believe in Jesus!'*

This is exactly what I mean about the way God uses his Word. The Spirit of God speaks through his Word in ways that can't be measured, explained or controlled. God's Spirit speaks through Scripture and gets into our bones and marrow and sinks into our consciousness in extraordinary ways.

How do we use the Bible in our evangelistic efforts? Christians often feel inadequate in evangelism because they haven't memorized enough Bible verses. Scripture memory is an invaluable tool in developing our Christian character, but frankly I have not found that sharing isolated verses with seekers is as effective as when we share the stories of Jesus or passages of Scripture that have moved us. In my experience that is when the Spirit operates with greater power.

Part of our preparation for doing evangelism is studying and meditating upon Scripture, allowing the Word of God to dwell in us richly. The more we gain insight from a passage and are moved by its meaning, the greater it enables us to communicate God's truth with power and clarity. It's amazing how often God uses our personal daily Bible reading to provide the truths we need to share with the person God leads into our lives that very day.

Another invaluable spiritual resource in evangelism is prayer. As we pray, God guides us into truth and sometimes shows us how to share that truth.

My experience with Kay illustrates how God uses both prayer and his Word. After reading the article about the 'medical intuitive', I had asked God what to say to seekers who might be led astray by reading such an article. I felt heartened by the Lord's answer and went to sleep. The next morning the Bible passage I read for my devotions was Luke 4. As I meditated in silence and in prayer on that passage, I was moved to tears by Jesus' profound commitment to restoring and setting people free from the ravages of sin. His purpose is for the blind to see, the lame to walk, the oppressed to be free and the captives to be released! But *never* did I imagine that only four hours later I would be quoting that very passage to a woman searching for God, a woman who had read the very same article as I had the night before.

I shouldn't be surprised. He is the living God who is always seeking and searching for his lost sheep. But what's important to note is this. Kay's manner while speaking to me was intense and sincere but very self-contained. It was only in the moment that I quoted the passage from the Bible that tears welled up in her eyes. Never underestimate how spiritually alive the Word of God is. I could almost hear its crackling power as I spoke it.

The Spirit chooses to work and speak through our human acts and words. God also speaks through his divinely appointed means of grace, such as preaching, prayer, the Bible, worship or the demonstration of our Christian life. As seekers come into contact with clear preaching, hear the Word of God, watch us at work and worship, and are the recipient of our prayers – watch out! Their lives may be changed.

13

Reaping the harvest in God's truth and love

All stories of conversion are different. Some conversions are dramatic, others quiet. Some people respond out of crisis, others in calm. But the common element in every story is that, one way or another, God reaches us. He comes through. He does not abandon us. But neither does he barge in uninvited.

In the more than thirty years that I have been a Christian, I have seen many people turn their lives over to God and be changed. And yet the awesome mystery of conversion never fails to move me. Any Christian who walks with God over a period of time witnesses the marvellous acts of God's mercy and power. We see him heal people of illness; we watch him restore the emotionally wounded to wholeness; we see him forgive and release from guilt those who have been in bondage to sin for years. Our lives bear witness to the countless prayers we have seen God answer, meeting the needs of the financially distressed, giving wisdom to those who seek it, giving grace and peace to those who suffer.

Yet for all the abundant evidence of God's power and grace, what could be more miraculous than seeing a person who was once dead in sin become alive to God? I believe the miracle of conversion is greater than the creation of the world. When God created the world, he had no sinful opposition to deal with. But when a person responds positively to God's call – even after the world, the flesh and the devil have all mounted their opposition – what we are witnessing is simply one of the greatest miracles there is. No wonder there is such joy in heaven over one sinner who repents!

Even more remarkable is that God invites us to be part of that process. We are his ambassadors. We not only have the honour of sharing God's message but we even have the awesome privilege of inviting a response.

Let's examine this glorious truth of God's work of transforming us. Then we will look at the marvellous resources God has given us as we learn how to declare God's truth, display God's love and depend on God's Spirit as we enter this final stage of evangelism.

Conversion: not information but transformation

The whole notion of our need for transformation rests on the premiss that we have a problem so serious that only God could solve it. But to benefit from the cure we need to understand the nature of the disease. As we saw in the last chapter, the nature of the disease, the ultimate source of human woundedness, comes from the dislocations of not making God the centre of our lives. Having put ourselves out of joint with God, we have wounded ourselves as well. In defiance and arrogance we have tried to be equal with God by putting ourselves in the centre instead of God. As the great prophet Ezekiel said in the eighth century before Christ, 'Though you are a man and no god, you try to think the thoughts of a god' (Ezek. 28:2, New English Bible).

What, then, can be done about our narcissistic, self-focused nature? We can't reach in and straighten a twisted nature. Though we are responsible for our condition of sin, we are powerless to change it. Can we overcome our addiction to ourselves by sheer willpower? What self-improvement course will give us the power to stop ourselves from being self-centred and self-absorbed?

It's at this stage of the journey that Jesus takes us by surprise. Just when we realize our poverty and our powerlessness, Jesus tells us to rejoice! Why? Because help is on the way! Only a power that is stronger than ourselves can help us overcome ourselves. That is why Jesus calls it the good news. He knew that the fatal human disease within our nature could be cured only by the Divine Surgeon.

Both the remedy and the proof of God's love and solution to our crisis are seen in the cross and the resurrection. The cross enables us to see our problem and how God solved it. The resurrection is where we see that human nature can be changed. Why does the resurrection give us confidence that we can be transformed? Because the very Spirit of God who raised Jesus from the dead and gave him physical life also enters our being when we are converted and gives us spiritual life. No other cure could solve our spiritual crisis but conversion.

Moral reformation, for example, looks at rules and how to conform. It focuses on our behaviour when what is needed is the reformation of our hearts. Spiritual transformation looks at Jesus and how to be transformed into his likeness! That's why moralism and legalism as solutions to sin are woefully inadequate. They may make us nice, but they don't make us new. Christ's cure is not, as C. S. Lewis wrote, teaching a horse exercises so he can jump higher and higher. 'Christianity,' says Lewis, 'is doing an operation on the horse so the horse can *fly*!'[1]

What makes humans fly? Or to put it less dramatically, what enables us to transcend our flawed human nature and live transformed lives? 'God's great secret, and the Christians' hope of glory ... that secret kept from the generations and the centuries past, is this: "Christ in you".'[2] When we receive Jesus as Lord and Saviour, God's Spirit takes up residence in our souls. That's what makes us a new creation. We now have within us not only our old human nature but God's new nature through his Spirit. This transformation does not happen overnight. But it could not happen *at all* unless God's Spirit indwelled us.

So, we cannot be transformed without being indwelt by Christ's Spirit. We cannot be indwelt with Christ's Spirit without being converted: We cannot be converted without surrendering our lives in faith to Christ. That is why our goal in evangelism is not merely to *tell* people about Christ; it is to *lead* people to Christ as well – so that their lives may be indwelt and transformed by God's Spirit, just as ours have been.

Seeing how vitally important conversion is, should we simply nail seekers to the wall and force them to repent and be converted? The truth is, only God converts the human soul. As Jeremiah, the crusty prophet of old, said, 'O LORD, You induced me, and I was persuaded' (Jer. 20:7, New King James Version). Pascal, the great French philosopher, mathematician and Christian, said, 'We shall never believe, with an effective belief and faith, unless God inclines our hearts, and we shall believe as soon as he does so.'³

So, in a strict sense, it is only the Spirit of God who can bring conviction of sin and liberate our will that has been deadened by sin. Does that mean, then, that we are off the hook? Have our responsibilities ceased once we have proclaimed the good news?

The truth is, the announcement of the gospel is not enough. As witnesses and servants of Christ, we are called to seek a commitment to Christ. We don't do this by force or manipulation. But at the right time and the right place we encourage seekers to respond to the truth. As ambassadors for Christ, we hope for conversions and even seek them, not by our power but in the power of God. We can be instruments of the Spirit in his work of persuasion and conviction. This doesn't mean, however, that we are responsible for the results. As Methodist authors Eddie Fox and George Moore point out, 'The only failure we ought to fear is that of failing to spread the gospel of the kingdom. The results are in God's hands.'⁴

Let's look at what we can do, then, to encourage seekers to commit their lives to Christ.

Reaping the harvest by declaring God's truth

What truths do we need to make clear to anyone seriously considering Christianity? How do we help people cross over the line into making a commitment for Christ? First, we need to make it clear that there is a decision to be made and that only they can make it. God will not force his love on them. He will not require them to have a reconciled relationship with him if that is not their choice.

Let's also help those considering Christ to understand that making a decision is not only how we enter the kingdom of God but it is also how we continue to grow in the kingdom. We must choose each day to love and serve God, to listen to Jesus and obey him. No-one drifts into discipleship, just as no-one drifts into God's kingdom. The seeker's need to make a decision simply mirrors what the life of discipleship is all about.

What, then, are the steps involved in making a genuine commitment to Christ? In the New Testament the primary elements of conversion seem to be a response of repenting, believing and receiving the Holy Spirit. To complete reconciliation with him, we must each admit that we have rebelled (Matt. 4:17), confess that we cannot be reconciled to God apart from what Christ did on the cross (John 1:12), and accept Christ's purpose, rule and power in our lives. Through prayer we can invite him to live in us (Rev. 3:20). Let's look at each aspect.

Repent. First, we repent of our sins. This involves asking God for forgiveness for our self-centredness as well as for our unbelief in not trusting who he is, for refusing his love and having chosen to go our way instead of his way. It also involves turning away from every behaviour that we know to be wrong.

Here again, let's help the seeker understand that to put our trust in Jesus does not mean that we will never struggle again with sin. The way we grow as followers of Jesus is by regularly confessing and turning from our sins. We need to be honest and admit that it's not easy to turn from sin. But seekers can trust God to help them not only to own and confess their sin but also to overcome it as well, for that is what he has done and is doing for us.

Believe. Second, we confess our faith in Jesus as our Saviour and our Lord. To be followers of Jesus means we acknowledge his absolute claim over our entire lives, and we accept that our faith must issue in obedience. We must be willing to give God first place in our lives and to live under his rule. Jim Wallis in *Agenda for Biblical People* writes that 'the great tragedy of modern evangelism is in calling many to belief but few to obedience'.[5] That is why Jesus frequently asked people to count the cost before they made a commitment. He wanted them to be sure they understood what they were committing themselves to.

Again, let us freely share that what is required of the convert is demanded of the disciple. We don't acknowledge Jesus as our Saviour and Lord in one second and then live as we please the next.

Two questions about evangelism that are frequently asked at this stage of the process are these. How much does a seeker need to understand in order to make a legitimate commitment of faith? When do we let him or her know about the implications of following Christ as Lord?

These are big issues and not all Christians are in agreement about the answers.[6] However, one thing seems clear. People who get into the Christian life without understanding the essentials of faith, or who have never been challenged to repent of their sins, are likely to remain stunted Christians at best.

This became painfully clear when I recently spoke to a Christian student convention. One young Christian student told me, 'Look, I cheat in my exams, and I feel kind of guilty about it. But I reckon it's all right because I really want to be a lawyer for Christ.' This kind of thinking reveals how little he understood of what it means to follow Christ when he became a Christian.

We must be certain that our evangelism is not divorced from an understanding of the content of the Christian faith. We must also help seekers to understand that we can't separate faith from how we live our lives. To follow Christ is to live under God's rule. Following Jesus means that every aspect of our beings, every dimension of our lives, will be directed, shaped and transformed by the holy presence of Jesus in our lives.

'But won't such honesty deter people from accepting Christ?' we may ask. My experience has been exactly what Mark Mittleberg describes in a magazine interview: 'There's a rumor that if you want to attract unchurched people, you've got to tell them what they want to hear. We've found just the opposite. People are looking for leaders who have the guts to tell them the truth.'[7]

Receive. Third, we receive the Holy Spirit by asking him to come into our lives. With the filling of the Spirit we are strengthened to live as new people who are called into a new way of life. We ask the Holy Spirit to come into our lives, to fill us with his power (Acts 1:8) and to fill us with his presence. The Spirit's presence seals what we have done in receiving Christ as Lord. However, our need for the Holy Spirit does not end at conversion. As followers of Jesus we will continue to need the fresh renewing of the Spirit to accomplish the various tasks and capitalize on the various opportunities that God gives us.

Potential converts also need to know before they decide for Christ how not to quench the Spirit's presence within them but rather what they will have to do to stay spiritually alive. Daily Bible reading and prayer are essential, as is belonging to a Christian community. Young Christians need to find a church that is faithful and alive, and they should meet with a small group of Christians regularly for Bible study, prayer and fellowship. They are to be baptized if they have never been so. We can help them for the first few weeks until they are more secure. It takes a long time to learn to live in God's world in God's way, so we need to be there to help them begin. And we must bring others along to help them too.

At some point we need to share not only the delightful privilege they have of helping others to find Christ but also the truth that they are called, as Robert Webber writes in his book *Common Roots*, 'to participate in Christ's victory over evil, to *extend* Christ's victory in every area of life in which they live and serve, to bring all of life under the reign of Christ'.[8]

Taking the final step

There is probably no experience more terrifying than the first time we lead a person to Christ. But there are few things more thrilling or that make us more aware of how true Christianity is. To see God's Spirit take control and beautifully change a person's life is one of the greatest miracles we will ever witness. So we must be willing to help people enter into a relationship with God if they are ready.

What do we do when seekers say, 'OK. I would like to be a Christian. How do I do it?' Or if *you* sense that the moment is right, you may say, 'Is there anything that would keep you from becoming a Christian here and now?'

Listen carefully to what they say. If they say they aren't sure or feel a bit reluctant, ask them if they'd mind telling you why. Once we hear their concerns, it's usually fairly easy to assess their readiness. For example, if they say, 'I just feel so unworthy,' all we need to say is, 'None of us is worthy. That's exactly the point. The Bible says that "while we were yet sinners Christ died for us".' Just be sure they understand that there is nothing any of us can do to make ourselves worthy. It's accepting what Christ has done for us on the cross (not what they can do) that opens the pathway to God.

Or they might say, 'I'm not sure I understand everything.' This is a good time to review the basic gospel truths. Do they believe they are sinners? Do they believe that Jesus died on the cross for their sins? Do they understand that asking Jesus to come into their lives is making a commitment to live in intimate relationship with Jesus as the Lord of their lives? If they understand and trust those things, they are probably ready.

Sometimes a person considering Christianity says, 'I believe the essentials of Christianity, but I still have unanswered questions.' We can reassure them that having faith in Christ doesn't mean we have all of our questions answered or that we never entertain doubts. If they seem to understand the essential truths, then we might say, 'Faith means you surrender everything that you understand about yourself to everything that you understand about God. Your knowledge of God and of yourself is not static. It will always continue to grow!'

After answering their questions, if you feel satisfied that they are ready, you may ask, 'Would you like to commit your life to Christ here and now?' If they say no, then do not pressure them. In fact, it's important at this point to reassure them of your genuine care. You might ask them whether you could pray for their continued journey toward God, asking God to reveal his truth to them. This communicates that they may still open the door to faith at a later date and that their needing more time to consider has not negatively affected your relationship with them. But if they give you a green light, then you have the extraordinary privilege of leading that person to Christ.

At this point I usually give some direction as to how to proceed. I suggest that we pray out loud together and ask if they'd like me to start first. The answer is nearly always yes. (I find that eases the awkwardness and also models how to pray in ordinary, everyday language.) I suggest that after I pray they may talk to God just as if they were talking to their best friend. If they ask me for guidance about what to say, I tell them to say simply, 'Lord Jesus, I am sorry for my sin of running my own life, and I turn from all my sins in repentance. I believe you died for me on the cross. I thank you for your love. Now I ask you, come into my life, Lord Jesus, and be my living Lord. Strengthen me to serve you with my whole heart.' Then we pray. After they have prayed, I then pray again, confirming

God's work in their lives and thanking God for entering their lives.

We need to remember one last thing: the joyfulness of what is taking place! Simply believing that Jesus lived, died and rose again for sinners does not make us a Christian. The devil believes the exact same thing! As one of my favourite preachers, Tim Keller, said in a sermon, 'What makes the Christian different from the devil? The Christian receives these truths *in joy*!' Keller said that the literal translation for the 'good news' is actually the 'joy news'! Let us remember, then, that what we are sharing with seekers is God's amazing 'joy news'. As G. K. Chesterton once said, 'Joy, which was the small publicity of the pagan, is the gigantic secret of the Christian!'⁹

One of the greatest thrills in life is leading a friend into a relationship with Christ. May God grant you the faith, the holy boldness and the experience of seeing the life of someone you know be transformed by him!

Reaping the harvest by displaying God's love

Evangelism involves an appeal to the whole person: mind, heart and will. When we explain the truth of the message, we are appealing to the mind. There is content to the Christian faith, and we do not expect anyone to make a blind leap of faith. When we ask seekers to commit their lives to Christ, we are making an appeal to their will. We know that no-one can come to the Father unless God calls them. At the same time we know that Jesus called people to make a decision. So we appeal to seekers to commit their lives to Christ not by pressure but by God-inspired persuasion.

But Christianity also appeals to the heart. We are inviting our friends into a love relationship with Jesus Christ. The Bible tells us, 'How great is the love the Father has lavished on us, that we should be called children of God!' (1 John 3:1, New International Version). We want seekers not only to understand the truth about God but to experience the love of God as well. How can God's love be expressed through us?

Life provides us with many opportunities to share our faith. Sometimes all that is required of us is short-term involvement. My experiences with Rick and Kay, whom I discussed in chapter 12, illustrate a short-term involvement. We struck up conversations sitting next to each other in a plane and a waiting-room. Perhaps one reason we developed quick rapport could be attributed to my outgoing nature. Yet I find many people are more likely to reveal themselves in short encounters with virtual strangers than they would to their next-door neighbours. We should expect it to take a little longer to develop trust with those with whom we live and work. That means we'll need to develop patience and take the time necessary to develop friendships in the places where we live.

In my experience, becoming friends with seekers who live in our immediate world takes time, energy and commitment. It takes time to know people, time for them to trust us. They need to see us in a variety of situations in order to know that we are real.

Even though my experiences with Rick and Kay were short-term and they were both remarkably open to the gospel, I don't want to leave the impression that everyone I meet turns to Christ on the spot. Far from it. I have many friends to whom I have witnessed and for whom I have prayed for years, and yet I'm still waiting for them to put their faith in Christ. But the wonderful news is that God continues to pursue us.

One of the most reassuring qualities of God is that he never gives up on us. He pursues us, and he will seek us until we draw our last breath. For it is God's deepest desire that no-one perish. As in Francis Thompson's famous poem, *The Hound of Heaven*, God relentlessly seeks to track us down. And when we finally turn to him, what we see are his eyes of love. This aspect of God's character that refuses to give up on people must be present in our character as well.

This insight really came home to me recently. About fifteen years ago I befriended Sue. We had many discussions about faith, we studied the Bible together and I prayed for her fervently. In the end she decided that Christianity wasn't for her. We had become good friends, and I was heartsick over her decision. She moved overseas, and though I had not seen her for years, I never stopped praying for her. Then, just in the past several months, she seemed to be continually on my mind, so I prayed for her with increased regularity.

Out of the blue I received a telephone call from a dear

Christian friend. Nancy told me that Sue had just moved to the town where Nancy lives, and so the two of them had reconnected. She said that Sue was considering faith again. In the past several years some difficult things had happened to Sue, causing her to reopen the question of God and faith. She had recently discovered an unread copy of *Mere Christianity* that I had given her fifteen years earlier. This time she read it and wanted to discuss it with Nancy. Nancy told me that she soon hoped to start a Bible discussion with Sue.

One of my fears all those years ago was that Sue's refusal of faith might have been permanent. But during those fifteen years Sue had experiences that had caused her to reassess her life. But most importantly, God had never stopped pursuing her. Will Sue respond this time in faith to God? I don't know. What I do know is that God nudged me to pray for her when I had no way on earth of knowing why. We do not evangelize in isolation. God delights in using all of his children to reach one lost lamb, even if it takes fifteen years – or a lifetime!

Another quality that demonstrates Christ's love is when we are willing to sacrifice for a friend. Maybe it is through the time we invest in listening to their pain, or in practical ways like babysitting for their children or cleaning up the mess after our flatmate has come home drunk.

I tell a story in my book *A Heart Like His* that reveals the sacrificial, persevering love that God longs to demonstrate to seekers through us.[10] As a college student, I went to L'Abri in Switzerland. It is a study centre and community begun by the late Francis A. Schaeffer for people from all over the world and from all walks of life who are searching for truth and reality. I had read Schaeffer's books, and I was curious as to what sort of person he would be. I hadn't been there a week when I found out.

My new roommate told me that she had been sexually abused by her father and brothers, had been diagnosed as an alcoholic at sixteen, and had been continually involved in the use of drugs. The message she had heard all of her life was that she was trash. When you hear that long enough, you believe it. And what do you do with trash? You dispose of it. That was what she was trying to do with her own life – dispose of herself in one way or another.

One night she came in drunk, and another night she was high on drugs. By the third or fourth night, she had taken some lethal combination of pills, and she had to be rushed to a medical centre.

Dr Schaeffer had been out of the country lecturing. He returned that night, exhausted and jet-lagged after a long trip. But when he discovered what serious trouble this newcomer was in, he immediately went to her and stayed by her side for many hours through the night. When she finally returned to our room several days later, the look on her face was almost impossible to describe. She looked at me with eyes as wide as saucers, and she said, 'Becky, he didn't get angry with me for breaking all the rules here. He held my hand. And he begged me to give God a chance. He had tears in his eyes when he heard all the junk that had happened to me. He cared so much for my pain. But he told me over and over, "Please, just give God a chance. He loves you. He can help you. Don't lose hope." I told him, "I have no hope. It's been beaten out of me." And he said, "I understand. Then hang on to my hope. Lean on *my faith* till you have your own. Trust my hope for what God can do in your life. Just please, please give God a chance." '

That woman stayed at L'Abri for a long time, and as she was slowly nursed back to physical and emotional health, her life was completely transformed. Her despair turned to hope not because she had the inner resources of her own at first, but because she was willing to open herself to God in whatever way she could, because she had seen God's hope and love through the eyes of someone else. She was able to give God a chance by leaning on the faith of someone else. Then one day her hope in Christ was truly her own.

What did Schaeffer offer her? He offered the sacrificial love of Christ. Not simply by talking with her and holding her hand through the wee hours of the morning even though he was exhausted, but by ministering to her for a whole year and a half until she was finally whole. It was a sacrifice for him and his staff of time, of money, of listening for hours and hours to her painful story until she was finally healed. But if Jesus, who was used to the company of God and angels, was willing to come to us and mingle with prostitutes and lepers, and subject himself to death – how can we ever talk about the cost of serving him?

If he was willing to be sacrificially involved in our lives, how can we do any less for others?

What is the moral of these two stories? Never give up! Always keep on praying. Even when you see no fruit or no spiritual response, the story is never over in a seeker's life until his or her last breath is drawn. Let us follow Jesus, who said, 'We must work the works of him who sent me while it is day; night is coming when no one can work' (John 9:4).

14

Reaping the harvest in God's power

How do we work in sync with the Spirit of God in bringing a person to Christ? First, by recognizing that conversion is a profound mystery. For one thing, the Holy Spirit is sovereign. He works as he pleases in his renewal of the human heart. That's why Jesus said, 'The wind blows wherever it pleases. You hear its sound, but you cannot tell where it comes from or where it is going. So it is with everyone born of the Spirit' (John 3:8, New International Version). In other words, conversion is beyond our ability to control. Again, it's a mystery, and 'mystery,' writes Flannery O'Connor, 'is a great embarrassment to the modern mind'.[1] Ernest Becker concurs: 'Moderns try to replace vital awe and wonder with a "How to do it" manual.'[2]

The mystery and the paradox of conversion is also seen in the fact that God does all, yet he chooses to save us in and through human decision and obedience. On the one hand, we cannot find God without God. It is God's grace that initiates our search and God's grace that completes our search. As Os Guinness writes in his book *The Call:* 'The secret of seeking is not in our human ascent to God, but in God's descent to us. We start out searching but we end up being discovered. We think we are looking for something; we realize we are found by Someone.'[3] On the other hand, the only way we can become a disciple of Jesus is through human decision.

So we approach this stage of calling seekers to make a decision knowing that by our own power and cleverness we cannot induce conversions. Jesus makes it clear: 'Apart from me you can do nothing' (John 15:15). Yet he has chosen us to be his instruments in his work of making disciples. How do we depend upon God's Spirit as we seek to lead others to Christ?

What we need most of all is boldness and faith. It takes faith *in* Jesus to lead a friend *to* Jesus. And faith is a gift from God that we are encouraged in the Bible to ask for.

When Peter and John were threatened by the Sanhedrin for evangelizing the Jews, they were understandably concerned. When they were released from prison after receiving stern warnings and threats not to speak or teach in the name of Jesus, the disciples turned to the Lord in prayer (Acts 4:24–31). They began praying by reciting God's characteristics and reminding God (and themselves!) of his nature and character. Then, after a lengthy preamble, they finally mentioned their problem: 'Now, Lord, consider their threats.' But it's what follows that is the surprise.

If you had been physically threatened and thrown in jail for preaching the gospel, wouldn't your prayer be more along the lines of 'Here I am, Lord – send Aaron'? Instead the disciples prayed, 'Now, Lord, consider their threats and *enable your servants to speak your word with great boldness.* Stretch out your hand to heal and perform miraculous signs and wonders through the name of your holy servant Jesus' (verses 29–30, NIV, emphasis mine). And God answered their prayer immediately by giving them supernatural power from on high that was evidenced by the boldness in their preaching the gospel and by God's power working through them to heal and lead others to faith in Christ.

To lead a person to Christ, we need to ask God freely to give us the boldness and faith that we need in order to reach the people that he has given us. It takes a special measure of faith to reach out to someone we have tried to win over a long period of time. It takes even more of God's strength when that person is a family member.

I know because it happened to me.

My father's story

I became a Christian in my teens. I tell most of my conversion story in my book *Hope Has Its Reasons*. One thing I don't mention in that book, however, is what happened to me the very first night I gave my life to Christ. That night began a story in my father's life that illustrates the joy of reaping that can be ours when we've faithfully cultivated and planted – and waited on the Spirit of God to act.

On my first night as a Christian, when I had gone to bed, in the dark I began to pray. All of a sudden I knew that God was speaking to me. The message was unmistakable: 'I want you to tell your father what has happened to you. I want you to tell him that I love him and that I want him to give his life to me.' I was horrified. My dad was, by his own admission, an atheist. He was also a highly successful businessman. He was the quintessential self-made man: self-reliant, justifiably proud of his accomplishments, feeling he needed no-one's help but his own. Furthermore, I knew he didn't talk easily about anything of a personal nature. The thought of telling him about my new-found faith was simply terrifying. I tried every way I could think of to weasel out of it and convince God it wasn't a good idea. But there was a relentlessness on God's part that made me know that I had to do this.

A few days later I asked Dad if we could talk. I felt awkward, embarrassed and uncomfortable, but I knew God had given me no choice. I told Dad in a very simple way that I had been searching for quite some time for answers to life's meaning. (That must have sounded comical coming from a young teenager to a middle-aged man.) I told him that I had surrendered my life to Jesus and that I had never known such joy and peace.

'How long ago did you do this, Becky?' he asked. He was not mocking or unkind, though it was clear from his expression that he believed it was merely a phase of adolescence.

'A week ago.'

When I told him that I hadn't wanted to share this but that God had pressed me to tell him, he was intrigued. 'Why is that?' he asked.

'Because I feel God told me to tell you something: God loves you, Daddy. He wants you to put your trust in him.'

He smiled at me sweetly and said, 'Well, it's kind of hard to teach an old dog new tricks. But I'll certainly think about what you've said.'

'Dad, is that all you're going to say? Why can't you … well, why can't you *just believe*?' I asked with characteristic teenage subtlety.

'Becky, you see everything around you?' he said, gesturing with his hand toward our home. 'Everything I've ever had, every accomplishment, everything you see in this home – no-one gave it to me. It wasn't a gift. It came from *me*. It's all a result of *my* hard work. I just don't understand why someone needs to depend on God when, with discipline, drive and a little luck, you can accomplish it all yourself. I'm sorry, Becky, but it doesn't make sense to me.'

As the years passed, my father recognized that my faith in Christ was permanent, that it wasn't a phase. He even admired my faith. And the Lord gave me other opportunities to share Christ with him. But Dad always perceived Christianity as being 'my thing', not something he could ever believe in. Even in those times in his life when I thought he might be the most open to God, such as when he and my mother divorced, he made it clear that faith just wasn't for him.

Nor was I the only one to witness to my dad. Dr John Alexander, the former president of InterVarsity Christian Fellowship, witnessed to my father once and prayed for my dad for years. My brother and my sister also came to faith and witnessed to Dad, but to no avail.

My father heard me speak publicly only three times in his life. All three times were when I addressed a big student missionary convention, which took place near my home town. Knowing that my father was coming to hear me speak, each time I asked the leaders on the platform to pray. I vividly remember the late Paul Little pouring out heartfelt prayers for my father to come to know the Lord. But there never was even an ounce of spiritual response on his part.

The last years of my father's life, however, became very difficult. Even though he was only in his sixties, he suffered a series of minor strokes that affected his short-term memory. Then he developed Alzheimer's. Tragically, his wife, Dorie, after valiantly taking care of him, had to place Dad in a nursing home when he was only sixty-nine years old. My once strong, witty, razor-sharp father, who was used to being able to control everything, was for the first time in his life dependent and afraid. It was so wrenching for all of us to see him in this condition that I begged God to bring something redemptive out of this tragedy.

As with many Alzheimer's patients, some days he would be coherent and able to follow and respond to what others were saying, and other days he seemed to be in a total fog. On one of his good days we were talking on the telephone, and he was terribly depressed. I tried to cheer him up, but finally I said in utter anguish, 'Dad, it grieves me to see you so lonely and depressed. If I could be there every minute, you know that I would, but I can't. But God is always with us. Dad, I just wish you could turn to God for help.'

To my utter astonishment, he replied, 'I've started praying; I've been asking him for help.' I honestly assumed that this had to be a sign of his further dementia. Evidently my speech-lessness gave it away, for my dad started to laugh. 'I know, it must be pretty bad for your dad to pray, mustn't it?' However, I knew it had to be true when my brother, Bob, phoned and confirmed that Dad had told him the same thing.

Jesus, yes!

Then one morning, many months later as I was praying, the Lord spoke to me. Clearly, unmistakably, I felt that God was telling me to go to my dad and appeal to him one last time to become a Christian. It was such a strong urge that I spoke to a close Christian friend and told her what had happened. I felt I needed to be sure if this was God's guidance. For one thing, what if I made the long trip and he was having one of his bad days and didn't understand what I was saying? Or what if he responded positively (which I could not in my wildest dreams imagine) but I couldn't tell if his response was genuine or just the result of his confused mental state? And even after all these years, even with my dad's diminished condition, I still felt weak at the knees at the prospect of witnessing to him. So my friend and I prayed for God's guidance.

I poured out my heart to God and told him how much I needed an extra measure of faith to be sure it was the right thing to do. How can one describe how God speaks to the soul? As we prayed, we both had an overwhelming sense that this was exactly what I was to do. I felt so strengthened in faith and courage that I arranged my journey immediately.

But on my way to see Dad all of my anxieties began to

resurface. I began asking the Lord, 'What if Dad isn't well enough? Or worse, what if he understands and says no? Or what if I blow it and don't explain things adequately?'

Then the Lord reminded me of what happened the night of my conversion. I had almost forgotten the experience, it had been so long ago. I felt the Lord quiet my fears and calm my anxieties by saying, 'You may have forgotten that experience, Becky, but I didn't forget. I asked you to go to your father over thirty years ago and you did. Now I'm asking you to go to him again. Don't worry; I'm in charge of this. Just be at peace.' With that I fell asleep for the rest of the flight.

The next day my dad's wife, my brother and I took him out to lunch. The nurses told me it was the best day he had had since they could remember. He was overjoyed to see me and called me by name. He laughed at our jokes during lunch; he participated in the conversation as best he could; he even remembered the name of a person the rest of us were trying to recall. It was a wonderful time. But it was only in the last ten minutes that I was actually alone with Dad in his room.

Somehow I always seem to end up in bathrooms in order to pray and build up my courage, and this time was no different! I went into my dad's bathroom and begged the Lord to continue to make his mind clear. I asked God to help him understand everything I was saying, and to let his response be positive.

As I emerged from the bathroom, Dad was sitting in a chair smiling at me. I pulled up a chair next to him. It is difficult to express in writing what he said because by this time he had difficulty in forming complete sentences and words, but I want to try to express it in the way that he actually spoke it.

I said, 'Dad, I have something important I want to talk about. It's about having faith in Jesus. Dad, you told my brother, Bob, and me that you pray now to God. Is that right?'

'Yes ... do now,' he answered.

'I'm so glad you pray. Dad, I don't know quite how to say this, but when I die and go to heaven, I want to know that we will be there together.'

'Me too,' Dad replied.

'Dad, do you know how you can be *sure* you are going to heaven?'

'No.'

'Do you believe that Jesus is God's Son?'

Dad looked out the window and I could tell it was taxing every ounce of his brain cells to think and then try to speak. 'Before … I … before … I … did … before, *didn't* believe. But then … so much happ … So hard… . Now … yes, I believe.'

As I listened to him struggling to speak, I couldn't help but be amazed. One of my dad's defining characteristics was his personal honesty. He could not tolerate dishonesty. It's why he always made it so clear that I was the Christian, and he was not. He didn't make the clarification out of meanness but out of integrity. And now, even at this difficult stage of his life, with so many brain cells deadened by this horrible disease, it was important to him that he was being honest. What he was saying was absolutely true: before his suffering, he did not believe. But as the suffering intensified, it had caused him to pray and turn to God.

I think it was at that moment that I realized how God had answered my prayer when I asked for something redemptive to come out of all of Dad's misery. The gift of Alzheimer's was finally evident to me: it had broken his pride. He finally had experienced something that he couldn't control, and through that he had seen his need for God.

'Dad,' I continued, 'Jesus loves you very much. Do you know that?'

'I just … hope so,' Dad answered.

'Do you know why you can be sure that Jesus loves you? Because he died on the cross for your sins. I have to ask you an important question now: Dad, have you ever made any mistakes?' I held my breath as I asked him this. For my father to acknowledge any weakness or culpability was truly repellent to him. Owning up to sin was always the biggest stumbling-block for him in regard to faith.

Up until this point my father had made perfect sense, but what he began to say now I could not follow. My biggest fear was that the Alzheimer's was too advanced for him to understand what we were talking about. I had told the Lord that if he began speaking incoherently, I would stop the conversation cold.

'Never mind, Daddy. We can talk about this another time,' I said as I started to stand up.

'No!' Dad replied so emphatically that it almost scared me. In fact, it was the only time he came close to using a complete sentence: 'Please, Becky. Want to say this. Let me try.'

'OK. Just take your time, Daddy.' I sat back down.

'It's ... there's ... road ... walk on it ...' he said, gesturing with his hands in a forward motion. 'But then road goes ...' then he gestured with one hand turning right, 'but I went ...' and he gestured with his other hand going left. 'Understand?' he asked me with pleading intensity.

'Yes, I understand. You are saying that life is like a road. You start off walking and everything seems fine. Then there's a fork in the road. You sometimes turned left when you should have turned right.'

'Yes! Yes!' he said, overjoyed that I had grasped what he was saying.

'OK, Dad, then I need to ask you the question again. Have you ever made any mistakes?'

Dad looked out the window for several seconds and then replied in absolute earnestness, 'Yes ... made ... one ... no ... two mistakes.'

I looked at him tenderly. I love my father dearly, but I know that, like all of us, he has made many more mistakes than two. My brother and sister and I have all suffered over many of my father's mistakes. Yet what amazed me in that moment was how little it mattered in light of eternity. Does Jesus ask us to understand the depth of our sinfulness before he will save us? Does he require a pound of our flesh before he forgives us? No, Jesus gave his *own* flesh so that we wouldn't have to.

'Dad, Jesus died for your two mistakes. That's why you can be sure that he loves you. But because he died, you need to tell Jesus two things: tell him that you are sorry for your two mistakes, and ask him to come into your life. Dad, that's called becoming a Christian. Would you like to become a Christian right now?'

Again he looked out his window, this time for an even longer period. In fact, I began to wonder if he had forgotten the question. So I started to repeat it. But he interrupted me by saying, 'Didn't forget.' Then he looked me right in the eyes and said, 'Yes. Yes ... want to.'

I realized at that moment that I had no idea how to lead

someone to Christ who had difficulty forming sentences, so I said, 'Dad, I know it's hard for you to talk. If you want, I will pray on your behalf. I'll speak for you. If you agree with what I am saying, then nod your head in agreement. OK?'

'OK,' he answered.

I took my father's hands in mine and for the first time in my life I prayed with my father. 'Lord, I am praying for my dad, Bob Manley. I'm coming to you now on his behalf. You know what he feels in his heart, and you know what we have just been talking about. So receive this prayer as if it were my dad saying it: Lord Jesus, I have made two mistakes in my life.' Dad nodded his head vigorously in agreement. 'Thank you for dying on the cross for me. I am so sorry I made those mistakes. Please forgive me.' Again he nodded his head. 'I believe you are God's Son, and I put my trust in you.' He nodded yes.

But then I stopped. I suddenly realized I had to. I turned to Dad, whose head was bowed, and I touched his arm as he opened his eyes and looked at me. 'Dad, you don't remember this, but you were once a very successful businessman. Something you always used to tell me was, "You've got to know how to close the deal." Well, Dad, I just realized that I can't take you beyond this point. You've got to close this deal for yourself. Dad, Jesus is with us now – he's right here in this room. Just tell Jesus what you have decided. But *you* will have to do it.'

My father looked at me in complete understanding, and bowing his head, he said in a voice that was uncharacteristically loud for him: 'Jesus, *yes*! ... and Jesus ... I love you!'

In my entire Christian life I never believed I would hear my father say those words. I looked up at Dad and he was beaming. The presence of the Lord in that room was astonishing and palpable. I threw my arms around him and through tears of joy I said, 'Daddy, you belong to Jesus! You belong to his kingdom for ever. Nothing can ever change that. I don't know when God will take you home, but I promise you, you don't have to be afraid. Jesus is with you now, and he'll take you by the hand when it's time to go to heaven.'

'Can ... can we ... go heaven together?' he asked.

'If you don't mind, Dad, I'd like to wait a bit. But when we see each other in heaven, it will be as though we were never apart. And Dad, just one last thing. I know sometimes you get frustrated and afraid. Try to remember just one word: Jesus. That's all you have to say. Just say the name of Jesus, and he will comfort you and help you. And even when you can't remember his name, don't worry because he'll come to comfort you anyway.'

I felt I hardly needed the help of a plane to fly me home the next day. I phoned my dad's nurses several times after that experience. I didn't explain why, but I asked them if they saw any observable change in Dad. 'Yes,' a nurse responded, 'your Dad used to get so agitated. But we've all noticed how peaceful and serene he seems.'

There's hope till the end

I saw my father several times after that. It was clear that what had happened on that trip couldn't have happened at any other time, for each time I saw Dad his condition had deteriorated. Toward the end he could barely speak at all, and yet even then, when I asked him if he'd like me to pray, he would smile and say, 'Yes, please,' and bow his head.

My father died on February 27, 1998 – less than two years after he accepted Christ. When I received the news, I turned to my daily devotional, *The Daily Light,* and read the passages for that day: 'He who hears my word, and believes on him that sent me, has everlasting life, and shall not come into condemnation, but is passed from death into life'; 'I give them eternal life; and they shall never perish, neither shall any man pluck them out of my hand.' All I could do was thank the Lord through my tears for being so merciful and for his extravagant love that never stopped pursuing my father.

There is nothing I can attribute my father's conversion to other than the sheer grace of God. But then, isn't that true of every conversion? There is a chasm between God and humans that has to be bridged, and the amazing news of the gospel is that God is willing to bridge it. My testimony is not that I never doubted Dad would be saved. To be honest, I frequently anguished over whether he would ever trust in Christ. Nor would I have ever described my father as a true seeker. He always seemed amazingly impervious to prayers or to the witness of others. I don't think that was entirely due to his being spiritually hard-hearted; it was also due to some deep emotional wounding from his childhood. Regardless, God got his attention. God responded to the prayers of so many that had spanned thirty years.

This deeply personal story reveals so much of what God is like. It also reveals the critical importance of the will, how terribly important our decision of faith is, even when our mental faculties are diminished. But most of all, it's a story about a God who loves us and who reaches out to us.

Perhaps some of you reading this are feeling grief because you think you are reading it too late. Someone you love has already died before you had the opportunity to witness to him or her. We are told in the Bible that 'the Lord is patient with you, not wanting anyone to perish, but everyone to come to repentance' (2 Pet. 3:9). God's desire is that no-one be lost and die without salvation. Tragically, some will. But no-one can know what takes place between God and the soul of a person in the last moments or hours before death. What we do have assurance of is that God will use every means possible to reach a person before it's too late. We can trust that if there is any way of saving a person without violating the person's will, God will do so. But my father's story also reveals how vitally important it is to witness when God gives us the opportunity.

Let us not hesitate, then, to share his glorious gospel. Yes, I grieved at my dad's funeral. But I grieved in the knowledge of hope, the hope that God, who had the first word, will have the last. Dad's conversion reminded me once again that all is of grace. 'What brings us home is not our discovery of the way home but the call of the Father who has been waiting there for us all along, whose presence makes home *home*.'[4]

15

Revealing truth through reason

Let's say Stephen Hawking, the world-renowned physicist, had a conversion experience. Now, for Hawking, facts are everything. But what if he suddenly declared to the public, 'I had this incredible experience last week while looking at my tulip patch. I'm now a believer. And I wake up early every morning and worship the tulip bulbs'?

I bet many people would say, 'Oh, wow, that's really beautiful, Stephen. I mean, as long as it works for you, then that's great.' Only a few would say, 'How do you know it's true? How do you know you're not creating your own little world and calling it reality?' We would check his facts in any other area but this one, because when it comes to faith, as long as we are sincere, then it is true enough. Or so we are told.

But something is wrong here. Hitler was sincere when he tried to exterminate the Jews and to subvert the German church for his own purposes. The people involved with the Heaven's Gate cult were sincere when they committed suicide because they believed they would be joining extraterrestrials travelling behind a comet. The cultists surrounding David Koresh were sincere when they met their fiery death in Waco, Texas, with their self-proclaimed messiah. Sincerity just cannot be an adequate basis for determining truth. Our concept of truth in general and of faith in particular has been so drastically reduced that something is true if it makes us feel good or comes from sincere motives. But as the adage goes, we need more than sincerity because we can be so sincerely wrong!

What we need is a faith that corresponds to the reality around us, that makes sense out of our world, that is internally consistent and hangs together. As Christians we do not have absolute proof for our belief in Jesus. There is in fact no absolute proof for any ultimate proposition, whether Christian or Buddhist or atheist or whatever. But the God of the Bible does not call us to leap in the dark; he does not require faith without evidence, for that is mere superstition.

As an agnostic, I used to feel frustrated asking truth questions of Christians when they always answered, 'It's just this feeling in my heart.' I would respond, 'But I need something for my head too!' And to my delight I found God offered both. He gives us the subjective experience of knowing him and objective evidence to act upon. It is not evidence that overwhelms us or answers every question, but it is evidence that is sufficient.

Apologetics and its limitations

The Bible tells us that we must give reasons for our faith as well as proclaim it. We should be prepared to give reasons for our commitment to Christ rather than to the idols of our age. Furthermore, we should try to understand what others believe in and think out the implications of our faith, especially so that we can give a compelling defence of why we believe the gospel to be true. Giving reasons for why we believe our faith to be true is what theologians call 'apologetics'.

When I look back to my early twenties, I think I almost believed that if I could just *convince* someone intellectually that Christianity was true, then that person would be converted. Both biblical revelation and life experience reveal such thinking to be wrong. We aren't saved by knowledge but by the grace of God, because the core of our problem isn't ignorance but sin. Even if we were able to persuade someone intellectually that Christianity is true, God would still need to awaken the seeker's will for the person to be converted.

Experience has taught me something else. Over the years I have been asked tough, honest questions from seekers whose motives sprang from a genuine desire for truth. But I have also spent countless hours discussing the evidence for the truthfulness of faith with seekers, only to discover later that truth was never their barrier to faith in the first place! For when I asked, 'If you could know without any doubt that Christianity was true, would you commit your life to Christ?' I was astonished by how often I was told, 'No, because even if it's true, I don't want to give up control,' or, 'No, because if I surrender to God now, I may miss out on some fun,' or, 'No, because even if it's true, I still have a bone to pick with God over how he mishandled something.' In other words, I've learned through experience that the real battleground between the seeker and God isn't in the area of the intellect – it is in the realm of the will.

Does that mean we abandon our attempts to use apologetics as a tool? Absolutely not. I don't believe, as some do, that we must abandon traditional apologetics altogether just because we live in a more experience-oriented culture today. To do that is to capitulate to our culture's excesses. However, I do believe we need to expand our understanding of the various ways we communicate truth in order to meet the seeker who is affected by the changing forces that shape our present culture.

Apologetics has a place so long as we recognize what it can and cannot do. We engage in apologetics because we take the seekers' questions seriously – maybe even more seriously than they do. We offer a defence of the faith because we long to intensify the seeker's hunger for the truth of God. We witness to the truth of the gospel in the hope that the Spirit will move that person to seek salvation. Yet we do so remembering that no intellectual argument can ever induce conversion. We cannot prove that Christ is the way to God, though we can and should make a case for faith's validity when we are asked to do so. But only God can quicken the human will that has been deadened by sin; only God can make the scales of unbelief fall so the blind can see.

In short, apologetics has its place and can be very effective, especially when it is combined with an effective presentation of the gospel. But it should be regarded, as Søren Kierkegaard suggests, as 'waving the carrot before the donkey'.

When we consider how to defend the truth of faith, however, we realize what unique challenges we face in our times. Much has been written about the culture of recent years, which is in the process of shifting from what has been called a modern culture to a postmodern culture. Our modern culture was shaped by the Enlightenment, in which reason reigned supreme and explanation led to experience. In our present postmodern culture we have become disillusioned with reason and disillusioned with the belief that technology can save us. Instead, the postmodern culture is seeking more spiritual and experiential answers to find meaning for life. The New Age movement is an example of this phenomenon.

The very fact that we live in such an experience-oriented culture leads us to ask: why and how do we defend the truth of our faith to people who often could not care less whether anything is true? What kind of apologetic do we use for someone who is put off by intellectual arguments and responds more to experience than to explanation?

Of course, not everyone we speak to has this postmodern mindset. There are exceptions, but it has been my general experience that the older a person is, the more he or she appreciates an appeal to the mind when considering faith. The professor on the plane, whom I mentioned in chapter 9, is an example of a person with more of a modern bent. He wanted to know what evidence there was to back up the Christian claims. He was drawn to and trusted intellectual proofs. He wanted to hear objective, rational evidence more then he wanted to hear my personal experience. He was also over forty. So what do we say to the person who wants well-reasoned answers and evidence that supports our claims that Christianity is true? Is faith based on something that one can examine, or is a person required to take a blind leap in the dark?

We will examine the first two areas of apologetics – philosophical and historical – in this chapter. These areas may be more effective with the cognitive, more modern seeker. In the following chapter we will examine the next two areas – sharing the biblical story and sharing our own story. These may be more useful for the postmodern type of person who is more receptive to hearing truth through experience before ex-planation. And then in chapter 17 we will turn to the last area of apologetics – depending on the resources of the Spirit. This one is a way to convey truth with everyone we seek to win for Christ, but it is especially appropriate when we are speaking to someone involved in the New Age or other alternative forms of spirituality. Let us feel free to use all the approaches whenever it seems appropriate.

Revealing truth through philosophical evidence

One thing that is encouraging to know is that the questions seekers raise don't vary much. For example, the commonly asked questions include these: How could a good God allow evil or hell? What is a human being? Are people basically good but simply misinformed and able to improve with the proper controls? How can we talk of absolutes (that something is 'good' or 'unjust') when everything is relative and has come about merely by chance? These are philosophical questions that Christians need to know how to answer.

When talking to seekers, see if you can get to the core of their beliefs by asking a few basic questions. It is surprising how few basic answers there are to life's ultimate questions. Listen carefully and sympathetically as they articulate their beliefs. The details of systems may differ, but most ideas can be put into a few slots. Here are some examples:

1. *The basic nature of the world.* Do people's arguments begin from the premiss that there is no God, that we started from nothing or from matter only? Or if they believe in God, what kind of God is it (personal or impersonal, finite or infinite, involved with human affairs or aloof)? This is especially relevant when we speak to those in New Age spirituality, who believe that God is in everything, that he is an impersonal energy that lies within each of us.

Discovering whether seekers begin from a naturalistic premiss or a supernatural one will determine a great deal. For example, if they do not believe in God and maintain that the universe is closed, mechanistic and impersonal, it would be impossible for them to believe in biblical miracles. If they do not believe in the supernatural, then it is pointless to keep arguing about something that their system could never accommodate. We should point out to them, however, that it is utterly consistent for us to acknowledge the possibility of miracles because our system allows for the supernatural. So instead of banging away at the possibility of miracles, we might ask: since they deny the existence of God and the existence of absolute truths, are they able to live consistently with such beliefs?

2. *Morality.* Closely related to the question of whether God

exists – and if so, what kind of God it/he is – is the issue of ultimate morality. If a God who is interested in matters of ethics does not exist, then there is no basis outside ourselves for determining what is right and wrong. I know many people who think in exactly that way, and they claim to be able to live consistently with that notion.

They advocate 'tolerance' in sexual matters, for example, saying that since there is no absolute standard of morality, sexual ethics is reduced to a question of taste and preference. Nevertheless – and this is the point – those same people are rigid moralists in opposing racial prejudice, child brutality, war and so forth. And why are they against such things? 'Because they are wrong, categorically and universally!' they retort.

But we cannot have it both ways. We must play by the same rules on different issues. We can legitimately and forcefully challenge them, 'If you say there is no such thing as morality in absolute terms, then you cannot say that child abuse is always evil; it just may not happen to be your thing. And if you find you are not able to practise your premisses with much consistency, then you need to re-examine your premisses.'

Most people's response to evil is one of horror. When we read of the Holocaust or of ethnic cleansing in the Balkans or of terrorist bombings, our immediate response is, 'That is wrong! It is evil!' Or when we hear of abject poverty or senseless torture, we say, 'That is unfair, unjust!' Or conversely, when we see a masterpiece, we say, 'It is beautiful.' In all this we are seeing people responding to the fact that they are made in the image of God – a good God, a God of beauty.

Our feelings of justice, of goodness and of beauty stem from the God who enshrines these very qualities and who made us like himself. As C. S. Lewis says, to call a line crooked still implies we know what a straight line is. Whenever people protest against evil, it tells us they have a strong sense of what is right and are angry to see it violated. So we must ask: where do our feelings of right and wrong, evil and good, come from? What is the origin of these qualities? Where did our culture derive these strong beliefs? Is it perhaps that we are made in the image of a God whose character is good, or is it that we developed such notions under an impetus toward cultural and physical survival?

Challenging our non-Christian friends on whether they live consistently by their own self-acknowledged principles is an effective way of casting doubt on their present beliefs. Some writers who deal with this same approach are James Sire in his book *The Universe Next Door* and C. S. Lewis in *Mere Christianity* and *Miracles*. Giving a reasoned advocacy of faith is a good thing; however, we must be careful, when we do so, not to act in a superior way. The main reason people find it hard to believe the Christian message is not ignorance but hardness of heart, which weakens their wills and makes their understanding foggy.

Therefore, let us humbly but enthusiastically reveal that the Christian worldview gives solid, intellectually profound answers to the very questions most people ask when they find their own answers are inadequate.

3. *Human nature.* Because we live in a world that has replaced belief in God for self, there is immense interest in the question of what it means to be human. So we will examine this at greater length. People want to know, as Sire writes in *The Universe Next Door*, 'Are we a highly complex machine, a sleeping god, a person made in the image of God, a "naked ape"?'[1]

To use apologetics in this area requires that we explain the Christian view of the nature of reality as it pertains to the human condition, addressing the problem of sin, where we find meaning and fulfilment, and so on. Our hope is that if seekers understand the biblical description of reality, they may come to see why their lives lack meaning. For example, why are people today unfulfilled in spite of having so many material possessions? Why do they still lack peace and meaning when we live in an age in which self is king? The task in apologetics is to help seekers understand that our misery comes *precisely* from placing ourselves at the centre of the universe. The biblical understanding of what it means to be human is that we exist for God, and when we fail to put him first, our hearts will always be restless.

An excellent illustration of how to apply apologetics in this realm comes from Stewart Ruch, the senior minister at the church we attend. Recently he went to the wedding of an old school chum. He asked for prayer that he might have an opportunity to witness to the people attending, especially those in the wedding party. The only person he knew was the groom. But he knew his friends would be just like the groom: in their mid-thirties, educated at prestigious universities, by nature very driven and all extremely successful. He left hoping for at least one opportunity to witness. He came back astonished by the fact that he was never able to initiate a single penetrating question. That is because once these men discovered he was a minister, *they* initiated every question! He feared they might be stand-offish because he was a minister. On the contrary, at the reception several men took him aside, saying, 'Listen, I hope you don't mind talking shop, but I'd really like to ask you some questions.'

Stewart said their questions initially ranged from 'Who wrote the books of the Bible, and can you trust their reliability?' to 'What do we really know about the person of Jesus?' In other words, they were asking for answers from the area of historical apologetics. But what they wanted to talk about more than anything else was the diagnosis of the human condition. What explanation does the Bible give for why the planet is such a mess? What are the roots to human behaviour that would explain why people can't find happiness and peace, and why do we do such destructive things? What is the explanation for evil? These are questions demanding answers from philosophical apologetics, especially as it relates to a Christian understanding of human nature.

Stewart said they were astonished to hear that the biblical explanation of the human crisis was spiritual in nature, not psychological or an issue of addiction. Not one of the men he spoke to had ever before heard of the idea of sin being a rebellious insistence on running the show rather than allowing God to be at the centre.

'But taking complete charge of my life is considered a *virtue* in my world, not a sin! What a revolutionary thought,' exclaimed one man.

Another man told Stewart, 'In these last ten years since university I have worked very hard and played hard. I've met all the goals I set for myself in my twenties, but I've discovered two things in the process. I'm not superman like I thought. And even with the success I've attained, it's just not enough.

What is it about knowing Christ that brings you such fulfilment?'

Another man asked, 'I'm in a business where I work with people with enormous egos. They don't believe in God because they think they are God. I see their deception and pride. But how do you conquer self-deception from a Christian perspective?'

Stewart talked to him about the resources we have that guard against deception. For example, he told him that we surrender to and check our opinions against the revealed truth in the Bible. 'Furthermore, we believe in a God who exists outside of us, who is transcendent and other and yet who speaks a personal word to his children through his Spirit. We learn how to listen to God. In fact, our church offers seminars on "listening prayer".'

'OK,' this man responded, 'but how do you know that what you are hearing is really God and not what you ate for breakfast? What protects you from *spiritual* self-deception?'

'Excellent question! I really wish I could take you to my church! Church is where we seek God, we worship him, we gather to be taught by his Word, and we come together to listen to God in prayer. If I am struggling to understand something, then I go to one of the prayer ministers during the service and they pray for me, or I go to my prayer partners and we ask God for guidance.'

'Wait a minute, you have people at your church who pray for anyone who needs it – right while the church service is going on?' the man asked incredulously.

'Absolutely! It doesn't mean we always get it right. But the church is one of God's marvellous resources against deception!'

The last thing the man said to Stewart as they were leaving the wedding party was, 'Listen, people like you have to go and find people like me so you can tell us these things. Otherwise, how will we ever know?'

Stewart astutely commented afterward, 'I'm so glad I didn't meet these men when they were in their twenties. Their openness and curiosity came out of the fact they had lived enough life to know they didn't have all of the answers.'

What fascinated me as I listened to Stewart was that almost every question he was asked dealt with the issue of what it means to be human. What is striking about modern people is how few truly cry out for solutions to metaphysical problems. We don't often encounter a person who asks, 'Tell me what the true nature of God is.' What we *do* hear is humanity's cry to be saved from the reality and consequences of sin.

When we hear people asking, 'Why am I not happy even though I'm successful?' or, 'How could our political leaders do such morally reckless things?' or, 'What possesses a person to bomb someone they disagree with?' or even, 'Why am I still confused, lonely and miserable even after years of counselling and recovery groups?' they are seeking to understand what is wrong with human nature. They are trying to make meaning out of the central ambiguity and contradiction of human nature. Why is it, they ask, that the same person can be capable of greatness and horror?

Apologetics is helping seekers grasp that the answer to their questions lies in the biblical understanding of the nature of reality. Evangelism, the sharing of the gospel, is the answer to their piercing cry and need.

Stewart's friends were asking questions about the human condition. These men understood that – whatever it means to be human – somehow we matter; we are significant. But sometimes we meet people who think a human being is only a set of chemicals, a piece of protoplasm. That is a valid philosophical position. But we may ask: can they live that way?

I had a biology teacher who stated on the first day of class, 'Man is merely a fortuitous concourse of atoms, a meaningless piece of protoplasm in an absurd world.' We were taught that having deep regard for random products of the universe where chance is king was inconsistent.

Some time later, however, that same teacher told our class in despair that his thirteen-year-old daughter had run away to live with an older man. 'She will be deeply wounded. She will be scarred, and I can't do anything to help. I must sit back and watch a tragedy,' he said grimly.

I raised my hand and said quietly that according to his system protoplasm could not be scarred.

His answer was devastating. '*Touché*. I could never regard my daughter as a set of chemicals, never. I can't take my beliefs that far. Class dismissed.'

No matter how hard we try, we can never escape the fact that we have been made in the image of God. Sooner or later our God-image will be revealed. When the point comes when people are not able to live according to their presuppositions, we must lovingly challenge them to stop escaping reality and live as they were created to be – children of God.

4. *The fundamental problem in the world and how we deal with it.* Everyone from physicists to poets agrees that something is wrong with the world. Philosophies, ideologies or explanations of the life process usually place the blame either on external circumstances or on individual decisions and actions. If they see the source as external, then they usually say the system needs changing. For example, an individual is not bad or selfish, he has just developed poor habits; she is a victim of an externally imposed evil. Whether the evil culprit is the capitalistic economic superstructure, as Marx suggested, or the environment, as behavioural determinist B. F. Skinner theorized, the focus of blame is outward, not inward. The alternative sees the problem as derived from some kind of internal chaos. Christianity says evil has permeated both levels and we must fight evil at both levels. But the source of evil is internal (Mark 7:14–22).

When we meet people, such as those involved with New Age, who believe humans are basically good, we must agree first. One pillar of our understanding of humanity is that God declared his creation good (Gen. 1). Our ability to respond with compassion, to be moved by the beauty of a Leonardo da Vinci painting or the soaring Austrian Alps stems from the fact that we were created with wondrously good qualities. But where do seekers with an optimistic view of human nature usually struggle? They have great difficulty understanding the problem of suffering. That is where the Christian explanation of reality is so satisfying because we are not naïve about the other aspect of our humanness – our sinfulness.

The Bible deals utterly realistically with both sides of us. We are not intrinsically cruel; God did not make us evil. But he made us free, and we rebelled. We are not now what we were created to be. By our own decision, we became abnormal when we chose not to be in relationship to God (Gen. 3).

So when seekers say that people are basically good, we must

ask them, 'How do you account for two world wars? For rampant bigotry that still exists in our age of enlightenment? How do we write off the atrocities of the Nazi or the Balkan experience?' We must not be naïve about the reality of evil. Nor can we afford to fail to put tough questions to those who say, 'All we need is a bit more education.' No-one should know or understand better the heights to which humans can climb or the depths to which we can succumb than a Christian. Therefore, we must force the world to take both human goodness and human evil with the utmost seriousness. And when their analysis of our dilemma is shallow or their solution is merely a sticking-plaster approach, we must help them see that.

To help people take a look at their view of what is the fundamental problem in the world is based in the recognition that everyone has a worldview – a conceptual framework in which they place people and events. We can capitalize on this because surprisingly few people recognize their own worldview or can articulate why they know their beliefs are true. Mostly their thinking is a smattering of ideas from a favourite teacher, a large residue from family background, a bit of opinion from their newspaper or their favourite television commentator, and so on. Our job is to help people develop their point of view more clearly, to recognize their beliefs and then push them to the point of conviction.

When we help people clarify their ideas, they will often be surprised to find out how unsupported they are by any hard evidence or how haphazard and inconsistent they now appear even to themselves. It is at this point that we can help people to push their ideas to their logical conclusions and help them to see why their positions are inadequate.

We need to raise questions that deal with the source of authority. In other words, we ask *why* they believe what they do. Is something true for them because it subjectively 'feels' right, or because of a tradition they were taught, or because they believe it is scientifically sound?

For example, a person may be at the point of questioning the goodness of human nature. Perhaps our seeking friend used to believe the best about human nature; now he is not so sure that we are essentially good and that with a bit more education we will conquer our foibles and flaws. We need to start where he is, explore his ideas about human nature, raise questions and suggest the Christian view about these various issues. Maybe that is as far as we should go in the first conversation or several conversations. But we have accomplished a great deal if we have been able to help him to see, for example, that we as people can create beauty, appreciate love, even respond heroically at times. Yet at the same time we cannot deny that we are deeply in crisis, that we struggle with greed and selfishness and that we hurt those we love, and that all the education and technology we have acquired cannot seem to curb this. Maybe we will be able to tell him God's solution to this dilemma in the first talk, or perhaps it will come later. But we must deal with each person's actual questions. And if he does not have any questions with his present position, we need to raise some for him.

Once I taught an eight-week course in evangelism to a Methodist church. One of the requirements of the course was to say to an unchurched friend, 'I'm taking a class on the Christian faith. We are examining what we believe and how to communicate our faith more effectively. Would you be willing to answer the questions the teacher gives us every week?' I made it clear that the questions were not to be used for manipulative purposes but genuinely to discover what their friends believe and to provide a basis for discussion. Every time I've taught this course, by the way, the results are the same. The seekers are *delighted* to be asked questions; it's the believers who are initially nervous about the assignment!

One week we were studying the Christian view of human nature. A person taking the course, Tom, asked his seeker friend that week: 'What do you think is the biggest problem in the world today?'

His friend answered, 'Universal greed and selfishness.'

'So what is the solution?' Tom asked.

'More education,' came the reply.

Now at that point Tom could have said, 'No, you idiot. Everyone knows education will not root out evil. The only one who can do that is Jesus!' But Tom was astute. He knew he had to bring his friend to the point of realizing that his idea was faulty. So Tom said, 'You say all people, everywhere, are selfish? And the solution is education? Well, if all people are selfish, then who is going to teach the class?'

His friend looked at him, smiled and said, 'You're right. It won't work. We must stamp out selfishness, but how? OK, so what does Christianity say can solve the problem of flawed human nature?'

Tom then explained to his friend that the core of the problem is sin and that sin can't be 'educated out' of us. Only God can change our hearts and our natures from the inside out. The man was ready to listen. Soon he came to an investigative Bible discussion, and eventually he gave his life to Christ. God, as it turned out, had been drawing him all along. But what helped to accelerate the process was the fact that Tom had listened to him carefully, explained the truth of the Christian position, and in so doing was able to show him the flaws in his own understanding.

We still need to remember that helping people to see the inadequacies of their thinking system will not convert anyone. Because, as we've said before, the power to transform a life spiritually does not rest in us; it rests with God. Furthermore, a lot of people are content to have conflicting beliefs floating around in their heads. But for some people, the realization that their beliefs are inconsistent or inadequate will make them willing to consider Christianity for the first time. That is why it is important to pay attention to the kind of person we are talking to. If this is a person who will not consider Christianity unless she knows that it is based on reasonable evidence, then that's where we start. The challenge is to communicate the whole gospel to the whole person: mind, emotions and will. But where we begin will depend in large part upon where the seeker's point of interest and need is.

So ask seekers questions about their position and help them see the holes in their own thinking. Then they may be ready to hear what the Christian perspective is. We may be led to communicate only one aspect of the gospel, or we may be led to share much more of it. That will depend upon the receptivity of the non-Christian and our sensitivity to the Holy Spirit.

Revealing truth through historical evidence

Have you ever encountered someone who discovers you are a believer and says, 'I think it's beautiful what your faith does for you. It's really your thing. I mean, it's not my thing, but it's so nice for you'?

To which we may say, 'But do you think it's true?'

People often respond with, 'No, I don't believe it's true, but what difference does that make?' Then we can continue the conversation in a number of ways.

One way is to say, 'How can a lie be beautiful? Either I am right or else I am hopelessly deceived. If I am wrong, then I have staked my entire life on falsehood. If I'm deceived, then it's ugly, not beautiful.'

Another way is to say, 'Despite your thoughtfulness in saying my faith is valid for me because it gives me such a warm feeling, all of the most tender feelings in the world cannot make a man rise from the dead. Either Jesus did or did not rise from the dead, quite apart from my feelings on the subject. And one of the best-attested facts in history is that his tomb was empty. The government was forced to issue a flimsy cover-up story because they couldn't find the corpse. Either Jesus was resurrected or there must be an explanation of what happened to his body. But neither conclusion depends on my warm glow to make it true. Jesus isn't true just because he makes me feel good.'

This moves us into the arena of historical evidences. And in this arena we face questions such as these. How do you know the Bible is historically trustworthy? Weren't some of the worst wars in history fought by Christians, such as the Crusades? Wasn't Jesus merely a good teacher? How do you know he was resurrected? Did Jesus even exist? Why Christianity and not other religions? What makes Jesus unique? Hasn't Christianity suppressed women? Haven't missionaries destroyed native cultures? These questions all require evidence – evidence that necessitates some knowledge of history.

The questions sceptics ask are remarkably similar. It would be helpful to have index cards with the problem stated at the top – 'Evidence for the resurrection' – and the basic arguments listed below. Also, there are excellent books that address all of these questions, and I have listed some of them in Appendix 2. Any of these books would be a good place to start learning how the common questions may best be answered. But first find out if your seeker friend really is interested in these questions. They are fair questions and there are good answers. Even if the seeker isn't interested yet, he probably will be once he is converted. I often find this type of apologetic is even more meaningful to the new convert than to the undecided seeker.

But in some cases seekers don't have any interest at all in historical or philosophical evidences for our belief. These are people imbued with the postmodern spirit that is abroad in the world today. Facts and arguments won't work with them, but something else will – something we're all fond of: storytelling.

16
Revealing truth through stories

A woman in her mid-twenties recently said to me, 'I'm not remotely interested in whether what you're saying is true – I want to know if it is *real*.'

'What do you mean by "real"?' I asked.

' "Real" means that you have actually *experienced* this truth in your life. It's not some dry dogma that exists only in your mind but has never touched your heart. I want to hear about what you have experienced, what makes life work for you, far more than I want to hear some didactic truth.'

Here is a typical postmodern perspective. How do we speak to a person who values experience over explanation? The issue here isn't how we can speak to postmodern people without using any categories of truth. Rather, it's how we convey truth by using forms they are more apt to understand and respond to.

One effective way of communicating God's truth (especially to postmodern folk but to others as well) is through the vehicle of storytelling – by telling God's story from the biblical narrative, and by sharing our story as well. In stories we explore how we and others have been affected by God's action in our lives. When people hear of our experience, they can often gain a better idea of the reality of the gospel. Let's deal with telling God's story first.

Revealing truth through telling God's story

How do we go about sharing God's story in the Bible? Do we just dive in with a stranger and begin reciting Bible stories?

First, we need to pay attention to the story of the seeker. We won't be able to make God's story relevant unless we understand his or her story first. It's always important to be sensitive to the needs and hurts of people. But in a postmodern, experience-oriented culture like ours, being able to discern individuals' needs is a vital skill if we are to help them see their need for Christ. Of course, what we know from the outset is that people are hungry for far more than they realize. Their dissatisfaction with life points to their hunger for God. Our ultimate aim is to help seekers understand that their problems in life, whatever they may be, cannot be solved unless they first resolve their bigger problem: getting their relationship with God right. But if we don't first listen carefully to their story, it will be difficult to draw their attention toward hearing God's story. As Ronald Johnson writes, 'Learning to listen as a part of our telling the gospel is a challenge because we are people who have been trained almost exclusively in the act of monological presentation.'[1]

I had an experience that illustrates this principle. As a birthday gift my family gave me a day at a health farm. Once there I was introduced to Jill, the manicurist. After talking for a few minutes, I said, 'Tell me what is it that you most enjoy about your life at the moment? What really gives you joy?'

She excitedly told me that she had just become a homeowner for the first time, and she shared all the joys and frustrations of that experience.

'Have you had a housewarming yet so your friends and family can celebrate with you?' I asked.

'Well, yes, though my mother didn't come. She never celebrates anything good that happens to me,' Jill answered with some bitterness.

This is a classic example of what happens in the course of a conversation. I had no agenda in asking her that question. I've never been the type of person who has five stock questions I always ask a person. I don't have a problem with people who do, but for me I find it impedes authentic interaction. I simply wanted to get to know her. The question popped into my head, so I asked it. Yet it led almost immediately to a revelation of deep pain in her life. Now what should I do? I decided to ask gently about her mother, and if she clammed up, then we'd move on to other topics. Only now I was praying for her as we spoke.

'I'm really sorry to hear that your mum isn't more supportive. That has to be painful. Has she behaved that way for long?' I asked.

'Yes, most of my life. My mum's a real pain,' she sighed.

'I wonder what her problem is?' I asked tentatively.

'You know, I've spent half my life trying to work that out. She is one of the angriest, most self-pitying people I've ever met. It's like, if anything good happens to anyone – even her own daughter – somehow it's always at her expense. She can't celebrate anything good that happens to me. She's always looking over her shoulder to see if I've got something more or better than her.'

'Wow, it sounds like a pretty deep case of narcissism and envy. It's amazing how destructive envy is. We don't hear much about it these days, but it really destroys the person who has it and hurts everyone around them as well.'

'I can't believe you're saying that, because that's just what I told my flatmate yesterday. It seems crazy, but I think my mum *is* jealous of me. Sounds like you've done some thinking about envy. What do you know about it?'

'Well, I did a project recently that involved researching the subject of envy, among other things. What helped me understand the nature of envy was reading the story of David in the Bible.'

'You mean David that fought Goliath? That's all I know about him, but did he have a problem with envy?'

'No, but King Saul certainly did. As you've been describing your mother, I've been struck by how much she has a personality profile just like Saul. He was profoundly envious of David, and Saul was always looking over his shoulder to see if David got more praise or attention. He could never celebrate anything good that happened to David for fear it was taking something away from him. In the end envy finally destroyed Saul.'

'That's incredible. There is somebody in the Bible who is like *my mother?* Wait till I tell my brothers. OK, tell me the story.'

For the next several minutes I told her the story of David and Saul. She listened to every word of how ferociously Saul pursued David, how Saul was eaten up with envy, hatred and eventually madness. What she wanted to know after listening to the story was this: how had David coped with being the target of someone's envy and hatred?

'Don't you wish David had kept a diary during all those years he fled from Saul? Wouldn't you love to know what he was feeling and how he coped with it all emotionally? Now *that* would be a page turner!' Jill said.

'Oh, but he did! We have the psalms, and many of them were written by David. When you read the books of Samuel, you get a fascinating historical account of what happened. But when you read the psalms, it's like reading David's personal prayer diary to God!'

'Well, what did he say? Wasn't he furious with Saul? Didn't he hate Saul? And wasn't David a bit fed up with God for not knocking Saul off so David could have some peace?'

'It's amazing to read, Jill. You find nearly every human emotion in David's prayers. Often he starts off very depressed and discouraged. Other times he begins with fury and anger. And you can't blame him. What Saul did to David was an outrage. David had looked to Saul as a father figure, and Saul turned on him viciously.'

'That's exactly where I am. Sometimes my mum makes me furious, and I feel nothing but hate. Other times I feel so depressed and alone. But I can't seem to climb out of it. How did David overcome his feelings of depression and anger? What did he do to keep himself going?' Then, looking at me with utter seriousness, Jill said, 'And there were no self-help tapes in those days either.'

'What I love about David is that he was so utterly human. When he felt pain, confusion, fear and anger, he acknowledged it. He didn't try to pretend. But David knew what to do with his humanity – he brought all of it right into the presence of God. He didn't blame God for his troubles; instead, he asked for God's help in his troubles. David didn't come to God in his Sunday best; he just poured out his pain and suffering right there in front of God.'

'And God wasn't offended by his honesty?'

'God loved it! God wants to have a warm, open, trusting relationship with us. God even called David a "man after my own heart".'

'So was David helped by being that open with God?'

'You bet he was! David's prayers often began from the bottom of the emotional pit. But, somehow, just bringing his pain and naming it right in God's presence caused David's spirit to rise. It's amazing how often he begins in sorrow and concludes in hope and even praise.'

'Did David ever forgive Saul?'

'Yes, I believe he did. David wasn't perfect; he made lots of mistakes. But slowly, over time, you see what happens to a person who gets to know God and chooses to obey him. David was deeply sinned against – just as you have been, Jill – but God helped David to forgive Saul and not to carry bitterness and anger in his heart. God helped David to let go of the injustices done to him and to wait for God to set things right.'

'Well, there is no way I could forgive my mum, not after all she's done to me. I hate her. I'll never trust her again. Anyway, why should I?'

'It's clear she's hurt you terribly. But you know why I think God asks us to forgive those who have sinned against us? Because he doesn't want us to carry around the cancer of unforgiveness within us. Not to mention the fact that *we* need God's forgiveness too!'

'Well, maybe it was easier to forgive people in biblical times. I don't think that many people do it today.'

'You know what? There was someone in my life that I had to forgive, and I desperately didn't want to. She was a person who caused enormous pain to people that I love deeply. I remember how shocked I was to discover one day that not only did I not want to forgive her, but I hated her. I didn't want to admit to the hate, but it was there, and it was deep.'

'Would you mind telling me about it?' Jill asked.

I spent the next several minutes telling her about a personal story of my own battle with hate. I was honest with her about the circumstances, and I didn't try to present myself as being above temptation. I told her how deeply I struggled and how much I didn't want to forgive this person. In sharing this it naturally came out that I was a Christian. I told her that God requires his followers to forgive, just as David had to learn. Finally, through God's help and grace and my willingness to obey, I had been able to overcome hate and to forgive.

'Jill, I don't know where you are with God, but I know I

needed God's help to be able to forgive. If you ever choose to forgive your mum, you'll need God's help too. I know from firsthand experience that we have to get our relationship with God in order before we can get the rest of our relationships straight. One thing I know, God cares deeply about your pain. He knows you've been sinned against and it's *not fair*, but he doesn't want to see you destroyed by being stuck in hatred like Saul was.'

'Becky, I'm going to tell you something. I'm still flabbergasted that there is a story in the Bible that relates so much to my situation. I always thought of the Bible as a book of "thee's and thou's". I never dreamed there were people in there who acted like my mother! But if you hadn't told me your own story, I would have tried to dismiss the story about David. But you've been through pain too. You didn't want to forgive any more than I do, but you did it anyway. OK, let's go back to David and tell me how he forgave Saul.'

'Jill, I'd love to, but our time is up!'

'Well, I've never seen time fly by so fast. Becky, honestly, sometime you should think about writing a book about David,' she said.

'Well, as a matter of fact, I have! That was the project I mentioned earlier. I tell you what – I'll bring you a copy sometime.'

I went home and my family said, 'Wow, Mum, you look great!' But when I replied, 'Listen, I *have* to go back. Really, it's for the sake of the gospel!' my children responded with rolled eyes and said, 'Oh, yeah, right. Now there's a good excuse!'

I did return, and when Jill saw me, she said, 'I'm so glad you've come back. That day we talked I was up half the night telling my flatmate about our conversation and about that person in the Bible. What did you say the name was – Sammy? Sally? Susie?'

'It was Saul,' I answered, trying to suppress my laughter.

'Oh, yes. Well, I went out and bought a Bible so as to read that story, but I didn't know where to look. I even told my brothers that there was someone in the Bible with a personality like our mother. They couldn't believe it either!' Jill reported.

Each time I have returned we have spoken at deeper and deeper levels of what it means to forgive, how one goes about it, how we need God's help to do it. We are now discussing what it means to be a Christian. Jill is considering what it means to forgive her mother, but I believe, even more importantly, she is considering Christ. And I might add that my nails have never looked so good!

I have reflected on this experience a great deal, and I believe there are several levels of meaning. First, I was struck by how God's truth spoke to Jill, how it got through. But why? How?

For one thing, Jill heard something in the biblical story that she connected with. The story of David slipped past her defences, caught her imagination, and she discovered she could identify with David. In other words, God's truth came across to her as personal and relational rather than didactic and distant. God's truth took on a human face and human frame through David. Through sharing the biblical narrative of David, Jill began to grasp that God cares about our problems, that God wants us to relate to him authentically and personally. In hearing about David's struggles, she began to consider why forgiving others is important. Most of all, she got a taste of what an authentic walk of faith looks like through the life of David.

Another interesting aspect of that experience is that, by conveying truth through the biblical narrative, it placed the weight of authority where it belonged – on God and not on me. For example, I was comfortable saying, 'You know, David really taught me how important it is to forgive,' or, 'David showed me that first we must get our own relationship with God sorted out.' Pointing to a third party for authority made it easier for both of us. I didn't sound like I was speaking *ex cathedra*, and if she disagreed with what I was saying, she could disagree with David and not me.

For example, at one point she got a bit heated over the idea of forgiving her mother and said, 'Well, I don't think David would have forgiven my mother if he really knew her.' She softened a bit later, but what I realized was that her responses were more authentic because she didn't have to worry about contradicting me – it was David she had the beef with. If I had said in a tone from on high, 'Well, the *Bible* says … !' I would have lost her. But when I said, 'You know, David really helped me understand something', it didn't seem like a cold, external code of beliefs being imposed but rather truth to be considered from what our, by now, mutual friend David had said. I sensed the weight of conviction and authority that comes through the Word of God, but she was able to hear the truth more readily because it came through a story about relationships.

Another reason God's truth got through to her was that she saw that we *both* stood under the weight of truth's authority. In sharing my personal story it became clear that the truth of forgiveness had been just as hard for me to hear as it was for her. God's truth had placed demands on me too. It demanded my own conversion, my own willingness to humble myself and obey. I was not preaching truth from on high; I was sharing truth that I had followed with my life. My testimony was that the process of obeying had been difficult but worth it. Once she knew that I too had problems, that I too had struggled to obey God's command to forgive, it brought about an almost instant camaraderie. It built an authentic relationship between us because she saw that we were co-participants, fellow learners on the human journey to obey God.

Parker Palmer writes that true learning always involves obedience to the truth for *all* the parties involved – for the teacher and the student, for the knower and the seeker. The problem, he says, is when 'we want to avoid a knowledge that calls for our own conversion. We want to know in ways that allow us to convert the world – but we do not want to be known in ways that requires us to change as well.'² I believe one of the most important aspects of my witness to Jill was allowing her to see my subjective struggles to learn how to obey the objective truth of God. But the entire experience was rooted in first listening to her pain.

Revealing truth through telling our story

My illustration with Jill reveals how helpful it can be to share our own story as well as God's story. The world hungers – perhaps without even knowing it – for examples of evidence in people's lives. They want to know if God works. Has he brought us identity and meaning? Have we experienced his love in ways that fulfil and complete us? We can do this when we learn how to share our own Christian experience.

Sometimes God will lead us to share the biblical narrative and then our personal story. At other times we begin with a personal story that leads us into sharing some aspect of God's story. However God guides us, it is the combination of the two that helps seekers, like Jill, begin to pay attention to what God is saying.

Sharing a personal experience with a seeker does not mean that it needs to be deeply private. For example, I met a woman not too long ago who described herself as a 'professional seeker'. She told me of her constant search to find meaning, peace and identity. But then she said, 'I think I'm on to something now, Becky. I've been listening to these tapes, and they are really helping me a lot!' I asked her to describe this new therapy.

'Well, every night before I go to sleep I play this tape that says, "You are beautiful. You are extraordinary. You are kind. You are loving. You are wonderful. People look up to you. Your friends count it a privilege to be in your presence."'

I asked, 'How many times do you have to listen to these tapes for them to work?'

'A lot!' she answered.

'Excuse me if this sounds rude, but how can such affirmative statements mean anything when the person speaking on the tape has never laid eyes on you? It's like saying, "Dear consumer, you sure are gorgeous."'

'Oh, but for an extra charge you can get a personalized tape with your name on it,' she answered.

'It sounds as though you really want to improve your life.'

'Oh, I really do.'

What was she searching for? On the surface she wanted to improve herself, but I believe that behind her desire for self-improvement was a profound need for love. What one 'heard' behind her words was the wistful hope that if she could just be good enough, then maybe someone would love her. She was trying to use self-help tapes to motivate herself into positive action that would fill the deep 'hole in her soul' for love through constant affirmation.

The Christian answer to this is that our need for love and our capacity for positive change ironically lie in our willingness to face the negative: owning our sin and then coming into a relationship with Jesus as Lord of our lives. However, she had already told me that she'd had a negative church experience, so instead of starting with a Christian explanation of the solution, I said, 'You know, the recovery movement says that the only way we bring about inner change is to first own our problem. What do you think of that as a change strategy?'

'Listen,' she said, 'I know what I'm listening to is a lie. It's just that these tapes kind of ... oh, I dunno, they just help me get through the night.'

Think of what she is actually saying. She is so lonely and so hungry for kindness and love that she is willing to pay money for a recording of a stranger's voice telling her lovely things that she knows have no basis in reality. I could have wept to hear it.

'What do you use, Becky, to get through life?' she asked.

'I have someone in my life, but he's no stranger. I don't have to pay him, because he already knows my name. He tells me the truth – that I am beloved and cherished. He also tells me where I'm in trouble and must change. But he never condemns me. Instead, he helps me overcome my weaknesses and enables me to become my true self, the self I am called to be.'

'Where can you buy such a tape?' my new friend asked incredulously.

'It can't be bought. It's free,' I answered. Then I shared with her the gospel and told her of the beauty of living in an intimate, loving relationship with God through Christ.

The point here is this: if I had tried to explain or defend the truth of the gospel by sharing the evidence for the resurrection, I would have lost her. She needed to hear that God longs to establish an intimate relationship with her, and that it is through Christ that she can experience wholeness and love. The way I communicated that truth was by sharing my own experience first, before I shared the gospel.

I have told many stories in this book – some of which have surprised me even more than the others involved. The changes God has worked in people always amaze me. But he has done good works in you too. Don't be afraid to tell people who you are and who you were before you met Christ.

True, some people only testify to themselves: 'Once I was a wretch. Now I'm great.' God sometimes drops out of the testimony altogether. Or all of their witness is simply personal – what God has done for them. 'I know he lives, because he lives within my heart.' We must direct people's attention outward to God in Christ loving and reconciling the world to himself by the death of his Son on the cross. But the subjective dimension is equally real and, when balanced by the objective and historical, is a powerful witness to who God really is.

The subjective dimension is equally important in talking with that category of postmoderns involved in alternative forms of spirituality. But their beliefs create special issues and so I have chosen to devote an entire chapter to sharing one's faith with these people. God loves them and is calling them to himself through us.

17

Revealing truth through the power of the Spirit

It is astonishing to reflect on the rise of spirituality in recent years. Twenty years ago we didn't even have names for spiritual categories and practices that are commonplace today, or if we did, they were considered so far out as to be inconsequential. Yet today these experiences are considered almost mainstream: near-death experiences, out-of-body experiences, visualization, channelling – to name but a few. And what was called the 'new consciousness' is now known as the New Age.

The challenge in our present 'spiritual' age is this: how do we define, communicate and defend, in a winsome way, spirituality from a Christian perspective – following Christ and making him Lord of all of life? That's a challenge because what is perceived as spiritual can include doing crystal therapy or life regression on Monday, finding our 'inner child' on Tuesday, meditating with zither music and Tibetan bells on Wednesday, having our sessions for Quantum healing on Thursday, and swimming with dolphins and getting aromatherapy massages on Friday!

This is an immense subject and far beyond the scope of this book to deal with in any thorough way. However, there are books listed in Appendix 2 that I encourage you to read if you are in dialogue with people involved with alternative forms of spirituality. My intention is merely to examine some approaches we may take in defending the truth of our faith, especially in our dialogue with people in the New Age movement.

Revealing truth through the Spirit

It has taken me years to appreciate that God reveals his truth through the power and demonstration of his Spirit. When I did campus ministry years ago, if I saw a seeker slip into an 'ordinary' Christian fellowship meeting, I'd get nervous. I was afraid it would be 'too Christian' or 'too spiritual' for the seeker to appreciate. Who knows? – maybe back then it was true. Perhaps it's due to the rise of spiritual interest in our culture today, but I have seen seekers won to Christ because they saw the unmistakable power of God's presence during a worship service. There is no greater spiritual power than the power of the Holy Spirit, and God reveals his truth through the resources of his Spirit.

Let us be clear that the work of the Spirit operates in all of the apologetic approaches we have been discussing. We need the Spirit's help when we offer a historical defence of the faith just as we need his help when we share a biblical story with a seeker. What we are examining in this section is how to avail ourselves of the Spirit's power as we witness to those involved in alternative forms of spirituality.

We must not forget that one of the most powerful apologetics we have to offer the world is the Spirit's work in our own lives. It is important to take the time to reflect on how God's Spirit has been with us at every stage in our pilgrimage, whether in the times of suffering and crisis or the times of joy and victory. Such an exercise can only lead us to render thanks.

We also need to listen to God's Spirit as we meet people. Our attitude needs to be one of expectancy. We should assume that God's Spirit is at work in the lives of those people we meet, seeking to draw them to himself. As we witness, let us remember that the Spirit was no doubt at work in that person's life before we met him or her, and the Spirit will continue to work after we are long gone. Our task is to be sensitive to what the Spirit is doing in that moment and to participate with him in the process.

Above all, let us be careful to not quench the Spirit. One of the primary ways we block God's Spirit is through being judgmental and critical of others. Even the right message given in the wrong spirit makes it difficult for the Lord to use us effectively. Remember that we are called to 'speak the truth in love' (see Eph. 4:15). A great deal of our Christian message runs counter to where our culture is. So it is natural that there will at times be conflict in the seeker who hears it. But if seekers sense the welcoming and loving presence of God's Spirit in us, they will be far more likely to hear what we have to say. It's tragic enough that the world assumes that Christians are judgmental and critical. Let's not exacerbate the problem by proving them right by our behaviour!

One of the ways we can facilitate the Spirit's work, and something I have emphasized in this book, is the need for us to listen. Effective evangelism requires it. It's not enough that we discover *our* style of communicating faith, as is popularly assumed, but we must also seek to understand the person we are speaking to. In other words, we need to understand the context of the seeker. As Alan Roxburgh writes in his excellent book *Reaching a New Generation*, 'Our problem is not the inadequacy of the gospel but the fact that we have forgotten how to read the gospel through the realities of the context. Adequate listening demands that we hear the deep concerns shaping our time.'[1] We listen carefully not so that we may create a gospel that simply matches itself up to the current trends. Rather, understanding the seeker's context enables us to rediscover and proclaim the gospel with power and clarity as God's good news for all times, and in particular for 'a time such as this'.

Promotion to godhood

What do we discover as we listen to those who are drawn to alternative forms of spirituality? A friend of mine who is a devotee of the New Age has taught me a great deal about why, for example, the New Age has such enormous appeal to people in our modern culture. She describes herself as someone raised in a mainline church but who has for years been trying, though unsuccessfully, to leave the Christian tradition. We have had several discussions about her beliefs, but it tended to be on a more surface and intellectual level. Then one day I got a phone call that changed all of that.

Anna called me on a day in which I was stricken with a virulent flu. I was vomiting every thirty minutes, and I had a pounding, violent headache. I was in bed, my children were at school and my husband was out of town when the telephone rang. I don't know why I answered the phone when it rang, but the minute I heard Anna's voice, I knew something was terribly wrong. Anna is a very strong, self-reliant person, so it was unnerving to hear her sound so frightened. 'Becky, I'm in trouble. I've been having medical problems, and I've just had a call from the surgery. It looks serious. I've to see the doctor tomorrow morning. They suspect it's cancer. Somehow I have to get through this night. I'm terrified, I don't want my children to see me so panicked, and I don't know what to do. Becky, would you please pray for me now over the phone?'

Knowing there was no way I could minister to Anna in my present condition, I urgently offered a silent prayer: 'Lord, I ask you in Jesus' name, please take away every symptom right now so I can pray for her.' *Instantaneously* every symptom vanished. And though Anna and I were friends, we certainly didn't have an intimate friendship, so I also asked the Lord to guide me into truth as I prayed and to calm her spirit and give her peace.

As I began to pray for Anna, something remarkable happened. I not only felt the presence of the Lord in a special way, but I found myself praying things that revealed a far greater level of intimacy and knowledge about her than I actually had. I knew such knowledge had to be coming from God.

After I prayed, I asked Anna if she would call me back in fifteen minutes so I could give her Bible passages to read. When she phoned again, she said, 'Becky, something extraordinary happened as you were praying. I felt as if God was speaking directly to me, letting me know that he knows me intimately. I could feel my anxiety just being lifted and taken away. It was almost a physical sensation. It was so powerful. I didn't tell you at first because I was sure by the time I called back for the verses I'd be a basket case again. But I have this *amazing* peace.'

The minute we hung up, my own flu symptoms returned, though not at the same level of severity. I couldn't help but pray, 'Er, Lord, not to be impertinent, but just for the record, would it upset some great celestial plan here if I could be rid of this flu?' As it turned out, I was just ill enough to have to remain in bed for the next twenty-four hours, which gave me ample time to pray for Anna! So I decided my diminished flu symptoms were a mercy after all.

Two days later Anna came to my house. After doing more tests the doctors discovered that she did not have cancer as they had thought, although she would still have to have an operation. However, for the first time she spoke candidly about what she believed. My praying for her had been both deeply meaningful as well as troubling, because now it forced her to re-evaluate her beliefs. What she told me was remarkable.

When she had received the upsetting phone call, I was not the first person she had turned to. Instead, she had called a New Age hotline. It is a New Age service that provides prayer and counseling for people in distress.

'Becky,' Anna said, 'it was a horrible experience. I told the woman who answered that I was desperate, afraid and needed prayer. But her prayers weren't personal; in fact, they sounded vague. I came in crisis needing real help, but all she did was pray an "I am the universe" and "I am God" kind of chant. I didn't need to pray to myself or to the cosmos – I needed help from God! But even worse, I think she was doing something else while she was praying for me. There wasn't an ounce of real love coming through. By the time we hung up, I was in worse shape than before the call. I knew I had to have someone pray for me who absolutely trusted in what she believed. So I called you. The difference between your prayers and the New Age prayers were like night and day.'

'Anna,' I replied, 'part of me wants to say to you, what did you expect? Even though it's hard to pin down New Age beliefs, we're on pretty safe ground to say that one major tenet is their pantheistic belief that God is in everything. They don't believe there is a God outside his creation, that he exists outside of us as a personal being whom we address. They believe God is an impersonal energy, a creative force that runs through all of creation and lies within each of us. That woman was being faithful to New Age beliefs by praying what she prayed. But you inferred correctly how impotent such a belief is in light of genuine crisis.

'Anna,' I continued, 'though I'm sorry you didn't experience compassion when you called her, I'm not surprised. I think one of the great counterfeits in the New Age is the lack of love. I know they talk a great deal about love, but frankly, the movement is very self-centred. Their emphasis has always been on finding the God within, but it ends up promoting self-absorbed practices under a religious disguise. It's Christianity, not the New Age, that calls us to truly love our neighbour.'

'Becky, there's something else. To be honest, I've experienced a power that operates through doing New Age spiritual practices. But when you began to pray, I experienced a power far greater than anything I've ever known through New Age. What underscored it was that I knew the power *had* to be from God, because you were too ill to have been its source. I was sure I was going to be awake all that night after I got the phone call from the surgery, but after you prayed, I slept like a baby. I had this sense that God was there holding me.'

'Anna, may I ask you something? You say you experienced the power of God and his love reaching out to you through the prayers of a Christian far more than you have ever experienced through the New Age. So what is it that still draws you to New Age?'

'I like their emphasis on the positive. I'm turned off by how Christians talk about sin. It's so negative. New Age encourages us to turn from anything that is negative. It's freed me to realize that there is no bad in me, only good. Because I am God and God is me.'

'But Anna, if God is simply you and the God-force intertwined, then *what kind of God gets cancer?* Not any God I would want to depend on. Didn't your cancer scare show you that you need a God who is outside of yourself and larger than your own psyche? How can you live in reality and not acknowledge that there is evil and sin? Don't things like cancer show us that we can't pretend everything in life is positive? What I love about Christianity is that it is rooted in reality. It acknowledges the problem of pain and evil; it tells us how we got into this mess in the first place and tells us what to do about it.'

'You know what really bothers me, Becky, is that I realized for the first time that I don't have a philosophy that teaches me how to make meaning out of suffering.'

'Oh, Anna, you've hit the nail on the head. Moderns are hopelessly inadequate when it comes to suffering because we think the purpose of life is for God to make us *feel* good. But what if God's purpose is to make us *be* good, to become godly people? Then suffering takes on a whole new meaning because God can use our difficulties to deepen our faith, strengthen our character and walk with us as we go through hard times.

'Anna,' I added, 'I forgot to ask you something. What did you think about the Bible passages you read?'

'I found them deeply moving, even strengthening. I just had to close my eyes when I hit words I couldn't handle. You know, like references to God being King and Lord.'

'What's wrong with that?' I asked, puzzled.

'It's the language of dominance and control that is so rooted in Western thinking.'

'Well, the Bible originated in the East, not the West. But what other language did you find offensive?'

'The language that suggested surrender and submission. I have a lot of trouble with that because it feels like the language of abuse. It grates on the ears of someone like me who believes in rights, choice and equality.'

I must confess that at that moment I was stunned. Here we were, two women who had been brought up in the same part of the country, who were about the same age and who had many other things in common. Yet language that I find deeply moving and liberating she found abusive and offensive. I realized as never before the challenge before us of communicating the gospel to today's ears.

All I could say to Anna was this: 'Maybe the language of surrender and submission only makes sense once you've seen the greatness, goodness and glory of God. Just to be in his presence, to experience even for a fleeting moment his majesty and holiness and goodness, makes the language of rights and choice seem laughable. Maybe what's needed is a new vision of who God really is.'

'Well, where do you go to find that? And don't tell me the answer is church. I've never found anything that seemed spiritually vital when I used to go to church. It felt stale, rigid and doctrinaire.'

'Oh, Anna, then come with me to my church! At our church the worship alone nearly punctures the ceiling!'

'Well, I gave up going to church because I have a real bone to pick with God. I begged him to heal the daughter of a close friend, and she died anyway. Then I asked him to help someone whom I deeply love, and her life is still a mess.'

'Listen, I'm sympathetic to your pain when your prayers aren't answered as you think they should be. I prayed for a person whom I felt had been a "mismanaged case" by God too.'

'What conclusion did you come to?'

'That I am not God. I can't see into a person's heart. I can't possibly see the big picture or what God will do in the future. But here's what I could say to God: I do not understand you in this situation, but I know your character is true and loving. Therefore, I can trust that *you* know what you are doing even though I don't.'

'Well, I'm not willing to say that, at least not yet. I think God bungled the job, and that's when I knew I needed to start taking more control.'

'Whoa! So what you're saying is that when God didn't do what you wanted, you found a religion that deifies self so that you can have more control? But your cancer scare made you realize that your God is too small. You know what your problem is, Anna? You're in a power struggle with God. And as your friend, I have to tell you this – you're not on the winning side. Life's great lesson is that God is God and we are not.'

It was fascinating to see, as we peeled the layers away, that what was really at the heart of her struggle was rebellion. That is perhaps not much of a revelation because all of us struggle with rebellion against God. It's just that one doesn't often see it so clearly.

I owe a great deal to Anna. Besides the fact that I love her and enjoy our friendship, she has helped me to understand today's struggles and longings. She is still wrestling with what to do. She told me recently that she feels she can't give up on traditional Christianity, but neither does she want to give up the New Age approach. But God has his hand on her life. He dramatically reached out to her once, and I'm sure in his great mercy he will continue to reveal his love to her.

Exposing spiritual deception

How, then, do we reach someone in the New Age movement, or someone involved in other forms of spirituality? The fact that they are searching for spiritual realities is a marvellous opportunity for us to share the gospel. How do we go about it?

First, we need to educate ourselves at least minimally about what they believe. Even though I am light-years away from being an expert on New Age beliefs, what I did know helped me enormously in my conversation with Anna. There are books listed in Appendix 2 that will help us understand the basic tenets of the New Age movement. Then we need to understand how their beliefs differ from biblical truth. For example, the New Age belief that God is an impersonal force is radically different from the biblical understanding of God being a transcendent personal Creator who speaks to us and to whom we can speak. There are vast differences in what we believe, and we need to know what they are. Then we can explore ways to answer their questions as well as defend our own position.

Second, in the New Age movement we see a search for spiritual power, spiritual experience and transformed lives. Yet we know that there is no greater power than the power of the Holy Spirit. How, then, do we point seekers to the reality of God's Spirit?

I believe part of the answer lies in what we will examine in the next chapter, namely, by allowing outsiders to see the spiritual vitality of our own Christian communities. Seekers need to see the life, love, joy and peace the Holy Spirit brings to Christians' lives. When seekers truly see people set free and healed by the power of the Holy Spirit, their curiosity is aroused. What better apologetic can we offer true spiritual seekers than that of a vibrant, worshipping church?

It was experiencing the Holy Spirit's power that arrested the attention of Anna. What fascinated me about that experience was that I could have never engineered this 'contest' between power centres. Nor could I have imagined that my being ill could be used by God to prove that it was his power and not my own. That experience reminded me once again that God truly is glorified in our weakness! So let us ask God to reveal the power of his Holy Spirit through our lives and communities.

We must be careful not to tempt God by capriciously seeking for signs, nor is it a guarantee that it will lead people to repentance and faith, but it is a valid avenue that we need to pursue.

Third, and most difficult, how do we reach people whose problem is not that their self is divine and king (as they believe) but that it is actually a prisoner? In other words, how do we deal with people who are spiritually deceived? Most of the alternative spiritualities seek to transcend Christianity by offering a superior, 'deeper' spirituality. How do we respond? We start by understanding what it is that draws people to these other avenues in the first place.

One reason, for example, they say, is that they long to transcend the separateness they feel from the universe, from each other and from God. That is why there is so much discussion in New Age literature about being 'connected' to the cosmic whole. Let us freely affirm their desire for a restored, unified creation. Indeed, the purpose of Christ's death and resurrection is to restore this broken earth with its marred people. Let us also agree with their notion that they feel separated. They are. We celebrate their desire for unity, their longing to overcome separateness, but we need to find ways of expressing how true unity with God is achieved.

The belief that our separateness can be *humanly* overcome is a spiritual deception from the biblical point of view. Sin indeed separates us from God. Sin brings disunity from the Spirit. True restoration cannot come from within the system. The only thing that brings us into unity with God's Spirit is confession of sin, repentance and trust in Jesus as Lord.

Another sobering aspect of spiritual deception in the New Age is their reliance on 'spirit guides' through whom they seek guidance from the spirit world. This is a practice that is clearly forbidden in the Bible (Deut. 18:11). Why aren't we encouraged in Scripture to contact higher spirits, employ them as guides and harness their wisdom or power for our human needs? Because God alone is to be our source of power, of wisdom and of knowledge.

This call to seek 'higher guidance' isn't new. The Gnostics of the second century taught that God was too exalted, too far away, just 'too busy' to be bothered with personal human affairs. They taught that other beings exist who are higher than humans but lower than God, whom we can contact for help.

But the biblical warning is stark: we are not to toy with the realm of spirits. There is only one God: there is no other. To seek guidance from anyone else – be it spirit guides, mediums, diviners – is blasphemy. God is our refuge, and it is to him and him alone we are to turn for help, guidance and wisdom. We do otherwise at our peril.

Besides spiritual deception, there is also the problem of self-deception in the New Age because the basis for evaluating truth is totally subjective. Evidence is not offered because it is not required in such a system. The only 'proof' required is subjective certainty. 'Because of its absolute subjectivity, the I-am-God or I-am-the-universe position remains beyond any criticism external to the subject.'²

So we return to our question: how do we break into self-deception and spiritual deception? Speaking rationally into deception rarely works because the origin of the problem is spiritual in nature and not intellectual. Spiritual deception requires a different strategy. Our primary strategy needs to be prayer. We must ask God himself to find a way to break through the spiritual deception and self-deception, to help those involved in counterfeit spiritualities to see their rebellion and to repent. We must ask God to break any experience of false fruit, such as feelings of unity and peace that are self-deceived. But what we *don't* say is, 'My goodness, you really are deceived and rebellious!' It is not something that we *say*; it is something that we *pray*!

Whether we begin by asking God to reveal his truth through the power of the Holy Spirit or begin by offering evidence or telling stories (as in the previous two chapters), let us remember that what motivates our apologetics is our desire to direct attention to Jesus. We want seekers to examine Jesus and his claims by what they see in our lives. Let us therefore offer the world models of head-and-heart-and-Spirit-filled Christianity.

Such models, however, do not spring solely from individual, personal witness. And that is why we must next turn to the witness to Christ that can flow from his body, the church, when it works as a co-ordinated whole.

18

The witness of community

We were not born to be alone. God created us for relationships. So we have been born first into the human family and then, as Christians, born again into the family of God. All of us, therefore, are members of some kind of community – our own family, school, friends, colleagues, neighbours or other social groups. As John Donne said, 'No man is an island.'

Still, we often feel like islands. Our professional commitments frequently lead us not only into geographical isolation but into emotional isolation as well. And so loneliness – the very opposite of community, the most crushing of all emotions – descends on us. There is an important reason for this. It is by design and not caprice that we find loneliness crushing. Only in community can we become fully alive, fully human, finding rest and completeness in the context of others. It is not enough for one individual to imitate the ways of God, for God is not alone; he is the Trinity. Therefore, it is the community of God's people who will represent him more fully and completely.

Furthermore, it is in community – in seeing ourselves juxtaposed with others – that we learn who we are. In community we can exercise the gifts God has given us. In all likelihood these gifts are gifts of ministry. For Christians especially, community is glorious, for it is in community that we can worship together, be nurtured and bear one another's burdens.

What, then, is the role of Christian community in evangelism? Some Christians feel that their community (be it a church, a Bible study, a small group or a friendship relationship) can prepare people to be launched out for witness to others. Certainly we need to be fed and nurtured and built up and trained. But we must remember, too, that our local

Christian community itself can be a powerful witness to our non-Christian friends. Communities of Christians who practise what they preach arouse and stimulate curiosity in Jesus. When the teaching of Jesus is heard and demonstrated, there will be an impact.

No lone rangers

We are not called to be 'Lone Ranger' Christians. We are called to love one another. Indeed, an understandable basis for rejection of belief in God, according to Jesus, is lack of love among Christians (John 17:20-24).

Unlike the solitary explorer, out there dodging the perils alone, we are called to be a close family that welcomes others into our midst. We invite people to come and share our love and our gifts. We are free to admit that we have not arrived and are far from perfect. But because we believe Jesus is the living centre of our group, we invite our seeker friends and acquaintances to hang around us and observe him.

I used to feel uncomfortable about the presence of sceptics in Christian groups. Would they feel weird listening to us pray and watching us read the Bible? As I said in a previous chapter, when I gave a talk to a group, I used to ask the leaders if there were any non-believers present. Upon reflection, I realized that even if there were, I would not change my message at all. The world is not as fragile as we think. Non-Christians can handle us in our natural habitat far more than we realize. All they need is to feel welcome and to be invited to come and see. In fact, people long to be a part of a community that will care for them (whether it is a Bible study group or a church).

Although that truth is ageless, it has never been more timely than today. For a variety of reasons, people are drawn in more often by the warmth of relationship than by the brilliance of apologetics. In fact, people are almost too vulnerable to community; if they feel loved, they will tend to believe anything. This situation is exploited to the fullest by a number of the fringe religious groups.

As Christians true to Christ, we do care about emotional needs, but we must be careful not to manipulate people through it. It is fine that unbelievers are drawn into our midst because they feel welcomed and cared for, but we must be as concerned for their minds as for their souls. We must offer not only love but excellent biblical teaching as well. There has to be solid truth taught in our warm communities or else our houses of faith will be built on shifting sand. The world needs both to feel God's love and to hear God's truth in us.

Communities, then, can be powerful tools to communicate the reality of Jesus. Let us take a closer look at some of the forms these communities take.

Christian small groups

Our witness as a community can be especially demonstrated through a small-group Bible study. The group should think of activities to which they could invite their friends. Bruce Erickson, who used to work among students, said that his small group learned of a man on social security whose house needed reroofing. Bruce suggested that each member bring a non-Christian friend and make it a 'roofing party'. Someone would have to be pretty desperate to go to a party like this, but a group spent the day together, working hard, caring for the man and just having fun.

Some of them eventually became Christians. Without realizing it these Christians had been witnessing all day by the way they cared for each other, by their concern for the man, by their ability to have fun. We need to invite people along to see us as we live. Things we take for granted (that we pray for each other, that we sincerely try to love each other, and so forth) can make a deep impression.

Another way we can make a lasting impression on the world is in our attitude toward possessions. Jesus talks about few things as much as our possessions. He tells us that no person can serve two masters (Matt. 6:24). To serve God as our first love means there can be no competing loyalties. We can stimulate a curiosity in the gospel when we demonstrate that we believe our money is God's, and we desire to use it to please him.

Lois (whom I mentioned in chapter 3) had her interest in the gospel stimulated when she came to a fellowship meeting and heard a Christian student say he had no money for his fare home. Immediately three fellow Christians reached into their pockets and gave him what they had. Later, when Lois wanted to go to a Christian student conference but had no funds, another Christian told her he would sell his camping tent. He loved camping, but he felt that her getting nurture for her young faith was more important. When we demonstrate a biblical attitude toward money and material possessions, the world stands up to take notice.

Or take another example. Once a woman told me her small group wanted to reach out to their seeker friends, but they could not think of what to do. Then she said quickly that she had to dash to pick up tickets for her group to see *Richard III* in which she was performing. When I told her that would be a great thing for them to take their friends to, she asked, 'What does *Richard III* have to do with God?'

'For starters, this play deals with the problem of evil. Is Richard responsible for his cruelty, or can he blame it on his "genes" and his crippled body? Any discussion of the nature of evil leads one to discussing ultimate issues,' I said.

So here we have an example not only of what to do but also of the importance of integrating our faith into our world. If we think God is relevant only in Bible studies, our witness will have little impact.

That means we need to be conscious of current political and cultural events. It is not necessary to see or read everything, but we do need to be aware of what our culture is listening to. Then we must develop our analytical skills in evaluating our culture from a Christian perspective. We need a 'Christian mind', as Harry Blamires has suggested. I know a woman who does not go to many films, but she reads film reviews regularly to gain understanding and awareness of her culture, and it helps her in talking with others. Unfortunately her example is an exception.

When through our small groups we reach out to our sceptic friends in love and bring them into our midst, when we live as Jesus would have us live, regarding people as infinitely more important than material things, and when we demonstrate sensitivity and insight rather than ignorance toward our culture, the impact will be great. Our Christian group, then, will not become ingrown and isolated from the surrounding society. Rather, we will demonstrate that Christians are real people who care deeply for others. We study and love the Scripture because it, too, is passionately honest about life and is loyal to the truth about us. We meet together as Christians and we pray and study God's Word because we celebrate the call to live in the real world and are not trying to escape from it.

Nevertheless, perhaps we feel bringing our non-Christian friends to a Bible study full of Christians would be too overpowering at first. We may feel they need something less threatening to start with.

Investigative Bible discussion

Sooner or later we must get our seeker friends reading the Bible. One effective way is to gather several sceptic friends with one or two Christians and discuss a passage that vitally confronts us with the person of Christ. This is a wonderful means of outreach to our neighbourhoods. Our seeker friends need to see Jesus as he walks through Palestine – watch what he does, listen to what he says, observe how he relates to people. This was how his disciples slowly became convinced of who Jesus was. Our friends, too, need to hang around the Jesus in the Gospels.

Many people blindly accept Christ's deity as a child, and then blindly reject it as they grow up, without ever realizing that Jesus comes to us first as a person. Our aim is to allow Jesus to come alive to them in the Scriptures to give them a feel of what kind of person he is.

When you invite your friends, assure them that no previous Bible knowledge is necessary. They do not have to believe in God or the Bible. The point is for them to read firsthand what the Bible actually says. If they do not believe, then, as my sceptic companion on the aeroplane said, for the sake of intellectual integrity they need to know what they are rejecting. We can assure them that it will not be churchy; we will not sing hymns. Rather, we will consider the passage as we would any historical document, arriving at conclusions that the text, not the teacher, demands.

This is an efficient way to present Jesus. Most people do not recognize their need for Jesus in a one-shot conversation. But when a Christian befriends them and eventually leads them into a study like this, they will grasp a much fuller picture of what it means to be a Christian. Even if we met only six times, we could look at (1) Jesus' sensitivity and compassion to people (John 4: the woman at the well); (2) his miraculous powers (John 11: Lazarus's resurrection); (3) who he claimed to be (John 14: 'I am the way, and the truth, and the life'); (4) how to become a Christian (John 3:1–21: Nicodemus); (5) the death of Jesus (John 19); and (6) his resurrection (John 20).

Most importantly, to lead this kind of discussion it is not necessary to have lots of experience or training as a Bible discussion leader. The leader needs to draw out the members as to what the text says, not lecture for an hour.

If you would appreciate help in knowing how to ask the right questions and draw people out, it is not hard to find. I have mentioned some helpful guides in appendix 2.

Evangelism through the local church

In the early days of my ministry I worked among students with the InterVarsity Christian Fellowship, the American equivalent of the UCCF. One of the many things I appreciated about InterVarsity was their clear emphasis on the importance of the church. They continually emphasized to students that parachurch organizations will come and go but that the church, the agent of God's action in the world, is for the ages.

Moreover, the church can offer to the world a model that a Christian student group never can. It can offer to the world a model of unity amid great diversity – diversity of age, race, occupation, ability, interest and so forth. There are inevitable limits to a model of Christ that includes mostly people who range in age from their late teens to twenties.

If you are reading this as a student and you are not associated with a local church, let me say this to you: go immediately and find one where Christ is exalted and the Bible is trusted and acted on, and begin worshipping there. For only there will you find the full scope of what Christian community can mean.

Clearly, one of the most effective ways to do evangelism is through the local church. John Stott has described evangelism through the local church as 'the most normal, natural and productive method of spreading the gospel today'.[1] Michael Green, Adviser in Evangelism to the Archbishops of Canterbury and York, wrote in his book *Evangelism Through the Local Church*, 'Whenever Christianity has been at its most healthy, evangelism has stemmed from the local church, and has had a noticeable impact on the surrounding area ... If local churches were engaging in loving, outgoing evangelism, within their neighbourhood, many of our evangelistic campaigns, missions and crusades would be rendered much less necessary.'[2]

The question is, then, how can churches become communities of faith reaching out and offering life to the world around them? I have often asked pastors how effective their congregations are in reaching out to their local area. Frequently they tell me they don't feel they are effective. Why is it, they ask, that when evangelism-training programmes end, sometimes so do the evangelistic efforts? What makes people become inwardly motivated to share their faith?

E. M. Bounds wrote, 'People are God's method. The Church is looking for better methods, God is looking for better people.'[3] What can pastors do then to encourage their flock to evangelize?

First, as pastors, teach your congregation to nurture an intimate walk with God. Help them to learn how to walk by faith, to pray boldly and to listen to the Spirit. That way your members will be able to share not only the gospel but also the real difference that Christ makes in their lives.

Second, remind them that success breeds success. The more they dare to open their mouths and witness, the more they will see positive results. Encourage them to take risks, to exercise boldness, for only through obedience will they truly know that God is there.

Third, encourage them not only to build friendships with seekers but to introduce their seeker friends to fellow Christians. One pastor I know who wanted his church to be actively involved in evangelism began by building small-group neighbourhood Bible studies. For the first time the members of his church began to trust each other, love each other and become involved in each other's lives. After they had met for six months, he then encouraged them to witness to their seeker friends. As they formed friendships with non-Christians in their neighbourhood, they genuinely wanted them to meet their friends in their Bible discussion. Soon the Bible-study members were bringing their seeker friends to their group and eventually to their church. The pastor told me that, for the first time during his ministry there, real evangelism was going on in his church.

There is a reason for this. Using systems like going door-to-door or handing out tracts or giving a prepared speech can be initially helpful, but such methods have limits. Going door-to-door may help you to get a hearing, but once you are inside the door, your orientation can never be the same again. You meet a stranger only once. From that first meeting, some kind of relationship will follow.

Asking a person a set of good, stimulating questions designed to draw out their interest in spiritual matters can be very effective. But once the questions have been asked, you can't use them again with the same person. The closer you become to an individual, the more awkward you feel using methods that are best suited for someone you don't know.

No matter how we initiate a spiritual conversation, what seekers ultimately need to see is the gospel fleshed out in a believer's life. Strangers, so long as they remain strangers, only hear a message and never see it lived out in human relationships. One of the greatest gifts (and evidence) that we give is the chance for others to see how Jesus lives his life through us. And the demonstration of his love, his holiness and his charity is especially powerful in a community of believers.

We live in a culture of people who feel like burnt ground. They have heard it all. They have been assaulted by every experience imaginable. And when our style or initial approach reminds them of all the others, Jesus is reduced in their estimation to merely one option among many.

I am not saying there is no place for contact evangelism. But I am saying that by far the most effective, the most costly and even perhaps the most biblical kind of evangelism is found in the person or groups who look at the people around them, those with whom their own life naturally intersects, and then begin to cultivate friendships and to love them. When churches start to reach out to their neighbourhoods through small groups, or whatever format works for them, the impact can be overwhelming.

How, then, is the church to become an evangelizing centre?

First, we have to believe there are people who are open to the gospel. In the Gospel of John we are told of an encounter Jesus had with a worldly, promiscuous woman. When the disciples saw that he was speaking to her, they were astonished. And Jesus' response to them was: 'Do you not say, "Four months more and then the harvest"? I tell you, open your eyes and look at the fields! They are ripe for harvest' (John 4:35, New International Version). Do we believe that the fields are ripe for harvest?

Several months ago I called a good friend, Adele, and asked her if she knew of a hair salon near my home. She suggested a place she had heard of. I went and a beautiful woman introducing herself as Meg told me she'd be the one cutting my hair that day. As we chatted, I asked Meg to tell me about her family. In doing so she casually mentioned that she had a brother who was a born-again Christian. Several minutes later she said he was also an avid reader. I didn't say anything then, but a few appointments later, having already told her I was a Christian, I mentioned that I had written a few things that perhaps he might have read. She said she'd make sure she asked him the next time they spoke on the phone.

When I came in for my next hair appointment, Meg said, 'My brother was over the moon that I am doing your hair. He read *Out of the Saltshaker* ten years ago, and he said it really changed his life. Isn't that an amazing coincidence that he has read something that you wrote?' she asked.

About one month later I was at the front desk paying Meg when one of the hairstylists nudged her, saying she should tell me something. I looked puzzled and Meg said, 'Well, I didn't tell you this before because I was afraid it might make you feel uncomfortable. But remember when I told my brother that I was doing your hair? After I told him, there was this long pause of silence on the phone. Then he said that all those years ago after reading your book, what struck him was the feeling that someone with a personality like yours would be able to help me find God. So he knelt down and prayed and asked God to please send someone like Becky into my life. Then he said, "Meg, ten years ago I asked God to send someone *like* Becky into your life. I didn't ask him to send Becky herself." Then he sort of got choked up.'

I stood there looking at Meg, whom I have come to genuinely love, and I could hardly hold back the tears myself. Then Meg said, 'I didn't tell you because I didn't want you to feel funny. You know, about the *pressure* of having to help me find God!' Then we all burst into laughter.

But as I got into my car I couldn't help thinking, *How does God do this?* From the outside it all looked so casual and haphazard. I asked Adele if she knew of a hairdresser, and she casually mentioned a place. I didn't even ask for a specific name when I called. I just happened to get the person who was free at that time, who just happened to have been the recipient of her brother's prayer ten years ago. What a brother! What a God!

Just at the time I met Meg I was invited to do a conference for a large seeker-sensitive church in the area where I live. They had read my book *A Heart Like His*, and the pastor wanted me to do a conference training the leadership of the church in the area of deepening faith and developing character based on the life of David. Then on Sunday I was to preach to all the services, which comprised both believers and seekers with little or no church background. As I was speaking that Sunday, it dawned on me that this might be just the right church for Meg. The service was God-honouring and lively, the music and drama were great and there were lots of people around her age.

Meg and I have spoken freely and easily about faith, so the next time I saw her I intended to bring it up. But I never had the opportunity because the first thing Meg said to me was, 'One of my clients goes to a church that she thinks I'd really like. She said you've just spoken there. Do you think I would like it?' Of course, it was the very place I was going to mention. That's the thing about God – you can never beat him to the punch! Naturally I encouraged her to go.

Then about a month later Meg said, 'Remember the church where you recently spoke and my client attends? Well, they are building a brand-new place because they've grown so large. And they're moving in soon.'

'Yes, I knew that, but how on earth did you know that?' I asked.

'Because their new building is opposite my house!' she exclaimed.

Are the fields ripe for harvest? Two weeks ago I took a much-needed break from my writing schedule. My children arrive home from school at 3:15 in the afternoon, so I quickly dashed out to buy some pumpkins and gourds so I could be back before they came home. I felt a bit brain-dead from writing all day, but when I saw the vast array of beautiful pumpkins lined up in a row, and flowers and plants of every hue, the sheer beauty of this autumnal vision took my breath away! Feeling my own spirit revive, I quickly selected what I wanted and went up to the counter to pay.

I had noticed when walking in how life-weary the woman at the till appeared. I was the only person at the counter, so I showed her all of my items with great delight. She managed a weak smile and said, 'You know, I forget to look at what I'm selling since I do it every day.' We continued to chat as I got out my chequebook. Out of the blue she asked me what I did for a living. When I told her I was an author and speaker, she said, 'I say, you aren't that famous romantic novelist who lives in this area, are you?'

I laughed and told her that I wasn't but that I knew who she was talking about because she is my neighbour and a good friend.

Then she said, 'Well, perhaps what I need just now is to buy a romantic novel. Then I could see what it feels like to have a happily-ever-after ending for once.'

'Oh, dear. Sounds like it's been a rather long autumn for you,' I answered.

'Not long autumn. Try long life,' she answered bleakly.

'Have you been in a relationship that recently fell apart or something?'

'I've been divorced three times. And I'm involved with someone now, but I know he's not committed. He's always telling me that you can't force love; it happens if it's supposed to,' she answered grimly.

'You're right, he definitely doesn't sound like a serious candidate. Why are you still continuing to see him?'

'Who knows? I guess it's because I'm lonely. Oh, I know, I've read all the self-help books that say you have to be able to live alone and like yourself before you're ready for a relationship. I know all about being my own best friend. I just wonder why none of it works,' she said dejectedly.

, 'Well, I think you have to take seriously your need for a relationship. Your very hunger for one tells you that you've been made for intimacy. The trick is finding how to meet that need in satisfying and constructive ways rather than empty and hurtful ways.'

'You're right there! Feel free to pass on any tips!' she said smiling.

'Well, I can tell you what's got me through the tough times,' I answered.

'Fire away!'

By now we had picked up the pumpkins and were carrying them to my car. 'First, it's developing a relationship with God. Once you turn to God, you find that he fills your need for love and intimacy in a way that enables you to develop much healthier relationships with others.'

'Which means you're not putting all your marbles in a basket that was never meant to hold them all in the first place?'

'Exactly! The second thing may surprise you, but what has really helped me is going to church. You meet some great people there, you get reminded every week of what is real, and you form friendships that make you realize that you're not alone.'

She looked at me in astonishment and said, 'I can't believe you just said that. I've been so depressed lately, but yesterday I felt I couldn't go on any longer. Then all of a sudden this idea popped into my head: *Why don't you go to church?* I haven't been to church in twenty years, but yesterday I thought maybe I should start going. So I'm amazed that you just said it!'

She told me that she'd already thought of a local church that she wanted to attend. I encouraged her to go straight away and even if it didn't feel comfortable at first, to not give up on it immediately. I told her that I'd come back again when it was time to buy some Christmas poinsettias and ask her how she liked church.

As I was pulling out of my parking space, she asked me, 'Do you think God knew that I was thinking about going back to church and he sent you here to confirm it?'

'God not only knew what you were thinking; it was God who put the thought in your head! And yes, I think God did want you to know that he loves you, that he cares about your problems, and he wants to meet you in church this Sunday!'

I walked in the back door of our home as my children were walking in the front. When I excitedly told them what had just happened, they shared my joy, but they also couldn't help but start laughing. One of our family jokes is how often I go somewhere to get some kind of service but return saying I absolutely must return there for the sake of the gospel. 'Well, now we know where we'll be buying our plants for the rest of our lives!' my children joked.

The fields are indeed ripe and ready to be harvested. What God needs are labourers. The issue before us is not whether we must all become adept at sharing the gospel with those who sell pumpkins! I've said it before, but I will say it again: God made us different. Some of us are able to connect to people and get into serious conversations quickly, while others of us need time and trust to be established before we feel comfortable sharing the gospel. The point is not that we imitate someone else's style but that we find our own style and then get on with the business of sharing the gospel.

The question that concerns us, however, is this: what kind of church experience will these women have if they decide to go? Will they find the church welcoming and warm? Will it feel like a safe place to them? I don't even know the name of the woman who sold me the pumpkins, but I know enough about her story to know that if no-one reaches out to her, if she feels judged or is made to feel she isn't good enough to be 'one of them', she'll never go back.

Even more important than our church evangelism training programmes is whether the people in our congregations demonstrate the love of Jesus to those who come through our doors. Is our church warm and welcoming? Do we practise hospitality and see it as a holy ministry? People today are desperate to connect in some meaningful way to others, yet modern life makes a deep sense of connection and personal integration terribly difficult. Before tracts and techniques, before programmes and pamphlets, we need to open our arms wide and let seekers know that they bless us just by being in our midst.

19

Without a vision the people will perish

How does the church reach out to seekers and become the evangelizing centre it was meant to be? Before we think of programmes or techniques, we need to be renewed in our vision of who Christ is and what God's purposes are for our world. Author Alan Roxburgh is right when he says, 'We have lost the vision of a cosmic, transforming Christ who addresses all of life.'[1]

We saw in chapter 3 that to call Jesus the Lord of life is to live under God's rule, which extends to all of life. To say we believe that Christ is Lord is to recognize that the purpose of Christ is the transformation of every aspect of our being and our world. How, then, do we live out this vision of a transformational reality in our churches? How do we translate our belief in the transforming lordship of Christ to those who are hungry and poor; to the homosexual; to the unmarried mother; to the marginalized ones who slip between the cracks in our cities; to the institutional structures that oppress; to the political structures that may cause good or harm; or to concerns for our planet and its resources? What is our responsibility as Christ's agents to participate with Christ as he seeks to restore all things into wholeness in himself?

Recovering our vision

Let us begin by renewing our vision of what it means to live as radical disciples of Jesus in this broken world. Let us seek to connect and submit every area of life to the authority and transforming intention of Christ, for by our doing so seekers cannot help but be drawn to us. For example, if Christ's transforming power is concerned with every aspect of what it means to be human, then what do we do with a seeker who is suffering from cancer? Jesus didn't offer healing only for those who believed in him; he healed people whether they believed in him or not. Yes, it's imperative that we share the gospel with seekers, but isn't part of our witness to pray for their physical healing as well as their spiritual?

Are there individuals in your church whom God has gifted in the area of prayer and healing? Then let them go to suffering people, be they Christians or not, and offer prayers to God for their healing. It is a powerful testimony to the nature of Christ's love for all humanity.

Or what about those who suffer from sexual dysfunction, be it heterosexual or homosexual? My home church has a powerful healing ministry to those seeking sexual wholeness. Mario Bergner, the author of *Setting Love in Order*, leads a ministry at our church called 'Redeemed Lives'. Many have received profound ministry and have been restored to sexual wholeness in the loving and welcoming context of our church community.

Or what about the poor and the isolated in our cities? What can we in the church do to reach those who feel isolated and alone?

We need a renewed vision of who Christ is and what he has come to do: to heal, restore and transform his creation! As we translate Christ's vision into practical realities, evangelism cannot help but happen.

Reading the signs of the culture

To be an evangelizing church also means we need to read the signs of the times in our modern culture in order to know how to reach people effectively for the gospel. We read these signs not so that we can water down the gospel to fit current trends. Rather, we listen to the modern cries for meaning while we plumb the depths of Scripture to see what the Bible says in regard to these issues. What we will discover is that we have far more to offer the seeker than we even realized.

The church and the hunger for community

For example, one of the cries we hear in our modern culture is the search for family, for a community, especially with the isolating, fragmentary nature of modern life. The longing for community arises out of a search for connectedness with God, with others and even with nature. The modern sense of being disconnected due to isolation, loneliness, broken relationships or simply the frenetic pace of modern life creates a profound longing for integration and a longing for a sense of place.

Alan Roxburgh asks the penetrating question: 'Where are the resources for building communities of Christian witness in a culture where life is profoundly alienating?'[2] He answers this in part by examining the work of historian E. R. Dodds, who addresses the fascinating subject of why Christianity, a small movement among a plethora of Eastern mystery cults, should come to triumph. Dodd believed it was due to the fact that Christian congregations were bound together by a common life. The early church was a 'context of hope, care and inclusion for widows, orphans, broken and destitute people in Roman society.'[3]

The need for community hasn't changed. In a magazine interview Mark Lauterback describes many touching and positive experiences he has had as a pastor seeking to be a witness to his community. However, he tells of one experience he and his wife had with a woman who came to help with the housework. She came from a terribly dysfunctional family and was studying different religions to see what she would believe. Mark had long discussions with her about the gospel, and she talked at length to Mark's wife. But in the end, much to their distress, she chose to become a Mormon.

As Mark probed to understand why, it became evident that she didn't understand much of Mormon theology. What drew her to Mormonism was their sense of family. She was lonely and searching for community, and she felt they loved her. Lauterback astutely points out, 'Our approach of assaulting her with truth was wrong. We should have taken her into our home.'[4]

As an evangelizing church, we need to ask ourselves: who are the poor and destitute, the widows and the orphans in our midst? How do we offer them the love and hope of Christ as a Christian community?

A divorced woman who was a single parent told me that she decided to return to the church after her divorce. She felt alone, afraid and desperately in need of a support system to help her bring up her three active boys. Most of all, she was seeking spiritual answers and needed to know if God was really there. She was initially afraid the people in the church might be judgmental. But when the pastor made his first pastoral visit, he simply said, 'What can we do to help? The Bible tells us to care for the widow and the orphans, and we truly want to do that. But you'll have to guide us in the practical ways we can show you the love of Christ.'

As they talked, the pastor began to see how the church could help. Some men in the church began to shovel the snow off her drive and worked on her car, families with sons offered to take her boys on camping trips, and there were women who just listened to her when she felt overwhelmed. Not only did the church see her through a difficult time but, because it behaved like a true community of Christ, she was led to make a commitment to Christ herself.

We also need to rediscover the sacred call of hospitality. My husband, Dick, told me a story that moved him deeply. Several years ago he was in a meeting that involved working on a large building plan. They had hired a very successful architect from another city. Dick had never met the architect, but as they began talking, he casually mentioned to Dick that he and his wife went to church. That opened the door to discussing their shared faith. Dick then said, 'What caused you to become interested in faith?'

'Many years ago,' began the architect. 'I had absolutely no interest in faith, but my wife decided she wanted to attend church. I told her that I'd go with her the first time but not to expect me to make a return visit. Church and church people held no interest for me whatsoever.

'To my surprise the sermon was pretty good. But afterwards a very distinguished, elegant older man came over to greet me. He asked me questions about my work and he seemed genuinely interested in me. Then he asked me if my wife and I had any plans for lunch. When I said we didn't, he then asked us to come to his home for lunch. I couldn't believe that a stranger was warmly inviting me to his own home. We had a marvellous lunch. It was clear to me that he was a very successful businessman – you could just tell by his quiet authority. But what struck me was the tremendous vitality of his love for Jesus. Just experiencing his kindness and seeing his faith made me know that I had to go back to church. We ended up joining, and I went every Sunday for the rest of the time we lived there. The man's name was Dick Evenhouse.'

Dick looked at him in astonishment. 'What, do you know him?' asked the architect.

'Yes, I certainly do. I was named after him. That man is my grandfather.'

The architect answered, 'Well, your grandfather had a profound spiritual impact on my life.'

'He had an even deeper impact on mine,' answered Dick.

And to think it all started with a simple offering of lunch. What a marvellous example of how to make the church a welcoming place! What an encouragement to all of us to pay attention to the newcomers and to greet them with the gift of hospitality!

What we have to offer a world that is lonely and searching for satisfying relationships is the community of Christ. Nicky Gumbel, the author of the Alpha course, made a fascinating observation in a lecture I heard him give. A man who had recently become a Christian told Nicky, 'I came from a very conservative Christian background, but I threw it all overboard because the unspoken message was that first I had to *behave*, then I had to *believe*, and then, if I was really lucky, they might let me *belong*.'

Nicky then challenged us Christians to model the exact opposite to seekers. First, give seekers a sense that they belong, that we are delighted to be their friends. Then pray they will come to believe. Then model and teach them how to behave. What a powerful inversion of what it means to be Christ's community!

To be a community centred in Christ means more than merely getting our own needs met. As Roxburgh writes, 'We need communities of God's people bound to one another because they have discovered the One in their midst who takes up their pain and gives it meaning in the larger call of a great journey toward a transformed and healed creation ... Community demands a pilgrim band who are on a journey, caught up in something fantastically bigger than themselves and their needs.'[5]

Lesslie Newbigin reminds us in his book *Foolishness to the Greeks* that the church 'is not meant to call men and women out of the world into a safe religious enclave but to call them out in order to send them back as agents of God's kingship'.[6] The church is to be focused not on itself but on its neighbourhood. We are called, Newbigin reminds us, not to remain isolated in fear from the world, nor to engage in ceaseless activities to keep the faithful busy. Our focus is to bring the glorious news of the One who said: 'As the Father has sent me, so I send you' (John 20:21).

The church and the quest for spirituality

Another prominent aspect of our modern culture is the search for spiritual meaning and spiritual experience. What do we have to offer people in their search for transcendence and mystical experience? What can we say to people who tell us they want to connect to a higher cosmic consciousness? What can the church offer such seekers?

First, as we invite seekers to come with us to church, what we hope they catch is a glimpse of the greatness and the glory of God. Our services should testify to the fact that God is far greater than we imagine. What comes across in a God-centred service is an indirect challenge to the self-absorption that permeates our age. We are there to bless God. All our attention is on him because he is the centre of the universe, not us. In our church service we are made aware, without ever saying it, that God is more important than we are – and such knowledge is liberating!

What means do we have to convey the greatness of God? First, we accomplish this by a clear proclamation of biblical truth. Nothing centres us or keeps us from confusion more than the Word of God.

Powerful preaching from the Word is a vital evangelistic tool. When I lived in Jerusalem, I met a woman who is a messianic

Jew, or a Jew who believes that Jesus is the true Messiah. As I got to know her and observe her in many different situations, I marvelled at the strength of her faith and her knowledge of the Bible. She had a very strong character. I could always count on Hannah to see things clearly and tell things straight.

One day I asked Hannah how she came to faith in Christ. She said that part of her nursing training required her to study in London for one year. She described herself at that time as a typical Israeli Jew: a sceptic, with almost no knowledge of the Bible, but faithful to her Jewish traditions. She became close friends with some women in the school of nursing who were Christians. They invited her to attend their church. She went once out of politeness, never intending to go back.

As she sat in the pew, however, she was astonished to find herself strangely riveted by the minister in the pulpit. 'I'm a very tough cookie by nature,' admitted Hannah, 'and I went in that day feeling intellectually superior to everyone around me, especially those needing to depend on some crutch to get through life. But as the minister began to preach, the first thing I noticed was his tremendous mind. He was so logical and lucid. And he understood my questions and doubts, my secular mindset. But more than that, there was an authority, a power that was impossible to deny.'

So she returned, Sunday after Sunday, for the entire year that she lived in London. 'I could have managed to escape cleverness or services oriented to entertain me, but what I couldn't escape from was the truth. And that man preached the truth of God's Word – faithfully and relentlessly.'

On Hannah's last Sunday before returning to Israel, the minister asked if there was anyone who hadn't made a commitment to Christ and who felt they were ready to come forward. 'It took an entire year of listening to him preach the Word of God for me to be ready, but I knew I had no other choice but to go forward. I gave my life unreservedly to Christ.'

That preacher happened to be the late Martyn Lloyd-Jones. And her Christian walk truly evidenced the blessing of having sat under such wonderful Bible teaching.

Let us never underestimate what a powerful evangelistic tool there is in the faithful preaching of the Word of God. Donald Bloesch makes the fascinating point that what brought thousands of people to faith in the eighteenth century were not the skilled apologists but the evangelical preachers who preached the gospel and reached the masses – preachers such as George Whitefield and John Wesley.[7] But that doesn't mean we don't take the time to read our culture. Rather, let us address the themes of our modern culture with the relevance of the gospel through the power of God's Word. Whenever I speak to denominational conferences for ministers, I always encourage them to take their preaching with the utmost seriousness. Excellent preaching not only builds up the saints but is used by God to convert the seekers as well.

The second aspect that speaks to the seekers in our midst is our eucharist and worship. I agree wholeheartedly with Alan Roxburgh, who writes, 'There is no more profound apologetic for the gospel than the vitality of a people at worship.'[8] In our experiential age we may shy away from anything that suggests an appeal to our hearts. And of course we do need balance. But John Stott, quoting Bishop Handley Moule, says 'Beware equally of an undevotional theology [that is, mind without heart] and of an untheological devotion [that is, heart without mind].'[9]

The truth is that Christianity is both deeply rational and deeply experiential. Our message requires not simply mental assent to a series of truth propositions; it also calls people into a love relationship with Jesus. We come to church to learn about the nature and truth of who God is, but we also come to church to experience being in God's presence. Again John Stott writes, 'There is a place for emotion in spiritual experience. The Holy Spirit's ... ministry is not limited to illuminating our minds and teaching us about Christ. He also pours God's love into our hearts. Similarly, he bears witness with our spirit that we are God's children, for he causes us to say "Abba, Father" and to exclaim in gratitude "How great is the love the Father has lavished on us, that we should be called children of God." '[10]

We need to have a worship life in our church that directs people to an experience of the transcendent God, who is present. It is God's desire to meet us in a deep and personal way. He does not want us to relate to him merely as the sum total of our rational theological beliefs but to connect with his being at a profound level of intimacy.

In our age, which hungers to be reconnected with God, we must realize that what we have to offer is the very presence of God in our midst! We celebrate the sacraments because we have the true bread of life to share. Roxburgh said, 'If there were a greater experience of God's presence, an expectation of intimacy, of knowing ourselves corporately connected to God and hearing ourselves addressed by God in ways not limited to a sermon, then our worship could be a means of mission to a spiritually hungry and disconnected culture.'[11]

Let us worship God with our minds, our hearts and our souls. And let us be sure that we invite seekers into the church where they will hear the Word of truth and experience God's Spirit. Where there is the spontaneous overflow of a community of praise and the radiance of a supernatural reality, there is transformational power!

Tailor-made evangelism

How can we find a way of doing evangelism that is right for our church? How do we go about finding a model that fits us?

First, as we have already discussed, we need to pay attention to our culture at large. What does it mean to be a seeker in a secularized, pluralistic modern world? This is a subject worth pursuing, and Lesslie Newbigin addresses this issue as well as anyone in his book *The Gospel in a Pluralistic Society.*

Second, we must pay attention to our own setting, to the seekers with whom we are in dialogue. We need to understand the place where we are ministering. What are the types of people that God has called us to minister to as a church? What kind of culture or cultures are involved? What are the cries of their hearts? In other words, we need to listen, and understand as best we can the context of those with whom we are sharing the gospel. George Hunter, in his very helpful book *How to Reach Secular People*, provides ten characteristics of secular people and strategies for how to reach them.[12]

The gospel is unchanging, but our context does affect the way we go about presenting the gospel. I have preached the gospel to prison inmates. I have also given evangelistic presentations at a prestigious country club. The gospel didn't change, but the way I presented it did.

The subject of contextualization in evangelism is an important issue and far beyond the scope of this book. Alan Roxburgh's *Reaching a New Generation* gives a splendid analysis of this subject.

Third, we need to understand who we are as well. One of the things I have learned, having travelled widely and spoken to many different denominations, is that every church has its own culture – its own language, its own traditions, its own ethos – and the people they are seeking to reach are different too. So examine who you are as a group. Are you a large, diverse inner-city church or a small rural church? Is your church made up more of elderly people or young ones? A form of outreach that works for one church may not work for another.

Does your church at least attempt to reflect the vision of a transformational community committed to healing lives and the world in the way that Christ intends? Or would you describe your church as ingrown and a place where only those from your own particular group would feel comfortable? Church was never intended to be a comfortable club for elderly Baptists or a fashionable spot for beautiful twentysomethings or an exclusive spa for middle-aged Anglicans. 'Our culture does not need any more churches run like corporations; it needs local communities empowered by the gospel vision of a transforming Christ who addresses the needs of the context and changes the polis into a place of hope and wholeness.'[13]

We all need to be stretched beyond our comfort zone as we reach outside the comfortable ghetto of the church to others. But arming ourselves with an understanding of who we are as a people will help us as we choose which evangelism strategy will work best.

Lastly, we must develop a clear mission statement as a church with concrete objectives as we set goals for evangelism. Does your church have a strategy for reaching unchurched people? Don't underestimate the need for training, as I initially did. My experience was very similar to what Ken Chafin describes: 'I watched women who had drive and ingenuity enough to make them excellent presidents of the PTA yet who were unable to tell the children in their class how to become Christians. I watched lawyers who were qualified to try cases before the Supreme Court who could not sit down in the living room of an interested friend and present a good "brief" for Jesus Christ ... I've discovered that most of the best people in the church need some help in learning to communicate their faith.'[14]

So how do we train people for witness? There are many ways to approach it. For example, I have seen some churches focus their evangelism strategy on a Billy Graham crusade. In the mid-1980s I was invited by several churches in France to give evangelism training to churches throughout that country in preparation for a Graham crusade. It was an electrifying time to be with the French churches as they geared up for what proved to be an enormously fruitful crusade. What made the training exciting was that there was a clear goal: all those who came to my evangelism seminars intended to invite their seeker friends to the crusade. They wanted help in developing their content and communication skills in order to share Christ more effectively.

The challenge after an 'event', of course, is: what does the church do next to continue its efforts? The goal is for people to share their faith as an integrated part of their everyday lives. But as part of your training be sure to include an evangelistic event to which our church can bring seekers.

It may be that your church decides to bring in a method of evangelism from the outside. For example, one highly successful effort is the Alpha course, a programme of suppers, lectures and conversation that is now the largest evangelistic effort in Britain and has spread to the United States and elsewhere. The Contagious Christian programme from Bill Hybels' Willow Creek Church is another good plan. The key is to decide which of these and other programmes best fits your people and the seekers you want to reach.

Don't be afraid, however, to develop a method that particularly fits your situation. In training churches in evangelism over the years, I have realized that there are well-defined categories. We need, as Gabriel Fackre once said, to *get the story straight* by learning how to give the content of God's story and ours. We need to *get the story out* by developing natural communication skills. We need to *take the story in* by learning to depend on the Spirit's power. And we need to learn how to *defend the story to others* by being prepared to answer the common questions people ask about the gospel.

Evaluate your church in light of these categories and see where the need is greatest so you will know where to begin. Then think through the format that would best serve your people. Should you kick off the evangelism training through a weekend conference or offer an eight-week course that meets one night a week? Should you study a book in many small groups or in larger classes?

What helps make evangelism successful is when the people of the church see evangelism as a way of life, not just an activity. It is discouraging to see people adopt an evangelism programme but then stop witnessing once the outreach is over. How do we prevent that from happening?

For one thing, the ministers need to model an evangelistic lifestyle. That is a great challenge when their lives are spent almost exclusively helping other Christians. But ministers who engage in personal evangelism give their church a tremendous boost.

One of the ministers in my church has been sharing his evangelistic encounters from the pulpit recently. Some of his experiences are hilarious, some are touching. But *everyone* is motivated to go out and do the same!

Evangelism succeeds better when the outreach or strategy is not the vision of the pastor alone. Effective evangelism always involves the congregation. The more it's a grassroots vision with many lay people involved, yet with enthusiastic endorsement and participation by church leaders, the more likely it will succeed.

Lastly, throughout this chapter and the last I have strongly encouraged the church to invite seekers to come and see what God is doing in their midst. I don't intend to change that stance, but I will add one word of clarification.

When we share the gospel, we need to be careful that we don't appear to be pushing people to go to our particular church. We don't want seekers to feel that all we're doing is canvassing for new members to sign up. If they don't have any church affiliation and they are interested, then by all means invite them to your church. But remember that the goal in evangelism is not to make people exactly like us. Our desire is for people to encounter God – not to become our clones.

Freedom to fail

We can learn a great deal of information, be full of zeal, master conversational skills, walk closely with God, participate in his community on earth and still blow it. That is one reason God told us so many stories of individuals in the Bible. He knew we would need the encouragement!

Take Peter. He loved Christ, and yet he constantly made mistakes. His most grievous error came in the last hours of Jesus' life. Jesus had told Peter he would deny knowing him, but Peter staunchly rejected the idea. After Jesus was arrested, Peter denied three times ever knowing him. He even invoked a curse upon himself if he knew him. As the cock crowed, what Jesus said had come to pass – Peter had denied the Lord.

Imagine how desolate Peter felt after Jesus' death. The last contact Peter had with Jesus was the scene of his own betrayal. In Jesus' most difficult moment, when he needed support the most, Peter had turned against him. Then a few days later Peter was told that the Lord had risen. Jesus was alive; his friends had actually seen him.

How did Peter feel now? He probably had ambivalent feelings. On one level he would be ecstatic, but on another afraid and ashamed. Maybe the Lord had given up on him. Maybe Jesus would feel Peter had made one mistake too many.

But God knew how Peter felt. He had a messenger tell the women who first came to the tomb, 'Go, tell his disciples and Peter' that he had risen (Mark 16:7, New International Version). 'And Peter' – two of the most beautiful words in the Bible. So the disciples went and said, 'Guess what? Jesus has risen! A messenger from God told us to go and tell you he's here. And, Peter, he said to tell you especially!' Only two words, but they brought a world of hope to a man.

And what did Jesus say to Peter when he saw him (John 21:15–17)? He asked, 'Peter, do you love me?'

And Peter said, 'Yes, Lord, I do.'

Jesus asked again, 'Peter, do you love me?'

Peter perhaps hesitated a bit, and then said, 'Yes, Lord, you know I love you.'

And then Jesus asked the third time, reminding Peter only too well of his recent painful history of thrice rejecting Jesus.

'Peter was hurt' and he said, 'Lord, you know all things; you know that I love you' (NIV).

Peter realized that Jesus knew who he was, his fallibility, his limits, his warts. And yet Peter loved Jesus. Jesus knew that too; he had known Peter's faults long before they ever dawned on Peter. And Jesus told him, 'Feed my sheep.'

Earlier Jesus had given Peter a nickname (Matt. 16:18). Of all the names to choose, Jesus picked the least likely: he called him Rock. We might have selected another, like Shifty or Quivery or Shaky. But Jesus chose Rock.

Jesus is telling us something through this. First of all, he knows us – me, you. He knows your limits, your broken promises, your failures. But he also knows that beneath all of that, you have a heart of love for him. He knows that you care. And Jesus also has a name for you, a name you would never have picked for yourself or dared to dream of. He sees what he is making you into; he knows what he has in store for you. And he gives you a name that suits what you are going to become. We are people of hope and not despair because we have a future that has been secured by God.

More important than our wobbly love for him is his absolute, unswerving love for us. When Peter told Jesus he would always remain faithful to him, Jesus knew his resolve would crumble. Nevertheless, he said, 'Simon, Simon, listen! Satan has demanded to sift all of you like wheat, but I have prayed for you that your own faith may not fail.' And he went on to say, 'When once you have turned back, strengthen your brothers' (Luke 22:31–32). Our Lord would not let Peter go. His love is the absolute of the universe.

Jesus knows our warts, but he also knows we love him. He knows what we will look like one day – not a grain of sand, as we so often feel, but a beautiful rock – and he loves us, eternally and mightily. And so he turns to us, as he did to Peter, and says, 'Feed my sheep.' It is that simple. Whatever gifts you have been given, whatever likes or talents, use them, give them, spend yourself on God's world as Jesus spent himself on you. Comfort his people.

Paul prayed as he wrote to the church in Corinth, 'Blessed be the God ... of all consolation, who consoles us in all our affliction, so that we may be able to console those who are in any affliction with the consolation with which we ourselves are consoled by God' (2 Cor. 1:3–4). Earl Palmer says that the word 'console' in this passage is most accurately described like this: a person is walking down a road alone, and he is then joined by another who walks alongside so he does not have to walk the rest of the road alone. And so we might retranslate the text this way: 'Blessed be the God who has walked alongside us, who walked alongside us in our affliction, so that we may be able to walk alongside others in their affliction with all the "walking-alongsidedness" that we have experienced.'

That is what God is like – he is the One who walks alongside. And that is what he calls his children to do. Regardless of age, temperament, fears, inhibitions, he bids us to feed his sheep.

What will we look like? We will look like a man I have only heard about. I met a student on one of the campuses where I used to work. He was brilliant and looked as though he was always pondering the esoteric. His hair was always unkempt, and in the entire time I knew him, I never once saw him wear a pair of shoes. Rain, sleet or snow, Bill was always barefoot. While he was a student, he had become a Christian.

At this time a well-dressed, middle-class church near the campus wanted to develop more of a ministry to the students. They were not sure how to go about it, but they tried to make them feel welcome. One day Bill decided to worship there. He walked into this church, wearing his denim jeans, T-shirt and of course no shoes. People looked a bit uncomfortable, but no-one said anything. So Bill began walking down the aisle looking for a seat. The church was quite crowded that Sunday, so as he got down to the front pew and realized that there were no seats, he just squatted on the carpet – perfectly acceptable at a college fellowship, but perhaps unnerving for a church congregation. The tension in the air became so thick one could slice it.

Suddenly an elderly man began walking down the aisle towards him. Was he going to scold Bill? My friends who saw him approaching said they thought, *You can't blame him. He'd never guess Bill is a Christian. And his world is too distant from Bill's to understand. You can't blame him for what he's going to do.*

As the man kept walking slowly down the aisle, the church became utterly silent; all eyes were focused on him; you could not hear anyone breathe. When the man reached Bill, with some difficulty he lowered himself and sat down next to him on the carpet. He and Bill worshipped together on the floor that Sunday. I was told there was not a dry eye in the congregation.

The irony is that probably the only one who failed to see how great the giving had been that Sunday was Bill. But grace is always that way. It gives without the receiver realizing how great the gift really is.

As this man walked alongside his brother and loved him with all that he had received from Christ's love, so must we. This man was the good Samaritan. He made Bill feel welcome, feel as if he had a home. So he also knew the secret of the parable of the prodigal son: there finally is a homecoming, because we really have a home to come to.

Appendix 1
Gospel outlines

The principle that must guide us as we seek to shape or share a gospel message for this generation is that we should be faithful to the core of the gospel truth and communicate it faithfully and clearly. At the same time we need to remember that even the New Testament writers were unable to reduce the gospel to a single metaphor. No one paradigm seemed to be able to convey the full reality of God's deed in Jesus Christ.

Furthermore, because people and cultures vary there will be many forms for communicating the message of the gospel. In other words we don't need to use a one-size-fits-all approach. But it is also important to be able to explain the essence of the gospel.

The following are some examples of gospel presentations. There are many more than those listed here. I encourage you to examine as many as possible until you find one you are comfortable with.

1. New Life for All

One widely used and helpful gospel presentation is the credo of the 'New Life for All' movement in Africa and Latin America.

1. God created all people for Life.
2. People, in their sin, have forfeited Life.
3. God came in Christ to offer people New Life.
4. People can receive this New Life by Turning
   ☐ from their sins
   ☐ to Christ in trust and obedience
   ☐ to the Community of New Life.

5. People knowing New Life are called to be faithful in all relationships.

Many denominations, traditions and movements use some version of this approach because, as George Hunter points out: '(a) It begins with creation – as the Bible does. (b) It includes the Church as part of God's saving provision. (c) It includes the Christian ethic and life-style as part of the message. (d) It begins with people's life concerns – a nearly universal point of contact. (e) Any Christian theological tradition can use it, and presumably in most any culture.'[1]

2. The Bridge

Another gospel outline that is in wide use in one form or another is the Bridge. This was originally developed by the Navigators, but the version below has been adapted by Sonlife Ministries, an evangelism training centre in Elburn, Illinois.[2]

It is possible to know God personally ...

In fact, the very reason God created us is so that we might know Him personally.

But ... to many people God seems very far away, distant, and impersonal.

Obviously there is a problem ...

The Bible teaches that God Loves You

'For God so loved the world ... that he gave his one and only Son that whoever believes in him will not perish but have eternal life' (John 3:16).[3]

And ... God wants you to know Him personally

'Now this is eternal life, that men may know him, the only true God, and Jesus Christ whom He has sent' (John 17:3).

But ... we are separated from God and his love

'God is on one side and all the people are on the other side' (see 1 Timothy 2:5).

Why do you think we are separated from God?

Figure 1. *The gap*

The Bible says our sins have separated us from God ...

'... your sins have made a separation between you and your God ...' (Isaiah 59:2).

'All have sinned, and fall short of the glory of God' (Romans 3:23).

God created us to know and love him. But we chose to go our own way and that relationship with God was broken (Romans 1:19-21). This attitude and its results are what the Bible calls sin.

This separation caused by sin creates some severe problems.

Figure 2. *Sin separating us from God*

Sin causes us to:

☐ Miss God's very best for life. 'Jesus said … I came that you might have life and have it to the full' (John 10:10).
☐ Face death and judgment. 'For the wages of sin is death …' (Romans 6:23). 'Those who do not know God … will pay the penalty of eternal destruction away from the presence of the Lord' (2 Thessalonians 1:8–9).

But … there is a solution.

Figure 3. *Sin bringing death and judgment*

Jesus Christ died and conquered death for you.

We deserve death and judgment, but Jesus took upon himself the punishment for our sins, so that we could have a personal relationship with God. 'God is on one side and all the people are on the other side, and Christ Jesus is between them to bring them together by giving his life for all humankind' (see 1 Timothy 2:5).

Jesus is the way to God.

'Jesus said, "I am the way, the truth and the life. No-one comes to God except through me"' (John 14:6).

Does this make sense to you? Still, it's not enough just to know this …

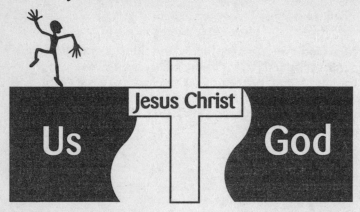

Figure 4. *Jesus Christ the Bridge*

Each of us by faith must receive Jesus Christ if we want to know God.

'To all who receive Him, He gives the right to become children of God' (John 1:12).

'For it is by grace you have been saved, through faith – and this is not from yourselves, it is the gift of God' (Ephesians 2:8).

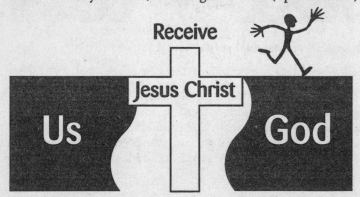

Figure 5. *Receiving Jesus Christ*

The 'A, B, C's' of faith involve:

Acknowledging your need – admitting you have sinned and desiring to turn from that sin (1 John 1:8–9).

Believing Jesus Christ died in your place and rose again to be your Saviour – providing forgiveness for your sins (1 Corinthians 15:3–4, 17).

Choosing to invite Christ to direct your life.

You can evaluate your current relationship with God by asking …

Which life best represents your current relationship with God?

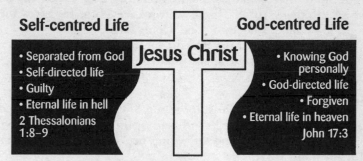

Self-centred Life

Jesus Christ

God-centred Life

- Separated from God
- Self-directed life
- Guilty
- Eternal life in hell

2 Thessalonians 1:8–9

- Knowing God personally
- God-directed life
- Forgiven
- Eternal life in heaven

John 17:3

Figure 6. *Self-centred life and God-centred life*

Which life would you like to have?

Your desire to have a personal relationship with God can be expressed through a simple prayer like this …

'Dear Lord, I want to know you personally. I am willing, with your help, to turn from my sins. Thank you for sending Jesus who died in my place and rose again to be my Saviour. Come into my life and lead me. Amen.'

Does this prayer express the desire of your heart? If it does, you can pray it now and begin your relationship of knowing God personally. If you are unsure, what is keeping you from receiving Christ now?

What happens when you receive Christ into your life?

The Bible promises:

☐ Christ comes into your life (Revelation 3:20).

☐ You become a child of God (John 1:12).

☐ Your sins are forgiven (Colossians 1:14).

☐ You have eternal life (1 John 5:11-13).
☐ You begin the adventure of knowing God personally (Philippians 3:8).

Am I to feel different?

It is important to remember that we rely upon God's Word, not our feelings, as proof of our having Christ 'within us'. 'If you confess with your mouth, "Jesus is Lord," and believe in your heart that God raised him from the dead, you will be saved' (Romans 10:9). 'To all who receive Him, He gives the right to become children of God' (John 1:12).

Regularly thank Christ for coming into your life ... and be sure to tell someone else about what you have done.

'New birth' certificate

I believe that Jesus Christ is the Son of God, and that he died on the cross, was buried, and rose again that I might have forgiveness of my sins and know him personally (1 Corinthians 15:3–4; John 17:3).

Today I have received Jesus Christ as my personal Saviour and desire to obey him as my Lord (John 1:12).

_____   _____

Date   Signature

How to grow in your relationship with God!

1. Talk to God about everything – this is *prayer* (Philippians 4:6–7).
2. Listen to God by reading the Bible – this is *Bible study* (Hebrews 4:12).
3. Spend time with others who know God personally – this is *fellowship* (Hebrews 10:25).
4. Help others to know God personally – this is *disciple-making* (Matthew 28:19–20).
5. Let God daily direct your life – this is *obedience* (John 14:15).

3. First steps to God

The following is an outline of the Christian message that was developed for students and staff in InterVarsity Christian Fellowship. Many have found it a useful summary to keep in mind as they share their faith. You may wish to copy this on the flyleaf of your Bible or photocopy this page and stick it on the inside cover.

God

☐ God loves you (John 3:16).
☐ God is holy and just. He punishes all evil and expels it from his presence (Romans 1:18).

People

☐ God, who created everything, made us for himself to find our purpose in fellowship with him (Colossians 1:16).
☐ But we rebelled and turned away from God (Isaiah 53:6). The result is separation from God (Isaiah 59:2). The penalty is eternal death (Romans 6:23).

Christ

☐ God became human in the person of Jesus Christ to restore the broken fellowship (Colossians 1:19–20a). Christ lived a perfect life (1 Peter 2:22).
☐ Christ died as a substitute for us by paying the death penalty for our rebellion (Romans 5:8). He arose (1 Corinthians 15:3–4) and is alive today to give us a new life of fellowship with God, now and for ever (John 10:10).

Response

☐ I must *repent* of my rebellion (Matthew 4:17).
☐ I must *believe* Christ died to provide forgiveness and a new life of fellowship with God (John 1:12).
☐ I must *receive* Christ as my Saviour and Lord with the intention of obeying him. I do this in prayer by inviting him into my life (Revelation 3:20).

Cost

☐ There is no cost to you; your salvation comes to you freely (Ephesians 2:8–9).
☐ But it comes at a high cost to God (1 Peter 1:18–19).
☐ Ultimately your response is a life of discipleship (Luke 9:23–24).

Appendix 2
Books for evangelism

In each of the categories below, the more general and basic books are listed first, the more specific and complex books last. All books listed are published by IVP unless otherwise noted. You can get more information on IVP books by requesting a free catalogue (IVP, Norton Street, Nottingham, NG7 3HR, telephone 0115 978 1054; fax 0115 942 2694; email ivp@ivpnottm.cix.co.uk) or by visiting IVP's website: www.ivpbooks.com

Books and booklets to be read and given to seeker friends

Basic Christianity. John Stott.
Becoming a Christian. John Stott.
Dead Sure. J. John.
The Evidence for the Resurrection. Norman Anderson.
Finding the path. Roger Forster.
The God Book. Charles and Peta Sherlock.
Is the New Testament Reliable? Paul Barnett (Hodder).
Making the Connection. Dave Richards.
Mere Christianity. C. S. Lewis (Collins Fontana).
Revealing the New Age Jesus. Douglas Groothuis.
The Universe Next Door. James W. Sire.
Why Believe? C. Stephen Evans.
Why Should Anyone Believe Anything at All? James W. Sire.
Why We Can't Believe. Paul Weston.

Evangelistic Bible study guides

The Big Story. Edited by Ro Willoughby.
Discovering Jesus. Ada Lum.
Knowing Jesus. Tricia Marnham.

More reading on evangelism

Evangelism and the Sovereignty of God. J. I. Packer.
Evangelism Made Slightly Less Difficult. Nick Pollard.
Explaining your Faith. Alister McGrath.
How to Give Away Your Faith. Paul E. Little.

Books on modern apologetics

Bridge-building. Alister McGrath.
Confronting the New Age. Douglas Groothuis.
Darwin on Trial. Phillip E. Johnson (Monarch).
The Francis Schaeffer Trilogy. Francis Schaeffer.
The Historical Reliability of the Gospels. Craig Blomberg.
In Defense of Miracles. Douglas Geivett and Gary Habermas.
Disarming the Secular Gods. Peter C. Moore.

Books on postmodernism

Guide to Contemporary Culture. Gene E. Veith (Crossway).
Postmodernity. David Lyon (Open University Press).
Truth is Stranger than it Used to Be. Richard Middleton and Brian Walsh (SPCK).

Books on the New Age

Confronting the New Age. Douglas Groothuis.
Revealing the New Age Jesus. Douglas Groothuis.
Unmasking the New Age. Douglas Groothuis.

Appendix 3
Study guide for individuals
or groups

Study 1. Sleepless in Spain (chapter 1)

1 Ask someone in the group to read the first paragraph of
chapter 1. Then ask: Can you describe how you have felt the
tension between the desire to be sensitive to people and the
desire to 'blast them with the gospel'?
2 Why was Becky surprised when her friends said they were
curious about her faith (p. 12)? How can we evangelize without
presenting the total gospel message all at once?
3 Becky found it difficult to predict what sort of person might
be most interested in coming to an investigative Bible
discussion (p. 13). How would you recognize or describe
someone who is spiritually open?
4 When Mary returned to Becky with questions and shared
some of her own life, Becky was slow to see that Mary was
'grappling with God' (p. 16). What are some signs that
someone is 'grappling with God'?
5 Becky says that whatever we fear the most, we will serve (p.
21). In what ways does fear of people determine how we relate
to (and serve) them?
6 Becky says our uneasiness often stems not from not knowing
the gospel message well but from not knowing how to be
ourselves (p. 18). Can you give an example of what she means?
7 What sorts of things have you shared easily with another
person (skills, books, hobbies, information), and how have you
done this? What can you learn from this in doing evangelism?
8 How does living out our lives honestly, so that people
recognize that we are far from perfect, actually speak positively
to the non-Christians around us (pp. 23–24)?

9 What are some ways we can turn evangelism from a project into a lifestyle (p. 24)?

10 Make a list of three non-Christian friends you expect to be with this coming week. How can you be more free with them?

Study 2. Jesus – the most human of us all (chapter 2)

1 What does the first paragraph of the chapter indicate is the essential point and purpose of this chapter?

2 How was Jesus a model of being open with people (p. 25)?

3 Summarize the ways in which Jesus identified with people (pp. 26–31).

4 Think of the people you've been in contact with during the last forty-eight hours. What needs do they have, and how might Jesus have identified with them to meet those needs?

5 What were some of the crises pointed out by Becky (pp. 31–35) that Jesus produced wherever he went?

6 We usually create a crisis or cause a controversy when our ego is being threatened or our needs are not being met. How is this different from the kind of crisis Jesus produced?

7 The religious people of Jesus' day were offended by him (p. 33). In what ways might you be disturbed by Jesus if he were with you today, even though you love him?

8 Give an example of a time when, with no forethought but simply acting on Christian principles, you (1) treated someone with compassion, (2) forced someone into a moral decision, (3) were able to be just plain, good company to a non-Christian, or (4) exasperated someone you were with.

9 This coming week, what are some ways you could try to act like Jesus, as described in this chapter?

Study 3. Jesus the Lord of love (chapters 3 and 4)

1 In chapter 3, Becky argues that the lordship of Christ is central to evangelism. In what way does the story of Lois demonstrate this close relationship (pp. 36–39)?

2 What are the four basic theological reasons that Jesus is Lord (pp. 40–43)?

3 Using the story of Cathy as a starting-point (pp. 43–45), what

are some specific decisions that you have made because Christ is your Lord?

4 What does Becky mean when she says to Jack, 'Whatever controls us really is our god' (p. 48)? Explain why you agree or disagree with this.

5 In chapter 4, Becky begins a set of three chapters on what Jesus valued most, beginning with his love for troubled people. What did Jesus think about the Pharisees' notion of how to please God, and what was his view (pp. 53–56)?

6 What is more important to you – getting to church on time or having a good relationship with others in your family on the way to church? Explain.

7 Becky reminds us (pp. 53–56) in the parable of the prodigal that the father saw in the son some attributes that the neighbour did not. Think of two people you love and enjoy. What do you think God likes best about them? Think of two people you can't stand to be around. What do you think God likes best about them?

8 After discussing the parable of the good Samaritan, Becky writes, 'Before any religious activity, our lives are to bear the stamp of profound love' (p. 57). List your religious activities in the past two weeks. List your acts of kindness within the same time period. What do these two lists reveal about who you are?

8 Why is it so easy to treat individuals as evangelistic projects instead of as people?

10 How does the story of Carla illustrate how we can look beyond someone's exterior background or image and see into their hearts?

11 Use the questions in italics on page 61 to guide you in thoughtful prayer.

Study 4. Questions of holiness and obedience (chapters 5 and 6)

1 What is so disturbing about Sonny in the film *The Apostle*?

2 Before reading this chapter, how would you have defined *holiness*? By this definition, would you have considered yourself holy?

3 How did Jesus and the Pharisees differ on what it means to be holy?

4 Becky writes, 'I frequently hear that the call to be holy and the call to demonstrate love to sinners are mutually exclusive' (p. 74). Rather, she suggests that what true holiness is all about is how we treat other people. Do you agree or disagree? Explain.
5 Becky reminds us that being under the lordship of Christ means having our compassion shaped by his moral absolutes and that 'sometimes it is the very love of God that demands that we speak painful truth to a friend' (p. 75). How should we communicate the wrongness of a friend's sin and our love and acceptance of that person at the same time?
6 In the story of Jake we see how honesty about our problems can actually be a part of holiness (pp. 76–77). How have you seen that to be true?
7 Moving on to chapter 6, what was the Pharisees' view of knowing God, and what was Jesus' view (pp. 79–84)?
8 What does Becky mean when she says that 'Knowledge must automatically translate into obedience' (p. 80)?
9 Look at the case of Sue and the desk (pp. 85–87)? What does this story indicate about the relationship between knowledge and obedience?
10 Is one of your friends interested in the gospel but not sure it's true? What would you think of issuing him or her with the same challenge Becky offered Sue? Explain.
11 What is the importance of understanding obedience as Jesus did for our evangelism and the way we call people to Jesus?

Study 5. Christ and his presence (chapters 7 and 8)

1 Chapter 7 considers three resources Christ offers us in evangelism. In the first subsection, Becky points out in the story of Mary and Martha that it is better to allow Jesus to serve *us* first (p. 91). What, exactly, does that mean? How are we to allow Jesus to serve us?
2 The second resource is illustrated by how the disciples allowed themselves to be limited by their apparently meagre resources and the story of Maggie and the ice-cream party (pp. 92–94). List your resources in evangelism, however limited you think they are. In what ways can you offer each of them to Jesus to use?
3 Explain or give an example of each of the three things Becky

mentions that we need to learn if we are to care for others (pp. 94–95)?

4 What practical difference does it make that the people we meet are created in Christ's image (p. 95)?

5 How is this illustrated by Mother Teresa, C. S. Lewis and the young nurse?

6 In chapter 8, Becky looks at four ways we can practise the presence of Christ: seeing people as Jesus does, loving them as they are, loving them as we are, and being salt and light in the world. To illustrate the first point, Becky tells of meeting a woman at the airport who wanted a drink (pp. 98–100). Give an example of a time recently when you felt someone had interrupted your plans. What would help you see such situations as divine interruptions?

7 How did Becky come to see beneath the crust of Betty (pp. 100–102)? Think of people you know who are closed or hostile to the gospel. How could you see beneath their crust?

8 Becky's relationship to Betty was a success in some ways and a failure in others. Do you think their relationship was a waste of time? Explain.

9 On pages 105–109 Becky discusses extroverts and introverts. In regard to evangelism, what are the advantages and dangers experienced by each of these types?

10 What are some strategies for minimizing the dangers?

11 Find a prayer partner who is also concerned about evangelism and covenant with each other about practising Christ's presence.

Study 6. Developing conversational skills (chapter 9)

1 How did your flatmate or spouse or sibling last let you know that you had done something he or she did not like? What does your answer illustrate about the importance of conversational skills?

2 How can our attitudes help in our presentation of the gospel or hinder it (pp. 115–117)?

3 Becky mentions a role-play exercise about telling a Christian what you are learning about evangelism and telling a non-Christian (p. 116). If you are studying this book in a group, try it now. If you are studying on your own, find someone this

week to do the role-play with. How did you feel about the difference in the two conversations?

4 What questions are you afraid a non-Christian will ask you? Why do these concern you?

5 What practical difference does or should it make to you that the Holy Spirit is the one who convicts people of sin and the need to turn to Christ?

6 What's the difference between exposing and imposing our faith (pp. 118–119)? Give an example of each.

7 Becky mentions terms that sound religious and have a special meaning to Christians (p. 123) such as *sinner, grace, salvation, justification, sanctification, regeneration, redemption* and *born again*. What other terms can you think of?

8 Now explain these terms in everyday speech.

9 Assume someone ridicules your involvement in a church or religious group. Make a list of good questions you could use to respond (pp. 123–125).

10 Some time during the next week, initiate a conversation with a total stranger, with no motivation other than trying to get to know something about that person. If you are studying this book in a group, tell about your experience next time you meet. If you are studying on your own, write out what happened.

Study 7. Witnessing and cultivating (chapters 10 and 11)

1 At the end of the last study (question 10), it was suggested that you initiate a conversation with a total stranger with no motivation other than to get to know something about that person. How did it go?

2 Becky offers a definition of evangelism from Michael Green (p. 130). Break down this definition into four or five parts and explain in your own words what each part means.

3 On pages 131–133, three ways of proclaiming the truth of the gospel are mentioned: declaring God's truth, displaying God's love and demonstrating God's power. Give a couple of examples of each that you have observed or participated in.

4 Why is it important at some point and in some way to put all three of these ways together?

5 In chapter 11, the first conversational model discussed is 'Investigate, stimulate, relate'. What are some good questions you could ask at the 'Investigate' stage?

6 When we 'stimulate' curiosity in unbelievers, we don't give them the whole gospel, but only part of it to arouse their interest. Give some examples from the book or from your experience, or create some examples of how this might be done.

7 In the 'concentric circles' model of conversations, give examples of questions that might be asked in each of the four layers.

8 How is the third layer, that of underlying issues, so crucial in conversations?

9 Conduct a role-play that moves a conversation through the four layers. (In a group setting, either divide everyone into pairs to conduct the role-play or have one pair role-play for the whole group, and then discuss what you observed and how the person playing the role of the Christian might have engaged the other person more effectively. If you are working through the book on your own, find someone this week to role-play with.)

10 How can it be helpful to raise the question of authority (as suggested in Model C)?

11 Why is demonstrating God's love so important during the first stage of cultivating an interest in Jesus (pp. 146–150)?

12 Take time to pray for God's power to be evident in your relationships and conversations with unbelievers in the coming week.

Study 8. Planting the seed (chapter 12)

1 Becky identified four main elements in the gospel message that she communicated to Kay (p. 159). Explain each element in a few sentences in your own words (without using God-talk).

2 Take time to write out in a page your story of how you came to Christ. Your story should cover at least the following three questions: What were the key events? What were the important truths you learned? How has it made a difference in your life? (If you are in a group, either break into pairs and share your story with your partner, or have several volunteer to tell their story to the whole group. If you are studying on your own, ask someone this week if you can tell him or her your story.)

3 Becky asks how we can communicate sin in ways that won't alienate people from the gospel. 'Christians have tended to deal with the subject of sin in one of two ways: either by being silent or by being judgmental' (p. 161). What is the answer to her question?

4 In her discussion with Rick, how did Becky communicate about sin clearly without alienating him?

5 Becky didn't define sin as being certain bad behaviours but rather a desire to control our own lives rather than be ruled by God. Do you think this is a helpful distinction to make with unbelievers? Why or why not?

6 Kay and Rick ultimately had different theological issues that were of most concern to them – Kay was concerned about evil and Rick was concerned about his own sin. How could some of the following issues be doorways for a non-Christian into theological issues and the gospel: (1) concern for the environment; (2) sensing a lack of community in one's life; (3) interest in equal rights for women?

7 Becky suggests that God often uses the Bible powerfully with others when we share the stories of Jesus and passages of the Bible that have had a deep effect on us. What are the stories that have affected you most and why?

8 Take time to access God's power in prayer by bringing to him those you know who need to have their hearts and minds opened to the truth of the gospel.

Study 9. Reaping the harvest (chapters 13 and 14)

1 There is nothing so terrifying as the first time we lead someone to Christ. Why might this be so?

2 How do you feel about the prospect of guiding someone to faith in Jesus?

3 Becky says conversion is not so much gaining information as going through transformation (pp. 172–174). Explain.

4 Give a brief explanation of the three steps of conversion: repent, believe, receive (pp. 175–177).

5 How do these three steps, properly understood, emphasize that becoming a Christian is a serious business and not a step to be taken lightly?

6 On page 177, Becky suggests that when we believe a person

could be ready to become a Christian, we should ask, 'Is there anything that would keep you from becoming a Christian here and now?' What reasons might be given for not taking this step, and how can we respond?

7 Becky says, 'I find many people are more likely to reveal themselves in short encounters with virtual strangers than they would to their next-door neighbours' (p. 180). Do you agree or disagree? Explain.

8 What can assure us and give us confidence about people (like Sue) who may not make a decision for Christ for many years?

9 How is it that calling someone to conversion is possible only through God's power and still involves us as messengers?

10 Chapter 11 describes the conversion of Becky's father. Why is it often most difficult to witness to our family members?

11 What can help us in these situations?

Before the next study: Ask a non-Christian friend, 'What is the biggest problem in the world today and what is the solution?' (The goal is not to convince the friend of the right answer but to simply find out what he or she thinks.)

Study 10. Revealing truth through reason (chapter 15)

1 What answer did you get to the assignment at the end of study 9?

2 What is the value of giving answers to questions people ask about Christianity, and what are the limits of the answers we might give (pp. 196–197)?

3 What are some of the differences between modern thinking and postmodern thinking (pp. 197–198)?

4 What are the most common questions you get about Christianity?

5 Which are the most difficult for you to respond to and why?

6 It is not uncommon to meet people who do not believe in absolute right and wrong. Becky says we can respond by saying, 'If you say there is no such thing as morality in absolute terms, then you cannot say that child abuse is always evil; it just may not happen to be your thing. And if you find you are not able to practise your premises with much consistency, then you need to re-examine your premises' (p. 200). Do you think this

is an effective response? Why or why not?

7 If a non-Christian were to ask you probing questions concerning your worldview, how would you explain: (1) the basic nature of the world, (2) morality, (3) human nature, (4) the fundamental problem in the world and how we deal with it (pp. 199–208)?

8 How do questions about the nature of true success or fulfilment in life reveal what someone thinks about what it means to be human (p. 204)?

9 'We don't often encounter a person who asks, "Tell me what the true nature of God is." What we *do* hear,' says Becky, 'is humanity's cry to be saved from the reality and consequences of sin' (p. 204). How can such discussions about human nature lead to discussions of the gospel?

10 Now think back to the answer you got to the assignment at the end of study 9. How could you possibly move from that answer to a discussion of the gospel?

11 Why does the historical nature of Christianity matter?

12 What can you do to be better prepared to respond to questions about the historical reliability of Christianity?

Study 11. Revealing truth through stories and the power of the Spirit (chapters 16 and 17)

1 At the beginning of chapter 16, a woman Becky met makes a distinction between what is real and what is true. Describe the difference and how valid you think this is.

2 Why are stories so helpful in talking to people who make this distinction between what is real and what is true?

3 Why is it important to start with the story of the person we want to share the gospel with (pp. 211–212)?

4 How does Becky suggest we do this (p. 213)?

5 How did the story of David fit in with the story of Jill, the manicurist (pp. 212–218)?

6 Becky says it is also important to tell our story. Why is it often so difficult for Christians to be honest about their problems and pains in life?

7 How can we overcome this?

8 In chapter 17 we are reminded how common alternative religious practices are these days. Which practices have you

encountered and how?

9 What is the difference between making accommodation to contemporary belief and understanding the context of non-Christians so we can more effectively explain the gospel to them (p. 224)?

10 Personal power is one of the main issues for people who follow New Age thinking. How does the story of Anna (pp. 224–229) show what the gospel has to say and offer about power?

11 How can we avail ourselves more of the power the Spirit offers?

12 On page 231 Becky notes that sometimes people are deceived spiritually in very serious ways. Yet she also says on page 224, 'It's tragic enough that the world assumes that Christians are judgmental and critical. Let's not exacerbate the problem by proving them right by our behaviour!' How can we reveal both the deception to others and God's love without being unnecessarily condemning?

Study 12. Community and vision (chapters 18 and 19)

1 How have you been affected and helped by being part of a Christian community?

2 If you are part of a small group, how could you reach out as a group to show love and care for, or just to have fun with, other people (pp. 235–237)?

3 What steps might you need to take to start up an investigative Bible discussion?

4 What could be done to help your church grow to be more of a place where non-Christians would be comfortable and welcomed?

5 Why is incorporating non-Christians and new Christians into a Christian community so important?

6 Nicky Gumbel (p. 250) mentions someone who thought the church expected people first to *behave* and next to *believe*, and only then might they *belong*. How would your church be different if it followed the opposite pattern, as Gumbel suggests?

7 Becky says that preaching and worship can be very effective

ways for the church to reach unbelievers (pp. 251–254). How can these be both nurturing to believers and attractive to unbelievers?

8 Becky gives three suggestions for finding the right evangelistic style or programme for your church (pp. 254–257). How would you respond to each of them?

(1) What are the types of people to whom God has called us to minister as a church? What kind of culture or cultures are involved?

(2) Who are we? Large? Small? Diverse? Uniform? City? Rural? Young? Old? Strengths? Weaknesses? Ingrown? Outgoing?

(3) How can we ask God for his guidance in the ways he wants us to change and reach out?

9 Do you feel you have the freedom to fail? Why or why not?

10 How does Peter's example (pp. 258–259) give you encouragement about your weaknesses and flaws?

11 Share how someone has walked alongside you, as Becky described the man who joined Bill on the floor of the church (pp. 260–261). What can you do this week to walk alongside someone else?

12 What one next step do you think God wants you to take regarding your witness? Take time to pray about this and commit it to him.

Notes

Chapter 2: Jesus – the most human of us all

1. G. K. Chesterton, *Orthodoxy* (New York: Image, 1959), p. 146.

Chapter 3: Jesus – the Lord of all

1. John Stott, 'Must Christ Be Lord to Be Savior? Yes', *Eternity*, September 1951.
2. D. Martyn Lloyd-Jones in a talk given to the General Committee of the International Fellowship of Evangelical Students in 1963.
3. C. S. Lewis, *Mere Christianity* (New York: Macmillan, 1969), pp. 54–55.
4. Thomas Oden provides an evaluation of modernity as representing four fundamental values: moral relativism, autonomous individualism, narcissistic hedonism and reductive naturalism. Thomas Oden, 'Back to the Fathers: Interview with Thomas Oden', interview by Christopher Hall, *Christianity Today*, 24 September 1990, pp. 28–31.
5. G. K. Chesterton, *Orthodoxy* (New York: Image, 1959).
6. Oswald Chambers, *My Utmost for His Highest* (London: Marshall, Morgan & Scott, 1927), p. 265.

Chapter 4: A question of love

1. Parker Palmer, *To Know As We Are Known* (San Francisco:

285

Harper & Row, 1983), p. xiv.

2. E. P. Sanders, *Jesus and Judaism* (Philadelphia: Fortress, 1985); E. P. Sanders, *Jewish Laws from Jesus to the Mishnah* (Philadelphia: Trinity Press International, 1990); J. D. G. Dunn, *Jesus, Paul and the Law* (Louisville, KY: Westminister John Knox, 1990), pp. 61–88.

3. S. Westerholm, 'Pharisees', in *Dictionary of Jesus and the Gospels*, ed. Joel B. Green, Scot McKnight and I. Howard Marshall (Leicester: IVP, 1992), p. 612.

Chapter 5: A question of holiness

1. William J. Bennett, *The Death of Outrage* (New York: Free Press, 1998), p. 123.

2. Gustave F. Oehler, *The Theology of the Old Testament* (Grand Rapids, MI: Zondervan, 1883), p. 18.

3. H. Wheeler Robinson, *The Religious Ideas of the Old Testament* (London: Duckworth, 1913), p. 40.

4. A. T. Robertson, *The Pharisees and the Jews* (London: Duckworth, 1920), p. 79.

5. John R. W. Stott, *The Message of the Sermon on the Mount* (Leicester: IVP, 1978), pp. 24–25.

Chapter 6: A question of obedience

1. Parker Palmer, *To Know As We Are Known* (San Francisco: Harper & Row, 1983), p. 43.

2. H. Wheeler Robinson, *The Religious Ideas of the Old Testament* (London: Duckworth, 1913), pp. 73–74.

3. Jim Wallis, 'Conversion: What Does It Mean to Be Saved?' *Sojourners*, May 1978, p. 14.

4. G. K. Chesterton, *Orthodoxy* (New York: Image, 1959), p. 154.

Chapter 7: Christ with us

1. Mother Theresa, 'The Poor in Our Midst', *New Covenant*

Magazine, January 1977, pp. 15-17.
2. C. S. Lewis, *The Weight of Glory* (Grand Rapids, Mich.: Eerdmans, 1949), p. 15.
3. Hope Warwick, 'Lady in 415', *Campus Life*, May 1976, pp. 50–52.
4. Mother Teresa, 'The Poor in Our Midst', p. 17.

Chapter 9: Developing conversational skills

1. Martin Luther, *Fastenpostille,* quoted in Donald Bloesch, *A Theology of Word and Spirit* (Downers Grove, IL: InterVarsity Press, 1992), p. 215.
2. Karl Barth and Eduard Thurneysen, *Come, Holy Spirit*, trans. George W. Richards, Elmer G. Homrighausen and Karl J. Ernst (Grand Rapids, MI: Eerdmans, 1978), p. 219.
3. Donald A. Bloesch, *Theology of Word and Spirit*, p. 244.
4. Dietrich Bonhoeffer, *The Cost of Discipleship*, trans. R. H. Fuller (London: SCM Press, 1959), p. 165.

Chapter 10: Three ways to witness

1. Michael Green, *Evangelism Through the Local Church* (Sevenoaks: Hodder and Stoughton, 1990), pp. 8–9, 11.

Chapter 11: Cultivating the soil

1. Sonlife Ministries, 526 N. Main, Elburn, IL 60119 or www.sonlife.com
2. Mark Petterson, 'Strategic Conversations', in *HIS Guide to Evangelism* (Downers Grove, IL: InterVarsity Press, 1977), p. 45.
3. Ibid., p. 47.
4. Donald Bloesch, *A Theology of Word and Spirit* (Downers Grove, IL: InterVarsity Press, 1992), p. 240.

Chapter 12: Planting the seed

1. Donald Bloesch, *A Theology of Word and Spirit* (Downers Grove, IL: InterVarsity Press, 1992), p. 13.

2. Helmut Thielicke, *The Trouble with the Church*, ed. and trans. John W. Doberstein (New York: Harper & Row, 1965), p. 50.

3. Kallistos Ware, *The Orthodox Way* (Crestwood, NY: St Vladimir's Seminary Press, 1986), p. 8.

4. Bloesch, *Theology of Word and Spirit*, p. 228.

5. Rebecca Manley Pippert, *Hope Has Its Reasons* (San Francisco: Harper & Row, 1989), p. 106.

6. There are various ways of understanding the doctrine of the atonement. What struck me on reflection was that Kay's and Rick's situations called for two (complementary) ways of looking at the atonement. Kay was drawn to an understanding of the cross that emphasizes the risen Christ's victory over the powers of evil that ravage humankind. She found great comfort in knowing that Christ had put down and destroyed evil by his death and resurrection, that God was in Christ reconciling the world to himself, and that Christ invites the saved to participate in his victory over evil by living under his rule and extending his victory in every area of life. This is an interpretation called the 'Christus Victor' theory of the atonement. For further exploration, see Gustav Aulén, *Christus Victor* (SPCK, 1970). By contrast, Rick was drawn to an interpretation of the cross that emphasizes the debt Christ paid. What deeply moved Rick was that God took our place and became our substitute when judgment had to fall. The sinless one stepped in for the sinful and accepted the penalty that we alone deserved. This is an interpretation of the atonement that is called 'penal substitution'. For further exploration, see John R. W. Stott, *The Cross of Christ* (Leicester: IVP, 1986).

7. John Calvin, *Institutes of the Christian Religion*, trans. John Allen (Philadelphia: Presbyterian Board of Christian

› Education, 1936), p. 90.
8. J. I. Packer, 'Children of a Larger God', *Leadership*, summer 1998, p. 110.

Chapter 13: Reaping the harvest in God's truth and love

1. C. S. Lewis, *Mere Christianity* (New York: Macmillan, 1969), p. 182.
2. Leanne Payne, *The Healing Presence* (Wheaton, IL: Crossway, 1989), p. 79.
3. Blaise Pascal, *Pensées*, ed. and trans. A. J. Krailsheimer (Harmondsworth: Penguin, 1966), p. 138.
4. H. Eddie Fox and George E. Moore, *Faith-Sharing* (Nashville: Discipleship Resources, 1998), p. 53.
5. Jim Wallis, *Agenda for Biblical People* (New York: Harper, 1976), p. 23.
6. The 'lordship salvation' debate is well covered in Dallas Willard, *The Divine Conspiracy* (London: Fount, 1998), pp. 43–50.
7. Mark Mittleberg, 'Evangelism That Flows', *Leadership*, summer 1998, p. 29.
8. Robert Webber, *Common Roots* (Grand Rapids, MI: Zondervan, 1978), p. 165.
9. G. K. Chesterton, *Orthodoxy* (New York: Image, 1959), p. 160.
10. Rebecca Manley Pippert, *A Heart Like His* (Leicester: IVP, 1996), p. 206–207.

Chapter 14: Reaping the harvest in God's power

1. Flannery O'Connor, *Mystery and Manners* (New York: Farrar, Straus & Giroux, 1969).
2. Ernest Becker, *The Denial of Death* (New York: Free Press, 1973), p. 164.
3. Os Guinness, *The Call* (Milton Keynes: Word, 1998), p. 14.
4. Guinness, *Call*, p. 14.

Chapter 15: Revealing truth through reason

1. James W. Sire, *The Universe Next Door*, rev. ed. (Leicester: IVP, 1988), p. 18.

Chapter 16: Revealing truth through stories

1. Ronald Johnson, *How Will They Hear If We Don't Listen?* (Nashville: Broadman & Holman, 1994), p. x.
2. Parker Palmer, *To Know As We Are Known* (San Francisco: Harper & Row, 1983), pp. 39–40.

Chapter 17: Revealing truth through the power of the Spirit

1. Alan J. Roxburgh, *Reaching a New Generation* (Downers Grove, IL: InterVarsity Press, 1993), p. 127.
2. James W. Sire, *The Universe Next Door*, rev. ed. (Leicester: IVP, 1988), p. 170.

Chapter 18: The witness of community

1. John R. W. Stott, *The Contemporary Christian* (Leicester: IVP, 1992), p. 241.
2. Michael Green, *Evangelism Through the Local Church* (Sevenoaks: Hodder and Stoughton, 1990), p. ix.
3. E. M. Bounds, *Preacher and Prayer* (Wheaton, IL: Institute of the Billy Graham Center and Worldwide Publications, 1993), p. 10.

Chapter 19: Without a vision the people will perish

1. Alan J. Roxburgh, *Reaching a New Generation* (Downers Grove, IL: InterVarsity Press, 1993), p. 127.
2. Ibid., p. 55.
3. Ibid., p. 56.
4. Mark Lauterback, 'Contact', *Leadership* (summer 1998): 36.
5. Roxburgh, *Reaching a New Generation*, p. 129.

6. Lesslie Newbigin, *Foolishness to the Greeks* (London: SPCK, 1986), p. 124.
7. Donald Bloesch, *A Theology of Word and Spirit* (Downers Grove, IL: InterVarsity Press, 1992), p. 237.
8. Roxburgh, *Reaching a New Generation*, p. 129.
9. John R. W. Stott, *The Contemporary Christian* (Leicester: IVP, 1992), p. 121.
10. Ibid., p. 127.
11. Roxburgh, *Reaching a New Generation*, p. 119.
12. George G. Hunter III, *How to Reach Secular People* (Nashville: Abingdon, 1992), pp. 44–72.
13. Roxburgh, *Reaching a New Generation*, p. 105.
14. Kenneth Chafin, *The Reluctant Witness* (Nashville: Broadman, 1974), p. 141.

Appendix 1: Gospel outlines

1. George G. Hunter III, *How to Reach Secular People* (Nashville: Abingdon, 1992), pp. 87.
2. Sonlife Ministries, *Knowing God Personally* (Elburn, IL: Sonlife Ministries, 1995).
3. Scripture references in the outline are quoted from the New American Standard, Living Bible and New International versions of the Bible.